Preferences
and Situations

Preferences
and Situations

Points of Intersection
Between Historical and
Rational Choice Institutionalism

Ira Katznelson and Barry R. Weingast
Editors

Russell Sage Foundation, New York

The Russell Sage Foundation

The Russell Sage Foundation, one of the oldest of America's general purpose foundations, was established in 1907 by Mrs. Margaret Olivia Sage for "the improvement of social and living conditions in the United States." The Foundation seeks to fulfill this mandate by fostering the development and dissemination of knowledge about the country's political, social, and economic problems. While the Foundation endeavors to assure the accuracy and objectivity of each book it publishes, the conclusions and interpretations in Russell Sage Foundation publications are those of the authors and not of the Foundation, its Trustees, or its staff. Publication by Russell Sage, therefore, does not imply Foundation endorsement.

Library of Congress Cataloging-in-Publication Data
Preferences and situations : points of intersection between historical and rational choice
 institutionalism / Ira Katznelson and Barry R. Weingast, editors.
  p. cm.
 Includes bibliographical references and index.
 ISBN 0-87154-441-5
  1. Social institutions. 2. Institutions (Philosophy) 3. Preferences (Philosophy) 4. Rational
 choice theory—Political aspects. 5. Historical sociology. 6. Political sociology. I.
 Katznelson, Ira. II. Weingast, Barry R.
HM826.P74   2005
306.2'01—dc22   2005048997

The paper used in this publication meets the minimum requirements of American National Standard for Information Sciences—Permanence of Paper for Printed Library Materials. ANSI Z39.48–1992.

Text design by Genna Patacsil.

RUSSELL SAGE FOUNDATION
112 East 64th Street, New York, New York 10021
10 9 8 7 6 5 4 3 2 1

Contents

Contributors

IRA KATZNELSON is Ruggles Professor of Political Science and History at Columbia University.

BARRY R. WEINGAST is senior fellow at the Hoover Institution and Ward C. Krebs Family Professor in the Department of Political Science at Stanford University.

RICHARD BENSEL is professor of American politics in the Department of Government at Cornell University.

DAVID W. BRADY is Bowen H. and Janice Arthur McCoy Professor of Political Science in the Graduate School of Business and professor of political science at Stanford University and senior fellow at the Hoover Institution.

CHARLES M. CAMERON is professor of politics and public affairs at Princeton University and visiting professor of law at New York University School of Law.

JON ELSTER teaches political science at Columbia University.

JOHN A. FEREJOHN is Caroline S.G. Munro Professor of Political Science at Stanford University and senior fellow at the Hoover Institution.

PETER A. HALL is Krupp Foundation Professor of European Studies and director of the Minda de Gunzburg Center for European Studies at Harvard University.

JAMES JOHNSON is associate professor of political science at the University of Rochester.

MARGARET LEVI is Jere L. Bacharach Professor of International Studies in the Department of Political Science at the University of Washington.

JAMES MAHONEY is associate professor of political science and sociology at Northwestern University.

JEREMY C. POPE is assistant professor of political science at Brigham Young University.

1

Intersections Between Historical and Rational Choice Institutionalism

Ira Katznelson and Barry R. Weingast

Despite their differences, historical and rational choice institutionalism have a good deal more in common as a result of their convergence on institutions than is ordinarily realized. The dissimilar strengths of these "schools" can advance each other's agendas, some aspects of which have been converging.

The characteristic ways of working by each group of scholars have generated important advances. Our ambition is not to erase these distinctions but to make the most of them. We believe there is much to gain from mutual engagement, not just better self-critical understanding about features of work that could strengthen each tradition in its own terms, but also genuine cross-fertilization and collaboration within the ambit of work on particular puzzles and cases. The chapters in this volume show, in practice, how many of the putative differences separating historical institutionalism (HI) and rational choice institutionalism (RCI) diminish, or even disappear, when they ask how institutional situations shape and help constitute and induce preferences people use to make judgments and choices about the present and the future at particular moments in time.

We first consider how this productive erosion of boundaries has developed, and what the implications are for how the two approaches might "learn" from each other. A shared interest in how context, situations, and institutions induce preferences has largely supplanted approaches that risked depicting agents who either are over- or undersocialized. We first review the turn to institutionalism by rational choice scholars, who often imputed ex ante preferences to individuals without worrying much about their larger sources, and by comparative-historical social scientists, who treated preferences as caused primarily by macro-level dynamics without much concern about the microdynamics of their interaction. We then show how the convergence by both on institutions, especially when conjoined with temporality, has opened fruitful grounds for collaboration, anchored by a common emphasis on how institutions stimulate and help generate preferences at particular times and places.

Nonetheless, significant barriers impede this goal. Although central to accounts of purposive action, preferences remain a relatively primitive category of analysis. Equally problematic is the inadequate attention paid to "a range of temporal processes that are common in political life" (Pierson 2004, 2). By diagnosing and addressing these obstructions in a fruitful engagement across approaches, *Preferences and Situations* demonstrates that HI's and RCI's approaches to politics, history, and social phenomena have many actual and potential points of contact and overlap. It also highlights how they might come to complement each other rather than contend with one another.

Our two points of departure are preferences and institutions. We focus on these concepts because they lie at the heart of some of the biggest apparent differences between HI and RCI scholars and because of what we see as the growing commonalities. Political science faces a range of such methodological differences and sites of intellectual tension. One is the ongoing debate between instrumentalism and constructivism in international relations. Another is the differences that distinguish the way groups of political theorists read and deploy texts. What follows, therefore, focuses on just one of many important controversies—one, though, that raises important issues at the heart of each of the discipline's subfields.

Preferences are foundational for any theory that relies on agency. We know too little about preferences, where they come from or how they are generated. As we see in the chapters that follow, historical and rational choice institutionalist scholars have been converging on the idea that because institutions often generate sufficiently strong incentives for actors, whether medieval kings or members of the modern U.S. Congress, we can derive a form of preference based on the compelling logic of institutions embedded in particular historical situations; or at least come to understand how a given institutional milieu both constrains and shapes the repertoire of available preferences.

Approaching Preferences

Building on the insights of Peter Hall (2000), we distinguish three ways preferences have been described and understood. First is that they are imputed to actors within the framework of assertive theory; that is, the theory posits a set of preferences for the relevant actors. Second is that they are caused by historical processes; that is, the theory attempts to suggest how historical developments cause a particular set of preferences held by a given actor. Third is that they are induced by strategic circumstances and human interaction; that is, the theory implies that specific patterns of relationship and interaction within institutions and or social processes encourage or persuade a given actor to possess a particular type of preference.

There are strong and weak versions of each. Theoretical imputation can simply assign bundles of preferences that either are unexamined givens or products of unobserved assumptions about human motivation. Alternatively, and more softly, it can introduce fixed actor preferences into a theory based on observation and induction. Likewise, in some causal accounts individuals are so powerfully inscribed within structures and role categories that they have no option but to prefer what specific historical or institutional roles designate. In less determinate form the sources of potential preferences are discerned probabilistically within the dynamics of social relationships that change over time. Similarly, induced preferences may be invoked forcefully by the logic of strategic interaction among actors within circumscribed institutional contexts. Less determinatively, these settings may actively affect aspects of preferences without uniquely shaping them.

We are partial to the less strong version of each. Good theory requires imputed preferences but better theory assigns preferences for the limited compass of the theory based on empirical learning. Good causal history cannot proceed without embedding individuals but better history works with more than one register of time and structure, understanding that preferences may variously be shaped, and that even the same structural constraints can be understood and interpreted from more than one perspective. Good analysis of strategic situations demands appreciation of how the production of social outcomes induces preferences, rather than just being a reflection of them, but better analysis leaves open the degree to which preferences are thus induced in a relatively durable manner.

Moreover, these approaches work best when their boundaries are crossed. Just as any good theory must do some imputing and any institutional analysis must grapple with how specific sets of rules and behavior within their ken shape and reshape the predilections of actors, assigning preferences and identifying institutional pressures and possibilities gain power by being nested inside compelling analytical histories that offer warrants for designating what actors want and the conditions within which they choose. In turn, accounts of historical causation insisting that the building blocks of preferences—including interests, desires, values, opinions, tastes, and morals—be located inside thickly inscribed temporal and spatial contexts gain power both from relatively focused designations of preference within processual accounts of institutional dynamics.

Further, it is our belief that the study and understanding of preferences has been advanced by the turn to the analysis of institutions by both HI and RCI, and thus to richer understandings of how preferences are induced within their ken. Before this shift, HI scholars had tended to stop once they had underscored how preferences are caused by macrohistorical change without showing clearly enough how, in a more fine-grained way, they also are induced within particular and often restricted institutional settings. RCI scholars were inclined to designate actor preferences by imputation rather than demonstrate how they had been institutionally induced. With the focus on institutions, both sets of scholars turned their attention to situationally induced preferences in a more focused manner, complementing but not replacing their prior emphasis, respectively, on caused and imputed preferences.

Fastening large-scale and often long-term processes to human relationships and patterns of power via the establishment of rules, signals, norms, and incentives, both schools have come to share the view that institutions solve key problems of human coordination and cooperation, offer frameworks for problem-solving, and confirm as well as establish political, economic, and social hierarchies. Institutions are not free-floating processes or cultures that provide milieus within which individuals and groups are most directly embedded for some or many aspects of their lives. Over time, they also help establish the identities and categories of actors and their range of possibilities, hence the scope and content of preferences.

Irrespective of their intellectual provenance, each of the chapters in this book seeks to make interconnected sense of preferences, time, and institutions. Because RCI and HI have moved to this focus from rather different starting points, because each is nourished primarily by different disciplines and research traditions, and because each situates its institutional analysis in distinctive ways, it often is difficult for practitioners to see just how much common ground for productive mutual learning they in fact have forged.

A key problem for rational choice scholars (most of whose work in noncooperative game theory is based on John Nash's pioneering idea that players adjust their strategies until none any longer can gain from shifting) "is not that Nash equilibria fail to exist" for particular profiles of preferences "but rather there are too many of them" (Austen-Smith and Banks 1998, 274). Historical institutionalists tend not to be surprised, not because a given game can generate multiple solutions, but because history throws up many games both in sequence and all at once. Because historical circumstances vary so widely, and because they develop over uneven spans of time as the result of an extensive array of causal chains, historical institutionalists have insisted as a signature claim that choices about feasible alternatives are structured by determinate situations regarding who the actors are and which choices are in fact on offer. This, as it turns out, is what rational choice institutionalists have been stressing and doing as well, especially when they attend to particular historical cases.

Much remains to be done to make exchanges across the RCI-HI divide fruitful. Perhaps the biggest difference between the two approaches concerns the types of questions they ask. Rational choice scholars especially prize the analysis of specific, time-bound, events—an election or a piece of legislation, for example. The penchant of historical institutionalists for longer temporal horizons spanning decades or more makes them a good deal more likely to encounter and analyze situations in which preferences on several dimensions evolve over time and in which the set of actors is less likely to remain stable. History, moreover, rarely stands still for any specific game, as actors and their preferences are entailed within many strategic and normative settings simultaneously, in layers. What historical institutionalists mean by the environment is rather more complex than the environments considered by most RCI collective choice and game theory models as they try to yield meaningful predictions. By contrast, historical social science is more concerned with guarded generalizations and post-diction, often under conditions of complexity and uncertainty.

Notwithstanding the distinguishing features of each approach and enduring differences of emphasis, we wish to stress the fair number of overlapping possibilities. The richer the historical story within which it is set and the more persuasive the attribution of preferences to actors, the more convincing is the selection of a given institutional game. Likewise, particular games played by particular agents with ascribed preferences can help drive and guide historical accounts of particular circumstances or longer-term dynamics, even if the primary causal movers may be assigned elsewhere.

But if we are to do more than take note of such points of connection, we need to overcome a number of stereotyped images of the other that continue to impede mutual consideration and potential collaboration. When HI scholars look at how rational choice scholars treat preferences, they still tend to see the traits Kenneth Shepsle described a decade and a half ago. Rational choice, he observed, is motored by "rational man" considered as "an atom unconnected to the social structure in which he or she is embedded," and is marked by theories that "worry hardly at all about the sources of preferences and beliefs." Further, he noted, formal theorists often deliberately repress institutional details, rejecting the "time- and location-bound" qualities of bureaus, courts, legislatures, and electoral arrangements as impediments to general theory (Shepsle 1989, 134, 135). This description identifies RCI squarely within the strong version of imputed preferences.

These, of course, are characteristics likely to produce a recoil by historical institutionalists who share commitments to chronology and temporality, to the specificity and particularity of situations, and to the importance of historical causation over more than very short periods when considering purposive action. From this vantage, they understandably are made nervous by any casualness about the specification of the origins and content of preferences or insouciance about assumptions concerning the stability and precision of assigned preferences. These features are especially apparent when relatively thin and often short-term historical accounts, deployed illustratively, are instantiated and mediated by very strong theory, or are considered one situation or one game at a time rather than within more complex temporal or institutional configurations.

In turn, RCI analysts still tend to see that preferences, so central to their own studies, are downplayed as an analytical category in historical social science analysis. They see scholarship that gives greater priority to the macroscopic tracing of historical cases and processes whose more general import or potential for cumulative knowledge often is unclear, and they fail to see the connection between long-term structural processes and the imputation of preferences to groups of actors based on their role in primarily structural historical arguments governed by their own versions of strong theory. Reading classics in comparative-historical analysis, RCI scholars observe that preferences often seem ascribed or imputed or caused too slackly, and, further, worry about the absence of strategic analysis of how preferences are aggregated into social outcomes. In other words, RCI sees the HI arguments about how historical processes "cause" preferences as undertheorized and often inadequate.

Both of these assessments are out of date. Their mirror-image caricatures are hardly baseless, yet each fails to appreciate the difference the turn to institutional analysis and induced preferences has made to both schools of analysis. The rational choice tradition has begun to attend more systematically to historical and institutional processes to better understand how actor preferences have been fashioned and how institutions have introduced biases or other distortions. Historical institutionalists have begun to study how preferences are deployed and reshaped in practice. Both, albeit with distinct links to other features of their work, have done so by placing institutions and preferences front and center in a new way.

Preferences and Circumstances

Preferences signify propensities to behave in determinate circumstances by people who discriminate among alternatives they judge either absolutely or relatively. But preferences may in considerable measure be the product of circumstances and institutions that, in mediating between the agency of persons and large-scale historical developments, can guide reasons for how people actually choose. Situated this way, preferences cannot be reduced to the conduct of persons or groups of individuals, nor can they be assigned to people by theory alone. Nor can they be read or inferred directly from the larger historical structures that help give rise to them. Despite the range characterizing the ways HI and RCI scholars examine politics, their approach to preferences gains power when their inquiries about such institutions as those of transitional justice, monetary union, court systems, voting, and candidate nominations are understood not just to be shaped by, but to convoke, human preferences.

As the new institutionalism within rational choice moved from an austere universe that had elided institutional details to a rich concern for the origins and particulars of specific institutional arrangements within which strategic action occurs, the status of preferences has undergone a significant change, particularly the standing of imputed preferences and the relationship between induced and imputed preferences.

Any rational choice model of human action is constituted by individuals, information, feasible options, and preferences. Whether the theory takes the form of social choice or noncooperative games, choices are understood to echo or reveal preferences held by persons, either alone or in collectivities. Before rational choice scholars turned to institutions, they tended to impute attributions about fundamental preferences—such as a wish to keep power, get rich, provide for one's family, or promote an ideology—prior to strategic situations or interactions. Such preferences thought to be deeply embodied by the person, as in claims that these are fundamental human desires, were offered axiomatically as durable, bedrock motivations. In this sense, they were transhistorical human traits that transcend particular cultures, settings, or institutions. These imputed preferences (imputed in part because they are impossible to determine with empirical certainty) neither were considered as caused or induced in the typical analysis, but rather considered as given, stable, precise, consistent, and exogenous. This treatment ranged from simple single-dimension linear vector models to more complex and inherently quadratic ones.

Within the new institutionalism, rational choice scholars have become far more empirical, conditional, and situational in deploying preferences. At some distance from the notion that the preferences of actors are constant and enduring, preferences now are treated as those of persons in interaction with other actors, in particular institutions, understood as game forms. No longer simply imputed by the theorist-observer, here the interactive play of the game itself in part induces actor preferences. Context and situations matter deeply, especially when players mutually anticipate the actions of others and select strategies that respond to those decided by others. These induced preferences concerned with instruments, such as strategy choices, at times can be observed with sufficient regularity that they can be legitimately imputed as ends toward an individual's fundamental goals or underlying preferences.

It is easy to miss this change. The typical RCI paper still begins by assuming a simple form of preferences and traces the consequences in particular institutional settings. The vast majority of RCI studies of Congress, for example, simply assert that members seek reelection. Looking at a single paper, it can appear that preferences are imputed by the theory alone as an unquestioned prior. But this characterization is inadequate. On closer examination it becomes clear these preferences were induced and, further, that a series of earlier works have shown how they are induced, how they vary across time, and in particular which institutional details explain their emergence. Not all RCI literatures have this cumulative quality, of course. In particular, papers that branch out into new topics such as the study of dictatorship have a different character. In those literatures, imputed preferences are more questionable as the papers are best understood as preliminary and exploratory. Moreover, RCI scholars typically give less status to conclusions based on imputed preferences over which there is no consensus than they do results based on preferences over which there is empirical work.

In more developed settings, such as work in American politics on Congress or elections, RCI scholarship moves differently. Scholars tend to build on the work of their predecessors, who in turn had built on theirs. Contributions do not reinvent the wheel. This holds for characterizations of behavior, such as the role of committees, but also for the form of preferences, such as the claim that politicians maximize the probability of being elected or reelected.

In these cumulative literatures, the issue of the form of preferences is often the subject of intense debate. This is readily seen in the early spatial model literature of the 1960s and 1970s, which used a range of different maximands. The same point holds for studies of Congress. Most RCI studies of Congress do assume maximizing reelection, a form of imputed preferences. These are not fundamental preferences, however. People are not born with the idea that they will run for Congress and seek to increase their probability of reelection. Rather, people who run for Congress with whatever set of motivations, and who thus wish to make a career of public life, must by virtue of the institution get elected and reelected.

This is not as truistic as it sounds, as demonstrated by *Congress: The Electoral Connection*, David Mayhew's classic work (1974) that helped forge the consensus among Congress scholars about the reelection hypothesis. Part 1 of the book traces the implications of the reelection assumption in the electoral arena and part 2 outlines them for behavior and institutions within Congress. Mayhew opens, however, with a contextual introduction that focuses on the reelection assumption itself, and discusses why this form of induced preference is reasonable to impute in the context of the United States, but not in Great Britain or continental Europe.

To this end, he examines various institutional details of Congress, contrasting them with the British Parliament. The institutions differ, he argues, in three critical environmental dimensions. The first is nominations. In the United States, any individuals meeting minimal qualifications can run for a House or Senate seat. Moreover, they typically can run as a candidate under the major party's label by a simple administrative procedure. Second, members of Congress attain many positions of power within the legislature, including committee and subcommittee chairmanships, in large part by virtue of service such as seniority. Third, financing elections is highly individualistic; members of Congress do not rely solely on their party for funds but typically raise their own (although this began to change at the end of the twentieth century). In contrast, political parties control all three features of political life in Britain. An individual needs permission of the party to run under its label for a particular seat. The party awards positions of power, such as ministerial positions. And the party controls electoral funds.

For Mayhew, the point of this contrast is twofold. First, it helps motivate the reelection assumption for the United States. To function as what at first appears simply as an imputed preference within the book's larger analysis, the electoral imperative is presented as having been generated endogenously within a particular type of legislature. Moreover, it is a time-sensitive preference. Congress in the antebellum era was different. Then, most members did not seek a career in Congress. A great many preferred local office, serving a only short time in Washington as part of their duty to the local party to get rewards from it. Second, the incentives induced by a deep, contextual understanding of the institutional differences between countries and their legislatures yields a comparative conclusion: The goals of MPs should differ systematically from those of MCs. MPs, for example, are necessarily more focused on their party and its fortunes than their counterparts in the United States.

This example indicates a heightened RCI sensitivity to the way institutional arrangements and rules not only interact with preferences to produce outcomes but also help generate the preferences themselves. It also identifies potential points of contact between HI and RCI. The reelection assumption did not emerge as an aspect of strong deductive theory. Rather, it came into view as a scholarly consensus following extended contextual-historical analysis, particularly the degree to which in the 1970s RCI types and traditional Congressional scholars came to believe they were engaged in the same enterprise and thus could draw on one another's findings.

In taking on a more nuanced and historically informed focus on institutions, RCI scholars have revised understandings first drawn from less institutional approaches. Their assumptions about preferences evolve as they trace consequences and test predictions against behavior. As an example, RCI scholarship on Congress has rejected an alternative assumption quite common among economists in the public choice tradition to the effect that politicians are rent-seekers (see, for example, Tollison 1982). Instead, they have drawn closer to the way HI writings insist that individuals often have preferences by virtue of being in an institutional and political environment with determinate characteristics. Thus, the assumption of reelection maximizing is causal and structural in the same sense that preferences sometimes are imputed for members of particular groups within HI analysis. Indeed, members without these preferences soon would cease to be members.

We can see this shift in emphasis regarding preferences in the new institutionalist RCI literature on bureaucratic behavior in the United States, which has gone through three phases with respect to preferences. In the initial stage, RCI scholars assumed that bureaucrats focused on themselves, seeking to maximize the emoluments of office or the size of their budget (see, for example, Downs 1967, Tullock 1965, and Niskanen 1971). Students of the next RCI generation, finding the predictions and explanations of the first literature inadequate, sought a new mode of analysis. This group emphasized the importance of other institutional actors in the bureaucracy's environment, such as interest groups, Congress, or the president. Initially, these models were dyadic in the sense that they studied the bureaucracy in the context of only one institutional actor: interest groups for George S. Stigler (1971) and James Q. Wilson (1980), the president for Terry M. Moe (1982), Congress for Morris Fiorina (1981) and Barry R. Weingast and Mark J. Moran (1983). In these studies, the bureaucracy was typically assumed to be an agent of a particular political principal that, by virtue of the pattern of rewards and punishments offered by the principal (Congress, the president, an interest group, depending on the given analysis), pursued policies favored by the principal.

By the middle to late 1980s, it was clear that these dyadic models were inadequate. A given bureaucracy could not at once pursue policies favoring both the president and Congress because, typically, they disagreed. The third phase of this literature, building on the second, regards bureaucrats as possessing preferences over policy and who act to further those preferences subject to a complex interaction with other institutions, such as interest groups, Congress, the president, and the courts (see, for example, Eskridge and Ferejohn 1992, Epstein and O'Halloran 1999). Individual studies on bureaucracy thus assume particular forms of preferences. This assumption, however, is not arbitrary, but subject instead to considerable debate, nuance, and evolution.

This research, like HI, makes the historical and situational analysis of institutions a central feature. RCI contextual analysis often proceeds through the analysis of comparative statics, studying how equilibrium preferences and behavior change as institutional details change. Because papers often take analysis one argument at a time, focusing on particular episodes (as in the many studies of how individual pieces of legislation were passed into law), the cumulative effect may be difficult to discern to those not steeped in the particular literature. Reading a paper in isolation gives no sense of the longer conversation through which consensus and understanding have emerged.

Too often, to our taste, these analyses suffer from the absence of longer time horizons, both medium and more extended. But some RCI scholars have begun to work with longer periods of time. Thus, in chapter 3, David W. Brady, John Ferejohn, and Jeremy C. Pope study the passage of the 1964 Civil Rights Act, but not from the more typical RCI vantage of the strategic interaction of members of Congress in that single Congress. Rather, they step back and observe that civil rights had been on the agenda for a decade and that two previous bills, in 1957 and 1960, were gutted so that they passed primarily as symbolic acts. What, they ask, made 1964 different? To address this question, they look at two hypotheses. First, preferences of members of Congress changed through elections that brought new members to Congress with different preferences. Second, public opinion changed so that members' induced preferences over policy changed. Their evidence favors the latter.

Still, the dominant trend with RCI is for the focus of particular models to be short term, relatively presentist, and closely linked to particular strategic situations with particular structures of payoffs. Although comparative statics allow the assessment of behavior over time and across changing contexts, the analysis works best when the particularities of situations—that is, the institutions within which interaction and choice take place—are very well specified. This is an advantage, because in such research exacting claims about historical distinctiveness, and the individuality and nonreplicability of specific historical moments and conjunctures, staples of historians and historical institutionalists alike, can contribute productively to the delineation of strategic players, games, and moves within substantial accounts of structures, institutions, and persons in determinate situations. In making these moves, RCI has come to help us understand when, why, and which institutions come into play. Thus, within RCI, attributions of the preferences of the relevant actors have become a good deal more than imputed "just so" ascriptions.

Shifting Analysis

Rational choice scholarship has moved from imputed preferences to accounts of institutionally induced preferences (some of which are sufficiently regular and durable to become imputed assumptions). Historically oriented social scientists have also moved—from a relative neglect of preferences to more structural emphases, or from a concern for how historical developments cause preferences to a tighter focus on induced preferences (which then can be deployed within macro-causal accounts more centered on agents and agency than were typical just a short time ago).

The classic precursors of HI today are the books of macroanalysis on a large scale written in the 1960s and 1970s by, among others, Reinhard Bendix (1964), Barrington Moore (1966), Perry Anderson (1974), Immanuel Wallerstein (1974), Charles Tilly (1975), and Theda Skocpol (1979). Despite differences in emphasis, questions, and spatial as well as temporal scale, these works shared a number of key traits. They all sought to tame the varieties, contingencies, and remarkable range of history by deploying strong theory, primarily Marxist, often modified by Weberian impulses, to focus on moments and processes characterized by change on the largest scale. (Tilly 1984) They studied how feudalism ended and capitalism began, how a Europe-centered and integrated global market developed, how pathways to different types of political regimes were forged, and how revolutions developed and concluded. The main goal was to identify and explain in relatively parsimonious ways the appearance and enlargement of the main features of the modern, especially Western, world after the fifteenth and sixteenth centuries. These features included state-making, large-scale organized warfare, capitalism, urbanization, increasing differentiation of the zones of life (state, market, and society; work and home), and the mobility of people, ideas, money, and power. Efforts at periodization sought to distinguish and understand moments marked by change on a massive scale and more ordinary times whose dynamics and pathways were shaped, perhaps even determined, by the processes and outcomes at moments of very high indeterminacy.

Such efforts found their handmaiden in rather holistic analyses that treated structures both as outcomes of large-scale historical processes and as causes that, alone and in combination, established fields of action within which human beings lived, cooperated, and conflicted. In the analytical hierarchy typical of these works, rather less attention was paid in the first instance to agents and their preferences. People and their preferences tended to be collapsed into categories established by the interplay of theory and history. Once defined, say, as peasants, kings, Protestants, bureaucrats or other such positions in the social order, agents were of course recognized as the bearers of preferences, but their content almost could be taken for granted. In a form of imputation, actors were constrained to possess a limited array of preferences inside strong theoretical and historical accounts.

These works, given the structural holism so prominent within them, seemed totally at odds with the microdynamics of rational choice as it then was emerging as a site of influence in the social sciences. If, from the vantage of this body of historical social science, rational choice seemed more concerned with deductive model-building than understanding vexing historical instances, then from the perspective of rational choice, the social science of "big structures, large processes, and huge comparisons" (Tilly 1984) lacked causal discipline, the capacity to cumulate findings, and, perhaps above all, the ability to identify and analyze microfoundations for historical developments.

Much as RCI has turned to institutions, so has HI, if from a rather different starting point. During the past quarter century, HI has developed as a somewhat narrower, more focused, offspring of the earlier body of historical social science. Its temporal sweep is shorter. The range of regimes it considers is more limited. It is interested as much in durable patterns as in immense change. It has developed more of a policy focus, concerned to understand, among other key issues, the political economy of capitalism in its many variants (Hall 1986; Streek 1992; Thelen 1991; Steinmo 1996; Hall and Soskice 2001; Swenson 2002), types of welfare state (Esping-Andersen 1990; Immergut 1992; Skocpol 1992; Pierson 1994; Huber and Stephens 2001; Hacker 2002), social movements and their popular bases (Katznelson and Zolberg 1986; Goldstone 1991; Banaszak 1996; Ritter 1997; Tarrow 1998; McAdam, Tarrow, and Tilly 2001), and the rise, persistence, or decline of authoritarianism and democracy (Downing 1992; Rueschemeyer, Stephens, and Stephens 1992; Ekiert 1996; Ertman 1997; Mahoney 2001).

Institutions have come to play three critical roles in this body of work. First, understood as historical products, they provide links between unsettled moments of great transformation and more ordinary times. Second, they constrain and shape human beliefs, values, interests and the way these are deployed to shape outcomes. Third, and this is the leading point of contact with RCI, they are understood to generate preferences. In these ways, institutions have come to provide the great connecting tissue between types of time and between levels of analysis within HI (Immergut 1996; Katznelson 1997, 2003; Pierson and Skocpol 2002; Mahoney and Rueschemeyer 2003). In so doing, they have changed the genre of historical social science.

Along the path of this intellectual shift in character and emphasis—indeed, in part prodded by it—has been the crisis of Marxism, both in the world at large and in the academy. In the precursor scholarship to HI, much of the work was accomplished or suggested by historical-materialist understandings of temporality, change, and the key units of structure and action. Purposive behavior largely was understood to be the product of structural imperatives. Even when Weberian themes were introduced into this scholarship—mainly by way of adding state-centered subjects to those of capitalist political economy—human action, preferences, and choice remained downplayed.

In part, the turn within HI to a serious engagement with institutions was a response to a loss of confidence in Marxism's master narrative. No longer was it possible to treat history as a singular process of successive types of social organization composing coherent social types. In a transition from Marxism (but not a rejection of Marxist subjects and themes), HI disaggregated such outsized concepts as the state and capitalism into more specific sets of interacting institutions. Images of distinct systems and transitions have become more plural, often moving to different rhythms of institutional change (Skowronek 1993; Orren and Skowronek 2004). Of course, there have been stronger reactions to the predicament of Marxism, including varieties of postmodernism that reject notions of reality in favor of signification and that decline or even reject the search for systematic regularities, patterns, mechanisms, and causes. HI did not take this turn. It never left causal social science, though at times it has engaged with more hermeneutical scholarship interested in constructing interpretations of human identity and diversity.

The new focus on institutions and the resources they offer, the connections they make across time, and the links they present that connect constraints and opportunities to choices and decisions has made it possible for HI scholars to bring agency and preferences to the fore rather more than in earlier historical social science (Wickham-Crowley 1992; Greenstone 1993; Clemens 1997; Sanders 1999; Goodwin 2001; Katznelson

2003). Their analyses that are concerned to make sense of the various kinds of action institutions facilitate or inhibit are based on a number of strong intellectual commitments. There is a devotion to understanding particular cases in depth. Individuals are always historical and embedded, never free-standing or the irreducible units of analysis. Institutions are understood to be both stable arrangements that endure over the long term and locations that can produce profound disturbances to the status quo. Institutions change probabilities of preference formation and action. People pursue projects based on their preferences within institutions, just as institutions delineate the scope of possible projects and help bring preferences forth (Collier and Collier 1991; Yashar 1997; Waldner 1999). For such work, institutions constitute social reality in ways that are complex and multiform.

Detailed attention to institutional histories and design, and to the way actors understand their situations, provide bases for inference within HI. Its various qualities by no means restrict HI scholars to qualitative methods of one kind or another. Rather, HI is methodologically permissive, even opportunistic. But only within bounds. HI views variable-centered views of the world skeptically when they imply relatively closed systems in which the causal torque of relationships between or among variables is assumed to stay relatively constant across a wide range of times and places. Though quite open to large-scale data sets and big-N scholarship, HI treats findings based on this kind of inference as guides to hypotheses and to questions that can only be parsed by the analysis of specific situations in which variables appear in distinct, sometimes unique, configurations. As a causal enterprise, HI seeks to understand how particular institutional arrangements in particular locations at particular times were fashioned as results of long-term historical developments. In this aspect of HI work, preferences are caused by these historical processes. In turn, HI scholars also consider how institutions that result from historical causes themselves induce the formation of preferences, and how it is that these preferences then recursively enter into the larger dynamics of historical development and change. Sometimes preferences are exogenous to institutions; at other times, they are the products of the process by which institutions endogenize preferences.

Within RCI, institutions have been seen primarily as sites of cooperation, in which problems of coordination and collective action can be overcome. To be sure, there have been RCI scholars (Moe 1987; Knight 1992) who have sought to make power and the uneven distribution of capacities and resources as constitutive of institutional analysis as cooperation, but this has been a minority trend. Within HI, by contrast, power is central. Institutions are always seen as distributive switchboards and as peopled by individuals and groups with a range of assets and possibilities. While some relationships within institutions cluster people who share attributes and are located in structurally equivalent places, others convene ties between people of different circumstances and abilities. In part, institutions normalize or naturalize these states of affairs but also provide arenas for contests and offer the potential for change (Douglas 1986; Haydu 1998).

Both RCI and HI, in short, have converged to institutions; one from the direction of microanalysis, the other from macroanalysis. For both, power and problem solving meet in institutional settings. Both prize particularity and credit the distinctiveness of situations whose rules they seek to understand as precisely as possible.

Inducing Preferences

These intellectual developments have set the stage for this book. Part of the broader trends we have underscored, here we are fascinated with the processes by which institutions in their wider historical settings induce preferences, and, in so doing, alter the character, qualities, and effects of human agency.

The contributions fall into three main groups: first, those that consider particular episodes, seeking to identify the paths and mechanisms by which preferences both emerge within these contexts and, in turn, motor historical developments; second, those that emphasize specific mechanisms and processes; and, third, those that reflect on types of occurrences. The book concludes with a reflection on how an accomplished research project would have profited from a closer integration of HI and RCI.

Situations

Richard Bensel studies the interaction of structural features and strategy in the 1896 Democratic Party Convention that ultimately nominated William Jennings Bryan. When it opened, no front-runner had emerged. The preferences of a great many delegates over the identity of the nominee had yet to clearly form, and no candidate had a majority. Bryan's speech was electrifying. By the time it and the subsequent demonstrations were over, he was the obvious nominee. Over the course of the speech and demonstration, most delegates came to support him. A strength of this paper is that, while written from the HI perspective, its principal insights can also be told from an RCI perspective of ex ante uncertainty, not about fundamental preferences (which involved winning the presidency), but over the instrument or strategy—in this case, the nominee—best placed to achieve that end.

David Brady, John Ferejohn, and Jeremy Pope are interested less in how preferences crystallize than in how they change. As noted, they study the evolving preferences of members of Congress for civil rights. Such legislation garnered insufficient support to pass in the 1940s, 1950s, and the early 1960s, but received enormous support in 1964 and thereafter. What accounted for this quite radical shift in member preferences? In assessing alternative explanations, they show how, in this instance, the major factor was constituency change. As the plight of southern blacks became widely publicized, many northerners came to believe in the injustice of the southern Jim Crow system. As constituents' attention and views changed, so too did those of their representatives. It was the institutional dynamics of political representation that generated the dramatic shift in preferences that made it possible to turn the demands of the civil rights movement into law. Among the contributions of the paper is a demonstration that standard statistical techniques in the study of congressional voting can be used to trace and estimate the degree and shape of changes in preferences.

Studying the decision of Edward I in 1290 to expel England's Jews, Ira Katznelson asks how we should understand not only the shift by the king from a program of integrating this minority more fully in English life but the radical disjunction from the preferences of prior English kings during the period of Jewish settlement that began at the end of the eleventh century. He gives pride of place to the manner in which thirteenth century kings, culminating in Edward, had to manage new normative and institutional relationships linking the crown to society, most notably the emergence of a body of rights after Magna Carta, and especially the robust development of Parliament following the Montfortian rebellion of the 1260s. Set within a larger framework of events—both international, especially shifts in geopolitics with the loss of territory in Normandy, and domestic, with the growth of a national identity in the context of efforts to extend the scope of English rule in Britain—the mechanism of political representation, the paper shows, fundamentally altered the manner in which Edward and his successors defined the situation and framed decisions about the Jewish minority.

Processes

All actors, whether individuals, groups, or collectivities like national governments, Peter Hall stresses, never have a singular interest or a sole identity. Any given issue may tap more than one interest and one identity. Thus, the formation of preferences concerning specific actions must include a process by which actors weigh the relative importance of different interests and identities. They make such judgments, Hall argues, by deploying causal ideas and persuading others to agree. Stressing how such preference development occurs in a series of events, and in circumstances of uncertainty, about which there is an unfolding narrative, he shows how these processes shaped the decisions taken by the British, German, and French governments regarding membership in the European Monetary Union (EMU) in the 1980s.

Barry Weingast studies a radical shift in preferences in colonial America. Weingast's purpose is twofold: methodologically, he uses rational choice tools to model the historical institutionalist's concept of critical junctures; substantively, he applies the model to the emerging rebellion against British rule. How and why, he asks, did an elite that largely took its Britishness for granted become potential revolutionaries? Specifically, why did American moderates switch sides from opposing to supporting the radicals to create the Revolution? Weingast addresses these questions by focusing on the interaction of the radicals' theories of the British and their actions. He shows how the Americans' world views combined with the evidence from British actions to alter the beliefs held by moderates about British malevolence so they came to support a revolution, thus creating a critical juncture.

Charles Cameron seeks to understand the quite remarkable growth of the federal judiciary in ways that were unanticipated at the founding of the United States. Rather than opt for one of the two dominant positions in the literature—that judicial state building was produced by Congress or that it was the product of actions and decisions by the Supreme Court, he develops a more inclusive model, offering a constitutive role to federalism, suggesting when majorities in Congress become the prime movers and when Congress recuses itself and the Court becomes the lead player in advancing judicial development. The essay develops its arguments by presenting analyses of key nineteenth-century cases, including the Fugitive Slave Act, the Removal Act of 1875, and those concerning state sovereign immunity.

Categories

Margaret Levi is interested in the problem of how diverse preferences come to be placed in a hierarchy within a given organization. Focusing on the International Longshore and Warehouse Union (ILWU) and the International Brotherhood of Teamsters (IBT), she asks how the preferences of their leaders were ordered. Why, in some instances did leaders put a higher priority on serving the union, thus producing open and honest institutions, rather than their personal interests, which can lead to closed and corrupt organizations? Why, in other instances, the reverse? These inherent tensions in preference formation, she stresses, occur not only at the level of the organization or competing groups within it, but at the individual level itself. Once a preference hierarchy crystallizes, with communication and signaling it can harden into a collective culture shaping outcomes.

Jon Elster explores how preferences are formed about transitional justice after the shift from a given regime to another, especially the creation or return to democracy after a period of authoritarian rule. Historically, responses vary widely, from ignoring previous crimes and actions, to granting immunity, to truth commissions, to paying reparations, to investigations followed by trials. Renewing a distinction of seventeenth-century French moralists, Elster distinguishes preferences motivated by emotions, impartial reasons, and interests in esteem, power, or money. He then parses each type, showing how it might come into play in different circumstances of transition, and illustrates the utility of his typology in treatments of a wide array of cases, ranging from French Revolution and post-Napoleonic era to the aftermath of Latin American dictatorships, from the German Democratic Republic to apartheid South Africa.

James Johnson examines the process by which the rules for excluding some citizens from the franchise were dramatically narrowed as a site from which to consider issues in how RCI studies the development of institutions. He especially fosters more self-consciousness on the part of RCI analysts concerning how to analyze, explain, and justify equilibria, understood as outcomes, by examining the emergence of universal suffrage as an equilibrium institution, and by considering normative and strategic motivations as distinct causal sources. These, he insists, must be kept separate. Because the expansion of the right to vote has a moral torque, it is all too tempting to account for this result in moral terms. Thus, in focusing on the problem of existing elites and voters' preferences over expanding the franchise, Johnson rebuts previous studies that emphasize the moral aspect of these preferences. Instead, he argues that franchise extension was mainly the result of strategic interactions amongst myopic actors with short timeframes who could not possibly have foreseen the outcome their dealings produced.

Synthesis

James Mahoney's reflections on the place of liberalism in political development in Central America make up the most self-conscious of the book's essays in seeking to show how, within a specific zone of inquiry about institutions and preferences, combinations of HI and RCI can offer better accounts than either on its own. Having written a major book on choices elites made selecting between radical policies and moderate reforms that was written mainly from an HI vantage (Mahoney 2001),

Mahoney now asks how RCI models can advance a more focused account of the nature and outcomes of these choices by key actors. He does so, moreover, without sacrificing historical depth or an appreciation for the importance of context; in this instance, the degree of political threat elites faced when making decisions at critical junctures.

Read individually and collectively, these papers advance our understanding of how productive points of contact between HI and RCI can illuminate important historical episodes, processes, and puzzles. But they also leave open, and thus invite further consideration of important questions about preferences as a concept and as a tool of research.

Preferences is a broad and capacious category. It encompasses a wide range of beliefs, values, interests, even emotions, and more than one type of choice situation. Is it too heterogeneous to consider from a single approach? Are the same conceptual distinctions and methods equally valid across the scale of decisions, ranging from the relatively trivial (which brand of black beans should I buy) to the large and critical decisions that individuals make about themselves and their societies (should one accommodate to a dictatorship or seek to overthrow it even at great personal risk), and the majority that fall in between (like the voting choices members of Congress make hundreds of times in a given session)? (Ullman-Margalit and Morgenbesser 1977; Ullman-Margalit 1984). Moreover, even within a particular zone of decision, individuals typically possess not a single, all-purpose ordering of preferences, or a simple distinction between ethical and subjective preferences (Harsanyi 1955) but hierarchies of preferences whose rankings can alter under specific institutional and historical conditions (Sen 1977). Such considerations, in turn, raise vexing issues about the conduct of research and the empirical determination of preferences—do we simply ask individuals, read their prose, conduct ethnographies, observe behavior, infer preferences from variations in outcome, or combine such approaches? Over what span of time and with which range of settings and institutions? What rules should guide such choices and potential combinations?

Postscript

We wish to close on a cautious and realistic note. This book focuses on preference formation and change, and reveals considerable points of intersection and overlap between historical and rational choice institutionalism. We have seen that much of this overlap is due to the ways in which approaches have focused on institutions, particularly the way institutions shape the incentives and preferences of actors.

Despite these points of contact and mutual learning, the two approaches have not come together as one. They possess different histories, instincts, questions, methods, and, dare we say, preferences. RCI tends to move from preferences induced within institutional settings to deductive theory in which, on the basis of its institutional findings, it feels confident in imputing preferences to actors within the theory's domain. By contrast, HI tends to move from preferences induced within institutional settings back to large-scale history, thus making the preferences produced inside institutions causal forces within generously proportioned analyses across relatively large swaths of time. There is little danger that communication and collaboration will produce methodological uniformity. But there are, we hope this volume indicates, many opportunities for fruitful sharing.

References

Anderson, Perry. 1974. *Lineages of the Absolutist State*. London: Verso.

Austen-Smith, David, and Jeffrey S. Banks. 1998. "Social Choice Theory, Game Theory, and Positive Political Theory." *Annual Review of Political Science* 1: 259–87.

Banaszak, Lee Ann. 1996. *Why Movements Succeed or Fail: Opportunity, Culture, and the Struggle for Women's Suffrage*. Princeton, N.J.: Princeton University Press.

Bendix, Reinhard. 1964. *Nation-Building and Citizenship: Critical Junctures in the Labor Movement and Regime Dynamics in Latin America*. New York: John Wiley & Sons.

Clemens, Elisabeth S. 1997. *The People's Lobby: Organizational Innovation and the Rise of Interest Group Politics, 1890–1925*. Chicago: University of Chicago Press.

Collier, Ruth Berins, and David Collier. 1991. *Shaping the Political Arena: Critical Junctures in the Labor Movement and Regime Dynamics in Latin America*. Princeton, N.J.: Princeton University Press.

Douglas, Mary. 1986. *How Institutions Think*. Syracuse, N.Y.: University of Syracuse Press.

Downing, Brian M. 1992. *The Military Revolution and Political Change: Origins of Democracy and Autocracy in Early Modern Europe*. Princeton, N.J.: Princeton University Press.

Downs, Anthony. 1967. *Inside Bureaucracy*. Boston, Mass.: Little, Brown.

Ekiert, Grzegorz. 1996. *The State Against Society: Political Crises and their Aftermath in East Central Europe*. Princeton, N.J.: Princeton University Press.

Epstein, David, and Sharyn O'Halloran. 1999. *Delegating Powers: A Transaction Cost Politics Approach to Policy Making Under Separate Powers*. New York: Cambridge University Press.

Ertman, Thomas. 1997. *Birth of the Leviathan: Building States and Regimes in Medieval and Early Modern Europe*. New York: Cambridge University Press.

Eskridge, William, and John A. Ferejohn. 1992. "Making the Deal Stick: Enforcing the Original Constitutional Understanding in the Modern Regulatory State." *Journal of Law, Economics and Organization* 8(1, March): 165–89.

Esping-Andersen, Gosta. 1990. *The Three Worlds of Welfare Capitalism*. Princeton, N.J.: Princeton University Press.

Fiorina, Morris. 1981. "Congressional Control of the Bureaucracy." In *Congress Reconsidered*, 2nd ed., edited by Lawrence Dodd and Bruce Oppenheimer. Washington, D.C.: CQ Press.

Goldstone, Jack. 1991. *Revolution and Rebellion in the Early Modern World*. Berkeley: University of California Press.

Goodwin, Jeff. 2001. *States and Revolutionary Movements: 1945–1991*. New York: Cambridge University Press.

Greenstone, J. David. 1993. *The Lincoln Persuasion: Remaking American Liberalism*. Princeton, N.J.: Princeton University Press.

Hacker, Jacob S. 2002. *The Divided Welfare State*. Cambridge: Cambridge University Press.

Hall, Peter A. 1986. *Governing the Economy: The Politics of State Intervention in Britain and France*. New York: Oxford University Press.

———. 2000. "Some Reflections on Preference Formation." Memorandum for the Workshop on Rational Choice and Historical Institutionalism. New York: Russell Sage Foundation.

Hall, Peter A. and David Soskice, eds. 2001. *Varieties of Capitalism: The Institutional Foundations of Comparative Advantage*. New York: Oxford University Press.

Harsanyi, John C. 1955. "Cardinal Welfare, Individualistic Ethics, and Interpersonal Comparisons of Utility." *Journal of Political Economy* 63(August): 309–21.

Haydu, Jeffrey. 1998. "Making Use of the Past: Time Periods as Cases to Compare and as Sequences of Problem-Solving." *American Journal of Sociology* 104(September): 339–71.

Huber, Evelyne, and John D. Stephens. 2001. *Development and the Crisis of the Welfare State: Parties and Policies in World Markets*. Chicago: University of Chicago Press.

Immergut, Ellen. 1992. *Health Politics: Interests and Institutions in Western Europe*. New York: Cambridge University Press.

———. 1996. "The Normative Roots of the New Institutionalism: Historical Institutionalism and Comparative Policy Studies." In *Beitrage zur Theorieentwicklung in der Politik- und Verwaltungswissenschaft*, edited by Arthur Benz and Wolfgang Seibel. Baden-Baden: Nomos Verlag.

Katznelson, Ira. 1997. "Structure and Configuration in Comparative Politics." In *Comparative Politics: Rationality, Culture, and Structure*, edited by Mark I. Lichbach and Alan S. Zuckerman. New York: Cambridge University Press.

———. 2003. "Periodization and Preferences: Reflections on Purposive Action in Comparative Historical Social Science." In *Comparative Political Historical*

Analysis: Achievements and Agendas, edited by James Mahoney and Dietrich Rueschemeyer. New York: Cambridge University Press.

Katznelson, Ira, and Aristide R. Zolberg. 1986. *Working Class Formation: Nineteenth-Century Patterns in Western Europe and the United States*. Princeton, N.J.: Princeton University Press.

Knight, Jack. 1992. *Institutions and Social Conflict*. New York: Cambridge University Press.

Mahoney, James. 2001. *The Legacies of Liberalism: Path Dependence and Political Regimes in Central America*. Baltimore, Md.: Johns Hopkins University Press.

Mahoney, James, and Dietrich Rueschemeyer, eds. 2003. *Comparative Historical Analysis: Achievements and Agendas*. New York: Cambridge University Press.

Mayhew, David. 1974. *Congress: The Electoral Connection*. New Haven, Conn.: Yale University Press.

McAdam, Douglas, Sidney Tarrow, and Charles Tilly. 2001. *Dynamics of Contention*. New York: Cambridge University Press.

Moe, Terry M. 1982. "Regulatory Performance and Presidential Administration." *American Journal of Political Science* 26(May): 197–224.

———. 1987. "Institutions, Interests, and Positive Theory: The Politics of the NLRB." *Studies in American Political Development* 2: 236–302.

Moore, Barrington. 1966. *The Social Origins of Dictatorship and Democracy: Lord and Peasant in the Making of the Modern World*. Boston, Mass.: Beacon Press.

Niskanen, William. 1971. *Bureaucracy and Representative Government*. Chicago: Aldine Press.

Orren, Karen, and Stephen Skowronek. 2004. *The Search for American Political Development*. New York: Cambridge University Press.

Pierson, Paul. 1994. *Dismantling the Welfare State?: Reagan, Thatcher, and the Politics of Retrenchment*. Cambridge: Cambridge University Press.

———. 2004. *Politics in Time: History, Institutions, and Social Analysis*. Princeton, N.J.: Princeton University Press.

Pierson, Paul, and Theda Skocpol. 2002. "Historical Institutionalism in Contemporary Political Science." In *Political Science: The State of the Discipline*, edited by Ira Katznelson and Helen Milner. New York: W. W. Norton for the American Political Science Association.

Ritter, Gretchen. 1997. *Goldbugs and Greenbacks: The Antimonopoly Tradition and the Politics of Finance in America*. New York: Cambridge University Press.

Rueschemeyer, Dietrich A., Evelene Huber Stephens, and John Stephens. 1992. *Capitalist Development and Democracy*. Chicago: University of Chicago Press.

Sanders, Elizabeth. 1999. *Roots of Reform: Farmers, Workers, and the American State, 1877–1917*. Chicago: University of Chicago Press.

Sen, Amartya K. 1977. "Rational Fools: A Critique of the Behavioral Foundations of Economic Theory." *Philosophy and Public Affairs* 6(4): 317–44.

Shepsle, Kenneth A. 1989. "Studying Institutions: Some Lessons from the Rational Choice Approach." *Journal of Theoretical Politics* 1(1): 131–47.

Skocpol, Theda. 1979. *States and Social Revolutions: A Comparative Analysis of France, Russia, and China.* New York: Cambridge University Press.

———. 1992. *Protecting Soldiers and Mothers: The Political Origins of Social Policy in the United States.* Cambridge, Mass.: Harvard University Press.

Skowronek, Stephen. 1993. *The Politics Presidents Make: Leadership from John Adams to Bill Clinton.* Cambridge, Mass.: Harvard University Press.

Steinmo, Sven. 1996. *Taxation and Democracy: Swedish, British, and American Approaches to Financing the Modern State.* New Haven, Conn.: Yale University Press.

Stigler, George S. 1971. "The Theory of Economic Regulation." *Bell Journal of Economics and Management Science* 2(spring): 3–21.

Streek, Wolfgang. 1992. *Social Institutions and Economic Performance.* Newbury Park, Calif.: Sage Publications.

Swenson, Peter. 2002. *Capitalists Against Markets.* New York: Oxford University Press.

Tarrow, Sidney. 1998. *Power in Movement: Social Movements and Contentious Politics.* New York: Cambridge University Press.

Thelen, Kathleen. 1991. *Union of Parts: Labor Politics in Postwar Germany.* Ithaca, N.Y.: Cornell University Press.

Tilly, Charles, ed. 1975. *The Formation of National States in Western Europe.* Princeton, N.J.: Princeton University Press.

Tilly, Charles. 1984. *Big Structures, Large Processes, Huge Comparisons.* New York: Russell Sage Foundation.

Tollison, Robert. 1982. "Rent Seeking: A Survey." *Kyklos* 35(4): 575–602.

Tullock, Gordon. 1965. *The Politics of Bureaucracy.* Washington, D.C.: Public Affairs Press.

Ullman-Margalit, Edna. 1984. "Opting: The Case of 'Big' Decisions," *Wissenshacftscolleg Jahrbuch.* Berlin: Wissenshacftscolleg.

Ullman-Margalit, Edna, and Sidney Morgenbesser. 1977. "Picking and Choosing." *Social Research* 44(4): 757–86.

Waldner, David. 1999. *State Building and Late Development.* Ithaca, N.Y.: Cornell University Press.

Wallerstein, Immanuel. 1974. *The Modern World-System: Capitalist Agriculture and the Origins of the European World Economy in the Sixteenth Century.* New York: Academic Press.

Weingast, Barry R., and Mark J. Moran. 1983. "Bureaucratic Discretion or Congressional Control: Regulatory Policymaking by the FTC." *Journal of Political Economy* 91(October): 765–800.

Wickham-Crowley, Timothy P. 1992. *Guerillas and Revolutions in Latin America: A Comparative Study of Insurgents and Regimes Since 1956.* Princeton, N.J.: Princeton University Press.

Wilson, James Q. 1980. *The Politics of Regulation.* New York: Basic Books.

Yashar, Deborah. 1997. *Demanding Democracy: Reform and Reaction in Costa Rica and Guatemala, 1870s to 1950s.* Stanford, Calif.: Stanford University Press.

PART I

Situations

2

A Cross of Gold, a Crown of Thorns: Preferences and Decisions in the 1896 Democratic National Convention

Richard Bensel

When the 1896 Democratic National Convention assembled in the second week of July, the delegates anticipated that two very different but equally important decisions would be made. One of these involved the adoption of a party platform for the coming campaign. The platform decision, in turn, was overwhelmingly dominated by a single plank on the monetary standard (whether the party would commit itself to the free coinage of silver). The other decision involved the nomination of a candidate for president.[1]

For some months before the convention assembled, both the delegates and outside observers anticipated that the platform fight would be a well-structured game in which almost all the participants possessed strong, publicly revealed preferences. And that is, in fact, how the decision was made. The contest for the presidential nomination, on the other hand, was a wide open race in which most delegates, when they arrived in Chicago, held soft sentiments about potential nominees. In many cases, in fact, delegates appeared to be indifferent toward two or more of the candidates. The result was a highly contingent process in which a speech by William Jennings Bryan, delivered in defense of the silver plank in the majority platform, played a critical role in shaping the preferences of the delegates. This "Cross of Gold" speech has ever since been widely acknowledged as one of the most moving oratorical performances in American history.[2] Because Bryan was at most a very dark horse candidate at the beginning of the convention (most observers saw him as nothing more than the favorite son of the small Nebraska delegation), any attempt to analyze the nomination contest must explain how his speech came to shape the preferences of a large majority of the delegates.

Thus we have two equally important but very different situations in this convention. Each involved the same participants within a decision process in which the stakes were very high. The decisions themselves were almost but not entirely separable; announced positions on the monetary plank of the platform were so strongly fixed and the plank was so salient that silver candidates for the nomination could not and would not have run on a gold platform, and vice versa. However, all silver candidates could have run on the silver plank that was adopted and all gold candidates could have stood on the hard money platform that was rejected. In addition, most (but not all) of the participants were party professionals, fully prepared to evaluate the signaling and other displays of sentiment constantly produced in this information-rich environment. Thus we can analyze two different decisions in the same convention, one of them known well in advance to closely resemble a structured game and the other expected to be a highly contingent process. The participants were the same in each case but interacted with each other and came to form their preferences in diametrically contrasting ways.

Overview

Delegate preferences on both silver and gold were strong in the sense that they directly implied votes for or against the silver plank, which ultimately (and predictably) came before the convention. However, with respect to the candidates, delegate preferences were weak in the sense that they were highly unstable and largely unformed. They also tended to be indirect because delegates often viewed candidates as means rather than ends. For example, as they surveyed the field, individual delegates and state delegations sometimes parked their support with favorite sons or other candidates unlikely to be serious candidates for the nomination. Thus publicly indicating that they were in play, these delegates and delegations could then bargain with the representatives of more viable candidates over things like patronage; these negotiations also clearly implied that the candidates were being treated as means rather than ends.

The primary purpose here is to indicate the varying utility of assuming fixed, strong preferences as a precondition for "playing the game" in more formal game theoretic models. Conflict over the party platform, for example, unwound in a context in which delegate preferences were both fixed and strong. As a result, the game, if formally modeled, would be very simple and relatively uninteresting; all that happened was that the silver delegates outvoted the gold faction and thus adopted the silver plank. Competition for the presidential nomination, on the other hand, was conducted in a context in which delegate preferences were highly unstable and weak. For that reason, the process through which Bryan won the nomination cannot be formalized in traditional game theoretic terms even though both the delegates and the candidates often exhibited instrumentally rational and strategically sophisticated behavior. The dissent, if there is one, is thus only from the assumptions that underlie more formal game theoretic models, not from the general principles of rational choice theory.[3]

A Digression on Rules

For the purposes of this analysis, the procedural rules that governed the convention will be assumed to have been fixed in advance of the actual deliberations. However, this working assumption is impaired by a number of instances in which these rules were either viewed as open to formal revision (in the sense that the convention could explicitly change the rule in question) or required remedial interpretation (in the sense that past precedents did not indicate how the rule would apply in the present situation). The most important uncertainties involved: first, whether the national committee would allow the silver faction to present an alternative to the gold man selected by the committee to be temporary chairman of the convention; second, whether the order of business that had prevailed in prior conventions would be followed in Chicago (most important, whether the adoption of a platform would precede the nomination of the presidential candidate); and, third, whether the unit rule and the two-thirds rule would be abandoned.

In the actual course of events, each of these decisions and rulings was made in a way that most conformed with past precedents and thus only marginally, if at all, upset the pre-convention calculations and strategies of the delegates and candidates. With respect to these rulings, we should conclude that most of the proceedings were highly structured by well-known and constraining rules even though, in some cases the delegates must have been a little uncertain as to how a rule would be interpreted. Few situations in ordinary politics are precisely governed by a fixed set of procedures; the 1896 Democratic National Convention, in practice, was perhaps one of the more well-behaved arenas, particularly in light of the extremely passionate preferences the delegates held with respect to silver and gold.

The Cross of Gold: Adoption of the Silver Plank

By the time delegates began to assemble in Chicago in early July, almost all observers expected that the party would endorse free coinage of silver in the platform.[4] Adoption of this plank was to cap the campaign that had led many state conventions to endorse free coinage and, in most cases, bind their delegates to that position. For many delegates, this formal commitment was probably unnecessary: "silverites," as those favoring free coinage were commonly known, fervently believed that the then prevailing gold standard had a malevolent impact on the American economy and should be replaced by silver. Be that as it may, the preferences of delegates with respect to silver and gold were well known and even published in detail before they arrived in Chicago. These preferences were viewed as unshakable as the convention opened, an interpretation that was repeatedly confirmed as the delegates deliberated.

One of the most detailed descriptions of the strength of the silver and gold factions was published in the *Chicago Tribune* on June 27, ten days before the delegates convened. Since the last of the state conventions had just adjourned, this was the earliest date at which the identities of all 930 of the delegates were known and, thus, the earliest date at which preferences on the monetary standard could be assigned to each of them.[5] The *Tribune* printed the names of each delegate together with the "instructions" with which their states had bound them or, if no instructions had been given, their individual preferences with respect to the monetary standard. Of the fifty-one states and territories represented at the convention, thirty-three had adopted resolutions favoring silver, sixteen had done the same for gold, and only two (Florida and the District of Columbia) had not adopted resolutions one way or the other. Most of the silver states had passed very similar resolutions, each of which was intended to be an iron-clad commitment to the "free coinage of silver at a ratio of 16 to 1 without waiting for concurrence by other nations."[6] Although the gold states had endorsed the yellow metal in resolutions that varied a little bit more in language, their commitment to sound money (a common euphemism for the gold standard) was equally strong.[7]

Because preferences with respect to the monetary standard were so well defined and strongly held, the strategic situation was relatively simple; all the silverites, who comprised an overwhelming majority of the delegates, had to do was approve the plank in the convention. In practice, the silver delegates took a number of steps to ensure, as best they could, that this decision would not become entangled in other issues. The first of these was to organize their forces just prior to the convening of the convention. In the meetings in which they coordinated their strategy, representatives of the various silver delegations agreed to support prominent silver senators as consensus candidates for the posts of temporary and permanent chairmen, thereby preventing the emergence of competing candidates.[8] Competition for the posts, the silver leaders felt, might have provided an opening that could have been exploited by the gold faction.[9]

The second most important tactical decision made by silver leaders was to suppress a proposed caucus of all the silver delegates; this caucus had been suggested as a means of deciding the major issues before the convention actually met. It would have excluded the gold delegates and thus would have prevented them from attempting to divide the silver forces by offering their votes or other blandishments.[10] The silverites were, quite reasonably, concerned that their parliamentary skills, the political prestige of their leaders, and the relative strength of their financial resources were overmatched by those available to the gold faction.[11] The exclusion of gold delegates from this preliminary caucus would have eliminated much of the danger that this imbalance entailed by allowing the silverites to agree upon a common agenda, an agenda that subsequently could have been rammed through the convention without delay or distraction from the gold faction (*Chicago Tribune*, July 2, 3, 1896).

The problem with this proposal was that the leading silver candidates for the presidential nomination also saw this preliminary caucus as an opportunity to pledge silver delegates to their own candidacy.[12] Because none of these candidates had anything approaching a lock on the nomination, the attempt to pledge the silver faction to a particular candidate might very well have sparked a long and bitter contest, a contest that might have seriously splintered the silver faction. For that reason, and because coordination was easily achieved on the platform and on candidates for temporary and permanent chairmen, silver leaders in the convention discouraged and ultimately blocked a preliminary caucus of the soft money delegates.

The last potential obstacle in the path of this structured game was the platform itself. Hoping to avoid divisive conflict over other issues, many silverites wished to restrict it (the platform) to a single plank demanding the free coinage of silver (in the formulaic terms already described).[13] In the end, this restriction was felt to be unnecessary because there were no other issues that even remotely approached the silver declaration in saliency.[14] Although the gold faction disliked the platform's endorsement of a national income tax and criticism of the use of federal court injunctions in labor disputes, these were very popular among silver delegates. Giving up the fight on these issues, the gold delegates chose to seriously challenge only two decisions by the committee on resolutions. One was the absence of what was usually a routine endorsement of a Democratic administration if the party controlled the White House. Because President Cleveland was despised by a majority of the delegates at the convention, a roll call on the minority report praising his administration lost by almost two to one. In this vote well over 90 percent of the silver faction opposed the resolution. Every gold delegate supported it—and Cleveland (for this roll call, see Dickinson 1896, 247). The second challenge was, of course, to the plank endorsing the free coinage of silver. In sum, because the alignment of delegates on most other issues was very close to that dividing the convention on the monetary standard, the silver faction risked little in opening up the platform to the full array of topics with which these declarations were normally festooned.

These three tactical decisions (the prior selection of temporary and permanent convention chairmen, the move to disconnect the declaration for silver in the platform from the presidential nomination, and the opening up of the platform to secondary issues) were very effective.[15] As shepherds of the preferences for silver, which they knew the delegates held as they arrived in Chicago, the silver leaders guided their flock to the platform decision with only, at most, six defections.[16] On the way, the silver faction picked up nine delegates who had previously indicated gold preferences, more than compensating for their losses.[17] When the convention faced the choice between the gold standard and free coinage of silver during deliberations on the platform on July 9, 1896, over 97 percent of the delegates voted as the *Tribune* had expected they would in their June 27 article (see table 2.1).[18]

The Contest for the Presidential Nomination

The contrast between delegate commitments on monetary policy and delegate ambivalence toward those who had entered the race for the presidential nomination could hardly have been more stark. With respect to the monetary standard, the preferences were strong and publicly identified well in advance of the decision. With respect to the various candidates who might run on the silver platform that the convention was certain to adopt, most delegates had only very shallow and tentative sentiments (Coletta 1964, 121). The public images of the candidates did not change very much during the proceedings, but the way in which delegates interpreted these images, matching them to plausible future developments in national and local politics, apparently changed quite a bit.

To be sure, the convention did have a front-runner in Representative Richard Parks Bland of Missouri, who had perhaps 100 delegates instructed by their states to support him. However, with instructions for 150 more delegates scattered among six other silver possibilities, the race for the nomination was still wide open. More than half of the silver delegates, in fact, were still uncommitted to any candidate.

Table 2.1   Announced Preferences of the Delegates on the Monetary Standard and Adoption of the Silver Plank in the National Democratic Platform

State	*Chicago Tribune* (June 27) Silver	Gold	Platform Roll Call (July 9) Silver	Gold	Discrepancy (if Any)
Alabama	22		22		
Arkansas	16		16		
California	18		18		
Colorado	8		8		
Connecticut		12		12	
Delaware		6	1	5	1
Florida	4	4	5	3	1
Georgia	26		26		
Idaho	6		6		
Illinois	48		48		
Indiana	30		30		
Iowa	26		26		
Kansas	20		20		
Kentucky	26		26		
Louisiana	16		16		
Maine	5	7	2	10	3
Maryland		16	4	12	4
Massachusetts		30	3	27	3
Michigan	28		28		
Minnesota	6	12	6	11	(1 absent)
Mississippi	18		18		
Missouri	34		34		
Montana	6		6		
Nebraska	16		16		
Nevada	6		6		
New Hampshire		8		8	
New Jersey		20		20	
New York		72		72	
North Carolina	22		22		
North Dakota	6		6		
Ohio	46		46		
Oregon	8		8		
Pennsylvania		64		64	
Rhode Island		8		8	

(*Table continues on p. 34.*)

Table 2.1 *Continued*

	Chicago Tribune (June 27)		Platform Roll Call (July 9)		Discrepancy (if Any)
	Silver	Gold	Silver	Gold	
South Carolina	18		18		
South Dakota		8		8	
Tennessee	24		24		
Texas	30		30		
Utah	6		6		
Vermont		8		8	
Virginia	24		24		
Washington	5	3	5	3	
West Virginia	12		12		
Wisconsin		24		24	
Wyoming	6		6		
Territory					
Alaska	6			6	6
Arizona	6		6		
District of Columbia	5	1	4	2	1
Indian Territory	6		6		
New Mexico	6		4	2	2
Oklahoma Territory	6		6		
Total	627	303	624	305	21

Sources: Delegate preferences were reported in the *Chicago Tribune*, June 27, 1896. The roll call on the minority report from the resolutions committee (supporting the gold standard) appeared in Dickinson (1896, 241).

Notes: Delegate preferences, as originally reported in the *Tribune*, have been adjusted to take into account the expansion of the delegations from the territories (from two to six delegates in each case) and the seating of one or the other of competing delegations after contests were decided. Because the monetary preferences of the individuals involved in these expansions and contests were already known, the consequences of these actions were well anticipated before the fact. The *Tribune* also adjusted individual preferences where a unit rule was expected to suppress a minority of a state delegation. For example, the Wisconsin delegation was split, with nineteen delegates favoring gold and five supporting silver. Because the state convention had bound all the delegates to gold, the *Tribune* reported the five silverites as favoring the yellow metal. In one instance, the state of Washington, the *Tribune* expected the unit rule to be enforced and, thus, that all eight votes would be cast for silver even though three delegates supported gold. When the rule was not enforced, the delegates split five to three for silver on the roll call, just as the *Tribune* had reported their individual preferences. Since the purpose of this table is to demonstrate the extent to which preferences had been accurately identified prior to the convention (and not to predict whether or not the unit rule would be enforced within a state delegation), the distribution of preferences have been entered in this table as the *Tribune* assigned them to individual delegates.

In addition to these leading possibilities, an additional half a dozen or so candidates were in the running, some supported by little more than rumors in the daily press. Others had more substantial reputations and followings. One, Senator Henry Teller of Colorado, was even a Republican, albeit a Republican who had bolted his party after the Republican convention had unambiguously endorsed the gold standard.[19] However, even among those delegates who had been bound by their state conventions, loyalties to particular candidates were usually weak. When asked who they were inclined to support for the nomination, most delegates would name two or more possibilities or, just as often, none at all.

Goals of the Delegates

A national party convention is, among other things, a political ritual in which the delegates collectively nominate a candidate for the presidency. As ritual, a national convention serves many organizational purposes, including sharing of information on strategy and tactics in the coming campaign, coordinating policy stances in the form of platform planks, and publicly pledging support for the nominee. These purposes are served even where the likely nominee is known far in advance of the actual meeting of the delegates. In such cases, the ritual aspects of the convention take on a very formalistic character (resembling, for example, the public ceremonies in which a monarch is anointed). When the identity of the nominee is far from certain, these rituals are still followed but they become the context within which delegates collectively make a decision and the setting within which candidates and their managers compete with one another.[20]

However, although the 1896 national convention was the setting within which a coordination problem was solved (with respect to naming the Democratic presidential nominee), the motives of the delegates who participated in this solution were much more complex and diverse. Some, for example, clearly ranked potential nominees by their relative strength as candidates in the general election. In doing so, their motives were a prospective share in presidential patronage, the enactment of particular policies by the federal government, or the collateral support a popular candidate would lend to state and local tickets, or perhaps some combination of the three. Other delegates were more oriented toward policy issues, desiring above all else, for example, that the presidential nominee possess a clear and sincere commitment to the free coinage of silver. Such delegates often ranked the competing possibilities differently from those who favored the strongest candidate for the presidency.

Many other delegates ordered the candidates in terms of their own career advancement. For some, this meant that they were more oriented toward the leaders of their state delegations than toward the candidates because the leaders were much more likely to influence their career prospects. As the leaders of the state delegations maneuvered for advantage in the convention, these delegates simply followed suit. Finally, other delegates were much more concerned with how their participation in the convention played at home than anything else. Positive coverage by newspaper reporters was the most important goal for these delegates.

Thus, while there was certainly a coordination aspect to the convention proceedings (in the sense that the delegates had to decide who the nominee would be), the aggregation of delegates into the necessary two-thirds majority was a multidimensional process in which individual delegates often ordered their preferences along more than one dimension and could only speculate on the motives (and therefore the preference orderings) of other delegates.[21] Moreover, the gold delegates, comprising almost one-third of the convention, probably preferred that the party nominate no one because the nominee, whoever he might be, would support the free coinage of silver. For these delegates, there was no coordination problem because they would have preferred a deadlocked convention.[22] The clearest coordination aspect to the proceedings, once the convention was underway, was that there was a tipping point at which the front-runner would become unstoppable because many delegates (for example, those most interested in presidential patronage or personal career advancement) would join his bandwagon.[23]

Displays of Preferences and Sentiment

Much of the activity by delegates in the days just prior to and during the convention involved public displays of support for one of the various presidential possibilities. The most reliable displays were those in which the delegate was bound by the instructions of a state delegation.[24] Such declarations were extremely likely to be translated into votes for the candidate, particularly during the early balloting. However, instructions by a state convention did not mean that the bound delegates personally favored the candidate. When the Texas convention pledged the delegation to Richard Bland of Missouri, for example, ex-Governor J. S. Hogg, one of the at-large delegates, declared that the instructions "would have no more effect on the Chicago delegation than the sniffs of a sand-hill 'possum."[25]

Much less reliable, although often more sincere, were public expressions of support given by individual delegates. As they arrived in Chicago, individual delegates were often debriefed by reporters as to their own and their delegation's attitudes toward the presidential possibilities. For example, as the *Chicago Tribune* reported on June 29, 1896, E. D. Matts of Montana, an at-large delegate arriving more than a week before the convention was to begin, declared that, although his delegation was not instructed, "he thought they would give their support to the Missourian [Bland]. He [personally] desires to see Bland nominated because, in his opinion, the bolting Republicans who want Teller, the Populists, and the Silver League people will be more likely to indorse him than any other Democrat."

Although campaign organizations consistently interpreted these expressions of sentiment in ways that most favored the prospects of their candidates, their task was not an easy one. Speaking to a reporter as he set up Bland's headquarters in the Auditorium Annex Hotel, George Washington Allen's "chief duty was to tell all comers Congressman Bland is already as good as nominated." Representing the front runner, Allen thus attempted both to stabilize sentiment that had already been attracted to the candidate and, if possible, expand such expressions of support to the "tipping point" where a bandwagon effect would make his nomination unstoppable.[26] Allen similarly praised ex-Governor Horace Boies as "our most formidable competitor" but said that he did "not think he can win," thereby implying that the Iowa man could not reach that tipping point. Noting that Bland already had a 100 or so votes bound to him by state conventions, Allen went on to claim about 250 votes for his candidate on the first ballot, with another 150 votes moving in Bland's direction on the second. As spokesman for the front runner, Allen was careful to both project victory and retain credibility as a political informant. Realizing this, he was quite specific in his claims, naming the states that he thought would support Bland on the opening roll calls. And, as favorable projections go, he was—as the *Chicago Tribune* reported on June 30 and July 3, 1896—both accurate and perhaps a little conservative (for other estimates of first ballot strength, see the July 4, 1896 issue). As to the presidential election itself, with Bland at the head of the ticket, Allen was less restrained.[27]

Strategic and Tactical Aspects of the Nominating Decision

In the sense that each of the delegates controlled one vote, the convention was a decentralized and level playing field. The diverse and often contradictory motives the delegates held reinforced this democratic and apparently chaotic political context; no one knew when or how the delegates would finally come to make a choice. However, there were at least four ways in which the convention exhibited a "lumpy" underlying structure. The first, as mentioned, was a tipping point at which delegates expected a bandwagon for the eventual nominee. Once this point was reached, delegates and candidates would end their posturing and the rituals associated with the nomination would begin (a motion for unanimity and an announcement of victory from the convention chair, for example). The second, as mentioned, was the fact that some of the state delegations were already bound by instructions to vote for particular candidates. Other delegations, although not bound by instructions, would cast their votes under the unit rule, meaning that a majority of the delegation would determine how all the state's votes would be cast. In these cases, the preferences of dissenting delegates would not be registered until and if the majority in their delegation disintegrated or they could form a majority behind their favored candidate.

The third structural characteristic to the nominating decision was the isolation of those delegates who supported the gold standard. Although they comprised almost a third of the convention, the gold delegates were considered pariahs by the silver faction.[28] Any attempt by a silver candidate to reach out to the gold delegations was deemed a treacherous compromise of the cause and, for most silverites, disqualified the candidate from further consideration.[29] Governor Claude Matthews, for example, was viewed as having extended a peace offering to the gold faction by publicly supporting the inclusion of a gold man in the otherwise silver delegation from Indiana (for a detailed account of the Indiana convention, see the *Atlanta Constitution* of June 25, 1896). His spokesmen were also rumored to have been quietly exploring cooperation with the gold faction as a means of winning the nomination. Both were said to have irreparably tainted his candidacy before the voting began.[30] After Matthews fell from grace, the other silver candidates apparently never opened negotiations with the gold delegations.[31] For their part, when the balloting on the nomination began, most gold delegates abstained from voting. Some, in fact, were not even on the convention floor.[32]

Finally, with information on delegate preferences coming in from a wide variety of sources, much of it of dubious quality and the remainder often so vague as to be useless, most delegates focused on a few large state delegations as landmarks of convention sentiment.[33] From this perspective, the most important delegation was from Illinois, led by Governor John Peter Altgeld. Because the gold faction controlled some 300 delegates in the convention, a silver candidate had to attract almost every vote among the 600 or so silverites to win the nomination under the two-thirds rule. With forty-eight delegates, Illinois was the largest contingent committed to silver and thus loomed as the most crucial delegation in the race for the nomination. The pivotal position of the state was enhanced by the fact that Altgeld was foreign born, having immigrated to the United States from Germany when he was an infant. Thus ineligible for the presidency, he was a free agent as leader of the Illinois delegation.[34] For these reasons, any early commitment by the delegation to one or the other of the candidates would likely be interpreted both as an objective evaluation of the likelihood that he would be nominated and a major step in that direction in terms of votes.[35]

The other pivotal state delegation was Ohio, which with its forty-six votes was only slightly smaller than Illinois. Led by John R. McLean and also pledged under the unit rule to his presidential candidacy, Ohio was not as free to play the field as Illinois. However, most observers felt that McLean's support for the nomination was more or less confined to his home state delegation and that McLean himself was well aware that his ambitions should be limited. A very wealthy man and a long-time supporter of silver as owner-editor of the *Cincinnati Enquirer*, McLean was widely viewed as someone who could balance the ticket for most of the other silver candidates. His money would help bankroll the campaign. Ohio, along with Illinois, promised to be one of the pivotal states in the general election. In this scenario, Ohio's votes were widely viewed as openly negotiable: in return for the vice presidential nomination for McLean, as the July 5, 1896, *Chicago Tribune* reported, the state would put the eventual nominee over the top. Because McLean could negotiate such an arrangement only once, he and his state delegation had to wait until the tide toward one of the candidates had firmly set. Thus, despite its pivotal role, the Ohio delegation did not produce useful signals for most of the convention. Until McLean was ready to pounce, his delegates remained nominally loyal to his presidential candidacy.

The Candidates

The delegates formed preferences very late in the nominating process for a number of reasons, two of them structural. For example, the rule requiring a two-thirds majority for a nomination set the tipping point for a bandwagon stampede much higher than it would have been with a simple majority. The impact of the rule was immeasurably strengthened by the presence of the three hundred or so gold delegates. Constituting almost exactly one-third of the convention, the hard money delegates, even if they had been so inclined, could not participate in a winning coalition because their support would have been a kiss of death to any silver candidacy. For this reason, observers attempting to handicap the race had to assume that a victorious silver candidate must attract the votes of almost every silver delegate to win the nomination. The number of announced candidates and the sizable delegations instructed to possibilities other than the front-runner (such as Ohio, Indiana, Kentucky, and Iowa) made, to all appearances, an early bandwagon literally impossible.[36]

The second structural factor was more or less related to the first. The deep split in the party between the hard and soft money factions closely followed sectional lines. Every state delegation from the Northeast, down to and including Maryland and Delaware, favored gold. Every delegation from the South and West, excluding Alaska and South Dakota but including West Virginia, Kentucky, Missouri, and the remainder of the Plains states, favored silver. Only the states of the Midwest were seriously split between the factions. As a result of this sectional alignment, the southern and border state delegations comprised almost exactly half of the 600 delegates in the silver faction. Given the pariah status of the South in national politics, almost all of the politicians from the southern and border states were, in practice, ineligible for the presidential nomination.[37] Generally hostile to southerners, northern electorates were particularly opposed to the numerous Democratic leaders from these states who had fought for the Confederacy during the Civil War. Confederate service, for example, was the most frequent objection made to Senator Blackburn of Kentucky, who otherwise would have been a much stronger candidate for the nomination.[38]

For decades, the Democratic party had looked to the North for men to place at the top of the ticket. Because of its size and pivotal position in most general elections, the party usually nominated someone from New York state. In the last three elections, that someone had been Grover Cleveland, the sitting president. In the 1896 convention, however, no prominent politician from New York or anywhere else in the Northeast was acceptable to a majority of the convention because they all backed hard money. In fact, because the northeastern leaders were so strongly committed to the gold standard, they probably would have refused the nomination even if the silver faction had, quite implausibly, proffered it. Thus the regional alignment on the monetary standard effectively excluded from consideration all otherwise plausible candidates from the traditional seedbed of Democratic presidential nominees while raising to national leadership a coterie of southern politicians who were practically ineligible for the nomination. As a result, the relative paucity of strong presidential possibilities from the West and Midwest made the convention's task much more difficult than it otherwise might have been.

Within this context, the Bland campaign had attempted to have its cake and eat it too. On the one hand, his managers stressed that Bland's home state of Missouri was oriented toward the South in national politics. Even though the state had been formally aligned with the Union during the Civil War, Missouri Democrats had been much more likely to elect former Confederates than Union veterans to political office, particularly once Reconstruction had come to a close. Furthermore, Bland's congressional district had contained some of the counties that had most strongly supported the southern cause. He was clearly comfortable working with former Confederates within the party and could not have succeeded in gaining and holding his congressional seat without their support. On the other hand, his organization also stressed that Bland had spent the Civil War in the West, where he saw military service as part of a punitive expedition against the Paiutes in Nevada. He moved back to Missouri only after the war ended and thus did not take sides during the bitter guerilla fighting within the state. Thus Bland could simultaneously pose as a southerner and a Union loyalist. However, by attempting to work both sides of the street, Bland's managers ultimately weakened their claims on both Union loyalists and Confederate sympathizers.[39]

Even so, Bland might still have won the nomination had he offered stronger personal credentials. For one thing, he could not have been better suited from a policy perspective as the nominee on a soft money platform. His single-minded devotion to silver throughout a long political career had produced an extremely narrow political profile, earning him the sobriquet "Silver Dick." On the one hand, this narrow profile was an advantage in that Bland's managers could more easily finesse other, possibly divisive issues. On the other hand, however, beyond his nickname and well-known dedication to the cause, Bland's people had "little to say in his favor." In fact, his contemporaries in Congress tended to view him as a rather obnoxious lightweight. One *Chicago Tribune* reporter wrote on July 7, 1896, that Bland's managers admitted as much, stating that they "do not attempt to deny that he is personally offensive to a great many people . . . that he never could lay claim to the title of a statesman, and, in fact, that even among his Democratic associates in the House he was [more] the cause of rather mild amusement than of any admiration."

In the opinion of many party leaders, this reputation meant that, regardless of the enthusiasm Bland's candidacy might attract among the rank and file, the Missouri man would eventually fall short in the balloting. When added to Bland's sterling record on silver, that expectation meant that opportunistic state delegations could park their votes under his banner while examining the rest of the field and awaiting further developments.[40] All of this meant that Bland's delegate counts were softer than they appeared; although few of the delegates counted in his totals would have deserted him had he ever approached the tipping point, many would readily turn to another candidate if one emerged from the rest of the pack. In terms of producing an early deadlock in the voting, the Bland candidacy could not have been better designed; here was a front-runner, holding almost half of the votes necessary to a nomination, who few delegates expected or wanted to win.

Populists and Silver Republicans

Once they had nailed down the platform and nominated their ticket, silver Democrats realized that the best they could hope for was the neutrality of the gold faction of their party. Even nominal endorsements of the national party nominees on a silver platform appeared out of reach and at least some open defections to McKinley and the Republicans seemed inevitable. To make up for these losses, silver Democrats hoped to attract both Populists and silver Republicans to their ticket. In fact, because there appeared to be no way in which the silver wing could placate the gold faction, a major third party effort in the presidential contest by either the Populists or silver Republicans would have doomed a silver Democrat. As a result, both Populists and silver Republicans held a practical veto over the various candidates; to nominate someone who would be unacceptable to either group would be to lose the election before the campaign began.

Silver Republicans were led by a coterie of western senators accustomed to office-holding and the pragmatic realities of incumbency. They were also more narrowly committed to free silver as an issue than the Populists or even the Democrats. In fact, to stand with McKinley and gold would have destroyed their party in any of the mountain states of the West. A third-party insurgency against silver Democrats, the Populists, and a regular organization remnant of their own party was even more suicidal. For these reasons, fusion with the silver Democrats on the presidential ticket on almost any terms was the only way these Republicans would retain their seats. The silver Republican leadership made it known that they would endorse almost any silver Democratic nominee. Although there was some uncertainty concerning how easily they could deliver rank and file voters to the silver cause, most Democrats assumed that, with an endorsement by western Republican leaders, their party nominee would easily carry the silver Republican states.

Much more problematic were the Populists, whose political agenda was much more varied, whose leaders were much less pragmatically adjusted to office-holding and incumbency, and whose rank and file were comparatively obstreperous.[41] The Populists had drawn a million votes in the 1892 presidential contest and, in the 1894 midterm elections, had emerged as a major, in some cases the dominant, party organization in most states outside the manufacturing belt of the Northeast and Great Lakes. However, unlike the silver Republicans, for whom the choice was fusion or political death, endorsement of a Democratic presidential nominee was viewed as suicidal by many Populists. This was particularly the case for southern Populists, who were engaged in rather bitter class warfare with their Democratic overlords. For them, endorsement of a silver Democratic presidential candidate was anathema, not because they did not support silver, but because fusion on the national ticket would fatally impair their often close cooperation with southern Republicans.[42]

For all these reasons, the Populists held a much more effective veto over the Democratic presidential nomination than the silver Republicans. The problem, seen from the silver Democrat perspective, was that no one was sure who could speak for those Populists who would entertain fusion.[43] Given the fragmented Populist leadership and the hostility of many rank-and-file party members to fusion on any terms, there was simply no one with whom the silver Democrats could bargain.[44] That a Populist endorsement of the Democratic nominee was essential to victory was assumed by almost every silver Democrat at the convention. Which of the candidates would be acceptable to the Populists, however, was very much in doubt: spokesmen for some of the more plausible choices openly claimed Populist support as they argued their cases; delegates backing less plausible alternatives simply kept quiet.

Bryan's Nomination

The man who eventually emerged from the pack, ultimately attracting votes from all the silver delegates, was of course William Jennings Bryan. A huge, spontaneous demonstration followed Bryan's "Cross of Gold" speech.[45] The cheering and general uproar continued for almost thirty minutes and Bryan himself was physically carried from the podium back to the Nebraska delegation on the convention floor. Most of the silver state standards were simultaneously brought over to the Nebraska delegation. From there, the excited delegates began to march in a circle around the center sections of that part of the hall in which the delegates were seated.[46] Clearly agitated by this eruption of sentiment in favor of the "Boy Orator of the Platte," Bland's managers were nonetheless amazed, as the *Chicago Tribune* of July 10, 1896, reported, "at the terrific rate at which the Nebraska boy covered the ground" previously separating him from the leading candidate for the nomination, jumping "from a nonentity to a first position."

Bryan had made no secret of his presidential aspirations but, as is clear from numerous *Chicago Tribune* reports June 29 and again on July 1, 3, 4, and 5 of 1896, most observers ignored or deeply discounted his chances.[47] Even when he began to emerge as a substantial candidate, he was often viewed as the stalking horse for one or more of the other possibilities, particularly Senator Teller of Colorado. When delegates flocked to his banner following the "Cross of Gold" speech, some of the party leaders who had helped manufacture his boom were said to have been appalled at the result.[48] Now that he was clearly a serious candidate for the nomination, Bryan retired to his hotel room to await the result (Coletta 1964, 142–43). On the fifth ballot, he received the nomination.[49] To say that he had come from behind in the presidential contest would have been a gross understatement.[50]

Conclusion

The major goal of this analysis has been to demonstrate how the formation of preferences can be either, in some cases, thoroughly exogenous and, in other cases, interactively endogenous to the making of a collective decision. Both types appeared within the context of the 1896 Democratic national convention. In the first, delegates voted for or against the silver plank as long-standing preferences were instrumentally translated into votes. In the most minute detail, those votes were predicted well in advance of the convention. In the second, William Jennings Bryan, who was not even considered a dark horse candidate by most observers as the convention opened, ultimately wound up with the presidential nomination. This outcome surprised all observers and delegates (with the possible exception of Bryan himself).

The roll call on the silver plank conforms comfortably with the tendency underlying much of the rational choice literature to treat collective political decisions, such as legislative voting, as the revelation of preferences. Seen this way, the votes for and against the silver plank simply translated firmly held and long-standing preferences that had been revealed even before the delegates arrived in Chicago. Because delegates had formed their preferences long before they came to the convention, the silver delegates' parliamentary decisions and strategies can be viewed as the instrumental execution of these preferences on monetary policy. The choice of parliamentary tactics, for example, was dictated entirely by the silver leaders' realization that a stable majority for silver existed, which—when properly directed and managed—would be enough to overcome the gold minority. There were, to be sure, subtleties associated with the choice of parliamentary tactics. But these were unrelated to the certainty that a majority of the delegates would display attitudes favorable to the free coinage of silver whenever called upon to vote. If we wished to do so, these strategies and the decision itself could be easily modeled in (very simple) game theoretic terms. In addition the imputation of (long-standing, durable) preferences from the votes, although unnecessary because delegates publicly declared their stances far in advance of the roll call, would have been sound.

If we were to consider how these preferences were formed, we would be compelled to trace them back to the political context of the states from which the delegates came. For some delegates, that context became a determinant factor years before the Chicago convention. For others, the state convention set the context for delegates just months, sometimes weeks, before the national platform was adopted. If we take the analysis another step or two backward, to the political and economic conditions from which the terms of intrastate party competition arose, then the emergence of preferences among the delegates can sometimes be traced back for decades. For these reasons, however, we would not try to explain the formation of preferences as induced by the strategic circumstances and interaction of the delegates at the convention. If anything, silver leaders carefully protected the preferences of their faction from just such factors as they guided their forces toward adoption of the silver plank.

The presidential contest, of course, was quite different. For one thing, although all the delegates participated in a common decision (the choice of a presidential candidate), they did not share a common context for that decision. For some, the choice of a candidate was an end unto itself because they passionately supported that candidate. For others, the goal was the selection of the most viable candidate, because patronage and other rewards would accompany party victory. Still others, almost all of them supporting gold, preferred that the party run no candidate. The radical diversity in fundamental goals meant that the delegates did not share a foundational orientation toward the decision facing them.[51] The absence of such an orientation, along with the unstable and poorly formed preferences to which it gave rise, renders some of the stock tools and expectations of rational choice theory inoperative.[52] For example, the notion of a tipping point in a nomination race depends on a more or less common orientation among the delegates that belonging to the winning candidate's coalition has some value, even if that value might be secondary to another goal. But, in the 1896 convention, many delegates strongly desired that the party nominate no candidate for the presidency or, if it should, that they remain aloof from the winning candidate's coalition. In addition, with respect to those delegates who expected to endorse the victorious candidate, their orientation often shifted from day to day and, during the roll calls, from minute to minute. On some days (and minutes), supporting the most viable candidate was salient, at other points the personal attractiveness of a candidate, and so forth. This kind of instability places a premium on a theoretical framework that can explain the generation of preferences, the hallmark of historical institutional approaches, as opposed to the strategic and tactical realization of preferences in a decision setting, the strength of rational choice perspectives. Finally, the role of passion, as raw emotional response to Bryan's speech, in the nomination of the candidate is largely orthogonal to both frameworks, with a slight edge to historical institutional interpretations, if only because the latter entertain a more eclectic variety of explanations and empirical problems.[53]

With respect to the presidential nomination, we could impute preferences from roll call votes but this would be a rather empty exercise because those preferences could have been (and often were) formed only minutes before they were announced and abandoned immediately afterward. We could, however, explain some of these preferences in terms of causal chains, some of them reaching back to the state conventions. The Nebraska delegation, for example, came to Chicago all but formally pledged to Bryan for reasons which obviously predated the opening of the convention. Such an analysis would certainly give us some idea which state delegations would exhibit the most stability in their public declarations and roll call support for one candidate or another. However, for the majority of delegates who formed preferences at the convention, an extended historical investigation would probably encounter diminishing returns very quickly; the context of the convention simply overwhelmed whatever prior considerations they had carried with them to Chicago.

Finally, although we could certainly conclude that the strategic environment of the convention in which the delegates signaled their changing preferences interactively induced the formation of those preferences, I am not sure what we would gain by doing so. For one thing, the strategic context of the nominating contest radically depended on what a delegate could see directly in front of him. During the Bryan demonstration, for example, the noise was so deafening that delegates could not communicate with one another. To interpret what was happening around them, they had to rely on what they could see—and because the convention floor was flat, they could not see very far.

Later, during the roll calls on the nomination, delegates near the Illinois reservation knew—because they could observe vigorous debate within Altgeld's contingent—that the state delegation's commitment to Bland was faltering. In contrast, those delegates farther away—who had only the regular announcement of Illinois votes for Bland to guide them—would have reasonably (and incorrectly) assumed that Altgeld's grip remained firm. In general terms, we could say that the delegates often did not share a common strategic context, which in turn could have influenced (induced) preference formation all at once and in the same way. If we understand preferences to be induced locally (that is, by way of what the individual delegate could immediately perceive in front of him), then the notion has some merit. But if we view inducement this way, the analysis would become extremely complex.

As analytical problems, the complexity of the Bryan demonstration and presidential nomination are probably beyond our conceptual reach.

In a trivial sense, this is because we do not have enough information as to, for example, the precise, immediate setting within which each delegate observed and acted. A far more serious difficulty is that the complexity of such situations was beyond the conceptual reach of the actors themselves. When, for example, Bryan gave his "Cross of Gold" speech to the convention, he paused at those points in his address at which he anticipated the delegates and spectators would cheer. But these points were not set down in the text of his address before he came to the podium. They were experientially read off the prior actions of the crowd as he spoke, interactively guiding him as he moved through his speech. Absorbing the collective and individual reactions of the convention, he instinctively adapted his performance to what worked.

Could Bryan have told us how he did this? The answer has to be no. We must credit his skill to the murky realms of talented, intuitive perception. But, if we concede that he did not know how he came to do what he did, can we analytically impose a rational, calculable frame upon him? Only up to a point. Bryan certainly knew that he was a skilled orator and fully trusted his talent. He also (correctly) identified the best point in the convention proceedings in which to unleash this talent, and which turns of phrase were likely to be effective in eliciting the passions of the audience. But the rest of what happened remains in the domain of the art of politics.[54]

The author would like to thank the other participants in the Conference on Preferences in Time for their advice and criticism. In my home department at Cornell, my colleagues in the Political Economy Research Colloquium, most particularly Kathleen O'Neill and Christopher Way, gave me invaluable suggestions on how to restructure this essay while saving me from the more serious gaffes which appeared in earlier versions. I alone, of course, am responsible for failure to correct all remaining errors.

Notes

1. Although the 1896 Democratic National Convention was one of the most important in American history, no detailed secondary account has been published. For brief descriptions which naturally stress the evolution of Bryan's prospects as a narrative backbone, often accompanied by minor errors of fact and interpretation, see Bryan and Bryan (1925, 103–15); Koenig (1971, 178–208); and Coletta (1964, 121–48). The overview presented in this article draws upon a book manuscript entitled *Passion and Preferences:*

Candidates and Policies in the 1896 Democratic National Convention (in preparation).

2. Bryan concluded his speech with this passage: "Having behind us the commercial interests and the laboring interests and all the toiling masses, we shall answer their demands for a gold standard by saying to them, you shall not press down upon the brow of labor this crown of thorns. You shall not crucify mankind upon a cross of gold" Dickinson (1896, 234). As he ended the first of these two sentences, Bryan symbolically brought his hands down about his head as if to place a "crown of thorns" upon his brow. As he ended the second, he extended his arms so as to imitate a crucifixion. His address was followed by what may have been the wildest demonstration of enthusiasm in the history of national political conventions. For descriptions, see the *Chicago Tribune* and the *Atlanta Constitution*, July 10–12, 1896; Coletta (1964, 141–42); Koenig (1971, 198–200).

3. For a discussion of these principles, see Tsebelis (1990, 31–39). Although Tsebelis states that positive theory becomes "less applicable" as "the actors' goals become fuzzy, or as the rules of the interaction become more fluid and imprecise," the decisions discussed in the following pages fall well within the parameters he sets out for rational choice explanations.

4. For a broad, colorful description of the campaign for free silver within the Democratic party, see the *Atlanta Constitution*, July 5, 1896. For an overview of the policies and politics of the period as a whole, see Bensel (2000, chap. 6).

5. At this point, the official size of the convention was set at 906 delegates but the Democratic National Committee had recommended in January 1896, that the size of the territorial delegations be increased from two to six delegates each and it was expected that the convention would accept this recommendation. The territorial conventions had accordingly selected six delegates to send to Chicago and the *Tribune* duly reported their names, along with their monetary preferences. As a result of these anticipated expansions, the total number of voting delegates was expected to be 930. For the January 16, 1896, meeting of the national committee in which the recommendation for expansion was adopted, see Dickinson (1896, 20–21).

6. The last clause, referring to other nations, eliminated any suggestion that free coinage should be postponed while the United States attempted to persuade Great Britain and other European powers to agree to the institution of an international bimetallic monetary standard. For a discussion of the issues and politics involved in bimetallist proposals, see Bensel (2000, 393–95). Louis Koenig described the language actually placed in the national platform, "the free and unlimited coinage of silver at the present legal ratio of 16 to 1, without waiting for the aid or consent of any other nation," as rapidly "becoming as familiar as the oath of allegiance" (1971, 188).

7. For the text of these resolutions, see the *Chicago Tribune*, July 4, 1896.

8. For detailed descriptions of the preliminary preparations for the convention made by prominent silver leaders, see the *Atlanta Constitution*, June 27, 29, July 1–8, 1896.

9. In order to separate the silver platform from the presidential nomination, only men who were not serious candidates were considered for either post. See, for example, the *Chicago Tribune*, July 6, 7, 8, 9, 1896.

10. In an open letter to the *Atlanta Constitution*, for example, Senator Ben "Pitchfork" Tillman contended that, "We must caucus and agree upon a candidate. Any candidate whose friends refuse to go into a caucus cannot get my vote. I am for no particular candidate. I want the best man and the man who the silver delegates agree upon. I will be no party to going into the convention and allowing the gold men, with the balance of power, to foist a weakling upon us. We want a man who stands for the issue and who we can elect" (July 5, 1896).

11. Leadership of the silver delegates was informally shared by a number of senators and governors, most of them from the South. For example, the five delegates who represented the silver faction as they negotiated with the gold-dominated national committee over the organization of the convention, were Senators James Jones of Arkansas, John Daniel of Virginia, and David Turpie of Indiana, along with Governors William Stone of Missouri and John Altgeld of Illinois. Although they collectively guided the silver faction through the proceedings quite competently and with little dissension, these men were not particularly influential in national politics. In fact, each was impaired by one or more flaws that limited their prominence. Jones and Daniel, for example, had served in the Confederate army, Altgeld had pardoned anarchists convicted in connection with the Haymarket Riot, and Stone governed what many northerners considered a "southern" state. While comparatively presentable as a national representative of the party, Turpie was sixty-eight years old and in poor health (The *Chicago Tribune*, July 2, 1896). As for the silver delegates, many were new to professional politics, having been drawn into party caucuses and conventions as part of a grassroots agrarian insurgency favoring the silver cause. As neophytes, the trip to Chicago was for many of them the first time they had ever been to a large city. For a possibly apocryphal story in which three Bland delegates climb a construction ladder to reach an unfinished elevated station and then wait fruitlessly for a train for which the tracks had not yet been laid, see the *Chicago Tribune*, July 7, 1896.

12. Because Bland was the front runner in the race for the nomination, his spokesmen welcomed a preliminary caucus of the silver delegates, hoping that their man would be endorsed as the soft money candidate. However, when neutral delegates and the representatives of the other presidential possibilities made it clear that they would strongly resent any such mixing of personal ambition with the silver cause, the Bland organization confined

their activities to promoting their man's availability and thus backed away from their previous support for a caucus (*Chicago Tribune*, July 4, 5, 7, 1896).

13. See, for example, the *Chicago Tribune*, July 6, 1896. Adopting this well-worn formula as the platform plank ensured that the language used to endorse silver would not be viewed as either a "carrier" for any other policy issue (for example, whether the individual states should be permitted to charter currency-issuing banks) or as indicating a tilt toward a particular candidate for the nomination (for example, because that candidate had previously expressed his views in similar language or had urged that the convention adopt that particular formulation of the plank). This formulaic statement thus permitted the delegates to see the silver platform as a policy goal uncontaminated by either side issues or the tactical maneuvering of candidates for the nomination.

14. The two issues that were most likely to have caused some friction within the silver faction concerned the issuance of currency by state-chartered banks and explicit condemnation of the Cleveland administration. For deliberations on that part of the financial plank concerning the banking system, see the *Atlanta Constitution*, July 9, 1896. For Senator Tillman's resolution condemning Cleveland and his withdrawal of that resolution during the convention proceedings, see Dickinson (1896, 208, 249, 250–56). For reports of hostility to Cleveland at the convention, see the *Chicago Tribune*, July 5; the *Atlanta Constitution*, July 6.

15. Their effectiveness was undoubtedly enhanced by the decision of the gold delegates to forgo dilatory parliamentary tactics and other forms of guerilla warfare over the decisions on presiding officers, contesting delegations, and the platform. In turn, the rather reserved behavior of the gold leaders was probably, at least in part, due to an awareness that the silver faction was well prepared to deal with such measures.

16. On July 3, the *Chicago Tribune* correctly reported that the Alaska delegation in fact supported gold, not silver as the paper had previously described on June 27. The Alaska delegates had personally announced their preferences the previous day as they disembarked from steamers in Seattle on their way to Chicago. While this represented an error in the *Tribune's* original report (an error shared by the *Atlanta Constitution* and probably due to lack of information on the Alaska convention), the monetary preferences of the delegation did not represent a defection from leadership of the silver faction and are not considered such in the text.

17. Only one delegate to the convention was actually identified in either the *Chicago Tribune* or the *Atlanta Constitution* as having changed his preferences on either gold or silver (*Chicago Tribune*, July 3, 5, 9, 10, 11; the *Atlanta Constitution*, July 3, 5, 6, 9, 10–12).

18. The exactitude with which the vote on the silver plank could have been predicted and the certainty that silver would prevail did not prevent the

delegates from displaying their preferences at almost every opportunity. During the convention deliberations on the selection of a temporary and then a permanent chairman, the decisions on contesting delegations, and adoption of a platform, the delegates cheered, stomped their feet, clapped, and waved umbrellas and hats whenever their monetary preference was mentioned. On the soft money side, the phrase "16 to 1" or reference to the large majority silver enjoyed usually sparked a demonstration. For the gold faction, the most common cues were Senator David Hill of New York and the casting of votes by the New York state delegation. For example, cries of "Hill! Hill!" filled the hall whenever a break in the proceedings permitted impromptu speeches by leading Democrats. However, once the platform had been decided and the convention had moved on to the selection of nominee, spontaneous demonstrations in support of one or the other of the metals largely ceased.

19.   For accounts of the decision of the Republican silver delegates to bolt and the bolt itself, see the *Chicago Tribune*, June 18, 1896.

20.   Michael Chwe describes public rituals as "social practices that generate common knowledge" by creating a context within which "audience members know what other audience members know." With respect to national party conventions, these rituals identify a "commonly-recognized" party candidate, utilizing procedures and language that is "often patterned and repetitive." In that sense, "the purpose of a ritual [for example, national convention] is to form the common knowledge necessary for solving a coordination problem [for example, collectively mounting a presidential election campaign]" (2001, 3–5, 26).

21.   One reason for this multi-dimensionality was that the eventual presidential nominee, whoever that might be, was often seen as the mediating agent between the delegate and some other goal (for example, the gratitude of the leader of the state delegation). Thus, delegate preferences for one or the other of the candidates treated, in many instances, the candidate as a means toward some other end, as opposed to an end unto himself. Another reason was that most of the silver delegates tended to rank the candidates very differently depending on these dimensions. For example, Richard "Silver Dick" Bland had built almost his entire career on support for free coinage and was thus seen as almost monomaniacally committed to silver. Of the leading prospects, he was thus ranked as the candidate most likely to vigorously pursue free coinage as a policy goal. However, his fixation with silver was also, along with other things such as his wife's membership in the Catholic church, viewed as an electoral liability. Other candidates, such as Horace Boies and Claude Matthews were viewed as much stronger candidates in electoral terms but, in part, their strength rested on a much weaker commitment to silver. Thus, when the silver delegates viewed Democratic prospects in the general election as bright, they would drift toward Bland;

if, as the rumor mill churned on, those prospects appeared to dim, these same delegates tended to drift toward Boies or Matthews. When prospects seemed very dark, some of the delegates even entertained the idea of nominating a Republican, Henry Teller, who, while firmly committed to silver, would probably have distributed much less patronage to the Democrats who elected him. Because these dimensions so strongly influenced the preferences of the delegates, manipulations of their saliency became a high priority for the men directing the campaigns mounted by the various candidates. Thus, the mantra for the Matthews campaign was that, one, Democratic prospects in the coming election were not very good and, therefore, the party needed, two, a nominee who could attract at least some support among eastern gold Democrats.

22.   Given that the nominee would support silver, the gold delegates had four options: hold their noses and endorse the party nominee; sit on their hands and endorse no presidential candidate; bolt the party and run a gold Democrat for the presidency in competition with the regular silver candidate; or endorse the Republican candidate, William McKinley. Once Bryan was nominated, each of these alternatives was chosen by at least a few gold Democrats but even those who endorsed the regular nominee would probably have preferred that the party had nominated no one for the office. Those choosing one of the other three options would certainly have preferred no nomination.

23.   For example, Chwe describes "coordination problems" as situations in which "each person wants to participate in a joint action only if others participate also." In a nominating decision, the tipping point occurs just before the stage in which delegates wish to jump on the eventual nominee's bandwagon. Once the tipping point has been reached, the nomination becomes "common knowledge" in that "everyone knows it [the candidate will be nominated], everyone knows that everyone knows it, everyone knows that everyone knows that everyone knows it, and so on." (2001, 8–10).

24.   With respect to the changing sentiments and preferences toward the various presidential candidates, there were two very different kinds of display. The most direct was the display of sentiment and preferences by the delegates themselves as they wore badges indicating support for a particular candidate, lustily cheered on the convention floor when that candidate's name was mentioned during the proceedings, gave a candidate the endorsement of their state delegation, or praised a candidate's availability in interviews with the press. Indirect evidence as to changing delegate sentiment can be gleaned from the tactics and strategies adopted by the various campaign organizations during the convention. For example, when a spokesman or candidate issued a statement which denied that his candidate was "unfriendly to labor," the natural inference was both that some report or rumor to the contrary was circulating among the delegates and that this

allegation was damaging the candidate's prospects because a friendly attitude toward labor was widely viewed by the delegates as an important criteria in selecting a nominee. For an example of such an announcement, see a telegram sent by Horace Boies to the *Atlanta Constitution*, July 2, 1896.

25. This was apparently a paraphrase of Hogg's statement. Texas, however, remained loyal to Bland until the last ballot made it obvious that Bryan would win the nomination. Hogg stubbornly protested his state's endorsement; in a caucus of the Texas delegation, for example, he questioned whether, in light of Bland's Catholic wife and children, he could in reality be considered the most available man (*Chicago Tribune*, June 25, July 6, 7, 1896).

26. On bandwagon effects, see Granovetter (1978). Granovetter, however, made two assumptions that are inappropriate for the analysis of the nominating contest in the 1896 convention. First, he assumed that preferences were formed before the event to be analyzed and that these preferences remained fixed until the event had ended. Second, he assumed that bandwagon effects involved dichotomous choices (for example, whether to join a bandwagon). Thus the construction of such situations (for example, how a candidate might come to attract enough support to become the object of such a bandwagon choice) remained outside the scope of his models. Both assumptions, if they were applicable in the contest for the presidential nomination, would have held only during the last half hour or so of the final ballot. Up until then, preferences were still being formed and more than two choices were still before the convention. From that perspective, almost all the politically relevant behavior before and during the convention remains beyond the reach of his models.

27. In the midst of these favorable projections, Allen was nonetheless compelled to defend Bland's support among the leaders of his own campaign organization. Sensing that the candidate's support was soft, even within his home state delegation, the reporter suggested that Governor Stone of Missouri in fact harbored presidential ambitions himself and was personally pursuing the nomination even while serving as the nominal head of Bland's campaign. "'That is nonsense,' replied Mr. Allen, somewhat warmly. 'Missouri is instructed for Bland and Gov. Stone will be here tomorrow working for him.'" For days afterward, Governor Stone was compelled to strongly deny these rumors in ever more emphatic terms (*Chicago Tribune*, June 30, July 1, 3, 1896).

28. Part of the hostility toward the gold delegates originated outside the convention. For example, James Weaver, the Populist Party candidate for president in 1892, stated that the Populists would support Horace Boies or any other man nominated by the Democrats "provided he was nominated by the free silver votes, but if a nomination came to [that candidate] by combination with the gold men the Populists would have nothing to do with it."

Since an endorsement of the Democratic nominee by the Populists was widely viewed as essential to victory in the national election, campaign managers for the various silver candidates approached the gold delegations very circumspectly, if at all. Most, in fact, avoided all contact with the gold faction (*Chicago Tribune*, July 7, 1896).

29. See, for example, the discretion and care with which the Boies managers attempted to reach out to the gold delegates (*Chicago Tribune*, July 6, 7, 8–11, 1896; *Atlanta Constitution*, July 8, 1896).

30. The managers of the Matthews campaign were caught between a rock and a hard place. On the one hand, they could not "howl too wildly for silver, for both Bland and Boies can beat them at that." On the other hand, they could not "make a deal for gold support, partly because they could not get it and partly because it would ruin all possibilities of getting the silver delegates" (*Chicago Tribune*, July 5, 1896). For the desire of his managers to find some way to reach out to the gold faction, see July 6, 8, 1896. This flirtation cost Matthews dearly. See, for example, the *Atlanta Constitution*, July 5, 6, 1896.

31. This lack of contact, however, did not prevent rumors concerning the sentiments and preferences of the gold delegates from running rampant. One of the most convoluted speculated that the gold delegates would not be unhappy to see Teller nominated because they could then bolt the ticket with impunity; because Teller was a Republican, voting against him could not be interpreted as disloyalty to the party. For this and other similar speculation, see the *Chicago Tribune*, July 5, 1896; the *Atlanta Constitution*, July 3, 4, 1896.

32. Even before the convention opened rumors abounded that gold Democrats were willing to bolt the ticket, voting either for McKinley or forming a third party ticket headed by a gold Democrat. As time went on, these rumors became increasingly specific (although many were denied by those who were mentioned in them), finally culminating in an avalanche of defections after the platform was adopted (*Chicago Tribune*, June 25, 26, 29, 30, July 1–12, 1896).

33. These delegations (more exactly, the leaders of these delegations) thus focused the attention of the convention in the sense that, whenever anything significant happened on the podium or somewhere else in the hall, observers would immediately turn to these delegations in order to evaluate the impact. In some cases, these delegations themselves generated these significant events (for example, when leaders from other delegations visited their places on the convention floor or when the state's standard joined a demonstration). However, only in the loosest sense of the term did these pivotal delegations serve as "focal points" for deciding who would receive the nomination. This was an information-rich environment in which the actors had many alternative ways in which they could coordinate their actions.

For that reason, intuition based on intuitive understandings of what might be an obvious or fair solution to a problem played a much smaller role than it would have in information-poor environments where communication between agents was difficult or impossible. On the other hand, a looser understanding of the term as "an inherently unstable . . . sign of where to look for the outcome" might encompass these pivotal delegations in that most observers believed they would be central participants in the bargaining which accompanied a nominating decision. The quote is from Schelling (1963, 112). On focal points generally, see pages 57, 112–13 in Schelling and Kreps 1990, 121–23.

34. Even if he had been eligible, Altgeld was viewed by many delegates as too radical for the nomination. As governor, he had pardoned in 1893 three of the anarchists who had been convicted of conspiracy in the Haymarket Riot. One year later he had vigorously protested President Cleveland's use of federal troops to put down the Pullman Strike in Chicago. The latter event had made Altgeld even more estranged from the administration than most silverites were and may have explained his and the Illinois delegation's indifference to Vice President Stevenson's availability as a silver candidate (see, for example, the *Chicago Tribune*, July 3, 1896). In any event, the Illinois delegation was initially viewed as completely free of tactical entanglements as it maneuvered toward an endorsement.

35. On July 4, three days before the convention was to meet, a poll of the Illinois delegation indicated a majority favored Bland. The next day, a caucus committed all forty-eight Illinois votes, under the unit rule, to his candidacy. This declaration followed several days of intense speculation that Altgeld and the Illinois contingent were leaning toward the Missourian. With delegates from the northern part of the state, particularly Chicago, favorable to Boies and those from the southern section partial to Bland, one reporter suggested that Altgeld was in a position to bargain with both candidates. One early, probably fanciful, rumor had it that Altgeld would deliver his delegation to the campaign that helped elect him temporary chairman of the convention. Another more realistic rumor speculated that Altgeld, in return for the early endorsement of Bland, received a promise from the Bland campaign that he would be appointed chairman of the National Democratic Committee and that the national party headquarters would be located in Chicago. The plausibility of this suggestion was reinforced by the likelihood that Illinois would play a pivotal role in the national election as well as the Democratic convention. For that reason, selecting Chicago as the national headquarters and, with less reason given Altgeld's radical reputation, the governor as national committee chairman would make good sense even if there had been no deal. The period immediately following the Illinois endorsement may have marked the high point of the Bland boom. One reporter, for example, even wrote that "the wave which is rapidly setting

in the direction of the old free coinage advocate" was so strong that "it will require something of a cyclone to disturb him" (*Chicago Tribune*, July 1–3, 5–7, 1896; see also the *Atlanta Constitution*, July 1, 5, 6, 1896).

36. After about half of the gold delegates had repeatedly abstained during roll calls on the nomination, the permanent chairman of the convention interpreted the two-thirds rule to mean "two-thirds of those voting." Given the gold abstentions, this clarification eased the impact of the rule in such a way that a silver candidate could now win the nomination even though about a hundred or so silver delegates voted for other candidates (whereas, under the earlier interpretation, almost any defection would have blocked a candidate). This interpretation was handed down just after the fourth ballot in which Bryan had for the first time taken the lead from Bland. Although probably unintended, the timing of the chairman's decision strongly reinforced the tendency of delegates to view Bryan as near or at the (now reduced) "tipping point." In fact, he won the nomination on the next ballot. For the decision, see Dickinson (1896, 322). Since the convention had more or less adopted the rules of the House of Representatives as its own parliamentary law and since those rules explicitly provided that a two-thirds majority (on, for example, a motion to suspend the rules) was calculated only on those voting, the permanent chairman's decision was relatively uncontroversial and, in some quarters at least, anticipated before the fact (*Chicago Tribune*, July 8, 10).

37. Putting the party's ability to win the general election above that of regional pride, many southern delegates in fact opposed the nomination of someone from their region as even a vice presidential candidate (*Chicago Tribune*, July 11, 1896; the *Atlanta Constitution*, June 25).

38. At the peak in the late 1870s, Confederate veterans held almost four out of every five southern seats in the U.S. House of Representatives. By 1896, this proportion had declined to about one out of every three but, of course, was much higher for senior members from the region who, on the whole, were old enough to have served during the war. Bensel (1990, 405–13). On ostracism of the South from the mainstream of national politics, see Bensel (2000, 2, 525). On the dominance of the southern wing in the national Democratic party, see, for example, Bensel (1987, 382–84). Confederate veterans were so prominent within the party that the Democratic National Committee rejected an earlier date for the convention because it would have conflicted with a previously scheduled conclave of the United Confederate Veterans in Richmond, Virginia. As one southern member of the national committee complained, if the two conventions were held at the same time, many Democrats would have been forced to choose between them. Dickinson (1896, 5–6). Reflecting this strong southern influence, the most popular song played in the hall, on the streets, and in the hotels during the convention was "Dixie" (*Atlanta Constitution*, July 10; the *Chicago Tribune*, July 4, 1896).

For reports that Blackburn's Confederate record fatally damaged his prospects for the nomination, see July 1, 2, 5, 1896.

39. Even before the convention opened, for example, the Boies campaign spread a rumor that the Grand Army of the Republic, an organization of Union Civil War veterans numbering in the hundreds of thousands, "had their knives out for Bland" because he had cast a vote against a major veteran's bill while serving in Congress (*Chicago Tribune*, July 3, 1896). For reports that Missouri's status as a southern state independently damaged Bland's prospects, even among southern delegates, see July 4, 7. Bland, in fact, was so closely associated with the South that one reporter incorrectly reported that he was a Confederate veteran (July 10).

40. The clearest example of such behavior involved the Georgia delegation. The delegation came to Chicago uncommitted with sentiment fairly evenly divided between Bland and Boies. However, none of the leading candidates attracted "any great degree of enthusiasm." As the convention opened, Georgia "threw out a temporary anchor on the Bland rock to await developments." However, immediately after Bryan's speech and well before the platform had even been adopted, Georgia abandoned its earlier endorsement of Bland and switched over to Bryan. That night Georgia placed Bryan's name in nomination with Hal Lewis delivering the nominating speech. Only two days earlier, without mentioning Bryan or his prospects at all, Lewis had predicted that either Bland or Boies would win the nomination (*Atlanta Constitution*, July 6, 8, 9, 11, 1896). For a general description of this tactic, see July 8.

41. For a description of the policy declarations of Populist and western Republican state conventions during this period, see Bensel (2000, chap. 3).

42. This summary vastly oversimplifies a much more complex political reality. For a succinct summary of Populist strategy toward the Republican and Democratic parties in the summer of 1896, including southern opposition to anything but a "middle-of-the-road" campaign, see Hicks (1961, 351–60).

43. Many Populists would have welcomed Senator Teller if the Democratic convention had nominated him. See, for example, an interview with Chairman H. E. Taubeneck of the People's Party National Executive committee which came out of St. Louis with a July 1 dateline, reprinted in the *Chicago Tribune*, July 2, 1896. Prominent members of the Populist party, among them Taubeneck, Ignatius Donnelly of Minnesota, "Sockless" Jerry Simpson of Kansas, and James Weaver of Iowa, openly lobbied delegates for Teller in Chicago (July 5–7).

44. In rather sharp contrast, the silver Republicans attended the convention in force. The most prominent among them were four western senators, Fred Dubois of Idaho, Lee Mantle of Montana, William Stewart of Nevada, and Richard Pettigrew of South Dakota. Dubois, in particular, was in close contact with Senator Teller and relayed messages from him to the convention.

45.   Schelling suggested that, in the absence of an "an apparent focal point for agreement, [a mediator] can create one by his power to make a dramatic suggestion," thus bringing about agreement between contending parties. (1963, 144; quoted in Chwe, 2001, 98). In some sense, this is what Bryan did in his speech; posing as a neutral advocate for the silver plank in the party platform, Bryan made a (albeit implicit) dramatic suggestion that he should be the party nominee. However, such an interpretation falls outside Schelling's point on several counts. First, however much he wished to pose as a mediator, he was hardly neutral with respect to the nomination. Second, his dramatic suggestion formed preferences within a context in which each of the candidates constituted an indivisible solution or outcome. For example, the delegates could not give half of the nomination to Bland and the other half to Teller. Within that context, Bryan moved the delegates to himself as the solution, not as a compromise between other candidates. Finally, Bryan did not immediately receive the nomination; his speech, while certainly dramatic and suggestive, only gave him the nomination after five long and equally dramatic roll calls. From this last perspective, Bryan's speech did not create an obvious focal point toward which the delegates immediately and, within the new choice situation he had created, naturally gravitated.

46.   As Richard Hall has noted, voting in most situations is flat in the sense that a vote does not reflect the intensity of a preference between two alternatives (aside from the weak contrast with abstention). An auction, by comparison, reveals the comparative intensity of preferences of two or more buyers through the amount of money they are willing to pay for an item or service (1995, 293). Delegates to the Democratic National Convention displayed the intensity of their preferences (what might be called passion in many cases) through cheers, clapping their hands, waving canes or umbrellas, throwing paper and other objects into the air, and standing on their chairs as they wildly moved their arms. Such displays could not formally affect an outcome because every delegate's vote was equally weighted, whether that delegate was barely over the indifference threshold or strongly committed to a policy or candidate. But these demonstrations could affect the preferences of other delegates in that they signaled something about the relative commitments of individuals, including how hard they would work for a platform or candidate in the coming general election. For that reason, they were closely monitored by political leaders. For example, during the demonstration following Bryan's speech, the leaders of the pivotal Illinois delegation (which had already declared for Bland) paid close attention to which state delegations were responding and which were sitting on their hands. "Governor Altgeld was on his chair, but he was not cheering. Hinrichsen, too, was standing on the highest pinnacle he could find. But these men were not cheering. They were keeping track of the weak places—one for

Bland, the other for Bryan" (*Chicago Inter Ocean*, reprinted in the *Chicago Tribune*, July 12, 1896).

47. For Bryan's own evaluation of his chances, see Bryan and Bryan (1925, 103). For general surveys of newspaper estimates of Bryan's strength as the convention opened, see Coletta (1964, 122); Koenig (1971, 177–78).

48. The *Chicago Tribune*, for example, attributed at least some of the convention's enthusiastic reception of Bryan's speech to the machinations of southern senators who, in reality, favored Teller. These senators had helped to stimulate sentiment for Bryan as a means of holding off Bland's candidacy. Bland was seen as perilously close to the "tipping point" as the result of the decision by many of the gold delegates not to participate in the roll calls on the nomination; their abstention, along with a favorable ruling from the convention chairman on the two-thirds rule, would dramatically reduce the number of silver delegates required for the nomination. Bryan, these senators hoped, could attract sufficient strength from the Bland candidacy so as to deadlock the convention and thus provide an opening for Teller. However, they "had no intention of placing in nomination a young man whose inexperience in life manifestly unfitted him for the position of President and whose headstrong character and repeated revolts against party discipline showed that he would be beyond personal control if once in the White House" (July 10).

49. Although the balloting cannot be described in detail, it should be noted that there was abundant signaling during the roll calls, with state delegations sometimes passing as they were called, sometimes asking permission to change their votes, and often cheering shifts in position made by other delegations. The most important of these signals was largely unintended. During the fifth and what turned out to be the last ballot, the Illinois delegation asked permission to retire from the hall in order to discuss its position. Since the delegation had previously been publicly and loyally committed to Bland, other delegates interpreted the request as a signal that Illinois was reconsidering its position and, since Bryan was growing stronger on every roll call, almost everyone concluded that the state had rebelled against Altgeld and would go over to the Nebraskan when it returned to the hall. Thus the state persuasively signaled its intentions, putting Bryan over the "tipping point," without making a public declaration. In addition, it should also be noted that preferences, in terms of votes for one or the other candidates for the nomination, were being formed and reformed well within the roll call itself. Individual delegates and their state delegations were changing their votes even as the balloting proceeded.

50. Bryan estimated that he had spent about sixty dollars during the convention, "a sum probably as small as anyone has spent in securing a presidential nomination" (Bryan and Bryan 1925, 107).

51. The ways in which delegates attempted to grapple with this complex, inter-

active, and rapidly changing political reality resemble the kinds of radically simplifying assumptions that Granovetter suggested might be necessary in his models in order to make falsifiable predictions (1978, 1433–41).

52. For example, the notion of ideal points for either the delegates or the convention doesn't make much sense when the preferences of many of the participants in a decision are in flux. Nor does the concept of a pivotal voter provide much leverage when preferences are unstable up to and even within the roll calls which determine a decision. In fact, almost all the heavier weapons in the rational choice armory are plugged by unstable preferences.

53. For more on this last consideration, see Richard Bensel, "A Crown of Thorns: Individual Calculation and Collective Passion during the 1896 Democratic National Convention," presented to the conference on Political Action and Political Change, Yale University, October 22–23, 2004.

54. In the same way, how delegates transformed their absorption in the events surrounding them into preferences was also conceptually incomplete. For example, delegates were emotionally moved by Bryan's performance but were unable, aside from platitudes, to tell reporters why their passions had been aroused.

References

Bensel, Richard Franklin. 1987. *Sectionalism and American Political Development, 1880–1980*. Madison: University of Wisconsin Press.

———. 1990. *Yankee Leviathan: The Origins of Central State Authority in America, 1859–1877*. New York: Cambridge University Press.

———. 2000. *The Political Economy of American Industrialization, 1877–1900*. New York: Cambridge University Press.

Bryan, William Jennings, and Mary Baird Bryan. 1925. *The Memoirs of William Jennings Bryan*. Philadelphia: John C. Winston.

Chwe, Michael Suk-Young. 2001. *Rational Ritual: Culture, Coordination, and Common Knowledge*. Princeton, N.J.: Princeton University Press.

Coletta, Paolo E. 1964. *William Jennings Bryan*, vol. 1, *Political Evangelist, 1860–1908*. Lincoln: University of Nebraska Press.

Dickinson, Edward B. 1896. *Official Proceedings of the 1896 Democratic National Convention*. Logansport, Ind.: Wilson, Humphreys.

Granovetter, Mark. 1978. "Threshold Models of Collective Behavior." *American Journal of Sociology* 83(6): 1420–43.

Hall, Richard. 1995. "Empiricism and Progress in Positive Theories of Legislative Institutions." In *Positive Theories of Congressional Institutions*, edited by Kenneth A. Shepsle and Barry R. Weingast. Ann Arbor: University of Michigan Press.

Hicks, John D. 1961. *The Populist Revolt: A History of the Farmers' Alliance and the People's Party*. Lincoln: University of Nebraska Press.

Koenig, Louis W. 1971. *Bryan: A Political Biography of William Jennings Bryan*. New York: G. P. Putnam's Sons.

Kreps, David M. 1990. "Corporate Culture and Economic Theory." In *Perspectives on Positive Political Economy*, edited by James Alt and Kenneth Shepsle. New York: Cambridge University Press.

Schelling, Thomas C. 1963. *The Strategy of Conflict*. New York: Oxford University Press.

Tsebelis, George. 1990. *Nested Games: Rational Choice in Comparative Politics*. Berkeley: University of California Press.

3

Congress and Civil Rights Policy: An Examination of Endogenous Preferences

David W. Brady, John A. Ferejohn, Jeremy C. Pope

In economics the fundamental methodological starting point is to look for explanation in structure rather than in preferences. Thus in partial equilibrium theories, economists examine comparative statics propositions—descriptions of shifting choices as wealth, prices, or technology change, holding preferences constant. The reason for starting with these parameters is not that preferences are unimportant for the explanation— the overall choice pattern will depend on preferences, after all. But many have argued (or assumed) that not much can be said as to how preferences are likely to change during processes of choice. We think this view is overdrawn. We believe that many important preference change phenomena might be approached with standard analytical tools or minor variants thereof. Indeed, we believe that there is already more explicated preference formation within standard models and descriptions than is commonly recognized.[1] We also believe that models with endogenous preferences might best be approached incrementally from within established modeling and descriptive traditions.

Here we attempt such an analysis by examining the dramatic political changes associated with the passage and support for civil rights legislation beginning in the late 1950s. Previous explanations and descriptions of these events implicitly take account of changing popular and legislative preferences, thus this seems a fertile area to begin an analysis of preference change. We try to account for the different reasons legislators update their beliefs inducing new public policy preferences, and compare this account with a simple electoral change model of induced preferences in which legislator preferences—and thus public policy—shift merely through replacement.

Standard explanations of the passage of civil rights legislation usually point to two interrelated factors: legislator replacement and institutional rules changes. During the late 1950s and early 1960s Democrats made significant gains in Congress. Additionally, urban districts—where Democrats were particularly strong—increased as a percentage of the House due to judicial-enforced reapportionment. At roughly the same time, the institutional structures within Congress that prevented race-oriented legislation from being voted on in both chambers began to crumble. The House Rules Committee moved into the speaker's orbit, and there was an increasing willingness of Senate leaders to work around conservative southern chairs—historically an important bottleneck for civil rights bills. Additionally, the Kennedy and especially the Johnson administrations increased their commitment to enact legislation. No doubt the growing number of Democrats and representatives with urban interests contributed to the breakup of the institutional logjam.

Was the emergence of civil rights legislation just a matter of breaking up institutional impediments that released pent-up demands for greater equality for black citizens? Should the best explanation focus on the battle for control of the Senate Judiciary and House Rules Committees? Or was there a kind of awakening either of the American public or of their elected representatives to responsibilities they had long ignored?

The descriptive institutional story has been pretty thoroughly explored by earlier congressional scholars such as James Sundquist (1968) and others,[2] but not enough serious attention has been given to explanations of preference change. In keeping with an attempt to find explanations in structure, we clarify and discuss the mechanisms by which congressional representatives might rationally have changed their induced preferences even when popular preferences may have remained fixed and find that the typical institutional story of policy change through electoral replacement seems wanting. We will have more to say about that in our conclusion.

It is also worth noting that racial politics have been very important in recent American political development. The sequence of political battles resulted in the transformation of American school systems, integration of many public and some private places, and an enormous, liberalizing reversal in American attitudes about race. In terms of politics, the struggle destroyed the long-standing political equilibrium of Democratic hegemony built on the pillars of solid Democratic strength in the southern states and liberal North. In historical context, civil rights is not only a fruitful place to begin examining endogenous preference change, it is one of the most important political developments of the past century.

It is undisputed that

the mid-1960s witnessed a fundamental change in [the New Deal coalition]. Racial concerns gained a prominent foothold on the national political agenda, and in the process, they took on a clear partisan meaning. Breaking with a tradition of a hundred years the Democratic Party gradually became the home of racial liberalism (Carmines and Stimson 1989, 116).

Myriad authors have noted this change. Another large set of social scientists have documented the increasing liberalization of American attitudes on race (Kellstedt 2000; Kinder and Sanders 1996; Schumann et al. 1997). They uniformly trace this racial evolution to a beginning point in the late 1950s and early 1960s. Even in the period, people understood that fundamental societal attitudes were changing, but slowly (Dye 1971). The picture is decidedly complex. A collection of Lou Harris and Angus Campbell poll questions from 1963 to 1970 illustrate this point (see table 3.1). Some of the questions show significant changes in a pro-civil rights direction (for example, questions about protests, restaurants, and hotels). Other questions see fairly little change, or even negative change, as in the question about white people having a right to keep Negroes out.

Because of the complex issues involved, other authors have argued

Table 3.1   Measures of Civil Rights Attitudes in the 1960s

Question Wording	1963	1964	1966	1968	1970
Federal government see to it that blacks get fair employment treatment[a]		33		33	
See to it that white and Negro children go to the same schools[b]		38		33	41
Blacks can go to any hotel or restaurant they can afford[c]		41		48	56
White people have a right to keep Negroes out[d]		29		24	21
Negroes have tried to move too fast[e]	64		70		
Justified to march in protests[f]	53		35		

Sources: Campbell (1971) and Brink and Harris (1966).
Note: All questions asked of whites only.
[a] Campbell (1971, 129)
[b] Campbell (1971, 130)
[c] Campbell (1971, 131)
[d] Campbell (1971, 133)
[e] Brink and Harris (1966, 220)
[f] Brink and Harris (1966, 222)

that it was congressional action and leadership that actually forced significant social change—as opposed to mass political protest or judicial-driven change. This background of complexity and uncertainty makes determining the precise mechanisms and causes of congressional preference shifting (or lack of them) both hard to determine and important. Why would representatives change their roll call voting behavior when the public had not yet clearly signaled a shift in preferences? We offer a view of change in civil rights policy that features preference change.

Typically scholars have thought of a fairly simple electoral model of preference change: member preferences are induced by their constituency preferences. This leads to explanations for changing public policy that focus on members of Congress being replaced or changing constituencies. We believe that where most accounts stop is the place that analysis should begin. Another way to think about preference change (that we thinks fits nicely with our theoretical discussion) is to see Americans as having a basic and underlying commitment to the broad values of justice, democracy, and equality. For more than two hundred years of American history these values have changed little in the abstract. But the public policy expression of those values has changed, and at times dramatically. The civil rights movement—one of the most dramatic changes—challenged Americans to compare their values with the way African Americans were actually treated. In short, the movement caused an updating of beliefs, which led to significant policy changes. Our story features citizens and their representatives shifting preferences as they update their views about how blacks were treated in regard to fundamental values of equality, fair treatment, and justice.

Endogenous Preferences and Theory

The literature on civil rights largely employs rational choice models committed to fixed preferences as explanatory objects—along with lots of nonrational choice preference-based explanatory models. Some literatures—such as the Chicago school of economics, sociobiological, or Marxist explanations—assume preferences to be linked to or fixed by materialist parameters (wealth, fitness, and the like). But even where such linkages are not assumed, preference-based explanations are said to explain behavior, patterns, institutions, or whatever in terms of fixed or exogenous objects.

Belief-based explanations have the same status insofar as beliefs can be understood as preferences over gambles or events. But in the classical model beliefs are supposed to be responsive to information or evidence and so it seems easier to understand beliefs as having important endogenous elements. But this endogeneity is limited by the requirement that initial or prior beliefs must assign positive probability to an event for any later belief to do so. Thus, in classical models, one cannot come to believe completely unanticipated things.

Of course, that preferences or beliefs are exogenous does not imply that they are unchanging, but whatever change occurs is exogenous or parametric. Someone's preferences about the way his steak is cooked could change, but such change arises through some process that does not depend on the person's choices. George Bush Sr.'s aversion to broccoli would seem a pure case. This distaste is, as far as we know, related to the density of a certain kind of receptor on the tongue—something that seems more or less fixed biologically. But, it may be possible, for all we know, that the density of the relevant receptors may decline with age or with the onset of some other condition leading Bush to be able to tolerate broccoli or even covet the vegetable. But any such mechanism is exogenous to Bush's choices. However, it is possible that the density of these receptors may be a function of previous choices—they could wear out, not likely in the case of the senior Bush, or become inaccurate through lack of use—in which case we would have an endogenous explanation of broccoli preference.

Stating the matter this way is already a caricature. It is easy enough to see income or wealth effects, or nonseparable preferences in the neoclassical model as instances of endogenous preferences. That economists derive these effects from properties of fixed preference orderings over a very large commodity space is best seen as a modeling convention. We choose to say, within the neoclassical framework, that preference orderings with certain properties will exhibit income or wealth effects rather than saying the preferences depend on wealth. Of course, as much recent empirical work suggests, this modeling convention is empirically restrictive: the neoclassical model cannot embrace all observable income effects or nonseparable preferences (see especially Kahneman and Tversky 1982). Besides, the artificiality of the neoclassical approach as a modeling convention becomes clear when considering temporal or risky choice in which the fixed preference ordering must be defined over time or event-dated commodities that do not yet and may never exist.

But even in more mundane settings, there is a sense in which neoclassical preference-based models use endogenous preferences in a less semantically contestable sense. The most obvious example involves preferences that are partly based on beliefs. Many preferences have belief-based elements. You might prefer to take Route 280 rather than 101 to San Francisco because you believe there is less likely to be traffic along that route. But, after learning of an accident on 280 your route preference may very well shift. Nothing about this is unfamiliar. You might prefer to drink water or milk with dinner rather than wine because you think it is healthier. But upon learning about the miraculous life giving properties of a good red burgundy, your preferences may (rationally) shift. We think political preferences are particularly likely to be filled with embedded beliefs. Your preference for a Republican over a Democrat is likely due to beliefs about how they would behave if elected to the presidency, or perhaps how others would respond to their leadership. Informational theories of legislatures emphasize this feature of legislative preferences: preferences over legislative proposals will depend in part on beliefs about their effects. On informational theories, insofar as information can be transmitted in the legislative process, preferences may be expected to shift in the course of debate and voting.

Political preferences seem especially likely to exhibit another kind of endogeneity—what might be termed strategic endogeneity. A member of a legislature might, for example, form preferences over bills and other proposals by taking account of how the passage of those proposals would be likely to affect policy. The theory of sophisticated voting may be understood as a theory of strategic preference formation, one based on the some specific assumptions about the voting process will proceed and on anticipations as to how people will choose in future votes. Empirically, killer amendments, position taking, and other forms of strategic action in legislatures have similar interpretations. If legislators are able to create innovative legislative proposals, preferences over other proposals could shift during legislative consideration.

Some thinkers have proposed hierarchical preference models in which agents have first-order preferences over consumption plans or states of affairs, but second-order preferences over possible first-order preferences. People may desire to have certain kinds of desires—to be able to appreciate fine wines (or perhaps to have cheap wine tastes if they are budget conscious), opera, or literature.

There is, of course, the practical problem of how to achieve the desired preferences. Addiction models are an easy special case: if you want to have tobacco addiction preferences, start smoking and a known and foreseeable biological process will kick in. But with opera it's not so clear. One of us thinks it works like an addiction; the other two can't get over the initial taste and doubt that there is any reliable causal process to be triggered. When it comes to wine, two of us switch roles and the third is a teetotaler and is consequently excused. Oh well. That just shows that when biology isn't there to help out, the practical problem for those with hierarchical preferences can be difficult.[3] And, in most interesting cases, there is disagreement among experts as to the biological processes. In any case, the hierarchical preference model is still neoclassical in structure. Higher-order preferences are trumps—in the sense that the present actor responds to them in choosing a course of action—

and so one engages in well-defined optimization with respect to these preferences, taking account of causal processes and other constraints (those gnarly practical problems). The first-order preferences you actually have (wine-hating opera buff) are induced in the sense of being the outcomes of a solution of this optimization problem.

So, we think that within the basic neoclassical framework, much progress can be made in understanding or at least modeling endogenous preferences. This is not to say that the problem is solved without remainder. No doubt there are endogenous preference phenomena that will elude neoclassical description and explanation. And there is no reason that others with insight as to how to understand such phenomena should not try their hand at explanation. And, no doubt, if such models are developed, their explanatory reach will overlap that of more orthodox approaches and we, as social scientists, will face some knotty problems in choosing among two successful explanatory programs. This would be a happy problem indeed—rather like having the luxury of having two top quarterbacks on your football team (it is often observed, however, that a surfeit of luxury produces headaches).

All of the above is, we think, uncontroversial and suggests that existing neoclassical thinking can already say a lot about situations in which preference change is a major element. This is true even when, as in our examples, we are thinking about individual choice issues. When dealing with issues of collective choice, things become more complicated and, ironically, more tractable for existing modeling approaches. This is because there is much more in the way of good social science research, both theoretical and empirical, that may throw some light on the way preference induction works. This is the point we hope to illustrate by considering the politics of civil rights.

Let's briefly consider theoretical issues first. Assume that agents have preferences over outcomes and that outcomes are the result of the actions chosen by all agents. Obviously, in such a setting, outcome preferences will lead to induced preferences over actions. If we prefer to not crash into each other when driving on dark and twisting roads, each of us will prefer action combinations in which both of us drive on the right or on the left. Note that these preferences over action combinations do not necessarily induce in us preferences over our own actions. I prefer to drive on the right if and only if others do, and so our induced preferences over actions may have a conditional structure. But, if the action to be chosen is not which side of the road to drive on but whether to enact a law requiring (or announcing) that driving shall be on the right, each of us will probably prefer such a law to none at all (at least if in the absence of such a law, there is reason to believe that coordination will be incomplete). So, while our induced preferences over individual actions may be complex and conditional, our preferences over collective actions may be well defined and complete. Note that this example resembles the individual choice problems considered above. Induced preferences are shaped by preferences over outcomes together with more or less foreseeable causal processes.

Much the same thing can be said as to preference over institutions or methods of choosing outcomes. Suppose we are members of a legislature and need to adopt a procedure for considering proposals. Assume, for example, that our choice is between an amendment procedure and an elimination procedure. In that case, if we resorted to some theorems about voting rules, we might reasonably take account of the fact that amendment rules tend to pick out majority winners when any exist, whereas elimination methods do not. That property of amendment procedures might be a reason for preferring it—for having an induced preference for such a rule or procedure. Again, induced preferences depend on preferences over outcomes or consequences together with foreseeable causal processes. But here the causal mechanisms run through others' choice of action.

From the more applied viewpoint of legislative studies, the basic idea is just as familiar but here there is also some empirical support for the ideas: congressmen are assumed to be sufficiently ambitious for reelection or advancement that the preferences they act on (in Congress or in their constituencies) may differ from those they hold as individuals—in this sense members have induced preferences. We may distinguish two circumstances. First, the relevant constituency may have a narrowly defined preferred position on an important issue (a median voter, for example). In such a case the congressman is probably constrained to take a position at or near that point (see Fiorina 1974). A second possibility is that there is no significant preferred position: here, depending on technical issues, the congressman may be less constrained. To give this possibility some practical sense, a district may have uninformed preferences that would not motivate them to defeat a member who strayed from the median point. Or it is possible that the actions of a member are so unlikely to gain attention in the district that the representative has the freedom to do as she pleases.

In any case, it seems that the constituency preferences play the same role as the foreseeable causal mechanisms in the previous section. For instance, a member taking action on personal preferences may trigger certain causal mechanisms—departing from constituency preferences may induce a primary challenge or an election defeat (Canes-Wrone, Brady, and Cogan 2001). Or a political leader might impose penalties or offer rewards such that a legislator updates his beliefs about the payoff structure. We next speculate about the mechanisms of preference change in the U.S. Congress, and then try to quantify some of the explanations for preference change with respect to the civil rights legislation of the 1950s and 1960s.

Mechanisms of Preference Change

With this idea of updating beliefs in mind, we turn to an examination of legislator behavior during the civil rights movement era. As will become apparent, there are many problems with using roll call data for this purpose. First, the legislative objects vary from one roll call to the next: contents of the bill change; is the vote on an amendment, or a rule or final passage? The analytical problems multiply. One might naturally assume that vote switches are most plausibly related to changed contents or strategic setting rather than to changed preferences. This is a natural and methodologically conservative assumption, but it does shift the burden of proof against the notion that beliefs about core values or preferences over policy to achieve those values might have changed. It seems possible that reformulating the proposal or question being asked might sometimes lead members to reveal induced preference in a way that could be interpreted as a preference change account. Here we will try to be more generous to belief-change explanations by leaving them "on the table" as long as possible.

Take one example, when the 1964 Civil Rights Act was being debated in the House, the conservative chair of the Rules Committee (Howard Smith of Virginia) introduced what he thought of as a killer amendment: he proposed that the bill prohibit discrimination on grounds of sex as well as race and national origin. The House leadership (sharing Smith's belief that the amendment might kill the bill) tried to persuade liberal Democrats to vote against the proposal. According to some accounts, many of these members would have been personally willing to do so if only such a vote could have been held in private. But the galleries were filled with women's interest groups who were there to observe behavior on any unrecorded (teller) votes and, at least in this case, liberal members were unwilling to go along with the leadership and vote down Smith's amendment. As it turns out the Smith amendment did not lead to the defeat of the bill but instead to including gender as one of a group of statutorily protected classes. We suspect that liberal congressmen were favorably disposed to prohibiting gender discrimination all along but that they would have preferred to follow the Democratic leadership if such work could have been done in the dark of night. That is in a secret vote, many would have had an induced preference to vote against the Smith amendment. However, the fact that the vote was to be public (in the sense of a standing or teller vote) and the presence of motivated interest group representatives probably induced these members to vote for the amendment. This is not an account of true preference change but one in which induced preferences—preferences that are revealed in specific strategic and informational settings—change because the setting changed.

As useful as stylized examples are, we need an enumeration of the processes by which preferences may have changed. And this enumeration needs to take account, as much as possible, of the motivation and process behind the preference change. As outlined, some induced preferences are purely tactical, depending almost entirely on the situation—for example, a member voting for a civil rights bill because the leadership has influenced or bought his vote. Other preference change may be more sincere (for example, a representative genuinely awaking to the injustice of Jim Crow, led to update her beliefs about policy effects and support a stronger civil rights bill). We will call this sincere category of change pure preference change. Thus it is possible to conceptualize types of preference change on a continuum stretching between pure preference change at one end and purely tactical preference change at the other end. Other types are in the middle. We list what we believe are the major categories.

> *Pure preferences* are evident when a representative changes her mind (her personal *preferences*) as to desirability of legislation in the area. She updates her beliefs. This could be due to a change in beliefs about the effects of legislative proposals, changing attitudes towards target or beneficiary groups, or changing views as to the extent of discrimination or of the proper role of government in dealing with it, for example. In the case of civil rights, we have reason to believe, given the strategy of the movement's leadership to peacefully publicize the injustice, that members of Congress updated their beliefs about the equity of civil rights policy.

> *Replacement* is retirement, electoral defeat, and the like of one member by another with (possibly) different preferences. Obviously retirements followed by the replacement of a like-minded member could be simple personal preference change. But we believe a much more common occurrence is a defeated or retiring incumbent followed by a member attempting to construct a new constituency. This is primarily what analysts have examined when considering the role of elections in legislative preference shifting.

> *Changing geographic constituencies*, such as when incumbent representatives are forced to run in constituencies that cared more about a given issue,[4] may induce new policy preferences.

Changing primary or electoral constituencies, such as when a congress-man chooses to construct a different supporting coalition within the geographic constituency, may induce a new set of policy prefer-ences. For instance party switchers of the Reagan era (Democrat to Republican) seemed to exhibit a more conservative voting record before the switch.

Progressive ambition may induce a member to support a policy to enhance the possibility of gaining future, higher office. For in-stance, being pro civil rights became more or less attractive for moving up to higher office (because of the ambition to represent a constituency with urban or multi-ethnic interests, or whatever).[5]

Observability of congressional votes and behavior increases back home in this period, perhaps inducing members to vote more in line with their district. The strongest possibility with respect to this mechanism would be the end of unrecorded votes (with the switch to electronic voting) in the mid-1970s, along with the other sun-shine provisions of that era.

Party leadership offering changed incentives to toe the line on issues important to the party, may result in revised beliefs about the mem-ber's voting preferences. As parties become more homogeneous, it might become easier to discipline committee or party leaders (see Rohde 1991; note particularly the fall of some chairs in the early 1970s and after the 1994 election).

Agenda mechanisms, that is, shifts in strategic preferences—whether due to the innovation of new proposals or amendments or perhaps the crafting of different procedures or rules—may induce a shift in preferences.

All of these mechanisms may have some role in describing preference change on civil rights. But only the first (pure preference change), which is the most difficult to measure, requires fundamental, internal prefer-ence change. As we will discuss, despite the difficulty of measurement, describing civil rights policy changes without some kind of pure prefer-ence change is difficult if not impossible. The second mechanism, re-placement, is easy to measure (was the member replaced?) but conceptu-ally not quite as clear, it could capture both electoral effects and a degree of pure preference change. But, we believe the most common type of preference change with respect to replacement takes place through elec-tions: voters—updating their own beliefs and preferences—choose a new, more representative member. Mechanisms 3 through 6—changing constituencies, ambition and observability—pertain to a member's style with the voters, as described by Fenno in his book *Home Style*. We believe for a number of reasons this type of preference change is difficult and therefore uncommon. Members have a reputation to maintain. They cannot simply switch from opposition of civil rights to support without appearing cowardly, or at least inconsistent. Even setting aside reputation considerations, it is probably personally difficult for a member of Congress to represent himself to the district (or a portion of it such as a primary constituency) in a radically new way.[6] In other words we believe members are by and large sincere people, not easily blown about by shifting political winds. Thus, mechanisms 3 through 6 are likely to be somewhat sticky, rarely yielding the kind of preference change required for a major policy change. Finally, party leadership and agenda (and to some degree observability) seem almost purely tactical: members reveal their preferences based on the legislative environment. Neither the member, nor her constituency is changing preferences about policy, merely over the tactics used to achieve goals. With these possible mechanisms in mind we turn to a description of preference shifting on civil rights during the 1950s and 1960s.

Preference Shifting With Respect to Civil Rights

We now discuss the available evidence for as many of the preference change types as we could address (beginning with replacement, moving to various mechanisms with respect to changing constituencies, and then concluding by discussing progressive ambition and leadership). This exercise is more descriptive than explanatory, because it is difficult to isolate causes of preference change and much more feasible to account for the categories of change. There is a great deal more evidence with respect to the replacement and changing constituency possibilities than with respect to other mechanisms, but we do try to discuss all of the possible mechanisms and emphasize again that our aim is to leave pure preference change "on the table" as long as possible.

We have tried to select similar roll call votes[7] to find moments in which a member would have the opportunity to switch positions. Obviously, time and differences in the bills make this strategy open to some questions. We believe, however, given the polarized nature of these issues during the period, and the increasing liberalism of the bills, that our choices are reasonable and that those who switched between bills really were expressing a different induced preference.

The point about increasing liberalism of the bills merits further explanation though, because it is central to some of the inferences we draw

Figure 3.1   Civil Rights Policy Proposals Arrayed by Degree of Liberalism
           >>> Conservatism

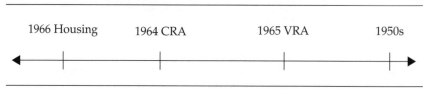

Source: Authors' compilation.

with respect to replacement and pure preference change. To identify true preference change, it is necessary to make some sort of assumption about the series of bills. Happily for our purposes, the bills consistently moved policy in a more and more liberal direction throughout the period.[8] The 1959 Civil Rights Act—toothless by many accounts—was still progress from the conservative status quo policy of the 1950s. The 1964 Civil Rights Act moved policy significantly to the left. Following Johnson's election in 1964, the 1965 Voting Rights Act moved policy further to the left. Housing acts later in the period—though not as powerful as the 1964 and 1965 legislation—extended the policy into new domains (figure 3.1).

Consider the change from the 1964 to the 1965 policy. If there were no preference change, this shift in proposed policy should have led some moderate members to stop supporting civil rights legislation. Conservative southern Democrats would have remained opposed, but some conservative Republicans and moderate northern Democrats should switch from a pro- to an anti-civil rights position, implying that the pro-civil rights margins should never increase over time. As the margins shift in the opposite direction, with more and more House members supporting civil rights. We feel confident inferring that some members updated their beliefs about the policy, consequently changing their preferences through one of the conversion mechanisms we have laid out. Our suspicion—admittedly difficult to prove—is that Martin Luther King Jr.'s strategy of rousing public attention to the injustice of civil rights policy worked, forcing people to update their beliefs. Once people had accepted the fundamental injustice of Jim Crow, people still disagreed about the most appropriate means to bring about equity. But despite the increasing conservatism of later years—the elections of 1966 and 1968, and onward into the 1970s bussing controversies and the Reagan era—the policy has never moved back to where it was before the civil rights movement.

As noted, simple replacement of legislators is a traditional explanation for preference change. Table 3.2 describes the districts that changed party

Table 3.2   Effects of Partisan Replacement on Voting on Civil Rights
          Acts, 1964 to 1965

		Yes	No	Did Not Vote
Northern districts that switched Republican to Democrat	Vote on 1964 Civil Rights Act	32	11	1
	Vote on 1965 Voting Rights Act	44	0	0
Southern districts that switched Republican to Democrat	Vote on 1964 Civil Rights Act	0	2	0
	Vote on 1965 Voting Rights Act	2	0	0
Districts that switched Democrat to Republican	Vote on 1964 Civil Rights Act	3	7	0
	Vote on 1965 Voting Rights Act	2	8	0

Source: Calculated by the authors based on *Congressional Quarterly Weekly Report* (1964, 1965c).

representatives in the 1964 congressional elections and shows how representatives from districts with partisan change voted on the 1964 Civil Rights Act and the 1965 Voting Rights Act.

Among districts that changed from Republican to Democratic representatives in 1964, all changes were in the pro–civil rights direction. The vote switches in districts that went in the Republican direction—predominantly southern districts—did not display any consistent direction. Overall, partisan replacement accounted for a pickup of thirteen votes for the Voting Rights Bill relative to the previous Civil Rights Act. Because the Voting Rights Act received forty-three more votes than the Civil Rights Act, partisan replacement could account for only a bit more than one-third of the total change.

In districts where the incumbent was replaced by someone from the same party (retirements, primary defeats, and so forth), there were six new northern Democratic civil rights votes, two more from southern Democrats and a loss of one Republican vote (see table 3.3). Thus, intraparty replacement can account for at most a switch of seven votes. Combining these figures with those in the previous table, replacements can generate less than half the total switching between 1964 (Civil Rights Act) and 1965 (Voting Rights Act).[9]

The final word on replacement is that it simply does not account for

Table 3.3   The Effect of Intraparty Replacement in Voting on
Civil Rights Bills

		Yes	No	Did Not Vote
Northern districts that switched Democrat to Democrat	Vote on 1964 Civil Rights Act	13	2	4
	Vote on 1965 Voting Rights Act	19	0	0
Southern districts that switched Democrat to Democrat	Vote on 1964 Civil Rights Act	0	7	0
	Vote on 1965 Voting Rights Act	2	4	1
Districts that switched Republican to Republican	Vote on 1964 Civil Rights Act	9	1	3
	Vote on 1965 Voting Rights Act	8	3	2

Source: Calculated by the authors based on *Congressional Quarterly Weekly Report* (1964, 1965c).

the majority of preference change that occurred between the 1964 and 1965 Civil Rights bills. Although some of the other data we examine will continue to touch on the issue of replacement, we can say at the outset that a replacement explanation alone is clearly not enough to describe the changing votes on civil rights.

Another possible mechanism for preference change is the construction of new constituencies. As more black voters came to the ballot box, southern politicians should have been more likely to want to include such voters in their primary constituency. Though we estimated several statistical models to see the effects of racial composition of the district on likelihood of switching, the low numbers of switchers did not yield statistically significant results. The data is consistent, however, with the notion that members do respond to a changing constituency. The average black proportion of the population in House districts where a member switched his vote (between 1964 and 1965) was 9.5 percent—not much different from the 11.4 average for all districts. But the district proportion of blacks for Democrats who changed their vote—likely to face a primary with an increasing number of black voters—rise significantly to 14.8 percent, and to a much higher 17.7 percent among southern Democrats. The last category of switchers (southern Democrats) was likely to receive the largest influx of new primary voters in the future

Table 3.4   Support for Aid to Education Bills in the 87th and
            89th Congress

	Pro-Pro[a]	Anti-Pro	Pro-Anti	Anti-Anti
Northern Democrats	99	4	2	2
Southern Democrats	7	10	3	39
Republicans	5	16	1	63

Source: Calculated by the authors based on *Congressional Quarterly Weekly Report* (1961, 1965a).
[a]Pro- indicates a yes vote on the proposal, and Anti- indicates a no vote. Thus a Pro-Anti legislator would be one who initially supported the bill, but shifted to opposition when the similar proposal was considered later.

elections because northerners likely already faced many black voters not disenfranchised by Jim Crow.

Constituency changes do not occur overnight,[10] so to account for a more gradually changing constituency (for example, a southern suburb getting slowly more urban) converting a member to a new position we examined some other votes from the civil rights era—excluding replacements—to see how much change we could see in some sequences of similar bills over time.

Here we begin with the 1962 proposal and the landmark 1965 Elementary and Secondary Education Act. Probably the most important political change was the election of forty-seven new Democrats in the 1964 elections. But, evidently, between 1962 and 1965 there was a substantial shift in support toward federal support for education occurring in both parties and across both north and south (see table 3.4). Given that neither of these bills contained a Powell amendment, the distributional explanation for change seems less plausible. This is possibly a circumstance in which some other mechanism(s) of preference change is doing the work.

Open housing bills from later Congresses offer another window on preference change. Proposals were voted on in the Democrat-heavy 89th Congress (after the 1964 elections) and in the somewhat more balanced 90th Congress (following substantial Republican midterm gains of 1966). By most accounts the second bill was actually somewhat stronger than the first, and might, on that account, be expected to lose support. Table 3.5 shows that that expectation was not realized.

As in the last table, open housing proposals picked up support across the board with those in both parties and regions switching in a liberal direction. As in the aid to education case in the 89th Congress, these data seem to point to a belief change explanation that is deeper than changing constituencies can account for. Of course, at this level of aggregation we

Table 3.5   Support for Open Housing Legislation in the 89th and
             90th Congress

	Pro-Pro	Anti-Pro	Pro-Anti	Anti-Anti
Northern Democrats	117	10	4	17
Southern Democrats	4	3	1	53
Republicans	44	11	3	65

Source: Calculated by the authors based on *Congressional Quarterly Weekly Report* (1965b, 1968).

cannot specify which of the mechanisms are most likely to be at work. But we can speculate.

The open housing votes came late in 1966 when candidates were looking to the elections. By this time the mood of the country had apparently shifted back to the right somewhat. Conversion (or, perhaps better put, apostasy) must account for some of the difference in voting patterns because 102 members who had voted for the 1965 Voting Rights Act voted against the open housing provision: thirty-one northern Democrats, eleven southern Democrats, and sixty Republicans. (One Republican switched against the tide.) Even though these members were unsuccessful in deleting the open housing provision, some nevertheless supported the bill on passage. Thirty-five members voted against open housing and then for the bill: seven northern Democrats, two southern Democrats, and twenty-six Republicans. This switching indicates not conversion in some psychological sense but the differential difficulty of the votes. In fact, voting responses on the roll calls form a near perfect Guttman scale. Of the 396 members who voted on all three roll calls, only four have nonscalar response patterns.

As noted, from the mid-1950s through the late 1960s[11] the House was presented with a succession of increasingly liberal, increasingly strong, civil rights bills and managed to muster majorities (sometimes slim) for all of them. Both replacement and conversion affected the size of these winning coalitions—though conversion cannot be accounted for completely without some appeal to pure preference change. A significant increase in the toughness of the measure at issue (as from the 1960 to the 1964 bill and from the 1965 voting rights to the 1966 open housing bill) occasionally led to a loss of pro–civil rights votes. However, when these tough bills were followed by equally or slightly stronger measures—as when the 1965 bill followed the 1964 act and the 1968 open housing bill followed the 1966 open housing measure—some kind of conversion or change in beliefs increased the size of the pro–civil rights coalition. Given that the bills grew successively more liberal, it is difficult to see how to account for continuing majorities without some degree of pure preference change.

In an attempt to analyze constituency-driven preference shifts another way, we looked at two votes within the same Congress—one on the Republican substitute to the 1965 Voting Rights Act and the other on the final passage of that act. Because both chambers had approximately the same two votes, we included the votes for both the House and Senate. In both bodies the only real change comes from Republicans, who voted for the weaker substitute and then in favor of the stronger act. In the Senate, fourteen Republicans voted for the (Republican Tower) substitute and then for the bill on final passage. Ninety-one House Republicans followed the same pattern as did two southern and four northern Democrats. In the House, eleven southern Democrats voted in favor of the substitute and then against the act.

The Republicans who voted for the weaker substitute must have preferred that to the actual Voting Rights Act and the Voting Rights Act to the status quo. Those Democrats who voted for the substitute and against the Voting Rights Act were located to the right of the voting act closer to the status quo. Analyses like these suggest that the members who voted for both the substitute and final passage were induced by the location of the act to vote for it over their preferred and more conservative opinion.

In sum, the pro–civil rights forces' impressive success during these years is attributable to the civil rights movement and the support it developed among urban whites. The movement, with the help of television, made civil rights a highly salient issue. Without the high saliency or the base of support, it is inconceivable that civil rights forces would have been able to command so much agenda space, much less present a sharply escalating series of proposals and win on all of them. Replacement cannot account for the success of the movement. In the 1950s, partisan replacement had little impact on the size of coalitions because northern Republicans and Democrats were equally likely to vote for civil rights legislation. By the mid-1960s, partisan replacement had a significant—but not decisive—impact because northern Democrats were much more likely to support civil rights legislation than Republicans were. In the 1950s, a true bipartisan pro–civil rights coalition opposed a coalition of primarily southern Democrats. Through the 1960s, as the measures got tougher and especially as the open housing issue come to the fore, it is true that more Republicans appeared among the opponents: on the key open housing vote in the 90th Congress, Republicans made up over half of the opposition coalition. But the key point is that an increasingly liberal policy carried majorities (often increasing majorities) through the 1960s and was never reversed by subsequently more conservative Congresses. At the risk of repeating the point too often, it seems unlikely that this series of bills could pass without some level of pure preference change.

Finally, with respect to the changing constituency mechanism, we should say something about redistricting. Our analysis made it hard to see redistricting, which is also a form of the changing constituency hypothesis, as a powerful influence on civil rights preferences. Despite the court-ordered redistricting of the 1960s, changing geographic constituency appears to account for very little vote switching—in part because many of the decision's effects would not have taken effect soon enough to matter. But to completely rule out the possibility, we looked at the proportion of changed districts within the stable voting categories (pro-pro, anti-anti) on the voting for the 1964 Civil Rights Act and on the voting for the 1965 Voting Rights Act as compared to the switchers (anti-pro, pro-anti). The results did not show any clear patterns, that is, there were not mean differences. As a further test we took the same two votes—passage of the 1964 Civil Rights Act and the 1965 Voting Rights Act in the Senate. Senators—perfectly insulated from the vagaries of redistricting, but not the influence of changing constituency preferences—show almost no propensity to change their votes. Southerners, except those from the more liberal Tennessee with its large black, franchised population, voted solidly against the bills. Northern Democrats and Republicans voted for them.

The House exhibited exactly the same pattern as the Senate. In both chambers only around 3 to 4 percent of members who voted on both bills switched votes (those in the anti-pro or pro-anti categories). Given this extremely similar result for both the House and Senate, it seems very unlikely that only the switchers in the House are being driven by changing constituencies caused by redistricting, because the Senate switchers could not be motivated by that. There is probably a separate cause—such as changing national beliefs—underlying this similar rate of change.

The last two mechanisms we can discuss are progressive ambition and leadership induced change. We examined the progressive ambition thesis by looking at members in the 88th, 89th, and 90th Houses who ran for higher office within a five-year window. The results did not show a significant difference for switchers running for higher office. Likewise those voting for Civil Rights bills were no more likely to run for higher office than those who voted against the same civil rights legislation. But such an analysis cannot be definitive because what is required to measure the phenomena accurately is a good measure of the district's views versus the state's views. But, at this point we do not see an obvious relationship between civil rights voting and progressive ambition.

Table 3.6   Median Adjusted ADA Scores in the Senate

	1960	1965	1970	1975	1980
All chairs	11.57	10.61	17.21	53.51	66.45
(Mean)	(24.09)	(26.19)	(30.84)	(42.32)	(62.07)
Democratic caucus	55.24	62.93	66.38	61.95	64.23
Floor	41.99	49.03	34.98	50.70	47.53

Source: Calculated by the authors based on data provided by Timothy Groseclose.

The final area for preference change we examine is leadership-induced preference change, and we focus on the changed incentives for committee chairs to line up with the party caucus—we begin with a non–civil rights example. Throughout the 1960s battles with southern chairmen over civil rights and after liberal legislation were legion. Seniority guaranteed members their hierarchical place on the committee roster, and thus institutionalized conservative southern Democrats. In the aftermath of the 1974 election, the Democratic caucus sent a strong signal by replacing four committee chairs—reportedly because of their unwillingness to yield to the liberal majority on public spending among other issues. Thus the expectation that post 1974 we would expect to see committee chairs more in line with the Democratic caucus preferences. In table 3.6 we show a comparison of Snyder-Groseclose-ADA scores for several Congresses across all committee chairs, the big three in the House (Rules, Appropriations, Ways and Means), the Democratic caucus and floor.

The results are clear that this does not account for preference change in the 1960s. Although it is true that by the 1970s the preferences of the committee chairs are exhibiting influences of the increasingly liberal Democrat caucus (no doubt due in particular to the influence of the class of 1974), the civil rights period shifts don't appear to hinge on committee chair changes.

Additionally, with respect to leadership, it is possible to find cases of specific rules or votes that the leadership might have used to delay or alter a civil rights vote outcome (for example, the cited Smith anecdote about gender protection). For instance in 1959 Johnson managed to win approval of a weaker civil rights bill by voting on the cloture rules before handing out committee assignments: several freshman senators previously committed to voting for a new cloture rule that would have made civil rights passage more likely changed their minds at the last minute. A few years later, in 1970, when pushing for reauthorization of the voting rights act the Senate leadership explicitly connected the vote to a law permitting 18-year-olds to vote. The House had defeated reauthorization, albeit by a four-vote margin. But when confronted with a bill including provisions for this new constituency, the House reauthorized the legislation by a vote of 272 to 132.[12] Despite these occasional anecdotes, a systematic story wherein the leadership consistently induces vote remains difficult to tell. We do not believe it was a critical cause for the changed civil rights policy.

Endogenous preference shifts accounted for some of the apparent preference change in the civil rights period—via some replacement and perhaps a small amount of constituency preference change. In other words, some members updated their beliefs based on one or more of the endogenous processes laid out above. But this accounting does not appear to explain all of the broad patterns.

Perhaps, given the nature of the times this should be expected. Bruce Ackerman (1991, 1998) has argued that Americans occasionally engage in higher lawmaking, a concept similar to what we are arguing here, because it involves the changing of the American creed: what was once permissible policy (institutional racism) is no longer seriously debated. During the civil rights period, the country was forced to reexamine the treatment of blacks; the public's beliefs about fair treatment for all Americans likely shifted during the period. This is consistent with the chamber-level measures of ideology. Despite the fact that the Democratic tide elections of 1958, 1964, and 1974 would seem to predict action on the racial agenda of liberal Democrats, passage of key civil rights bills never appears to quickly follow from those elections. Key civil rights legislation was passed and reauthorized at times either before or after—but not concurrent with—moments where the chambers shifted in a liberal direction.

Additionally, when we note that preference change occurs across regions and across parties and that it seems consistent with changing national election returns (as when Democratic victories in 1964 may have induced some vote changes, see footnote 5), we are forced to ask if a more national force is at work. We briefly mentioned the power of television and the mass media above. It may be that as people began to see the effects of Jim Crow and discuss it the national beliefs about what policies were necessary to achieve equity changed, ending the tolerance for institutionalized racism.

Conclusion

We have only scratched the surface of what is probably a vital future topic for political scientists. Recent work in the field has greatly expanded what we can say and model regarding measures of representation and preferences. NOMINATE scores, interest group scores, polling, and other technological developments make it possible to characterize the legislative and public distribution of preferences and beliefs.[13] Legislatures are designed to reflect public preferences—or "refine and enlarge" preferences, to use James Madison's language. Thus it should not surprise us when we find shifts of the sort depicted here: given time, national preferences will shift.

Our effort to account for preference change in the U.S. Congress has illuminated some of the possible causes of preference shifting. We began by listing the mechanisms by which legislators might show new or changed preferences in their voting record. Having left pure preference change on the table as long as possible, we can now say that a description of civil rights policy and politics requires some kind of pure preference change beyond replacement or other conversion mechanisms such as constituency change or leadership inducements. We speculate that legislators updated their beliefs along the lines Ackerman suggested. Although it is difficult to prove that possibility, we can confidently say that some kind of pure preference change must be accepted to account for the success and stability of the civil rights legislation.

One small, but interesting poll finding is evident in table 3.1. In 1963 the majority of whites thought that protesting over civil rights was justified. Three short years later only a third did. In the intervening time three things happened: the Congress passed two landmark civil rights bills; the president who backed those bills won in a landslide election;[14] and the face of the civil rights movement began to change from Martin Luther King Jr. to Rapp Brown. There is not enough evidence (nor clarity of theory, yet) for us to clearly label 1964 a critical or ratifying election, like the ones in 1896 or 1932. After all, the elections of 1966 and 1968 scarcely continued support for the administration and party that enacted those policies. But the civil rights policy has continued more or less unchanged since it was passed, despite the bussing that angered northern whites, the violence and continued protest of the 1960s and early 1970s, and the affirmative action that continues to anger many whites. Congress simply maintained the policies.

We believe that our accounting effort falls somewhat short (without accounting for pure preference change) because public beliefs changed regarding the effects and morality of the civil rights policies. In fact the chamber-level evidence of preferences is more consistent with that explanation than with a simple electoral-based model.

The technology already exists for political scientists to begin thinking about endogenous preferences, by considering the processes through which members update their beliefs. This paper points out some of the issues related to an endogenous preferences research agenda. We believe it will be a significant and ultimately valuable project. There is certainly much more to consider. We have only touched on such topics as the role of elections in conveying information to legislators about what their induced preferences should be; chamber differences in preference shifting; the fickle nature of public opinion in more normal political settings;[15] or the technological changes that allow members to better understand their district-level attitudes. There is much work to do and with luck the ideas presented here clearly introduce effective channels of research. We suggest that others in the field consider that legislatures by their nature will see many different kinds of preference shifts. It is the job of good political scientists to study those shifts and their causes, not simply hold them constant.

Notes

1. Gilligan and Krehbiel's informational model where the median legislator may update his beliefs about the effects of public policy is one example. Electoral models where a voter updates his beliefs about the candidates based on the campaign might also involve some kinds of preference change.
2. Also see Thomas Edsall and Mary Edsall (1992) for good historical work on the politics and policy coming out of the civil rights movement and Arthur Stevens, Arthur Miller, and Thomas Mann (1977) for the best analysis of the Democratic Study Group's influence on these events.
3. There may of course be biological or neurophysiological processes to call upon when developing wine or opera preferences. Wine and music appreciation seems to depend in part on the ability to discriminate among similar sensations and this is probably connected to hardware issues such as density of various taste receptors or the capacities of the auditory system. These features may set the upper limit or capacity for appreciation. But the ability to appreciate music or wine may also depend on the development of neural structures that may be much more plastic and subject to manipulation or training by explicitly adopted policies.
4. In the late 1980s Pat Williams (D-Mont.) knew that his state was likely to lose one of its two congressional seats in the redistricting following the 1990 census. He represented the more liberal, industrial party of the state but in anticipation of the need to run in the entire state he began spending time in the western, more conservative, agricultural section of the state. He held onto that seat following the redistricting.
5. Hale Boggs is certainly a candidate for this category. A strong Southern conservative at the beginning of his career, Boggs had converted for some reason—perhaps for leadership office in the Democratic Party—by the end of his career.

6. Though it is possible that if some congressmen actually had a change of heart—or indeed if they had pro–civil rights preferences all along (surely this is the story of Fulbright. and perhaps Frank Smith or Lister Hill)—conditions described in possibilities 3 through 6 may have made it safer to act on them.

7. All roll call vote information is taken from *Congressional Quarterly Weekly Reports*. We have listed voters as "for" or "against" depending on their definition of "paired for" or "paired against." But we have not accepted CQ Polls to ascertain a position. Unless otherwise noted in the text we are discussing final passage votes in the chamber.

8. See figure 3.1 for a rough approximation of the liberalism of several important civil rights policies. The important point is that time and liberalism of the policy are negatively correlated.

9. We reiterate that the bills were different in purpose and strength. We still aim to leave preference-shifting on the table as long as possible.

10. Though gradual changes seem like more likely, we did investigate the possibility that the election of 1964 had a significant and immediate effect on Southern Democrats and their willingness to switch. A logit model of either district switching (which obviously includes replacement) or personal switching (which does not include replacement) finds that the interaction term between LBJ's vote margin in the district and a dummy variable for South is positive and highly significant—even when controlling for political party and member ideology (via NOMINATE scores). In other words, as Southern members saw that LBJ remained very popular in their district—despite his support of the 1964 CRA—they became more likely to switch their vote to favor civil rights. This result is consistent with the idea that members updated their beliefs about the preferences of the district. Following an across the board Democratic victory in 1964 they were, for any number of reasons, willing to then change their vote.

11. In another version of this paper we looked at votes on aid to education between 1958 and 1966. All of that analysis was consistent with what we present here: members were unlikely to switch positions, but the group of switchers was bipartisan and came from both North and South.

12. The vote on the amendment to include the reduced voting age in the House bill was closer, but not that close: 224–183.

13. Obviously the greatest advancements will probably only come when the field is better prepared to link measures of public and legislator preferences.

14. A landslide so large and against such a weak opponent that it, if anything, overemphasized the level of public support for LBJ's program.

15. It is probable, after all, that civil rights is hardly a representative case study for simple preference shifting. That is what makes it such a good candidate for an Ackerman-based explanation appealing to notions of higher lawmaking.

References

Ackerman, Bruce. 1991. *We The People: Foundations*. Cambridge, Mass.: Harvard University Press.

———. 1998. *We The People: Transformations*. Cambridge, Mass.: Harvard University Press.

Brink, William, and Louis Harris. 1966. *Black and White: A Study of U.S. Racial Attitudes Today*. New York: Simon & Schuster.

Campbell, Angus. 1971. *White Attitudes Toward Black People*. Ann Arbor, Mich.: Institute for Social Research.

Canes-Wrone, Brandice, David Brady, and John Cogan. 2001. "Out of Step, Out of Office." In *Continuity and Change in House Elections*, edited by David Brady, John Cogan, and Morris Fiorina. Stanford, Calif.: Stanford University Press.

Carmines, Edward, and James Stimson. 1989. *Issue Evolution*. Princeton, N.J.: Princeton University Press.

Congressional Quarterly Weekly Report. 1961. Roll Call Information. XIX(35): 1536–1537. Congressional Quarterly Inc. All rights reserved.

———. 1964. Roll Call Information. XXII(7): 334–35. Congressional Quarterly Inc. All rights reserved.

———. 1965a. Roll Call Information. XXIII(14): 600–601. Congressional Quarterly Inc. All rights reserved.

———. 1965b. Roll Call Information. XXIII(28): 1312–13. Congressional Quarterly Inc. All rights reserved.

———. 1965c. Roll Call Information. XXIII(29): 1402–03. Congressional Quarterly Inc. All rights reserved.

———. 1968. Roll Call Information. XXVI(15): 842–43. Congressional Quarterly Inc. All rights reserved.

Dye, Thomas. 1971. *The Politics of Equality*. Indianapolis, Ind.: Bobbs-Merrill.

Edsall, Thomas, with Mary Edsall. 1992. *Chain Reaction*. New York: W. W. Norton.

Fiorina, Morris. 1974. *Representatives, Roll Calls and Constituencies*. Lanham, Md.: Lexington Books.

Kahneman, Paul, and Amos Tversky. 1982. *Judgment Under Uncertainty: Heuristics and Biases*. New York: Cambridge University Press.

Kellstedt, Paul M. 2000. "Media Framing and the Dynamics of Racial Policy Preferences." *American Journal of Political Science* 44(2): 245–60.

Kinder, Donald, and Lynn Sanders. 1996. *Divided by Color: Racial Politics and Democratic Ideals*. Chicago: University of Chicago Press.

Rohde, David. 1991. *Parties and Leaders in the Postreform House*. Chicago: University of Chicago Press.

Schumann, Howard, Charlotte Steeh, Lawrence Bobo, and Maria Krysan. 1997. *Racial Attitudes in America: Trends and Interpretations*. Cambridge, Mass.: Harvard University Press.

Stevens, Arthur, Arthur Miller, and Thomas Mann. 1977. "Mobilization of Liberal Strength in the House, 1955–1970: The Democratic Study Group." In *New Perspectives on the House of Representatives*, 3rd ed., edited by Robert L. Peabody and Nelson W. Polsby. Chicago: Rand McNally.

Sundquist, James. 1968. *Politics and Policy: The Eisenhower, Kennedy, and Johnson Years*. Washington, D.C.: The Brookings Institution.

4

"To Give Counsel and to Consent": Why the King (Edward I) Expelled His Jews (in 1290)

Ira Katznelson

With full power for themselves and the whole community of that country to give counsel and to consent for themselves and that community to those things that the earls, barons, and other magnates of the realm shall then cause to be agreed upon, as the king has been requested by the earls, barons and other magnates of the realm concerning certain things, regarding which the king wishes to have colloquy and treaty with them.
  —Summons of June 14, 1290, for knightly representatives to be sent from the shires to parliament by July 15 (cited in Stacey 1997, 90)

Of the business transacted in the assembly called for the 15th of July, we have no formal record; but it is shown by what follows to have been of a financial character, and comprised the grant of a fifteenth of all moveables, made by clergy and laity alike. It would appear that the king proposed this to the parliament, and also demanded a tenth of the spiritual revenue. At the same time, by an act done by himself in his private council, he banished the Jews from England: the safe conduct granted them on their departure is dated on the 27th of July . . . .The boon of consideration of which the new grant was made is stated by the annalists to have been the banishment of the Jews, a measure which was popular.
  —William Stubbs (1897, 127–28)

Edward I resolved to expel his kingdom's Jews in the early summer of 1290 when parliament was in session. His expulsion order was promulgated on July 18. The exodus began on October 12 and was completed, as the king had ordered, by the end of the month. Disturbed only by minor violence, the Jews set out from England's southern ports for

France, Spain, or Germany. By best estimate, they numbered only two to three thousand, down from a peak of some five thousand, in a population variously estimated in the range of two to three million. During the two centuries of their presence, Jews had settled in more than eighty locations, ranging from hundreds living in London, their initial place of residence and sole burial site until 1177, to isolated individual persons or single families living in peasant villages and some towns (Russell 1948; Mann 1986, 400; Mundill 1998, chap. 2). The majority lived in small communities numbering in the tens, rarely more than one hundred, that sustained a synagogue and a cemetery. Once ejected, Jews remained absent for nearly four centuries until they were invited back by Cromwell in December 1655.[1]

On the face of things, this history might not be grasped as very significant. Writing in this vein, Lionel Abrahams observed in 1895 that the "expulsion of the English Jews was an event of small importance alike in English and in Jewish history. In England the effect that it produced was barely perceptible." The Jews, he further claimed, "were driven from a land which thirty-five years earlier they had begged in vain from being able to leave. . . . The loss of their inhospitable home in England was but one episode in their tragic history" (Abrahams 1894/1895, 458). This perspective, reflected in the meager attention mainstream English medievalists have paid to Anglo-Jewish history (Stacey 1987b, 63) is plausible, but wide of the mark. Jews played a role that was far more important than their tiny number might suggest in shaping England's economy, social geography, and fiscal capacity in the twelfth and thirteenth centuries, and their standing evoked recurring interest and concern that also was disproportionate. Further, if, as we will see, their growing insecurity, culminating in eviction, was critically affected by the establishment of rights and the creation of political representation at the national level in the early stage of the globe's first proto-liberal regime, the Jewish expulsion seven centuries ago hardly is a minor event. The challenge of explaining the links between these institutions and the expulsion lend this history an ever more urgent quality in light of the unfortunate resonance that ethnic cleansing has come to have in our time, despite the great differences separating the circumstances of mass democratization in the nineteenth and twentieth centuries from the political and social state of affairs that prevailed some seven centuries ago.

The compulsory Jewish departure is not well understood. There are two primary puzzles. The first is strategic. Set within a framework of royal ambition, how did kings assess the advantages and risks of protecting or expelling the Jews? The second is temporal. When, and why, did the Jewish condition shift so that extrusion could become an option? What brought Edward to prefer a nation without Jews?

Echoing William Stubbs, England's great nineteenth-century constitutional historian, a leading scholar of the expulsion recently has urged students of the expulsion to focus on the king's dispositions, arguing that their exit "was Edward's own decision. . . . Thus the final decision for expulsion seems to lie essentially with the king" (Mundill 1998, 253, 268). In the constitutional sense, it was, as Stubbs put the point, "an act done by himself." Because they were the king's Jews, their fate, of course, was overwhelmingly in the hands of the monarch. Other than belonging to the crown, they had no particular status (Richardson 1960, 134).

Yet a person-centered, solipsistic reading of royal preferences generally, or of Edward's in particular, with regard to the Jews is unlikely to be satisfying should it ignore either the timing and setting of the expulsion order, or, equally important, if it were to beg the question of how the larger circumstances in which kings governed affected their dramatic choices to uphold, modify, or overturn the practice of sovereign protection for the Jews.

The chance to consider these issues can help us think about this book's central analytical themes. Edward's break with precedent, reversing the insistence by prior kings that even Jews who wished to exit should be prohibited from leaving, provides an opportunity to consider the formation and transformation of preferences, the individually held "reasons for behavior . . . that account for the actions [taken] in given situations." Treated here, more specifically, as "the manner in which individuals construe situations (or, more narrowly, the way they frame a decision)," I probe how political institutions, mediating between individual agency and large-scale change, can elicit preferences that, in turn, reshape the larger environment (Bowles 2004, 99).[2]

In the Balance

Edward's decision often has been thought to contradict royal interests. "How was it," a late nineteenth century historian of the expulsion inquired,

> that, at a time when trade and the need for capital were growing, the Jews, who were reputed to be among the great capitalists of Europe, were expelled from England? How did Edward, a king who was in debt from the moment he began his reign till the end, bring himself to give up the revenue that his father and grandfather had derived from the Jews? How could he, as an honourable king, drive out subjects who were protected by a Charter that one of his predecessors had granted, and another had solemnly confirmed? (Abrahams 1894/1895, 75)

Over the course of their residence, as England developed a robust economy and emerged as Europe's most capable and effective administrative and fiscal state, Jews did prove a considerable asset. As sources of capital, they helped propel the growth of markets, towns, and networks of trade. As sources of revenue for the king and state, they helped fund ventures that enhanced English power and institutions. By the late twelfth century, their taxes were important enough to be collected and recorded separately. Under the ordinances of 1194, an exchequer of the Jews was created, a registry cataloging all Jewish holdings, centralizing financial control over their transactions, and making Jewish resources more amenable to effective taxation (Cramer 1941; Elman 1952). These regulations were detailed, specifying towns where contracts with Jews could be drawn and registered, and stipulating the supervision of record-keeping by Jews and Christians, including how keys should be held for the chests in which they were to be stored (Leonard 1891, 156–59; Poole 1951, 422–23). That year, "the Jews of all England," as a remarkable surviving record details, offered gifts of nearly 4,000 pounds, listed both by their town of residence and by individual names when the king returned from Germany (Leonard 1891, 162–64). Later, on a far larger scale, the Jews provided vastly disproportionate funds when John fought to keep the country's holdings in Normandy and Henry III struggled unsuccessfully to restore them. Jews, moreover, offered kings outposts of dependent populations and valuable sources of information located at the center of major towns, serving, in effect, as early warning indicators of opposition or insurgency.

Notwithstanding the advantages the presence of the Jews could offer, Edward's decision is, in fact, explicable in terms of royal interests. They were expelled despite these instrumental contributions. The Jews were a noticeable and widely disliked minority: for their religious stubbornness, perceived clannishness, self-enclosure, disassociation from the various institutions of a largely landed social order, and economic activity. If Jews offered benefits to the crown, they also identified kings with a pariah population, making them potentially less legitimate and more vulnerable to the claims, authority, and demands of vital interlocutors, including church leaders, rural notables, and urban elites.

Kings thus had to construe the situation and frame strategic calculations about the Jews by appraising how the primarily economic advantages they offered competed with the threat their presence posed to the quest for effective and legitimate rule. If the basic terms of this choice remained constant, weighing up the balance produced quite different results over time. The key challenge is therefore that of understanding why, when, and how one hierarchy of calculations was supplanted by another. Ultimately, why did Edward favor Christian homogeneity at the cost of a financial asset?

To account for these results, this essay offers the following propositions:

> After the loss of Normandy at the start of the thirteenth century, English kings responded to a configuration of geopolitical, economic, associational, and religious pressures that had decreased the security, autonomy, and legitimacy of the monarchy by consenting, with great reluctance, to remake the national regime's institutional topography.

> Singly and in combination, these efforts to reduce royal insecurity, which included the West's inauguration of liberal rights and the practice of regular political representation in parliaments, weakened the commitment kings had to save their Jews from harm. Jewish well-being as a value diminished within the hierarchy of royal preferences.

> As a consequence of growing societal pressures and a diminution of assured protection by kings, the Jewish condition declined over the course of the thirteenth century. Royal safeguards and a far more decent pattern of coexistence with Christian neighbors than existed in most places of Jewish settlement on the Continent, especially during periods of crusading, gave way to heightened physical, fiscal, and religious vulnerabilities.

> In due course, a more radical change from moderated protection and a raised level of jeopardy to the possibility of exclusion was induced by the institutional arrangements of rights and representation to which kings had assented. Two tightly linked mechanisms were at work. The first was that these new "liberal" institutions moved the relationship of state and society from layered fealty to one of negotiated transactions, a process that powerfully altered the manner in which monarchs viewed the kingdom's Jewish communities. The second was that revenue for key royal projects, especially warfare, now could shift from taxes fixed by custom to supplement income generated by royal landholding to taxes, mainly on moveable property, based on negotiation and consent, a shift that diminished the relative standing of Jews as contributors to the fiscal health of the crown.

> Within the strategic logic of this new polity, the shift in royal preferences regarding the presence of the Jews is best understood as a

constitutive part of Edward's successful efforts at state-making and nation-building. As he learned to negotiate inside the terms and bounds of the parliamentary kingship to achieve the monarchy's most cherished preferences for sovereign control over territory and people while guarding its standing and legitimacy and securing ample funds for key projects, he came to consider the situation of the Jews, and the range of options for dealing with their circumstances, in a new way.

Prospectively, Jewish deportation was not wholly determined by the country's new institutional environment. There is strong evidence that as late as mid-June 1290 Edward was planning to obtain a new fiscal exaction from the Jews, as he sought to find means to reduce his court's unsupportable level of debt (Stacey 1997, 89–90). What transpired in Westminster in the month before Edward's directive was a negotiation between the king and an enlarged parliament that demonstrates the power of the mechanisms of transaction and taxation to convoke a basic change in preference.

Over the course of the thirteenth century, kings responded to the tests posed by geopolitics, town growth, civil society, and national identity unevenly, with varying degrees of competence and success. By the time Edward finally expelled the Jews, it already was clear that he had managed the new form of kingship to successfully build an adept state, unify an English nation, extend the country's power and territorial reach, raise the necessary resources, and win consent for public action. His success and the tragedy of English Jewry thus were entwined, as in a braid. The historian David Carpenter puts the point, if a bit limpidly, this way (2003, 466):

> His achievement lay in establishing a new tax-based parliamentary state, and making the monarch for the first time since 1066 at one rather than at odds with the Englishness of its people. Edward by these means gained the power to wage his wars against the Welsh and the Scots. There also were certain internal victims of his rule. The Jews were expelled from England in 1290.

It is the tightness of this connection that has not fully been explored to date. Most students of the expulsion tend to account for the decision to eject the Jews by focusing either on their decline as a fiscal asset (Elman 1937; Veitch 1986), as if this capacity might not have been resuscitated, or point to shifts within the religious sphere (Langmuir 1990, 57–

133), as if they could not have been resisted, as so many papal and church pressures were, by the crown (Stacey 1999). Rather, the condition of the Jews was fundamentally conditioned by a change in the probability space for the development of royal preferences, a space that was affected most fundamentally by the trials the regime faced and royal responses to those challenges. Alterations and adjustments to the institutional situation of kingship, in short, not fiscal or religious factors as such, produced the sea change in royal preferences about the Jews that led to their excision.

Although this kind of focus on regime change is not the usual way the ejection of the Jews is explained—that pride of place, we will see, belongs either to fiscal causes or religious motivations and enthusiasms—it does appear as a key theme in small number of evocative articles. Writing in 1891, George Hare Leonard offered evidence that "parliament dearly wished to be rid of these aliens," stressing how the connection of Jews "with the Crown could not fail to be very objectionable to the constitutionalists of the day," and showing how "the politicians of the day pressed the constitutional grievance" (Leonard 1891, 103, 111, 129). Some nine decades later, Barnett Ovrut lamented that historians, rather than taking up Leonard's theme, had "neglected to place the expulsion within its proper perspective: a conscious act of an aggressive and far-sighted government made in response to a number of political and constitutional factors which were playing an important role in the development of the English state" (Ovrut 1977, 224). His own rather general sketch contended "that the king's decision to expel the Jews should have come when it did was primarily due to political-constitutional factors," but, unlike Leonard, he thought these to be issues "in which the Jews were only indirectly related," notably pressures on baronial landholding, the result of debts to Jewish moneylenders, that produced demands for parliamentary redress (Ovrut 1977, 229). More recently, the most important historian of medieval English Jewry, Robert Stacey, has written an indispensable account of the "evolving political bargain" that was negotiated between Edward and the representatives who had assembled at Westminster in the summer of 1290, arguing that the expulsion of the Jews "was conceded specifically to the shire knights in Parliament, in turn for their consent to a tax for which Edward had already been negotiating with his magnates for some weeks" (Stacey 1997, 78).

In returning to the largely neglected line of reasoning pioneered by Leonard, this discussion falls between Ovrut's suggestive but rather vague plea that more attention should be directed to constitutional and political issues and Stacey's valuable pointillist treatment of Edward's give and take with the magnates, burgesses, and knights in the period immediately preceding publication of the king's order to expel the Jews.

What follows, then, is a political sketch that divides the history of the two centuries of Jewish settlement into three epochs. First was a long era, initiated by the Norman Conquest, of successful state-building based on property redistribution, town growth, and the growing capacity of public authority in a system of centralized feudalism. Second was a half-century spanning the baronial revolt of the 1210s through mid-century to the start of a new epoch of civil war, dominated by the decisive loss of territory in France, the creation of a political society that possessed irrevocable rights, and the governing autonomy of towns. Third was a tumultuous critical juncture of three decades in which a monarch was deposed, only to be returned on the basis of a new regime placing the king in parliament at the core of government and its ability to raise revenue in a process of negotiation with the representatives of an expanded political nation that included magnates, knights, and burgesses; and in which an English cultural and linguistic nation began to be constructed with ambitions to command all of the British Isles and participate actively in European crusading as a distinctively English force.

At each of these moments, the fate of the Jews utterly depended on the country's kings. Their preferences were constituted in the main by the ways they could deal with royal insecurity and by the play of the new institutions they unwillingly had conceded to keep the monarchy intact. Whereas the first long moment proved virtuous for the Jews because kings construed situations and framed decisions about this group as a buffer and helpmate for the combination of feudalism and state-making in which they were engaged, subsequent developments radically altered the parameters characterizing their regimes. In consequence, kings developed preferences about the Jews that led first to a steady relaxation of royal defenses against elite and mass pressures on Jewish life, and ultimately to circumstances in which expulsion could be considered and accomplished.

Thirteenth-century revisions in governance produced a far-reaching doctrinal, administrative, and institutional reframing for the position of the king as a ruler and head of state. In turn, these fundamental alterations entailed a thoroughgoing shift to the way John, Henry III, and Edward came to take decisions about the Jews. More precisely, the institutions they created to deal with royal insecurity at home changed the way they ordered their preferences. Jews, who never were liked in medieval England, persistently faced pressures that sought, by religious accusation, economic and social boycott, symbolic degradation, and violence to constrict their settlement and reduce the scope for their remunerative activity. Kings were regularly challenged to lift their protective umbrella. Until the second decade of the thirteenth century, they resisted these pressures, placing their responsibility to shield the Jews ahead of considerations that might have made the group more vulnerable. This ordering of royal preferences changed, however, during the last eight decades of Jewish settlement, in a manner that significantly devalued the guardianship role of kings. By late century, this shift had moved expulsion as a policy from a location outside the ken of feasibility into a space where it became an increasingly probable outcome.

Royal Sufferance

At the time of the Norman Conquest, the country did not have a Jewish community. No Jews had been on the island since the days of Roman rule. They began to arrive in small numbers from Normandy, primarily Rouen, after suffering in 1096 at the hands of Crusaders preparing to leave for the Holy Land (Golb 1998). The refugees first settled in London, their sole place of residence for some four decades. After 1140, with the blessing of the country's kings, Jews came to live in trade and market center towns all across England, where they tended to cluster in Jewries, though there were no spatial ghettos that confined or walled them in. Not Christian, not part of feudal relations or a wider network of social relations, and not free to pursue most occupations, they were confined mainly to moneylending, a visible and theologically odious economic niche[3] (Helmholz 1986). Providing capital to small as well as large landowners, religious establishments, urban merchants, and to the crown itself produced widespread indebtedness to Jews, often affecting such institutional arrangements as feudal landholding as a result of how debts were discharged (Stacey 1985).

From the start, Jews existed on royal sufferance. Formally, they were the property of the crown, thus exposed both to routine taxation and targeted special expropriations. "The Jews were under the special protection of the king who in turn could tallage them at will" (Poole 1951, 422). As vulnerable residents, they were protected by royal decisions authorizing their rights to residency, property, and travel. They required special protection because they were external to the basic seignorial and communal mechanisms of English feudalism (Bartlett 2000, 351). From Henry I forward, they were sheltered by Charters based on earlier models established by Carolingian Emperors of the ninth century and the Holy Roman Emperors of the twelfth. Henry's *Magna Carta Judaeorum* stipulated that "Jews have free residence in England and Normandy, and may hold lands, fiefs, pledges, gifts, and purchases" (Leonard 1891, 331). Like these precursors, this type of arrangement shielded Jews, at least formally, from others who wished them ill, while defining them vis-à-vis the king, the broader polity, the economy, and society as residents rather than as subjects. The king was responsible for defending the

Jews, whom he recognized and forced others to acknowledge as a distinct entity free to organize as a largely self-governing religious community. Under this arrangement, local sheriffs, as delegates of the king played a particularly important role, as "their support was essential to local Jewish communities when danger threatened" (Hyams 1974, 275).

The initial twelve decades of Jewish settlement, though punctuated by a small number of allegations of anti-Christian ritual killing and extensive popular assaults in 1189 and 1190, were a time of relative prosperity and coexistence. William II, Henry I, Stephen, Henry II, Richard I, and John sheltered a steadily extending Jewish community, a population these kings considered a valuable resource as they sought to develop their recognizably modern ambitions. Like their successors, they were jealous and determined about frontiers, dominions, and powers. They sought to reinforce their internal rule by external success, and make external success possible by strengthening internal rule. They acted to establish a combination of independence from potentially powerful actors, whether religious or secular, and achieve durable supremacy over territory and population.

Although there had been earlier efforts to consolidate royal authority and integrate the kingdom, including exertions to secure its place under Danish rule in Anglo-Saxon England from the early eleventh century, struggles to hold the island's polity together rarely had been successful for long. By contrast, through a series of audacious acts, most notably land redistribution, the Norman monarchs fashioned a remarkable system of feudalism, combining a high degree of layered local autonomy with clear fealty and obligations to the center, the focal point of which was of course the king. By contrast with various continental models, English feudalism was characterized by an uncommonly clear hierarchy of loyalties buttressed by coherent public administration, policing capacity, and, above all, by the wholesale reallocation of property. All feudalisms are parcellized, but this decentralization was quite exceptionally counterbalanced by royal centralization. It was this system, combining property, authority, and loyalty that did more than protect the Jews: it gave them a role as engines of urban and market expansion integral to this system of centralized feudalism (Reynolds 1999; Waugh 1999; West 1999). It also set in motion a series of dynamic developments—including an emergent civil society and potential political nation both on the land and in towns, debt at significant interest that would come to be seen as onerous, and popular resentment at examples of Jewish prosperity and visibility at the center of English towns—that, under changing conditions, later would haunt both the kings and the Jews.

The new Norman rulers, who deployed an itinerant style and served both as king of the English and duke of the Normans, sought to secure and where possible expand the territory under their dynastic control on their various English and French frontiers to take in more resources of all kinds, including a larger subject population. Seeking to stabilize governance and reduce uncertainty, these kings sought to create durable and effective institutions of rule by establishing networks of loyal officials and instituting a net of communication linking the enlarged territories under their control. During the second half of the eleventh century, the Norman kings brought their new kingdom under control by integrating its administration with that of Normandy, often moving key individuals from roles on one side of the Channel to the other (Le Patourel 1976, 222–78), and by marshaling a potential armed force of some six thousand knights to garrison the many new castles they built (Dyer 2002, 86). Most important, "Englishmen were expropriated by the hundreds and thousands" (Reynolds 1994, 343), and their lands were assigned to Norman landowners, thus creating a ruling class linked across the lines of property and political power (Thomas 2003, 105–37).

This radical act, "the largest transfer of property ever seen in English history" in which "a whole upper class was displaced" (Dyer 2002, 80) fashioned a new aristocracy and a new social hierarchy (Dyer 2002, 85):

> In place of the pre-Conquest hierarchy of wealth consisting of a few super-magnates towering over many modestly well-off thegns, the new social order established about 200 substantial tenants-in-chief, earls and barons holding directly of the crown, who together owned about half of the land. Below them were another 1,000 landholders with land worth at least 5 pounds, and 6,000–7000 lesser men, some resembling pre-Conquest thegns, many with only a hide.

Having distributed immense estates in wholesale fashion to their followers in the form of royal grants, the new large landholders, in turn, were free to distribute parcels to their own followers (Reynolds 1994, 345). It was this hierarchical arrangement that was recorded so meticulously in the Domesday Book, the astonishing census of grants and landholding that William I ordered to be compiled in 1086. Overall, the land did not belong to the king, but landholders owed their place in the chain of property to the crown, thus creating a powerful tool of social and spatial integration for a monarchy based primarily in London.

This was a period in which landowning conferred many more duties than rights, including that of military service. Norman rearrangements in property went hand in hand with a military system combining the obligation "on all free men in the kingdom to serve and defend" the king "against his enemies both within and without England" with a reliance on household troops, paid soldiers, and knights who particularly owed military service as a result of their economic and social status. This dual system produced effective means to extend, protect, and police territory and its population, the hallmark of modern sovereignty. It also was a powerful fiscal instrument. Scutage, or payment for failure to serve in a particular military campaign, though often disputed, became a reliable source of income, one that complemented the period's other major source of taxation, the danegeld, a customary tax on property that was assessed on royally granted lands, counties, and towns, and collected by the justices of the kings who traveled throughout the kingdom for this purpose. There were downwards pressures as these funds were raised, for magnates would impose fees on their knights to help them pay the levy as well as discharge the debt they owed to Jews (Reynolds 1994, 352, 361–65; also see Green 1986).

None of the state-building ambitions of the eleventh and twelfth century post-Conquest English kings could have been pursued effectively without the existence—new to this period—of a sphere of the economy situated mainly in towns, based on money and trade rather than land and barter to which kings could achieve privileged access (Elias 1939/ 1994; Pirenne 1937; Abrams 1978; Hohenberg and Lees 1985; Bairoch 1988; Benevolo 1993). By realizing an ability to effectively tax the surplus of this dynamic sector, kings could secure their advantage over other actors with whom they potentially competed for political control. With access to a money economy as a source of revenue, kings gained means to equip and deploy military force, build administrative capacity, and police the behavior of others. In this manner, as Michael Mann has observed (1988, 86), early urban capitalism combined with systematic taxation and special exactions made it possible to build and integrate state structures. On the Continent, some cities and states became competitors (Tilly 1990; Tilly 1994; Spruyt 1994), but in England they developed a powerful synergism.

Understanding this opportunity, the Normans encouraged the growth of towns as loci of security, dynamic economic sites, and ecclesiastical centers where the church could be constrained. Towns emerged, often under the grant of royal charters, as distinct collectivities with rights of association and other personal freedoms, access to self-governing apprenticeships and crafts, mercantile possibilities, and the prospect of self-government for their burgesses. Integral to feudalism (arguably, without towns feudalism could not have thrived), towns also fashioned a distinctive free space, where Jews could reside and to whose economic roles and prosperity they could contribute.

Living in these settings, Jews were not just direct financial assets to kings, but important indirect sources of revenue to the extent that their moneylending and bullion-dealing contributed to the robust economic development of the twelfth century. Their provision of widely accessible credit to the country's wealthiest institutions, including landowners, urban commercial interests, and the church, made sources of economic lubrication available that otherwise either would have been absent or more difficult to obtain. These funds also enlarged sources of revenue for the crown. Kings thus had strong incentives to safeguard the Jews in circumstances in which the loyalty of the country's rural and urban elites to the crown, in the main, remained continuous (key exceptions concerned disputes over dynastic succession), where state-building was taking place, population and prosperity were advancing, a money economy and town development progressed, and lands were held in reasonably secure fashion by a cross-Channel dominant class in the context of an Anglo-Norman kingdom that was well integrated into larger European dynastic and religious establishments. The Jews may not have been liked but, from a royal perspective, the gains of their presence rather dramatically outweighed any price to be paid.

Until 1189, there were very few episodes of local anti-Jewish mobilization. Even though no intrinsic value was placed on group diversity apart from its pragmatic implications, and even as the emergence of ritual murder accusations in Norwich (1144), Gloucester (1168), Bury St. Edmunds (1181), Winchester (1182), and Bristol (1183)[4] and the renewal of crusading placed Jews on a plateau of apprehension, their condition was sheltered effectively by the crown.

After Henry II's death in 1189, England was swept by popular anti-Jewish violence. In September, thirty members of the London Jewish community were killed during the coronation of Richard I. Soon, with the king out of the country (he spent only six months of his ten-year rule in England; otherwise, he either governed in France or served as a leading participant in the Third Crusade), brutal assaults on the Jews spread to Lynn (later Kings Lynn), where the whole community was killed, and, in sequence, to Norwich, Bury St. Edmund, where fifty-seven Jews were murdered on Palm Sunday and the survivors were expelled, Stamford, where all the Jews who failed to reach the castle were killed, Lincoln, Colchester, Thetford, Ospringe, Winchester, Dunstable, and, most famously, York, where nearly all the town's Jews died by self-immolation in Clifford's Castle.[5] In all, this wave of violence resulted in some 500 Jewish deaths, or between 20 and 25 percent of the group's population at the time (Dobson 1974). There appears to have been something of a common pattern, in which the events were "instigated by . . . a number of the nobles who were heavily indebted to the Jews, or were pressed by the Royal Treasury which had taken up the debts to deceased Jews" (Jacobs 1893, 381, 389–90).

These depredations had violated articulated law, repeated in the following terms in 1180s:

> It should be known that all Jews, wheresoever in the realm they be, ought to be under the protection of the king's liege. Nor ought any of them place himself under any rich man without the king's licence; because the Jews themselves and all theirs belong to the king, And if any detain them or their money, let the king, if he will and can, ask it back as if it were his own. (cited in Leonard 1891, 68)

Where the king's representatives were able to move quickly, as at Lincoln, violence against the Jews was stemmed, and, as a contemporary, William of Newbury, observed, "the rising quickly subsided." By contrast, he wrote, "the men of York, were restrained neither by fear of the hot-tempered King nor the vigour of the laws, nor by feelings of humanity, from satiating their fury with the total ruin of their perfidious fellow-citizens and from rooting out the whole race in their city" (Leonard 1891, 117).

After the coronation violence, Richard quickly reasserted his custodial responsibilities. Ringleaders of the 1189 London riots were arrested. Three were hung. In a proclamation conveyed by letter to sheriffs in each English county to affirm the protected status of the Jews in March 1190, the king confirmed, in the words of this new Charter, "all their customs and liberties just as the Lord King Henry, our father, granted and by his charter confirmed to the Jews of England and Normandy, namely to reside in our land freely and honorably . . . and we command and order you to ward and defend and protect them" (Leonard 1891, 134, 136). In 1190, Jews took refuge in the royal castles of Norwich and Stamford. They were protected by royal officers in Lincoln, and provided with an armed royal escort when they left Bury St. Edmunds. The king, who was in France during the events in York, responded by sending the Bishop of Ely to take action. "The deeds done at York," William recorded that year, "were soon carried across the sea to the prince, who had guaranteed peace and security to the Jews in his kingdom after the rising at London. He is indignant and in a rage, both for the insult to his royal majesty and for the great loss to the treasury, for to the treasury belonged whatever the Jews, who are known to be the royal usurers, seem to possess in the way of goods" (Leonard 1891, 132–33). Eighty magnates and burghers were arraigned, severe fines imposed, and estates confiscated. Jews soon returned to York. Within three decades, the town again housed one of the England's most significant and prosperous Jewish communities.

Four years after the ascension of John in 1201, a new Charter of Liberties was issued, echoing the language in prior charters of the Jews: "Know that we have granted to all the Jews of England and Normandy to have freely and honourably residence in our land, and to hold all that from us which they held from King Henry, our father's grandfather, and all that now they reasonably hold in land and fees and mortgages and goods, and that they have all their liberties and customs just as they had them in the time of the aforesaid King Henry, our father's grandfather, better and more quietly and more honourably" (Leonard 1891, 212). This document reaffirmed that Jews could freely travel within England, possess property, sign contracts, maintain inheritance rights, and be free from tolls and customs duties. The charter also regulated legal dealings across the Christian-Jewish boundary, stipulating that Jews need only appear in royal courts, nonroyal cases against Jews were to be judged by Jews, plaintiffs of either religion required witnesses from both, and Jews could clear charges against them when they lacked witnesses by taking an oath on the Torah.

With the renewal of royal protection by Richard and John, Jews once again came to live in a climate of reasonable coexistence, marred, until the mid-1210s, only by an 1192 ritual murder accusation in Winchester. Fatefully, this era of peace was shattered by the targeting of London's Jews during the Baronial Revolt against King John in 1215, an episode famous for culminating in Magna Carta. Until that moment, with the temporary, if awful, exception of 1189 and 1190, a royal umbrella had assured Jewish safety despite the Christian population's only grudging forbearance. Certainly, they had lived with a significantly higher degree of safety than their continental brethren. Ephram b. Jacob, a Jew in Bonn at the time, observed in his documentation of the persecution of Jews in France, Germany, and Spain during the crusading of 1146 to 1148, that during the reign of Stephen "in England the King of Heaven saved the Jews through the King of England. He turned his heart so that he protected them and saved their lives and property" (Leonard 1891, 239).

Transformations

The increasingly unsettled relationships linking the English crown to the country's elites in the thirteenth century brought the long period of relative Jewish security to a close. A series of quite remarkable developments—including external territorial contraction followed by internal expansion, the considerable extension of towns and an urban-propelled money economy, the growing self-consciousness and capacity of the class of rural barons, and the early, tentative, but tangible emergence of an English nation with which kings had to identify and negotiate—radically unsettled the prerogatives, security, and authority of the monarchy and literally forced kings to concede an extension of existing constraints on their prerogatives that already had emerged within common law. During the thirteenth century, rights were codified for members of an emerging and partially autonomous civil society, and representative institutions in early but recognizably modern parliaments made the central state permeable to societal preferences. In turn, these broadly liberal entitlements and arrangements generated key preferences that thirteenth century kings developed about issues of nation and state, as well as their preferences about the country's Jews.

Over the course of the twelfth century, the post-Conquest landed class together with a growing free town population came to constitute the main sources of royal revenue and support. Later, however, as English kings faced the constellation of dramatic and intersecting challenges of the thirteenth century, these two social groups fashioned the nucleus of a civil society that challenged the standing and autonomy of the crown (Newman 1988). As a result, a monarchy that had stood on the shoulders of their support no longer could count on it. Precisely the features that had led to the integration of the dominant social classes and had produced far more social cohesion and integration than existed in France or the German lands now facilitated the growth of an antimonarchical society, one based on a sense of shared fate and loss, effective communications networks based on family ties, common experiences, a kingdom with relatively fine roads, and many emergent town centers.

The first engine of change was geopolitical. The key episode was the loss of the English dynasty's French lands in the first two decades of the thirteenth century. At the decisive battle of Bouvines in 1214, the excision of English holdings in Brittany, Anjou, Maine, Touraine, and especially in Normandy—in all, territory about three-fourths that of England itself—was confirmed (Powicke 1913). Over the course of the next four and a half decades, efforts to regain these areas failed. Finally, in the Treaty of Paris, agreed in 1258 and ratified the next year, Henry III recognized this defeat to be permanent. This dramatic territorial diminution replaced both the Anglo-Norman state and an Anglo-Norman nobility with an English focus and an English landed class. "England was now assuredly the centre of the political firmament of the kings in England in a way which had not been true since the Norman Conquest" (Davies 2000, 20).

These dramatic changes generated powerful effects. They made the crown the target of disenchantment, as losses in France profoundly harmed landowners who had been as essentially French as English. They, and others, especially town burgesses, who had helped fund the unsuccessful military ventures across the Channel, resented the high cost of their fiscal burdens that had produced such a resounding defeat. In trying to win resources to regain lost lands, John had successfully experimented with new types of taxation (Holt 1992, 43), and increased his tax revenues, which more and more were directed at individuals, to fund a dramatic growth in spending, which ran at the remarkable rate of 25 percent each year between 1207 and 1212 (Carpenter 2003, 271). Some of John's heaviest demands were mounted before his last unsuccessful attempt at Bouvines to recover the kingdom's French lands, and they were enforced by the use of extreme measures where necessary (Holt 1992, 191). Further, when he turned to the Jews for significant sums, he also put new pressure on those in debt to them. In these circumstances, both the rural and urban social forces that long had been bulwarks of support for the monarchy rather rapidly became available for mobilizations that made claims and favored privileges against the crown and its prerogatives. One target of this mobilization, we soon will see, was the king's Jews.

The intensity of discontent associated with the loss of Normandy brought John face to face with the prospect that his denuded regime might be overthrown. During the last half-decade of his reign, that is from 1212 to 1216, John faced the century's first potent insurgency by a coherent civil society in the countryside and in the towns, That violent baronial revolt was not just directed against the person of the king, but against the monarchy and its prerogatives. There had been revolts before, like that of 1170 to 1174 against Henry II, but these typically had been fought as battles about dynastic rights within the royal house. By contrast, the failed effort by barons to murder John in 1212 and the countrywide revolt after Bouvines sought to force a change to the basic terms of the regime itself.

John dealt with this powerful insurgency and the striking increase in royal insecurity it engendered by conceding unprecedented rights to his subjects; as Chapter 63 of Magna Carta put it, "that the men in our realm shall have and hold all the aforesaid liberties, rights and concessions well and peacefully, freely and quietly, fully and completely" (Holt 1992, 473). The rights he granted at Runnymede in 1215, a charter of liberties based on an explicit contract between the king and his subjects that conceded permanent constraints on what not just he, but all future kings legitimately could do, drew on ideas that had been developing within the baronial and knightly classes in the prior generation. Though the document was precipitated by the failings of John's government, especially abroad, Magna Carta was more than a negative appraisal of his rule, but "a criticism of a system of government" marked by unfettered royal discretion (Holt 1955, 2). As a potential political nation developed in the upper reaches of rural and urban society, its members came to resent, then resist, heavy fiscal exactions, the terms and often repressive enforcement of loyalty, and they came to think that the king's oaths to govern according to law were insufficient in circumstances where the king possessed extensive but not very well-defined powers and the boundary between law and will was inexact. Further, with the growing enhancement of the administrative tools at the monarch's command, a language of tyranny accusing the crown of behavior that contravened both law and custom was becoming more common.

Magna Carta codified limits to these powers, and thus clarified what the king could not do. Royal orders would no longer depend simply on the king's will. Chapter 1 proclaimed that "the English church shall be free, and shall have its rights undiminished and its liberties unimpaired." Chapters 38 to 40 established that trials must be supported by credible witnesses, that justice cannot be delayed, and that, most famously, "no free man shall be taken or imprisoned, or dispossessed or outlawed or exiled or in any way ruined, nor will we go or send against him except by lawful judgment of his peers or by the law of the land." Overall, the charter focused on the details of royal transactions with society, especially terms of inheritance, debt, and taxation, including the regulation of scutage, weights and measures, and obligations to military service, and included prohibitions on confiscations of timber, corn, horses, carts, and other goods, and freedom of movement for merchants within England and in leaving and entering the kingdom, other than in times of war. It further promised to restore liberties and rights from which subjects had been deprived. All this, it directly averred, had been granted "for the reform of our realm and the better settling the quarrel which has arisen between us and our barons" (Holt 1992, 449–73).

A striking feature of this constitutive document is the prominent place of Jews in the provisions concerning debt. The relevant clauses, the tenth and eleventh, modified these obligations:

> If anyone who has borrowed from the Jews any sum, great or small, dies before the debt is repaid, it shall not carry interest as long as the heir is under age, of whomsoever he holds; and if the debt falls into our hands, we will not take anything except the principal sum in the bond.
>
> And if a man dies owing a debt to the Jews, his wife may have her dower and pay nothing of that debt; and if he leaves children under age, their needs shall be met in a manner in keeping with the holding of the deceased; and the debt shall be paid out of the residue, saving the service due to the lords. Debts owing to others than Jews shall be dealt with likewise.

In seeking to enhance the crown's revenues, John had made it a practice to take the debts owed to the Jews after the death of a creditor. J. C. Holt's classic study of Magna Carta observes that, "since 1210 especially these had become a major source of income to the king and one of the main instruments of financial persecution of the aristocracy" (Holt 1992, 211). In August 1212, just two days after discovering the main plot on his life, John relaxed these debts as his first concession. The articles of Magna Carta thus extended this undertaking, modifying, and easing the burdens caused by this source of finance. Strikingly, once John's reign ended, these chapters were omitted from the texts reissued in 1216 and 1217 as part of a larger effort to cleanse the document of the clauses that had most offended the royalists (Jordan 2003, 34); under pressure, they were confirmed anew by Henry III in 1236.

The Jews were urban dwellers. During the thirteenth century, the towns they inhabited grew, as the urban nodes of the English economy came to be ever more important with the expansion of the country's commercial sector and the network of markets and fairs in towns, the rise of trade, and the acceleration of manufacturing. As new towns were founded and older ones expanded, the country came to be covered by a network of linked urban places. Almost all contained Jews, whose provision of credit was an integral feature of these settings.

After Magna Carta, Christian citizens of towns gained more rights to jurisdictional autonomy, town defense, and self-government. Towns were the country's first zones of societal liberty. Freedom was "the essence of town law." This included liberal provisions for the sale and inheritance of property, exemptions from tolls, but it "was also personal: town air could make a villein free" (Bartlett 2000, 337). Although responsible to the crown, towns developed robust forms of urban government, including financial autonomy, distinct laws, town officials, representative bodies of aldermen, and a sense of proud local identity. They also were loci of a variety of collective organizations, including guilds and mutual aid societies. Towns were the first organized venues for the formation of a recognizably modern public opinion and institutions of collective choice (Bartlett 2000, 337–42).

With their growing role in the economy and social structure of England, kings increasingly had to manage their relationships with towns carefully and negotiate their exchanges with local leaders and officials, especially because the towns were sources of unrest and collective mobilization. Sometimes, kings responded with repressive acts via police powers enforced by sheriffs, but more often, over time, they learned to accommodate to urban power. Beginning in the early 1230s, towns used this capacity to expel their Jews. From the perspective of these urban centers, Jews represented a constitutional anomaly. Towns had no direct control over them despite their pattern of residence, economic importance, and high visibility. Further, it was in towns that resentment of usury and religious objections to Jewish practices concentrated (Leonard 1891, 134).

In the course of trying to arrive at an equilibrium in his relationship with the towns, Henry III relaxed the crown's control over local affairs. Especially where urban opponents of royal absolutism were strongest, they were given scope to expel their Jews. The baron Simon de Montfort, an opponent of royal absolutism who later led the century's most important insurgency, oversaw the expulsion of Leicester's Jews in 1231. Soon, other towns took the same course of action. In the decade spanning 1234 to 1244, these included Newcastle, Warwick, High Wycombe, Southampton, Berkhamsted, Newbury, and Speenhamland. There also was a revival of religiously motivated accusations in this climate of reduced royal oversight: burning a Deacon who had converted to Judaism and married a Jewess, in Oxford in 1222; charging a Jew with forcibly circumcising the son of a convert, in Norwich in 1234; (he was tried by a church trial with no Jews eligible for the jury); an allegation that the body of a dead child had been cut to write Hebrew, in London in 1244 (he was buried near the high altar at St. Paul's); accusations of ritual murder in Norwich in 1251, and Lincoln in 1255 (the famous case of Little St. Hugh of Lincoln that later made its way into the *Canterbury Tales* [Langmuir 1990, 237–62]). With royal protection in the towns diminished in favor of local policing, there also were episodes of violence and the confiscation of synagogues in London in 1239, 1240, and 1243, and in Oxford in 1244. In this context, a royal order of January 1253 refused permission to Jews to extend their settlement to towns where no current community existed, and explicitly stipulated that no Jew could stay in England unless the person's presence was of direct benefit to the crown (Richardson 1960, 59).

The increasing autonomy and ability of towns and their governments, a site and source of societal liberty, thus proved hazardous to the Jews in circumstances where the king had been forced to widen the scope of rights for his subjects. More broadly, the growth of rights was replete with danger for rights-less Jews, when John and especially Henry relaxed their guard as they pursued "the better settling of the quarrel" with the society they governed. Negotiated rights for Christians went hand in hand with a change in how kings framed their decisions about Jews that led to a retraction of royal protection. Though still in place, the terms of the various charters that were meant to define and secure Jewish freedoms and status became increasingly hollow.

It was in this context that church leaders came to have more capacity to regulate Jewish life, and to act on their growing doctrinal suspiciousness about Jews. These developments took place in an environment that

featured increasingly unfriendly religious preaching. Throughout the period of Jewish residence, the church tended to oscillate between two
views: one that welcomed the physical presence of Jews as a confirma-
tion of the truth in light of their place in Christianity's grand narrative,
and another that regarded Jews who refused to convert as stubborn
primitives who should pay a price for refusing this truth. Over the
course of the thirteenth century, the second position gained ground, and
was reflected increasingly in onerous provisions (Langmuir 1990). The
Council of the Province of Canterbury that met in Oxford in 1222 limited
Jewish employment in churches, placed restraints on the construction of
synagogues, cut off social intercourse with Jews identified as usurers,
and reinforced the requirement, initiated by the Bull issued by Innocent
III at the Fourth Lateran Council of 1215, that Jews wear a distinguishing
badge.[6] In 1240, Jewish books and all known copies of the Talmud in
England were seized and burned by papal decree. That year, a church
synod at Worcester, and others at Chichester in 1246 and Salisbury in
1256 renewed anti-Jewish regulations. In 1251, Jews were ordered not to
eat meat during Lent. In a reversal of earlier practices, the king now
personally sanctioned local outrages against Jews. In 1255, after the ritual
murder accusation that followed the discovery of a boy in a cesspool
during a Jewish wedding, the case of Little St. Hugh, Henry traveled to
Lincoln to order that the accused be hung.

The post–Magna Carta situation of transactions between the king and
his subjects also tilted the fiscal burden in a Jewish direction. When
Henry fought difficult battles in Wales, undertook losing ventures in
France that failed to reconquer lost territory, and developed enhanced
itinerant ceremonial features of kingship throughout England, the only
group with considerable wealth without recourse to peaceful or violent
resistance was the Jews. Rather than heighten the risk of further revolt,
it made sense for the crown to ratchet up Jewish charges. In the 1230s,
Jews were taxed at three times the rate of the 1220s. Between 1227 and
1259, they faced tallages of some 170,000 pounds, plus other levies, including an exaction in 1244 of 40,000 pounds on the pretext of ritual
crimes.[7] A high tax on the Jews was levied in 1245 to rebuild Westminster Abbey. In 1250, the king compensated for reducing the tax burden
on his restless barons by accelerating Jewish assessments. By some estimates, the king confiscated fully half the total wealth of the Jewish community in the 1240s and 1250s (Carpenter 2003, 349). In turn, these exactions put enormous financial pressure on individuals who owed money
to Jews, since, ultimately, they had to finance these obligations. Five
years later, the fiscal noose tightened further as two Jewish financiers
were appointed to oversee the community's economic matters as if they
were in bankruptcy.

The Ninth Crusade, launched in 1271 by Edward on the eve of his kingship, was funded primarily by tallages on the Jews. Having been taxed so heavily in prior decades, however, they were unable to meet their full assessment. Falling short by one-third, their share was compensated by Edward's uncle, Richard of Cornwall, to whom the Jews were assigned as security for one year. This levy was quickly followed by two additional tallages, marked by repressive enforcement: a final charge by Henry III in 1272 and a first, confiscatory exaction of just under 170,000 pounds by Edward, as he returned to the Crusade that had been interrupted by his father's death. With their moveable assets wiped out, many Jews found they could not pay a vastly smaller tallage in 1275. Some were imprisoned, and their wives and children deported. In 1287, the Jewish community could only pay one-third of the 12,000 pounds Edward demanded.

These growing religious and fiscal pressures underpin the most familiar explanations for Edward's decision to expel the Jews. One line of reasoning stresses the radical transformation to the ambitions and worldview of the Church with the advent of crusading and its fervent culture. It also takes into account the rise of fundamentalist mendicant orders, the stimulation of local religious enthusiasms, an increasingly rigorous and insistent hostility by religious leaders to usury, and umbrage at the central and visible urban location of this self-consciously different and alien group. A second, even more dominant, view highlights how the fiscal capacity of the Jews diminished over the course of the thirteenth century, so that they no longer constituted a resource worth defending. At times, these historiographical strands combine, as in Paul Hyam's conclusion that "Edward's own actions were guided . . . by his sincere religious bigotry, but his constant concern for royal interests would never have permitted him in this self-indulgence had not the royal revenue from Jewish sources dropped far below the halcyon days before the Barons' Wars," and now "was near to exhaustion" (Hyams 1974, 288).

Certainly it is not possible to apprehend the normative and strategic circumstances of kings without coming to terms with the profoundly Christian character of their realms or the growing institutional and doctrinal antagonism of the Church. But kings and their actions cannot be trimmed down to religious compulsions and motivations. Monarchs often maintained their policy of protection in the face of episcopal pressures on occasions when bishops lent their authority to mass anti-Jewish feelings. Henry III, for example, ordered his sheriffs to put a halt to economic boycotts of Jewish communities that had been mandated by the Church (Hyams 1974, 288). In any event, at no time did the English Church call for Jewish expulsion. Nor did monarchs ever simply respond to anti-Jewish mass and elite pressures which were present in one or another form throughout the period of Jewish residence. Moreover, there is little evidence that the generalized opprobrium Jews faced when Edward decided on expulsion was dramatically greater than the ill-favor that had prevailed over the course of this history, especially during such periods of high stress as the widespread wave of assaults on Jews in 1190. Then, we have seen, Richard I protected his Jews and further regularized their relationship to the monarchy. A century later, there was no direct mass or religious pressure on Edward to expel his Jews.

In all, though this line of reasoning about religious pressure illuminates the milieu within which royal decisions were made, it was not the primary source of the choices made by English and French kings to expel the Jews. Leonard thus was right to observe in 1891 that "the religious feeling of the day evidently influenced the King as it influenced his people, but in neither case can it be considered paramount" (Leonard 1891, 129). The key issue is not the character or intensity of pressure from below, but why royal protection receded over the course of the thirteenth century. That question has to drive us back to the political realm.

Because kings had overstretched their Jewish resource with increasingly punitive exactions, a spiral of economic collapse had set in. "It is therefore clear," Peter Elman concluded, "that the Jews were expelled because from an economic point of view they were no longer performing that function which was their sole raison d'être in the circumstances." Likewise, John Veitch claimed that "by 1290 the Jews were no longer an important source" of finance, "allowing Edward I to appropriate their property at little cost" (Elman 1937, 252; Veitch 1986, 33).

Yet without being nestled inside a larger consideration of state and regime, the fiscal account, like the religious, cannot bear the causal weight put on it. Recent research rethinks whether the economic situation of England's Jews, while diminished, had become quite as dire or irremediable as this line of analysis argues. For sure, the Jewish community had come under a great deal of fiscal pressure as a result of confiscatory tallages and legislation in 1275 banning their participation in moneylending. Nevertheless, the combination of a growing role for Jews in the expanding wool trade, shifts to other forms of urban commerce, and a tolerated, if semi-clandestine, continuation of loan-making created circumstances that had begun to reconstitute Jewish wealth sufficiently to renew their potential as a source of revenue for the crown. That ability might have been nurtured further (Mundill 1998, chaps. 4 and 5). In France, Jews had suffered a worse financial fate, yet recovered. During the reign of Louis IX, they had been subjected to extraordinary taxation in 1223, 1227, and 1230 to pay for the king's crusading, faced restrictions on usury, and, especially harmful, experienced the steady withdrawal of support by public authorities for the recovery of their loans. Despite this concerted assault on its economic circumstances, the Jewish community survived, and began to flourish once again when Philip IV eased restrictions on Jewish credit and allowed a renewal of the group's main economic activities. On this example, the financial exhaustion of England's Jews might have proved ephemeral. Edward's preparation for a new Jewish tallage in June 1290 lends credence to this possibility. So too does clear evidence that in 1285 and 1286 he had actively considered a major reform that would have legitimated while closely regulating Jewish moneylending as an alternative to the formal ban that had been enacted in 1275 as a means to placate restive debtors, especially the knights, while restoring the Jewish community as a successful economic asset for the crown (Stacey 1997, 99).

Further, the fiscal line of investigation begs a key question. Why did kings permit, even facilitate, a deterioration in the economic circumstances of the Jewish community? Which stresses narrowed royal time-horizons so that kings substituted assertive searches for revenue in the short-run regardless of longer-term consequences? Which pressures changed the larger matrix of political calculations within which kings made decisions that altered the fiscal situation of the Jews? The fiscal argument, in short, also becomes persuasive only if placed within a larger set of political considerations.

New Maps

Magna Carta did not so much settle key issues about the character of the monarchical regime as fuel a struggle to define the terms of the new relationship between state and society. As the historian William Jordan comments, "Henry III's reign was lived in the scholarly shadow of Magna Carta. Any move he made that provoked opposition raised the spectre of an appeal against him to the principles of Magna Carta" (2003, 236). These tensions became more acute as decades of effort to restore English possessions across the Channel came to naught.

Henry's quest to roll back French gains by seeking and paying for expensive alliances with opposition movements in France, and, his aggressive stance of expansion within Britain were terribly expensive. Further, the price of buying support grew as he built a kind of theater state (Powicke 1950; Colvin 1971; Geertz 1980) marked by visible spectacle to enhance royal legitimacy. These features of his reign placed enormous fiscal pressure on all those in England who had the capacity to fund the state, including the Jews. Together, these developments demanded more and more royal revenue, yet also more and more caution by kings as they sought funds from landed and urban feudal elites.

From Bouvines to the formal acceptance of this new reality, in 1259, in the Treaty of Paris, a distinct, if still early and sketchy English identity began to take shape. Although the French language was not replaced by English in government or in the courts until the fourteenth century (Parliament started to hold its sessions exclusively in English only in 1362), the recrudescence of an English identity that had been crushed by the Norman Conquest was now initiated (Kohn 1940, 69). For this, the loss of Normandy proved pivotal. Whereas the twelfth century baronial elite had been Anglo-Norman, with the loss of their lands in France, as David Carpenter has noted, it "would be born, brought up and based exclusively in England. So would the king. Families might still retain memories of their Norman ancestry, but the logic of embracing an entirely English identity was now overwhelming." As a result of his setback in Normandy, John "was the first king to drop altogether the 'French and English' form of address in his documents. His subjects were now all English" (Carpenter 2003, 8). The English language revived in moving up the ladder of the social structure to take in the gentry and nobility, so that by the middle of the thirteenth century "there seems little doubt that even the highest aristocracy could speak English. Henry III's brother, Richard, Earl of Cornwall, certainly did so. So indeed did Edward I." Earlier, English had been the language of most ordinary residents. Now its fluent use rose up the hierarchy. French gave ground, and, like Latin, increasingly became a language that had to be taught. By mid-century, this process was well advanced. Living almost entirely in England, Henry "was far more English than any king since 1066" (Carpenter 2003, 353).

Nonetheless, in the face of a growing English national sentiment, he was widely viewed as an alien king, in part because of his dynastic ties on the continent, a charge that condensed and helped organize diverse currents of discontent against what, increasingly, was an unpopular reign—for its geopolitical failures, expensive tastes and high taxes, high-handed administration, abuses by his sheriffs, and limited access to the court and its decision making (Carpenter 2003, 350–54). Before Edward seized the mantle of Englishness, however, his father was still widely viewed as French. As a result, tensions between the king and society, which often took the form of disputes about the meaning and enforcement of Magna Carta, sometimes took on the character of a national conflict against alien rule.

Simultaneously, the royal map of power became more English. Under Henry III, dramatic shifts advanced the standing of England on its side of the Channel, within the British Isles. Under Henry III, "an effective modus vivendi . . . [developed] in the relationship between the English kingdom and the rest of the British Isles under non-English rule," as the "native rulers of Ireland and Wales had adjusted their ambitions to the practical reach of their power" (Davies 2000, 21–22). Ireland was now ruled by the English king stylized as lord of Ireland (a title Henry III passed to his son in 1254), and "most of the country was now, directly or indirectly, under English rule; parts of it were densely settled by third- and fourth-generation English colonists; and the essential features of English law, institutions, land tenure, economic practices, ecclesiastical habits, and culture had been transplanted to the island" (Davies 2000, 76). Wales was increasingly integrated as a dependent territory (though not fully conquered until the 1280s), neither to be separated from the English crown nor eligible to be a separate country. To the north, the growth of a distinct political identity in Scotland made it easier for English kings to assert their sovereignty on their northern borders; at the same time, the English aristocracy extended its family networks and property holdings into Scotland. In all, English hegemony over the British Isles advanced considerably during Henry III's reign, a development that reinforced tensions about the costs of empire and the definition of Englishness.

Concurrently, town growth continued apace, creating stronger bonds among its residents as local government continued to develop. Towns had their own officials and courts, raised revenues, administered services, and possessed legal identities. As self-governing entities with rights formalized in charters with the crown, and with growth in the number and scope of guilds, urban associational life was enriched, thus providing further sources of potential mobilization in opposition to the crown. Political liberties, including elections and representative assemblies, first were practiced in the towns, where they became durable institutions, as well as for demands insisting that equivalent institutions be created at the national level. For the oligarchy of merchants and landowners who dominated the towns, free spatial, social, and political patterns became important resources when insurgent impulses against the king turned, as they did in the late 1250s and 1260s, into a full-blown rebellion, then civil war.

With the early development of a tangible if limited national identity, the extension of the country's rule in the British Isles following a half-century of episodic warfare in France, and the development of towns, Henry faced a more potent opposition than John had some four decades earlier. The breach between politically active subjects and the monarchy widened.

Ever since the 1240s, proto-parliamentary councils gathered by the king from time to time had demanded more authority over taxation and royal appointments. A 1244 paper constitution making such claims served as the basis for a successful, if short-lived, constitutional revolution in 1258. Under physical pressure when the Earl of Norfolk led a group of magnates dressed in full armor to confront Henry at the West-minster, the king "thought he was a prisoner. Instead, he was made to accept a general reform of the realm" (Carpenter 2003, 360). These rules stipulated that the governmental decisions would now be made by a committee of twenty-four, half chosen by the barons. Further, at the par-liaments that met in Oxford in 1258 and 1259, the work of reform in-cluded stipulations that sheriffs, the king's key agents, henceforth would be chosen from the community of local knights and serve for a limited term, and that parliaments would assemble at least once a year.

These Provisions of Oxford—a series of memoranda concerning re-form—constituted a revolutionary transformation (Maddicott 1994, 159–63). Under their terms, the king lost control of royal castles to the barons, and the hands of government passed to a council of fifteen (appointed by the twenty-four), that included Simon de Montfort, his leading oppo-nent, with the capacity to select ministers and superintend the adminis-tration of the realm, and with the charge to govern collaboratively with parliament "to deal with the common business of the realm and the king together" (Carpenter 2003, 369).

The king soon reneged on his acceptance of this new political order. The provisions, he argued, had been enacted by barons in their narrow, not public, interest. By 1261, the provisions had been overturned and Montfort had retreated to France, but the king's revival of his customary powers proved temporary. Montfort returned in 1263 as the leader of a self-designated English rebellion to which the king surrendered, commit-ting the crown to expel foreigners and appoint only the native born to office. The provisions were reenacted, placing the king once again under the control of a council and parliament.

Edward led the counterattack on behalf of his father and the preroga-tives of the crown. Divided into armed camps, the kingdom was torn by civil war when Montfort and his followers rejected a ruling, favoring Henry, made by France's Louis IX, who had been called on to arbitrate. In May 1264, Henry and Edward were taken prisoner on the Sussex Downs. The provisions were restored and the council was reimposed on the monarchy by parliament in June. Now, Montfort effectively ruled in the king's name while Henry was held in London without real power. One of his most important decisions enlarged the political class to in-clude knights, who joined the June parliament, and town burgesses, who were made eligible to send representatives to parliament for the first time in 1265.

The revolutionary government lasted until August. Magnates siding with Henry led a counterattacking military coalition that killed Montfort at Evesham. Restored, Henry was not prepared to govern under the terms imposed at Oxford. But he also understood that he could not simply restore the status quo. To secure enough of a social consensus to govern and renew stability, he endorsed and coopted the demand for regular parliaments that were based on election, representation, and consent (albeit by a very small slice of the population). In so doing, he achieved something of the balance that John Brewer described for the English state of the late seventeenth and eighteenth centuries, a first example of a state strengthened by the paradox of parliamentary constraint on the monarch as a result of a liberal institutional shift that "lent greater legitimacy to government action" (Brewer 1988, xix).

This turbulent transition to a parliamentary kingship placed England's Jews in considerable hazard. Wherever the rule of the king was supplanted or significantly curtailed, attacks on the Jews usually followed quite quickly. Without royal protection, especially in the context of a politicization of Jewish debt by insurgents, truly ugly events ensued. The Jewish quarter of Canterbury was burned in 1261. London's Jewry was sacked in 1262. In a great massacre, hundreds were killed there two years later. Deadly rioting also was directed against the Jews in 1264, during Montfort's ascendancy, in Canterbury, once again, and in Worcester, Bristol, Bedford, Winchester, Lincoln, and Nottingham. It was, Jordan remarks, "a particularly bloody civil war for English Jews, whom some of the dissident barons and their supporters saw as royal flunkies, insofar as the profits of their money-lending, exacted from their baronial debtors among others, were often appropriated by the Crown" (Jordan 2003, 238). Relief from subjugation produced oppression in another form.

One feature of these assaults was the confiscation by rebels of the archae, the chests where records of indebtedness to Jews were stored by delegates of the Exchequer of the Jews. These seizures stood in a lineage of claims demanding the alleviation of debts owed to the Jews. Such reform, promised by the Oxford Provisions, became a centerpiece of Montfort's program over the course of his rebellion, when it provided a key inducement for support by lesser as well as greater landowners. In the eight months between October 1264 and June 1265, Montfort's government pardoned the debts and interest owed to Jews by sixty of his followers. "The number and novelty of these writs," his biographer remarks, "suggests that there was a policy here. Its object was to gain popularity for Montfort's government, at no cost to himself, but at the expense of the Jews and of the king who was lord of the Jews" (Maddicott 1994, 316). Whenever the king was pressed hard, as in Magna Carta, one of his first concessions was to release debtors from obligations to repay Jewish loans or soften their terms.

It soon was clear that by bringing society into dialogue with the king in parliament about the situation of the Jews, their lives would alter for the worse. An early harbinger was the bargain struck by Henry as his son, Edward, prepared a crusade between 1268 and 1270. Henry "negoti-ated with parliament after parliament, summoning to them knights and on at least one occasion burgesses as well. In the end, he secured a tax, after imposing restrictions on the Jews," legislating the Provisions of Jewry that curtailed their rights to hold land (Carpenter 2003, 382).

Expulsion

In a general summary, the historian Bernard Guenée observed that Euro-pean "medieval monarchy was limited by theory but not controlled by institutions" (1985, 86). The last years of Henry's kingship and the reign of Edward, by contrast, marked the first period when English kings in-deed were controlled, or at least strongly constrained and influenced, by an institution—parliament. The much-revised constitution made the prior framework, within which kings made choices about the Jews—how much they should be taxed, whether to endorse or permit local expulsions, the degree to which royal protection should be proffered, how to deal with demands about Jews by notables or the Church—obso-lete. The new politics that regular political representation convened made the country's Jews radically more vulnerable by reshaping the manner in which Edward framed his decisions about resources and po-litical legitimacy.

The main precursor to parliament were the aristocratic councils, some-times joined by church leaders, that Henry III had convened in the 1240s to secure funding for his military ventures that customary income could not sustain. Exchanges there typically took the form of proposals for levies offered by members of the king's retinue, with counter-suggestions by barons who usually demanded fidelity to Magna Carta as the price of their backing. Primarily forums for speech (parler), however, these bod-ies only loosely could be called parliaments in the sense of a modern legislature (Jordan 2003, 237).

The central institutional result of the Montfortian revolt was the estab-lishment of parliament as an assembly with the capacity to legislate on matters of taxation and warfare. By regularizing political representation for subjects in civil society, and by conceding bargaining power over the fiscal capacity of the monarchy, Henry and especially Edward crafted parliamentary kingship, a model that strengthened ties between state and society on the basis of regular exchanges between kings and an in-creasingly settled core of representatives that included magnates, bur-gesses, and knights. Although far short of an organizationally developed legislature, late thirteenth-century parliaments included such innova-tions as a process for petitions, committees, a growing judicial role, su-pervision and oversight of royal administration, and a prominent place for the king's ministers in parliament (Richardson and Sayles 1931; Bisson 1969, 354).

Parliaments became the key site for negotiations between a plural set of authorities, and thus utterly altered the conditions of government. During his first full thirty-five years as king, the first in which parliaments were present throughout, Edward summoned parliament forty-six times, almost always attending in person (Field 2002, 49). Parliaments had become "the means of vesting the king's government with consent, of mobilizing general support behind it, and of neutralizing discontents aroused by its policies" (Miller 1970, 6).

England's regime now was based on negotiation. A critical example was the issue settled by the Quo Warranto, a statute parliament passed early in the 1290 parliament that sat when the Jews were expelled. Ever since he had ascended to the throne, Edward had pushed to return rights, including the right to collect revenues, to the king that once had been passed to notables, or had been taken by them, when royal claims could not be documented in writing. Many notables resisted, claiming that these rights had been passed to them by oral agreement. The statute conceded that the king's entitlement to recover could go back no further than the start of the reign of Richard I, in 1189. This compromise was emblematic of the new order. Popular discontent and royal legitimacy now were mediated by parliamentary conciliation undertaken within a legislative process.

By far the most important set of policy innovations these new arrangements produced was the growth of noncustomary national taxation (Harriss 1975, 40ff; Levi 1988). Edward had expensive habits, not least his efforts to extend English hegemony. He pacified Wales between 1277 and 1284 by persistent warfare and the construction of a network of massive castles, and annexed the territory in 1284's Statute of Wales that parliament approved (Mann 1986, 424–30). It was within parliament that he had to obtain the resources necessary for this and other state-building ventures. Parliamentary taxation was not his only source of revenue—monies were raised from the church, from customary duties, and from income from royal lands—but it increasingly funded the state. What was novel was that these funds were the outcomes of explicit agreements based on negotiation. The political nation had to consent to be charged.

Edward emerged as one of the great lawmakers in English history. Stubbs's *Constitutional History* celebrates him as a king whose parliamentary statutes became "the basis of all subsequent legislation, anticipating and almost superseding constructive legislation for two centuries." Likewise, the twentieth century constitutional historian T. F. T. Plunkett argued that "a thorough commentary upon the statutes of Edward I would be in effect a history of the common law from the thirteenth century down to the close of the eighteenth" (Stubbs 1870, 171; Plucknett 1949, 156; cited in Hogue 1966, 216).

As it turned out, this new form of government strengthened the king and state by advancing royal legitimacy and increasing the sources of revenue that made it possible for the administrative and military features of the state to grow. One indicator of this étatist modernization was the separation of the household from the chancery in the early years of Edward's parliamentary kingship, with the chancery becoming a key institution promoting the capacity of the executive state with the consent of the governed, who approved the key policies it carried out for the king.

"In administration, finance and justice these years tell the same story," a historian of parliament from the start of Edward's reign has summarized. It is one "of a dramatic increase in the scope of government which impinged on the interests of a substantially wider sector of the community but at the same time provided facilities for subjects to assert and defend their rights." In this way, "parliament came to fulfill its unique function as both an instrument of royal government and the voice of the community" (Harriss 1981, 35), albeit soon to be a community without Jews.

Edward's period in office also was marked by a deepening trend of internal empire. He settled a new map for Britain by bringing the fragmentation and continuing turbulence marked by earlier episodes of war to an end. Guarded by his new forts on the periphery, Edward emplaced English settlers in the outer parts of Britain, and practiced symbolic as well as violent intimidation, notably in his extended victory march through Wales in 1284.

These adjustments to political life created a radically new environment within which royal preferences were shaped. Edward's inclinations and policies toward the country's Jews were primarily induced by these altered institutional dynamics. Actively pursuing the internal imperial project, he was the first king to establish "a new tax-based parliamentary state" that negotiated resources and terms of rule with civil society, and he was the first since 1066 to make the monarchy "at one rather than at odds with the Englishness of the people" (Carpenter 2003, 466).

In securing English rule over more of the British Isles, Edward made the Jews seem even more foreign. By the time they were expelled, Edward could justify the renewal of war against France with the claim that "the French wished to destroy the English tongue." Here, Carpenter notes, "the English language was being used as synonymous with the English people in a way that would have been impossible even a hundred years before" (Carpenter 2003, 8–9). With the extension of use for the English language, the growth of an English national identity developed in contradistinction not only to the French, or to the Welsh, Scots, and Irish, but to the Jews. Their everyday French speech, use of French in conducting transactions with the wider society, and conduct of internal religious and communal affairs in Hebrew, made them seem ever more strange both to their immediate neighbors and to those officials who increasingly identified with, indeed were part of, the push toward Englishness that the Jews could not join. The prodigious religious barrier that already separated Jews from the great majority now was entwined with national and linguistic elements. As English identity intensified and became politicized, Jews ever more were on the outside (Thomas 2003, 307–22).

Within a country governed by negotiation, royal protection flagged. Little was done to prevent the pillaging of London's main synagogue in 1272, or the anti-Jewish riots in Southampton and Bristol in 1274 and 1275. Indeed, local expulsions now carried a form of royal sanction. The Queen Mother's dower towns of Marlborough, Gloucester, Cambridge, and Worcester expelled their Jews in 1275. With the erosion of royal safeguards, Jews also were more exposed to Church provisions that aimed to further segregate them, as in the Statute of Pillory of 1267 that forbade Christians from buying meat from Jewish butchers.

But why were the Jews expelled? Even within this menacing environment in which the conditions of Jewish life had weakened and the degree of security the crown offered England's Jews had diminished, they continued, in the main, to lead peaceful and resilient lives. Had Edward chosen to enhance their physical and economic security, they might well have continued to be of assistance to his various royal projects. Despite a history of local expulsions in England and France, no national model for the wholesale removal of Jews yet existed.

The expulsion of 1290, in short, was not inevitable. But its likelihood had vastly increased with the shift in institutional arrangements and in state-society relationships since Montfort's rebellion. The growth of a new political society, the rise of parliament, the augmentation of Englishness, and the pressing need for revenue together altered the way in which the king came to frame the Jewish question. This shift radically altered the period's matrix of possibilities, opening the way for expulsion to become a real option.

Robert Stacey's reconstruction of the summer of 1290, when "the largest single grant of taxation conceded by parliaments to any medieval English king" was enacted, helps us see how the shift to a parliamentary kingship radically changed Edward's preferences about the presence of Jews as a permanent population. This was a pivotal parliament, not just for the Jews. It was here that the fiscal basis of the state decisively shifted to taxes on moveables, with the amount increased to a level that might close a persistent gap between revenues and expenditures (Willard 1913).

Jewish expulsion became part of this basic change in ways that "could not have been foreseen," even when the specific negotiations of that summer began (Stacey 1997, 78).

During that parliament, the type of bargain that had been evolving between the king and his society with regard to rights, representation, and resources advanced dramatically. The part of the king's negotiated understanding with parliament completed first was the Quo Warranto, followed by Quia Emptores, a law adopted during the second week of July that protected the rights of wardship and custody of lords when their tenants wished to sell their lands. These two pieces of legislation were negotiated with a parliament dominated by magnates, and did not directly involve any bargaining about the fate of the Jews. The knights, the period's House of Commons, then were summoned to join parliament from July 15, to make it possible for the king to enact his new type and level of taxation with their participation and agreement. The session's earlier concessions had "sealed the king's bargain with his lords; and in return for it," Stacey observes, "the magnates were prepared to recommend to the Commons that they grant the king his tax" (Stacey 1997, 92).

The knights who arrived in mid-July quickly and successfully exacted Jewish expulsion as their price. For the prior two decades, England's knights, as lesser landholders most susceptible to the costs of forfeiture, had been demanding legislative relief from the burdens imposed by Jewish debt. After his return following Montfort's death, Henry III restored the Jewish loans that had been revoked during the revolt. Numerous such debts had passed to the king after so many Jews had been killed by the rebels. In turn, Henry assigned many of these obligations to loyal followers and members of his family, who, by enforcing repayment, could acquire the lands of those without means to repay (Stacey 1997, 93–96).

The larger magnates had two forms of protection: influence at court and alternative forms of credit. As a social class, the knights thus were most vulnerable, so it is not surprising that they regularly pressed their complaints about Jewish moneylending on the parliamentary agenda. When parliament gathered between June 1268 and August 1270, the knights persistently raised the issue, and were not prepared to concede the taxes requested by the king until legislation was drafted by Henry to manage Jewish moneylending and annul fee-rents that subsequently would fall into Jewish hands. In 1271, again at the demand of the knights, Jews were prohibited from owning land.

Edward's massive tallage on the Jews in 1274 placed enormous downwards pressures on the knights. At a parliament gathered in October of the next year, the knights agreed to a new tax but only in exchange for a formal ban on Jewish moneylending. Yet the effect of the statute was mainly to drive much of this lending underground, so that pressures on the knights continued. By 1290, they demanded nothing less than the eviction of the Jews. Framed as part of a larger resolution to a parliamentary negotiation, Edward assented and the Jews soon had to leave.[8] "On 18 July . . . expulsion orders were issued to the sheriffs, and in return the Commons representatives gave their consent to a fifteenth on the lay movable property of the kingdom. By Friday 21 July the bargaining was done, and the king left Westminster for a six-month journey to the north" (Stacey 1997, 92). Stacey persuasively concludes that from 1268,

> legislation against Jews and Jewish lending was the essential precondition upon which local society in England was prepared to vote voluntary taxation to the monarchy; and because the king concluded in 1290 no lesser measure would secure the consent he needed. Edward got his tax, and in return the Commons got the expulsion; and it was on these terms that the tax was justified to the countryside. By and large the country considered it a fair bargain. There is noticeably less complaint about the pressure of taxation in 1290 than there had been, for example, about the significantly lighter taxation of 1275. (101)

The development of Parliament as a site of negotiation did not alter the fundamental state-building preferences of the king, which remained quite consistent. But this institutional transformation did reshape royal preferences with regard to Jews in tandem with the political exigencies of the moment, most notably the goal of establishing a stable and productive modus vivendi with the barons, knights, and urban burgesses that could secure for the king a reliable and modern tax base. Once established, at the expense of the Jews, the arrangement negotiated by Edward that was geared to these goals endured despite enormous changes to England's political economy in the following centuries.

As a result, every monarch before the English Revolution sustained Edward's decision to exclude Jews from the kingdom. The manner in which the situation of the Jews was reframed within the ambit of England's new regime proved durable, almost certainly because it would have been impossible for his successors to have governed with the consent they needed if they had tried to reverse his course. When, as in 1310, Jews petitioned for a return, they were rebuffed. A Jewish homecoming had to wait until Cromwell's forces badly needed fresh resources if they were to have a chance to endure.

So this is an unsettling history, one that raises thorny questions about how the doctrines and institutions of the Western liberal tradition—the globe's strongest guardian of cultural, religious, ethnic, and racial plural-ism—could have actively accommodated and advanced religious bigotry and minority group punishment. Taking a long view, we would do well to acknowledge the difficulties as well as the promise.

Notes

1. From the sixteenth century, there was a small, discreet Marrano community of practicing Jews who had converted to Catholicism before their expulsion from Spain in 1492 (Katz 1994, 1–14).
2. Of course, the relevant attributes that comprise preferences include a broader range, and may include values, beliefs, habits, emotions and psychological propensities, norms, commitments, and tastes. For a useful discussion, see Bowles (2004, chap. 3).
3. Jews are also recorded to have been corn traders, fishmongers, cheesemon-gers, goldsmiths, physicians, and pawnbrokers. A few others were scholars, as chronicled by Roth (1949).
4. In their nature, ritual murder accusations were directed against named indi-viduals, not the group. For a striking account of the form such accusations took, in a book that focuses on a slightly later period and on the continent, see Rubin (1999).
5. William of Newbury has left a contemporaneous account of the anti-Jewish violence of 1190, including the murder of the Jews at Lynn, that records the connection between monetary motives and religious piety: "Bold and greedy men thought that they were doing an act pleasing to God, while they robbed or destroyed rebels against Christ and carried out the work of their own cupidity with savage joy and without any, or only the slightest, scruple of conscience. . . . The first outburst against them occurred, as we have heard, at Lynn, a city renowned for its thriving commerce, where many of this people dwell, overbearing by their numbers, the greatness of their wealth, and the protection of the King. . . . Their houses were stormed and pillaged by the Christians, and burnt by the avenging flames and many of them fell victims to the fire or sword of the enemy" (Leonard 1891, 113–15).
6. We mostly remember this Council gathering in Oxford for the origins of academic regalia worn at commencements and other university ceremonies. In the twelfth and thirteenth centuries, the new universities were established with tight ties to the Church. Clerics, or aspiring clerics, mainly taught eccle-siastical and theological subjects in institutions that obtained papal charters. Academic caps, gowns, and hoods familiar to us grew out of the clerical dress of the period. In 1222, Stephen Langton, England's leading medieval archbishop, decreed that clergy should wear a closed, flowing gown. Both Oxford and Cambridge fell within the province of Canterbury; thus clerks in

these institutions met the terms of this decree. Later, the dress of the clergy changed, and the cappa clausa became exclusively academic.

7. A tallage "was an intermittent tax paid either in money or in kind by the direct feudal subjects of rulers and was spent at the discretion of the ruler" (Green 1997, 240).

8. From the evidence at hand, it is not possible to know precisely whether Edward responded to the knights or offered the arrangement in anticipation of their well-known wishes.

References

Abrahams, Lionel B. 1894/1895. "The Expulsion of the Jews from England in 1290." *The Jewish Quarterly Review* 6(part 1) and 7(parts 2 and 3): 75–100, 236–58, 428–58.

Abrams, Philip. 1978. "Towns and Economic Growth: Some Theories and Problems." In *Towns in Societies: Essays in Economic History and Historical Sociology*, edited by Philip Abrams and E. A. Wrigley. Cambridge: Cambridge University Press.

Bairoch, Paul. 1988. *Cities and Economic Development: From the Dawn of History to the Present*. Chicago: University of Chicago Press.

Bartlett, Robert. 2000. *England Under the Norman and Angevin Kings, 1075–1225*. New York: Oxford University Press.

Benevolo, Leonardo. 1993. *The European City*. Oxford: Blackwell Publishers.

Bisson, Thomas N. 1969. "Consultative Functions in the King's Parliaments (1250–1314)." *Speculum* 44(July): 353–73.

Bowles, Samuel. 2004. *Microeconomics: Behavior, Institutions, and Evolution*. Princeton, N.J.: Russell Sage Foundation / Princeton University Press.

Brewer, John. 1988. *The Sinews of Power: War, Money and the English State, 1688–1783*. New York: Alfred A. Knopf.

Carpenter, David. 2003. *The Struggle for Mastery: Britain, 1066–1284*. London: Allen Lane.

Colvin, Howard Montague, editor. 1971. *Building Accounts of King Henry III*. Oxford: Oxford University Press.

Cramer, Alice Carver. 1941. "The Origins and Functions of the Jewish Exchequer." *Speculum* 16(April): 226–29.

Davies, R. G., and J. H. Denton, eds. 1981. *The English Parliament in the Middle Ages*. Manchester: Manchester University Press.

Davies, Robert Rees. 2000. *The First English Empire: Power and Identities in the British Isles, 1093–1343*. Oxford: Oxford University Press.

Dobson, Richard Barrie. 1974. *The Jews of Medieval York and the Massacre of March 1190*. York: St. Anthony's Press.

Dyer, Christopher. 2002. *Making a Living in the Middle Ages: The People of Britain, 850–1520*. New Haven, Conn.: Yale University Press.

Elias, Norbert. 1939/1994. *The Civilizing Process: The History of Manners and State Formation and Civilization*. Oxford: Blackwell Publishers.

Elman, Peter. 1937. "The Economic Causes of the Expulsion of the Jews." *The Economic History Review* 7(2, May): 145–54.

———. 1952. "Jewish Finances in Thirteenth-century England." *Transactions, The Jewish Historical Society of England* 16: n.p.

Field, John. 2002. *The Story of Parliament in the Palace of Westminster*. London: James and James.

Geertz, Clifford. 1980. *Negara: The Theatre State in Nineteenth-Century Bali*. Princeton, N.J.: Princeton University Press.

Golb, Norman. 1998. *The Jews in Medieval Normandy: A Social and Intellectual History*. Cambridge: Cambridge University Press.

Green, Judith A. 1986. *The Government of England Under Henry I*. Cambridge: Cambridge University Press.

———. 1997. *The Aristocracy of Norman England*. Cambridge: Cambridge University Press.

Guenée, Bernard. 1985. *States and Rulers in Later Medieval Europe*. Oxford: Blackwell Publishers.

Harriss, G. L. 1975. *King, Parliament, and Public Finance in Medieval England to 1369*. Oxford: Oxford University Press.

———. 1981. "The Formation of Parliament, 1272–1377." In *The English Parliament in the Middle Ages*, edited by R. Davies and Jeffrey Denton. Manchester: Manchester University Press.

Helmholz, R. H. 1986. "Usury and the Medieval English Church Courts." *Speculum* 61(April): 364–80.

Hogue, Arthur R. 1966. *Origins of the Common Law*. Bloomington: Indiana University Press.

Hohenberg, Paul M., and Lynn Hollen Lees. 1985. *The Making of Urban Europe 1000–1950*. Cambridge, Mass.: Harvard University Press.

Holt, J. C. 1955. "The Barons and the Great Charter." *The English Historical Review* 70(January): 1–24.

———. 1992. *Magna Carta*, 2nd ed. Cambridge: Cambridge University Press.

Hyams, Paul. 1974. "The Jewish Minority in Medieval England, 1066–1290," *Journal of Jewish Studies* 25(Summer): 270–93.

Jacobs, Joseph. 1893. *The Jews of Angevin England: Documents and Records*. New York: G. P. Putnam.

Jordan, William Chester. 2003. *Europe in the High Middle Ages*. New York: Viking.

Katz, David S. 1994. *The Jews in the History of England, 1485–1850*. Oxford: Oxford University Press.

Kohn, Hans. 1940. "The Genesis and Character of English Nationalism." *Journal of the History of Ideas* 1(January): 69–94.

Langmuir, Gavin I. 1990. *Toward a Definition of Antisemitism.*. Berkeley: University of California Press.

Leonard, George Hare. 1891. "The Expulsion of the Jews by Edward I: An Essay in Explanation of the Exodus, A.D. 1290." *Transactions of the Royal Historical Society.* New Series 5: 103–46.

Le Patourel, John. 1976. *The Norman Empire.* Oxford: Oxford University Press.

Levi, Margaret. 1988. *Of Rule and Revenue.* Berkeley: University of California Press.

Maddicott, John R. 1994. *Simon de Montfort.* Cambridge: Cambridge University Press.

Mann, Michael. 1986. *The Sources of Social Power,* vol. 1, *A History of Power from the Beginning to A.D. 1760.* New York: Cambridge University Press.

———. 1988. *States, War, and Capitalism.* Oxford: Blackwell Publishers.

Miller, Edward. 1970. "Introduction." In *Historical Studies of the English Parliament. Volume 1: Origins to 1399,* edited by E. B. Fryde and Edward Miller. Cambridge: Cambridge University Press.

Mundill, Robin R. 1998. *England's Jewish Solution: Experiment and Expulsion, 1262–1290.* Cambridge: Cambridge University Press.

Newman, Charlotte A. 1988. *The Anglo-Norman Nobility in the Reign of Henry I: The Second Generation.* Philadelphia: University of Pennsylvania Press.

Ovrut, Barnett D. 1977. "Edward I and the Expulsion of the Jews," *The Jewish Quarterly Review* 67(April): 224–35.

Pirenne, Henri. 1937. *Economic and Social History of Medieval Europe.* New York: Harcourt, Brace, and World.

Plucknett, T. F. T. 1949. *Legislation of Edward I.* Oxford: Oxford University Press.

Poole, A. L. 1951. *Domesday Book to Magna Carta, 1087–1216.* Oxford: Oxford University Press.

Powicke, Maurice. 1913. *The Loss of Normandy, 1189–1204.* Manchester: Manchester University Press.

———. 1950. *King Henry III and the Lord Edward: The Community of the Realm in the Thirteenth Century,* 2nd ed. Oxford: Oxford University Press.

Reynolds, Susan. 1994. *Fiefs and Vassals: The Medieval Evidence Reinterpreted.* Oxford: Oxford University Press.

———. 1999. "How Different Was England?" In *Thirteenth Century England VII,* edited by Michael Prestwich, R. H. Britnell, and Robin Frame. Woodbridge, Suffolk: The Boydell Press.

Richardson, H. G. 1960. *The English Jewry Under Angevin Kings.* London: Methuen and Company.

Richardson, H. G., and George Sayles. 1931. "The King's Ministers in Parliament, 1272–1377." *The English Historical Review* 46(October): 194–203.

———. 1963. *The Governance of Mediaeval England from the Conquest to Magna Carta.* Edinburgh: Edinburgh University Press.

Roth, Cecil. 1949. *The Intellectual Activities of Medieval English Jewry.* Oxford: Oxford University Press for The British Academy.

Rubin, Miri. 1999. *Gentile Tales: The Narrative Assault on Late Medieval Jews.* New Haven, Conn.: Yale University Press.

Russell, Josiah Cox. 1948. *British Medieval Population*. Albuquerque: University of New Mexico Press.

Spruyt, Hendrik. 1994. *The Sovereign State and its Competitors: An Analysis of System Change*. Princeton, N.J.: Princeton University Press.

Stacey, Robert C. 1985. "Royal Taxation and the Social Structure of Medieval Anglo-Jewry: The Tallages of 1239–42." *Hebrew Union College Annual* 56: 175–249.

———. 1987a. *Politics, Policy, and Finance Under Henry III, 1216–1245*. Oxford: Oxford University Press.

———. 1987b. "Recent Work on English Jewish History." *Jewish History* 2(Fall): 61–72.

———. 1997. "Parliamentary Negotiation and the Expulsion of Jews from England." In *Thirteenth Century England, VI. Proceedings of the Durham Conference 1995*, edited by Michael Prestwich, R. H. Britnell, and Robin Frame. Woodbridge, Suffolk: The Boydell Press.

———. 1999. "Crusades, Martyrdoms, and the Jews of Norman England, 1096–1190." In *Juden und Christen zur Zeit der Kreuzzuge*, edited by Alfred Haverkamp. Sigmaringen: Jan Thorbecke Verlag.

Stubbs, William. 1870. *Select Charters and Other Illustrations of English Constitutional History from the Earliest Times to the Reign of Edward the First*. Oxford: Oxford University Press.

———. 1897. *Constitutional History of England*, 4th ed. 3 vols. Oxford: Oxford University Press.

Thomas, Hugh. 2003. *The English & the Normans: Ethnic Hostility, Assimilation, and Identity, 1066–c.1220*. Oxford: Oxford University Press.

Tilly, Charles. 1990. *Coercion, Capital, and European States, AD 990–1990*. Oxford: Blackwell Publishers.

———. 1994. "Entanglements of European Cities and States." In *Cities & the Rise of States in Europe, A.D. 1000 to 1800*, edited by Charles Tilly and Wim P. Blockmans. Boulder, Colo.: Westview Press.

Veitch, John M. 1986. "Repudiations and Confiscations by the Medieval State." *The Journal of Economic History* 41(March): 31–36.

Waugh, Scott L. 1999. "The Third Century of English Feudalism." In *Thirteenth Century England VII*, edited by Michael Prestwich, R. H. Britnell, and Robin Frame. Woodbridge, Suffolk: The Boydell Press.

West, Francis James. 1999. "The Colonial History of the Norman Conquest?" *History* 84(April): 219–36.

Willard, James. 1913. "The Taxes Upon Moveables of the Reign of Edward I." *The English Historical Review* 28(July): 517–21.

PART II

Processes

5

Preference Formation as a Political Process: The Case of Monetary Union in Europe

Peter A. Hall

Given that social science focuses on building and assessing models that simplify a more complex reality, accusing contemporary political science of being overly simple is hardly a telling criticism. Because they treat some phenomena as problems yet deal with others by assumption, all theories direct our attention toward some issues and obscure others, creating a distinctive "play of light and shadow" we should heed (Jenson 1989). Here I am motivated by a concern that contemporary political science casts too many shadows over the process of preference formation, thus diverting attention from factors crucial to determining political outcomes. By preference formation I mean the processes by which social actors decide what they want and what to pursue.[1]

The Antinomies of Contemporary Political Science

Although there are exceptions to any generalization about the field, including this one, contemporary political science is gripped by a neomaterialism even more reductionist than that of the Marxist analyses of the 1960s and 1970s. A reformed-Hegelian, Marx was never naive about the complexity of the process through which actors develop conceptions of their interests. He acknowledged how widespread "false consciousness" is, analyzed its origins, and developed the concept of praxis to explain how experience shifts a group's understanding of its situation and what would now be described as its preferences. Antonio Gramsci (1971) used his time in Italian prisons to produce an even more sophisticated set of formulations about such processes, which Louis Althusser (1971) and others have extended (Katznelson and Zolberg 1985).[2]

By contrast, although founded on neoclassical economic theory rather than the labor theory of value, many works in political economy explain political outcomes as a direct result of the material interests of the relevant actors defined more or less directly in terms of the benefits economic theory predicts will ensue.[3] These works constitute an influential research program, as defined by Imre Lakatos (1970), in materialist political economy. Among many examples is the powerful analysis of Jeffry Frieden and Ronald Rogowski (1996) about the effects of increasing international economic openness on domestic political coalitions (see also Rogowski 1989). The value of such analyses lies in the attention they pay to the clash of material interests underpinning many political outcomes (see Lasswell 1950). The principal limitation lies in how little attention they pay to differences that arise between what used to be termed the objective interests of the actors, as posited by some economic theory, and the actors' perceptions of their own interests as well as to the processes that aggregate such perceptions of interest into political action.

Two other lines of research respond directly to these lacunae. The first are the influential works of rational choice institutionalism that dwell on the importance of strategic interaction to political outcomes. These studies distinguish between the actors' fundamental preferences, which are usually specified by an overarching (and often neomaterialist) economic or political theory, and their strategic preferences, which are those that take into account the likely behavior of other actors with potential influence over the outcome. Institutions assume an important role in that they condition the types of strategic interaction feasible in equilibrium, thereby specifying the outcomes that can occur and driving a wedge between the actors' fundamental and strategic preferences.[4] This research yields important propositions about how institutions, understood as the accepted rules governing action, condition the formulation of (strategic) preferences, with an emphasis on how the institutional setting affects the sequencing of choices, the flows of information pertinent to those choices, and the capacities of actors for making credible commitments to each other (see North and Weingast 1989; Hall and Taylor 1996; Bates et al. 1998; Milner 1997). It is largely silent, however, about processes affecting the formation of fundamental preferences and emphasizes only some dimensions of the institutional setting.

The other prominent response to neomaterialism comes from research centered on the contention that ideas of various types have a causal impact on political outcomes in interaction with institutions and material circumstances. In its most radical versions, this work is constructivist, emphasizing that even basic categories of thought are social constructions and insisting on understanding political outcomes as the result of processes whereby these categories are constituted (Krotz 2002; Risse

2002; Wendt 1999; Katzenstein 1996). Less radical variants bring ideas into the analysis as focal points that draw strategic actors toward an equilibrium, as moral visions conditioning basic preferences, or as informational technologies specifying the means most likely to serve a given set of ends (Garrett and Weingast 1993; Berman 1998; Hall 1989). Some researchers take Judith Goldstein and Robert Keohane's minimalist position (1997), that the impact of ideas on political outcomes should be treated as independent of material interests and incorporated into the analysis only as a residual after the impact of material interests has been determined. Others see ideas as constitutive of actors' perceptions of their material interests and as interacting closely with material forces (Hall 1993; Blyth 2002). Because this research takes fundamental preferences as constructed rather than given and shifts the focus of analysis toward that construction, it is quite valuable for understanding preference formation. Its principal limitation is evident in the bifurcation between constructivists with highly sophisticated conceptions of how ideas might matter but limited empirical purchase on that problem, and those who demonstrate the impact of ideas with more empirical effectiveness but conceptualize the political role of ideas in more limited terms.

In sum, the field of comparative political economy has seen successive research programs focused on the role of interests, institutions, and ideas in politics, each with important insights (Hall 1998). Because these developed seriatim, however, they speak to each other only occasionally, and the results have not always advanced the study of preference formation because that process is marked by the interaction of ideas, institutions, and material factors. All too often, the literature counterposes explanations based on interests, ideas, or institutions as if they were alternatives, when effective accounts of preference formation require an exploration of how such factors interact (see Hall 1998).

Of course, the challenge is to specify precisely how this interaction occurs. My goal here is to make a modest contribution to that task. My focus is on the fundamental preferences of an actor, that is, those over potential courses of action that are pre-strategic in that they do not yet fully take into account the possible actions and strategies of other actors. As such, they are more basic than the choices the actor ultimately makes and distinguishable from the strategic preferences often said to be structurally induced by institutions (see Shepsle 1989).

In many accounts, it is customary to construe these fundamental preferences as fixed and general desires for well-being, utility, or power (see Sen 1978). Much of the institutionalist literature is built on an image of preferences with two components, namely fundamental preferences construed in these general terms and strategic preferences generated by the institutional context for interaction and the strategic moves other actors make in the context of them. But there is a substantial gap in this account, between fixed aspirations of such generality and the concrete behavior of human beings, that institutions alone cannot fill. In that gap sit a set of preferences over specific courses of action analogous to those portrayed in the pay-off matrices from which many game-theoretic analyses begin. These are fundamental preferences in the sense that they precede the strategic preferences on which we often focus, but, because they reflect preference orderings over specific courses of action, they are less general than the conventional dualist image implies. Many analysts are beginning to suspect that it is in explaining this dimension of preferences that explanations for much of the variance in many kinds of outcomes must lie. I suggest that actors often approach a decision with preferences over specific courses of action that are induced in the sense that they are influenced by the context in which decision making is undertaken but not necessarily induced by strategic interaction or institutions. The problem, then, is to understand how fundamental preferences of this sort emerge.

Understanding Preference Formation

In an effort to transcend the antinomies dividing the field, I begin from basic postulates about the situation facing an actor who has to form preferences over an action, applicable to individual actors and, with some qualifications, to collective actors such as organizations or governments. From those postulates, I deduce some key features of the process of preference formation in which ideas, institutions, and material factors all figure. This approach permits me to take advantage of the intuitions available to individuals, noting that, although the preference formation of a collective actor such as a government poses additional issues, some of the same problems confront individuals and collective actors. I have chosen propositions that should seem intuitively obvious for two reasons. On the one hand, it is beyond the scope of this essay to offer an extensive justification for them. On the other, many analysts ignore these propositions, perhaps because they are obvious.

Multiple Effects and Multiple Interests

I begin with the observation that every actor has multiple interests, many of which can be engaged by a single issue. In addition, every action has multiple effects. Although obvious, the point that every action has multiple effects is important because it means that, when forming a preference over some action, the actor has to assess its net costs and benefits across all of them. In some cases, that may be relatively simple. Drinking a milkshake for breakfast may be pleasing in sensory terms yet it is also fattening. To form a preference, the individual must consider both effects. In other instances, the effects may be more complex. Entry into monetary union provided Germany with guarantees that its principal trading partners could not lower the price of their goods relative to German ones by devaluing their currencies against the deutschmark, but it also deprived the German government of tools for managing the German economy and destabilized the German industrial relations system by replacing an activist central bank focused on German wages with one less likely to intervene in German wage negotiations (Hall and Franzese 1998).

Although less obvious, the point that every actor has multiple interests is equally important. The preference function, even of an individual, is multivariate, and preference formation entails a process whereby the actor decides how much weight to attach to each of the variables in that function potentially affected by the issue at hand. When deciding whether to drink the milkshake, the individual must weigh his interest in sensory pleasure against an interest in maintaining his waistline. When deciding what position to take on monetary union, British officials have to weigh the nation's geopolitical interests against its economic interests.

In many cases, an actor's multiple interests are closely associated with his multiple identities. When asked to vote in a referendum about day care, a voter has to decide how much weight to assign to interests that may evoke key aspects of her identity, whether as a woman, mother, taxpayer, Republican, citizen, or neighbor. Therefore, the process of forming preferences is intimately bound up with the process of forming and expressing identities. At such moments, the politics of interest and of identity come together in a single process. By choosing to weight one variable more heavily than another, the actor is simultaneously choosing to assert one dimension of her identity more strongly than another.

Even this simple account points to two features of preference formation worthy of more attention. The first is the process of aggregation, whereby an actor attaches weights to his multiple interests in a potential outcome. In the case of collective actors, such as governments, some agencies may speak with special strength for some interests, and the process of interest aggregation can take the form of an organizational politics, mediated by the institutional rules within which it occurs. A nation's central bank and its foreign ministry may each give more weight to different national interests. Political structures that condition the relative influence of agencies and the groups they represent will affect the preferences and positions a government adopts.[5]

Based on these premises, we should also expect framing to play an important role in the process whereby such preferences are formed. A "frame" is an effort to portray an issue in terms that link it to other beliefs (Schön and Rein 1994; Bleich 1999). By linking an issue to some sets of interests, frames downplay the resonance of that issue for other interests. Joining monetary union can be presented as a matter of economic advantage, as an issue of national sovereignty, or as an effort to secure international peace. In this context, appeals to identity can be prominent and potent. By framing an issue in terms designed to evoke a specific identity, the partisans of a particular position appeal to those who value this identity highly. In most political settings, this is a central feature of coalition-building. In a faculty meeting, I may respond to a student's case one way, when it is presented as a matter of compassion designed to evoke my identity as a humane person, but differently if it is presented so as to evoke my identity as a guardian of intellectual standards. When partisans secure broad agreement about how an issue should be defined, they acquire a powerful instrument. I can still choose which of my identities to assert. But, as a collective construct defined to some degree by the views of others, an identity is not entirely under one's control. Therefore, regardless of my beliefs about the statement I make by taking a position on the issue, my identity in the eyes of others will be determined by how they see that issue. Such considerations can be especially influential among those seeking political advancement.

In sum, forming preferences entails a process of aggregation in which the net costs and benefits of the multiple effects of the action must be assessed and weights attached to each of the interests potentially affected by the action. This process can be affected by how the issue is framed—by the identities salient to the actor, and by an organizational politics in which units with specific interests conflict with one another.

The Ubiquity of Uncertainty

Anyone analyzing preference formation should also bear in mind that one of the most important features of the political world is its uncertainty.[6] Equipped with the benefit of hindsight, social scientists tend to treat actions whose outcomes are known as if the latter were equally obvious in prospect. But to do so is to neglect a fundamental feature of politics. Every political action entails a risk-laden judgment about what will follow from it, which can be difficult to form with accuracy. Unintended consequences are endemic to the political world.

Research focused on how institutions structure strategic action has exploited this observation with great success, showing how actors use an institutional context to assess and control strategic uncertainty—that is, uncertainty about how other actors will behave. But a paradoxical side-effect of these advances has been to divert attention from other sources of uncertainty and how actors cope with them. Central here are the means-ends schemas used to assess whether a specific set of actions will produce the intended results, what Goldstein and Keohane (1993) term causal ideas.

Such causal ideas are constitutive elements of fundamental preferences, defining what game theorists sometimes term the pay-off matrix that precedes judgments made about the likely behavior of others. All too often, this matrix is specified with the benefit of hindsight, as if the actors faced no uncertainty at the time, or by an economic or political theory familiar to the analyst but not necessarily faithful to the ones used by the actors whose behavior is being explained. Ironically, our new-found capacities to show how institutions reduce uncertainty have inspired many explanations for the presence of institutions that assume the historical actors knew precisely how they would operate, though that too is often subject to uncertainty (see Bates 1988; North and Weingast 1989).

Political science still asks all too rarely why an actor believed the means he adopted would have the effects he anticipated and where those beliefs originated. When we say that an actor, whether an individual or a government, took a particular set of actions to further his interests, even if we know what his interests were, we need to know why he had any reason to believe such actions would serve those interests well. Even with regard to economic matters in which relevant theories are well developed, the formation of preferences can entail serious quandaries about the likely effects of an action. After fifteen years of debate, many of the British officials most expert about monetary union still admit that they do not know whether joining the European monetary union would serve the nation's interests. Even five years after its inception, the effects of monetary union remain unclear to many most interested in understanding them.

In sum, the formation of preferences involves processes through which the actors form judgments about which means are likely to advance their ends, involving the development of causal ideas and efforts to persuade others of their validity. In broader terms, these processes entail the formation of technologies of control, through which causal relationships within the relevant parts of the social or natural world are posited.

The Centrality of Interpretation to Preference Formation

It is but a short step to the observation that interests are not given unambiguously by the world but must be interpreted. Equipped with some economic or political theory and a retrospective sense of the state of affairs, any analyst can impute a set of stylized interests to a group of historical actors. But, if we are interested in understanding what the preferences of those actors were, we must acknowledge that the world does not hand them their preferences. Preferences are instead developed through a process in which the actors attempt to interpret the world and their situation in it (see Somers 1996).

In general, interpretation entails a gradual "making sense" of one's situation and options, using each new piece of information, as it is discovered, to refine and extend existing systems of belief, and to apply them to new problems. The process can be described in Bayesian terms as one of updating prior beliefs on the basis of new information, using a heuristic to specify the pace at which new information will be allowed to alter existing beliefs (see Bates, de Figueiredo, and Weingast 1998). At the heart of interpretation lies this fundamental tension between existing belief and new information, and the core problem is how to manage that tension, that is, whether to abandon existing beliefs in the face of new information or to stretch those beliefs to cover it. Much depends on the elasticity of existing beliefs and the tenacity with which they are held, which is related to how much past information has confirmed them, the availability of alternative beliefs, how they are linked to identity, and the scope of the challenge the new information poses (see also Lakatos 1970).

The Eventfulness of Preference Formation

This perspective points to what might be described as the fundamental eventfulness of preference formation (see Sewell 1996; Kingdon 1995). In the political world, new information typically comes in the form of an evolving series of events, each of which may confirm or challenge existing beliefs. That is how material developments such as the onset of recession or war enter into the process of preference formation. They inspire a reevaluation of the beliefs underpinning existing preferences. But events are rarely meaningful in themselves. Much depends on how they are interpreted, which turns partly on the context in which they occur. In short, new events inspire a double-sided reevaluation in which the meanings of those events and of existing beliefs are reinterpreted in light of each other.

These considerations imply that preference formation may have a narrative character in two senses of that term, especially important when governments are forming interpretations of the national interest. On the one hand, such interpretations display a forward flow: conceptions of national interest move as one event gives way to another in the nation's history. On the other hand, like the preferences of individuals, conceptions of national interest have a narrative quality in the sense that they must link present purposes or events to a larger story, in this case a story that ties the nation's past experiences and presumptive character to new purposes. These narratives do not have to be stories about manifest destiny but have to have something of that character: they make sense of current policy by linking it to a larger sense of the nation and its history.

The intrinsic dualism of this formulation should be apparent. Conceptions of national interest are rooted in and moved by real-world events. If fictitious, they are historical fictions. But, as surely as a nation is an imagined community, such conceptions are based as much on the interpretations given critical events as on the events themselves (Anderson 1991). What this means is that, to understand how governments form preferences over policies, we need to employ something like the eventful sociology William H. Sewell (1996) proposes. We have to trace the process through which critical events or experiences shift perceptions of the problems a nation or its government faces and of the available solutions for those problems. The implication is that policy is driven only partly by material forces and the institutional structures developed to cope with them. Its route also depends on the sequence of events a nation experiences and on the grand narratives devised to explain what it should do in the face of such events.

The Case of European Monetary Union

To assess whether this perspective gives us any explanatory leverage over political problems, I turn now to the decisions the governments of Britain, France, and Germany made about whether to enter an economic and monetary union (EMU). There were two stages to the formation of their preferences over EMU. One corresponds to the formation of what might be described as fundamental preferences about the desirability of establishing and entering a union, formed largely by December 1989, when these governments agreed to hold an intergovernmental conference before the end of 1990 to agree on a transition to monetary union. The second encompasses negotiations between that summit and the agreement at Maastricht in December 1991 on a new treaty for the European Union, when the member states formed and acted on strategic preferences about the precise shape of the new union. To delimit the analysis, I focus on the first stage—in which the fundamental preferences of these governments were formed, because these are said most often to be given by material circumstances.[7]

In many respects, the decision to embark on EMU is a hard case for the propositions I have advanced. It lies in the realm of economics and geopolitics, in which there are strong reasons to believe that material factors should dictate the preferences of governments and well-developed theories specifying what those preferences should be. If preferences can ever be imputed to governments without an exploration of how they are formed, that should be possible here. However, I begin by arguing that such approaches are not viable. I then show how illuminating it is in this case to see preference formation as a political process. Of course, such a brief account cannot be dispositive, but I believe it is usefully suggestive.[8]

The Inadequacy of Neomaterial Approaches

Materialist explanations for the fundamental preferences governments evinced toward monetary union usually take two forms. One emphasizes the national interest. That interest is deduced from an assessment of the nation's economic or geopolitical position at the relevant moment and a standard economic or political theory about the effects of entry on a nation in that position (Grieco 1995; Garrett 1993). The other, more sophisticated in institutional terms, expects the government's position to be driven by pressure from groups inside the polity whose interests are most affected by entry and whose organizational position gives them influence over policy—that is, by sectoral interests (Walsh 2000; see Moravcsik 1993). Political structures are said to condition the influence of each sector, but economic theory is used to deduce the preference of each sector from its characteristics. Let us consider each type of explanation.

Based on economic theory and the situation of these nations in the 1980s, it is difficult to conclude that entry into a monetary union unambiguously served the national economic interest of the nations that joined it. By joining, they gave up the ability to mount an autonomous monetary policy and to devalue against the other member states to mitigate the effects of an economic shock. Optimal currency theory suggests that monetary union will be advantageous only when the economic shocks its member states experience are broadly symmetrical, but evidence suggested this was not the case for many of the nations entering EMU (Eichengreen 1997, chap. 3). Thus, with entry, the capacities of the member states to respond to economic fluctuations were reduced. Control of inflation could be seen as the primary goal. But inflation had declined in Europe during the 1980s, well before agreement on monetary union, and its resurgence seemed unlikely. The savings in transaction costs associated with the union were relatively small. EMU did not offer its members substantial economic advantages beyond those already achieved by the European Monetary System (EMS), and it brought some economic disadvantages (see Fratianni and von Hagen 1992; Eichengreen 1997). In short, from a purely economic perspective, the advantages of monetary union were at best debatable.

Materialist explanations built on the salience of sectoral pressure are equally indeterminate. In a pioneering analysis grounded in contemporary monetary theory, Frieden (1991) argued that the sectors most likely to support a monetary union are export-oriented producers of tradable goods and internationally oriented traders and investors. However, Mark Duckenfield (2000) and James Walsh (2000) have shown that the positions taken by the relevant sectoral associations in Britain, France and Germany corresponded only rarely to such predictions. In Germany, sectors likely to be disadvantaged by monetary union expressed some support for it, while sectors in Britain that could be expected to benefit did not support it (see Verdun 2000).

As Andrew Moravcsik (1998) has shown, standard geopolitical considerations of the sort generated by realist models of international relations do not take us much further toward understanding the preferences these nations developed. By tying the economies of its member states together, monetary union may have enhanced the prospects for enduring peace in Europe, but Britain, which did not enter, had scarcely less interest in these prospects than its counterparts across the Channel. By entering EMU, France secured greater influence over continental interest rates, but only on a small scale, and Germany entered even though it lost some of its influence.

Economic and geopolitical factors certainly conditioned the decisions of these governments. No account of preference formation in this case can leave them out. But the key point is that they did so by a complex calculus that does not yield clear predictions ex ante about governmental preferences. To explain those preferences we have to consider the process through which the many cross-cutting economic and geopolitical considerations were interpreted and then weighed.

The proposal to establish a monetary union was first considered seriously by the member states of the European Economic Community in 1970 when a group led by Pierre Werner, then prime minister of Luxembourg, was commissioned to produce a report outlining how such a union might be developed. At that time, no agreement could be found on the issue. How do we explain the preferences that emerged by December 1989, when the member governments agreed to move toward monetary union? The extended process that took place in the intervening years displays many of the features I have associated with preference formation.[9]

The Role of Economic Events and the Policy Response to Them

Although the preferences of national governments over monetary union cannot be read directly from material factors, such factors had a role in the process of preference formation, which is best seen as a chain of events formed out of the intersection of economic developments and the policy response to them. In the decades after 1970, four sets of economic events began to shift the views of governments about the desirability of entering a monetary union.

The first set was precipitated by the collapse, in 1972, of the Bretton Woods regime of relatively stable exchange rates. The European governments responded by attempting to operate new monetary regimes, initially based on a so-called snake that allowed broad bands of fluctuation, and later on a European Monetary System (EMS) established in 1979 that specified narrow bands and more concerted arrangements for coordination. EMS is important because it became the status quo against which the value of entering a monetary union was to be judged.

The 1970s also saw increasing rates of inflation followed by higher levels of unemployment and lower rates of growth, ending thirty years of rapidly rising prosperity. It is difficult to overstate the impact of these events on the direction European preferences would take. On the one hand, the experience of double-digit inflation provoked a durable shift in the weight economic policy makers assigned inflation in their preference functions. On the other hand, the experience of stagflation led many to conclude that the Keynesian economic policies practiced during the 1960s and 1970s had failed. This set in motion a search for new approaches to policy (Hall 1993).

Governments once eager to take credit for rising rates of growth found themselves presiding over stagnant economies. They sought economic revival and relief from responsibility for high levels of unemployment. Therefore, with varying degrees of enthusiasm, many turned toward policies that intensified market competition and economic ideologies that attributed unemployment to market conditions rather than to the quality of the government's demand management. The international reflection of this "move to the market" was agreement among the members of the European Community (EC) on the Single European Act of 1986, which mandated the removal of trade barriers among the member states by 1992. The development of this single market changed the operating environment for European business; many firms shifted their strategies to take advantage of it. In so doing, they acquired stronger interests in stable exchange rates, if not monetary union.

The Single European Act envisioned the removal of controls on flows of capital across national borders and, as international flows of capital increased and became increasingly difficult to control, the European governments finally reached agreement in 1989 to eliminate exchange controls. Although a boon for European business, this step made exchange rate management more difficult. Without such controls, a nation's exchange rate is more vulnerable to speculative attack and governments wishing to maintain a stable exchange rate have to dedicate their monetary policies to that task rather than target rates of growth or employment (Mundell 1962). Therefore, once exchange controls were removed, the member states of the EMS found that monetary policy was no longer so effective a tool for managing the domestic economy. This is consequential because an autonomous monetary policy was precisely what nations entering monetary union were being asked to give up. If such policies were no longer effective, to lose them would not be a major sacrifice.

Several features of this chain of events are notable. Only two—the collapse of Bretton Woods and the stagflation of the 1970s—have roots so international that they can be described as exogenous to national policy. The others are all grounded in policy initiatives designed to respond to evolving economic challenges (Cohen 1996). In short, the path to monetary union was blazed by developments in the international economy and a succession of policy initiatives taken in response to them, and together these events generated the conditions to which monetary union was a response.

How these events were interpreted was often as consequential as the events themselves for the preferences governments were to develop (see Blyth 2002). The interpretation given to the stagflation of the 1970s had especially wide ramifications. Even though many factors generated it, stagflation was widely seen as an indication that activist demand management was ineffective and the problems of the European economies structural, that is, rooted in a Eurosclerosis that could be addressed only by rendering European markets more competitive. That interpretation fueled the single market initiative, and persuaded some governments that they would not lose important weapons against unemployment if they gave up fiscal and monetary authority to European agencies.

Evolving Technologies of Control

Preferences turn heavily on prevailing theories about cause-and-effect relationships and such theories are indispensable in the economic sphere, since we do not see the economy with the naked eye but live in the imagined economies constructed by economic theory. Accordingly, as Kathleen McNamara (1998) has argued, fundamental developments in economic theory also played a key role in shifting the preferences of European governments toward monetary union.

Throughout the 1980s, Keynesian theories gave way to a new set of monetarist and new classical theories built on rational expectations assumptions that became increasingly popular among economists and the officials they advised. Three postulates of what became the new conventional wisdom fed directly into the preferences of governments over monetary union. The first specified that activist fiscal policy is unlikely to improve rates of growth or unemployment—because time-lags make it difficult to set policy correctly, rational economic actors are said to be able to negate the real effects of any policy they anticipate, and nations have natural rates of unemployment determined by the structure of labor markets. The second suggested that monetary policy cannot have lasting "real effects" on unemployment and that efforts to reflate the economy will simply increase rates of inflation. The third maintained that monetary policy will be more effective against inflation where governments can commit credibly to it, by placing control over policy in the hands of a central bank independent of political influence (see also Cukierman 1993). The implications of these postulates for the appeal of European monetary union were profound. Told that monetary policy has few effects on the real economy, governments were more willing to give up control over it. They were persuaded to address the natural rate of unemployment through supply-side measures rather than demand management. The prospect of a European central bank independent of political control seemed increasingly attractive.

In short, a shift in the belief-systems specifying economic technology rooted in theoretical developments in the relevant policy community during the 1980s conditioned the preferences of European governments with regard to monetary union. Here, we see how experience conditions interpretation. The credibility of monetarist ideas was greatly enhanced by the apparent failure of the Keynesian alternative and by the plausibility with which monetarism could explain contemporary events (see Hall 1982). Monetarist ideas gained adherents partly because they offered a coherent rationale for the economic calamities of the 1970s, the success of the British economy under Thatcher, and the strength of the German economy under a highly independent Bundesbank (see Oliver 1997).

Establishing the Weights in National Preference Functions

These developments in the economy and the belief systems associated with it pushed all the European governments toward monetary union. If they had been fully determinative, however, Britain would have joined—and it did not. Moreover, as late as 1988, the political leaders of France and Germany still had doubts about the value of the project. There is clearly more to the story. Each nation interpreted the events of the 1970s and 1980s differently, partly because those interpretations were filtered through the prisms of distinctive national histories and nationally-specific chains of events.

France   In large measure, it was agreement between Germany and France that made monetary union possible. Once these two powers had resolved on it, the pressure on other members of the European Community to agree became intense. What were the critical experiences that shifted the preferences of the French government in this direction?

Like the rest of Europe, France experienced stagflation during the 1970s, and the electorate voted out the government presiding over it. Its successor was a socialist government under President François Mitterrand, whose initial response was to try to jump start the economy with a redistributive Keynesianism founded on wage increases and public subsidies to industry (Hall 1987). Although those measures failed, they put downward pressure on the exchange rate that France's partners in the EMS accommodated grudgingly only until the spring of 1983, when they insisted on deep spending cuts if France were to remain in the exchange rate mechanism (ERM). Forced to choose between dirigiste policies or more intense European integration, the Mitterrand government faced a critical turning point. Advised that dirigiste policies would not preempt austerity and disillusioned with their fruits so far, Mitterrand chose Europe. He reversed the direction of policy and began to promote a strong exchange rate dubbed the franc fort (Aeschimann and Riché 1996; Hall 2001). To justify this reversal in course, his officials promoted a rhetoric insistent that France's best chances for prosperity lay in deeper integration into European markets, soon reaffirmed by French support for a single continental market. With these steps, France embarked on a set of policies that made membership in a monetary union more attractive and, in tandem with policy, the orientation of French business shifted toward integration.

Note the eventfulness of these developments. Although pressured by economic developments, Mitterrand could have decided to take France out of the EMS and nearly did so. He admitted that he did not fully understand the economic choices he faced in 1983 (Dyson and Featherstone 1999, 137). There is an element of contingency in this. But once the decisions had been taken, these were seen as eventful developments in a second sense of that term: the French understood that the nation had taken a fateful step in 1983. The government did not simply reverse its policies. To justify them, it also began to tell a new story about how the economic fate of France was tied to the success of a single European market. Although the government showed little initial interest in monetary union, its new story affirmed a conception of French national interest that was ultimately congenial to that union.

Two other developments pushed the French government further in that direction. The first was the decision of the U.S. Federal Reserve Bank to offset the inflationary effects of the Reagan deficits by raising American interest rates, taking the dollar exchange-rate to new highs during the 1980s.[10] The Europeans were forced to raise their own interest rates, lest their depreciating currencies import inflation. Not only did this experience dash Mitterrand's hopes for reflation, it also intensified French resentment about the status of the American dollar as a reserve currency, which allowed the United States to run large trade and budgetary deficits with impunity while imposing economic austerity on Europe. French officials began to express interest in seeing a European currency that would have as much international leverage as the American dollar, a theme that would subsequently animate French support for a single currency.

Here, we see the importance not only of events but of how they are interpreted. Although German officials were concerned about the turbulence of American policies and agreed to the Plaza Accord of September 1985, designed to bring down the dollar exchange rate, they attached little importance to the idea of creating an alternative reserve currency. However, France had a national narrative built around its aspirations to remain a world power, nurtured by President Charles de Gaulle, into which proponents of monetary union adroitly fit their own aspirations for a common currency. During the 1980s and 1990s, the French debate about monetary union was dominated by claims that the new euro would end American dominance of the international monetary sphere (Dyson 1999, 182, 190; Howarth 2001, chap. 2).

Monetary developments inside the EMS also influenced the trajectory of French opinion about EMU. Underpinned by Germany's highly-independent central bank and robust economy, the deutschmark had long been strong relative to the French franc. However, alarmed by the inflationary implications of large capital inflows during the 1980s, the Bundesbank raised interest rates to levels that France had to shadow to remain in the exchange rate mechanism. At the same time, speculative pressure that had been growing with flows of international capital targeted the weaker French franc, putting further pressure on the French authorities to pursue austere policies and precipitating periodic negotiations about the realignment of rates in the EMS that were invariably tense, as the Germans sought to avoid an appreciation that would damage their exports and France tried to avoid the inflationary effects of depreciation (Szász 1999, chaps. 8, 11; Ungerer 1997, chap. 15).

Such tensions raised questions about the long-term stability of the EMS. Realignment in April 1986 was followed by another in January 1987, which inspired the Basle-Nyborg effort to improve coordination in the EMS. These experiences increased the interest of French officials in monetary union, on the grounds that a European central bank (ECB) over which France had some influence might free them from the dominance of the Bundesbank and provide monetary policies more conducive to growth (Dyson 1999, 188–89).[11] Partly with this in mind, Edouard Balladur, the French minister of finance, mooted the prospect of monetary union in June 1987. In November, Mitterrand proposed a Franco-German economic council to coordinate policies, and, in January 1988, Balladur (1988) sent his fellow finance ministers a memorandum proposing steps be taken to create a monetary union.

Note the importance of the sequencing of these events. If the French government had not committed itself to a "European" strategy in 1983 and deepened it by agreeing to the Single European Act of 1986, its response to subsequent tensions within the EMS might have been to withdraw rather than seek monetary union. The interpretation French officials developed in response to the events of 1983 conditioned how they would react to subsequent events. If France's future lay within an integrated European economy, the appropriate response to problems was more effective integration. Keynesianism in one country had been tried and rejected in the early 1980s. It was not given another chance.

Electoral politics also figure in this dynamic, but primarily as a motor accelerating developments that might have come more slowly if inspired only by expertise or international developments. Balladur's memorandum was issued on behalf of a government of the right a few months before presidential elections, at a time when a quarter of the French electorate regarded the construction of the European union as the most important problem facing the nation (Balleix-Banerjee 1999, 32). Mitterrand expressed public support for monetary union partly to avoid being outflanked on the issue. In June 1988 he endorsed the formation of a committee of European central bankers chaired by Jacques Delors to report on the feasibility of monetary union to the Madrid summit of June 1989 (Dyson and Featherstone 1999, 156).

Despite these moves, however, Mitterrand and other French ministers were still not fully convinced that rapid movement toward EMU was desirable (Szasz 1999, 115). A third set of events in the autumn of 1989 sealed the issue. When the communist regime in East Germany collapsed and the prospect of German reunification loomed, the French government's interest in deeper European integration intensified. A unified Germany would be a powerful and potentially unpredictable actor. Germany had invaded France three times since 1870. French officials wanted to ensure that a unified Germany would remain committed to an integrated Europe, and they saw monetary union as a vehicle for that commitment. Accordingly, Mitterrand took advantage of France's veto over reunification to pressure Chancellor Helmut Kohl to set an early date for an intergovernmental conference (IGC) to agree on the details of transition to monetary union (Attali 1995, 326, 353; Genscher 1995, 378, 390).

In the course of these events, France became a driving force behind monetary union.[12]

Germany   It is not difficult to cite reasons why German governments might have had a preference for European monetary union. Burdened by a history that limited their assertiveness in international relations, successive German governments had come to see the European Community as their best route to international influence, and the German public had become committed Europeans (Markovits and Reich 1997). The German government's support for EMU was closely coupled to its interest in deeper political integration; and joint support for EMU was a vehicle through which to reaffirm Franco-German leadership of the EC, a key feature of the German strategy for influence within Europe (Genscher 1995, 390–91). EMU also offered German industries guarantees that their principal competitors in Europe would no longer be able to undercut their prices through devaluations.

Although it is easy to attribute clear-cut interests such as these to actors, competing considerations belie such simple pictures of the German case. Fearful of inflation and impressed with its postwar record, the German electorate was deeply attached to the deutschmark and the Bundesbank that defended it. A majority did not want to see them replaced with institutions susceptible to the influence of more profligate governments such as those of France and Italy (Duckenfield 2000). To undermine the Bundesbank was to threaten the stability of the German industrial relations system (Hall and Franzese 1998). The powerful Bundesbank itself was apprehensive about monetary union. Well into the late 1980s, the preferences of the German government remained indeterminate. What shifted them decisively toward EMU were the events of that decade. Some changed the opportunity costs of not agreeing to EMU. Others changed the actors' cause-and-effect assessments of the alternatives.

Prominent among the latter were tensions within the European Monetary System. Although Germany held the upper hand there, periodic pressures for realignment during the 1980s led German economic officials to wonder whether the system could remain stable and German foreign policy officials to worry that the tensions engendered by negotiations over realignment might undermine the Franco-German axis of cooperation they valued so highly (Dyson and Featherstone 1999, 321). As in France, the experience of operating the exchange rate mechanism, while largely successful, generated growing concerns about its long-term viability. Its collapse could pose serious problems for a German economy deeply integrated into Europe. At the same time, the June 1988 decision of EC finance ministers to abolish the remaining exchange controls helped persuade the Germans that a single currency area might be feasible (Grant 1994, 119).

Geopolitical events were also important to German calculations. The advent of reform in the Soviet Union under Gorbachev intensified the view of Hans-Dietrich Genscher, Germany's long-standing foreign minister, that the EC had to integrate politically to respond effectively to developments to its east, and he saw monetary union as a vehicle for such integration (Genscher 1995, 378; Dyson and Featherstone 1999, 307). In February 1988, Genscher came out strongly in favor of EMU (Genscher 1988). Just as in France, electoral politics then lent force to this development. As the leader of the Free Democrats, the junior partner in the governing coalition, Genscher was competing for votes with the Christian Democratic party of Chancellor Helmut Kohl. To show that he too was a committed European, at the Hanover summit of June 1988, Kohl supported the proposal of Jacques Delors to establish a working group to plan for transition to monetary union.

By 1988, then, the German government was moving cautiously toward monetary union, showing strong interest without complete commitment. The final set of events consolidating this commitment came with the collapse of the East German regime in October 1989 that offered Kohl an opportunity to secure German reunification. To do so, he needed the agreement of France, and Mitterrand insisted on securing an early date for an IGC to agree on monetary union before accepting reunification. Kohl himself was deeply interested in seeing a unified Germany tied closely to Europe. His main reservation was that the issue might present difficulties in the German election of the fall of 1990 (Attali 1995, 345). But with the terms of reunification hanging in the balance, he agreed in December 1989 that the first steps toward EMU could be taken in July 1990 (Genscher 1995, 390–91).

Great Britain   In this context, the British story is about the dog that did not bark. Until October 1990 the British government was still locked in internal debate about whether to join the exchange rate mechanism of EMS. Well into the 1990s it evinced no interest in joining monetary union, and its main goal in the negotiations leading up to Maastricht was to ensure Britain could opt out if EMU proceeded. Precisely because it is so different, however, this case also offers insights into preference formation.

Some aspects of the prevailing national narrative can be cited to explain why Britain's leaders were less likely to think that monetary union would serve the national interest. Like France, Britain had an interest in containing Germany, but its governments had reason to hope that this might be done better through a strong Atlantic alliance than through

European integration. Britain had twice rescued the continent from German conquest by eliciting the support of American governments, and its leaders attached great value to their "special relationship" as the pivot between Europe and America. These views were more deeply rooted in history than the realities of contemporary geopolitics, but the concept of a small island nation standing up against the large European powers was an important component of the British national narrative.

However, material considerations also set Britain apart from the continent. Because many British voters were homeowners with variable-rate mortgages, the British electorate was more sensitive to changes in interest rates than continental electorates. Prime Minister Margaret Thatcher was reluctant to enter the ERM partly because that would entail giving up her control over interest rates; and, by virtue of this decision, Britain lacked the experience of trying to operate the ERM that persuaded many French and German officials to support EMU.

However, such considerations were far from dispositive. There were equally good reasons to think it would be in Britain's interest to enter monetary union. By the late 1980s, the overseas sterling balances were no longer large and a majority of Britain's trade was with Europe. As a financial center, the City of London was as likely to gain from entry as to lose, and the economic shocks afflicting Britain were not especially asymmetrical to those of many member nations. The Thatcher government had supported the development of a single European market. To the extent that EMU would enhance the operation of that market, it should have been congenial to Britain. Considerations such as these led subsequent Labor governments to look with more favor on entry into monetary union.

Why did the Thatcher government not do so? The personal opposition of the prime minister is part of the answer, but her position was not singular. On EMU, the government was relatively monolithic: even cabinet ministers who favored entry into ERM, such as Nigel Lawson and Sir Geoffrey Howe, opposed entry into monetary union (Lawson 1992, 892; Stuart 1998). The issue of monetary union touched on many British interests, and the British government ultimately attached more weight to those militating against entry than to those favoring it. Chief among these were concerns about maintaining British sovereignty. EMU was widely seen as a double-edged sword that would enhance the operation of the single market but increase pressure for political integration. The governments of France and Germany attached substantial value to political integration. The British government did not.

These considerations are apparent in the statements of British officials at the time. After agreeing reluctantly to the establishment of the Delors committee in June 1988, on the premise that, as members of it, the central bank governors of Britain and Germany could blunt the force of its recommendations, Thatcher was disconcerted by speeches Delors gave in July (to the European Parliament) and September (to the British Trades Union Congress) in which he declared that "in ten years, 80 percent of economic legislation—and perhaps tax and social legislation—will be directed from the Community" (George 1998, 193; Gowland and Turner 2000). In a landmark response at Bruges in September 1988, Thatcher explained why she would oppose monetary union. Warning that Europe must not become an agent for "creeping back-door Socialism," she said:

> We have not successfully rolled back the frontiers of the state in Britain, only to see them reimposed at a European level, with a European super-state exercising a new dominion from Brussels. . . . Europe will be stronger precisely because it has France as France, Spain as Spain, Britain as Britain, each with its own customs, traditions and identity. It would be folly to try to fit them into some sort of identikit European personality. (1993, 744–45)

Her statements exemplify the views expressed by other members of the British cabinet in 1988 and 1989.

As such remarks reveal, calculations of interest are often influenced by issues of identity. Across the channel, EMU was presented as an expression of Germany's European identity or as a vehicle for enhancing France's international stature. But Thatcher and many of her compatriots had a conception of British identity that was distinctly not European (Young 1998, chap. 9). She treated monetary union as a zero-sum project that might bring economic benefits but would challenge British sovereignty, describing it in her memoirs (Thatcher 1995, 506) as "a modern equivalent of the Carolingian Empire." This approach had wide resonance in the universe of British political discourse. As late as 1998, two-thirds of Conservative members of parliament agreed that "joining the Euro would mark the end of the UK as a sovereign nation" (Gamble and Kelly 2002, 105).

The character of domestic political alignments mattered here as well. Thatcher had worked hard to give the Conservative Party a new identity—as the party of free markets arrayed against state intervention. Her approach to European integration was designed to reinforce this identity, by supporting efforts to expand market competition in Europe but opposing any expansion in the authority of European agencies. With this stance, Thatcher's aligned her party's identity with the commitment to sovereignty prominent in British national identity, thereby reinforcing both (Dyson 2000).

My point is not that an actor's identity always determines how much weight is given to various interests in its preference function, because identities are neither primordial nor entirely fixed. They can be responsive to evolving events. Thus, the choice of which interests to weight most heavily is made simultaneously with a choice about which identities to assert, and the two sides of this process must be considered together. Of course, having taken a position on which interests to weight heavily, a government uses related appeals to identity to build coalitions around the issue. This is a potent type of politics: once identities are evoked, compromises that might be agreed when purely material interests are at stake become more difficult. In the British case, Thatcher's decision to treat European integration as a matter of identity politics left deep divisions within the Conservative Party and successive governments with an uphill battle when they decided to mobilize public support for the EU.

Conclusion

This chapter can be read as an argument for retaining the historical dimension of historical institutionalism, understood not as an effort to uncover features of the distant past that condition preferences but as an effort to study how the unfolding events endogenous to a decision-situation influence the preferences of actors over alternative courses of action. Even preferences that are fundamental, in the sense that they are not driven primarily by strategic interaction, evolve as events unfold. The key feature of the world that generates this dynamic is the ubiquity of uncertainty. I am not arguing, as some do, that ideas always trump material factors in the process of forming preferences. But I am suggesting that material interests rarely arise unambiguously from the world. As a result, the process of forming preferences is one of interpretation, in which the relevant actors gradually develop, out of experience, a set of beliefs about their interests, whether material or otherwise.

Of course, to urge attentiveness to the role of evolving context in the process of preference formation is to introduce some unpredictability into the analysis. Contingent events play a role in such processes. Without the collapse of the Soviet Union and the prospect of German reunification, the advent of EMU might have been delayed, if not preempted. However, this chapter is not a cry of concern about contingency. From the analysis of European monetary union, we can draw durable generalizations about the types of factors that condition preferences, which contrast with those emphasized by alternative modes of analysis. From some optics, these factors can be construed as the mechanisms involved in fundamental preference formation (see McAdam, Tarrow, and Tilly 2001).

Noting that actors have multiple interests and actions many effects, I have argued that an actor's preferences depend on how heavily he weights each of the interests in his preference function, presenting this, not as a decision made once and for all at a particular moment, but as a fluid evaluation that responds to experience and the framing of issues. Accordingly, when attempting to explain an actor's preferences, we should look at how the relevant issue is being framed, something that is partly under the actor's control and partly dictated by the structure of public discourse about it. Frames acquire importance because, when asserting his interest in a matter that carries material import or moral valence, an actor is often also asserting a specific identity. Once again, while the actor has some influence over the identity he chooses to assert, there is a structural dimension to this process because it is through an identity that the actor recognizes himself and others recognize him, and it is the structure of social discourse that generates recognizable identities. Accordingly, this analysis directs our attention to the frames assigned to specific issues and the identities recognizable within a national community.

From this perspective, preference formation, whether by an individual or a government, is a process in which the actor tries to make sense of his actions in his eyes and those of others. It is a weighing of multiple interests, often linked to multiple identities, in which competing considerations are balanced. By virtue of this, when the actor is a government, national histories are highly salient to preference formation. To explain their actions to themselves and others, actors commonly reference a set of narratives that draw heavily on past experiences and the interpretations of them that have authority in their community. Of course, some actions can be presented as a radical break with the past, but even these need to be linked to a narrative of past failures. More often, courses of action are chosen with an eye to how well they fit into national narratives of previous success.

National history, then, is a factor structuring the process of preference formation. French officials were attracted to European monetary union partly because it seemed to be a vehicle for enhancing the international stature of France, long one of their most important concerns and one readily recognized as legitimate by the national community. On this point, the differences in how EMU was presented in national debate during the 1980s and 1990s are revealing. If monetary union was often seen in Britain as a threat to national sovereignty, in France it was usually presented as a vehicle for enhancing the nation's influence in Europe and the world, while Germans tended to discuss it as an exercise in enlightened restraint. Each formulation resonates with prominent facets of the national narrative; and, although there is always room to maneuver within such narratives, they ultimately render some courses of action more appealing than others.

I have also argued that beliefs about cause-and-effect relationships are central to establishing fundamental preferences over specific courses of action. Our opinions about the desirability of a course of action turn on our views about its effects, and that, in turn, directs our attention to the critical role that experience plays in preference formation. Causal beliefs are rooted in theories about how the world works, but the credibility of those theories turns on our experience of using them (Hall 1993). As experience shifts, so do our causal beliefs. The monetary theories that inclined many European officials toward EMU were unlikely to have been persuasive if the experience of stagflation during the 1970s had not discredited previous Keynesian beliefs and the experiences of the 1980s affirmed the value of monetarism (McNamara 1998; Blyth 2002).

In short, preference formation is a process in which experience and interpretation intertwine. Each is adjusted in light of the other, as events unfold and give rise to new experiences. Out of that process emerge both an interpretation of recent experience and a reinterpretation of existing beliefs. In some instances, the process can be seen in informational terms, akin to Bayesian updating but, in others, there is a moral dimension to the judgments being made. To deny the reciprocal character of this process of mutual evaluation simplifies the analysis but at the cost of missing its true character. That is why preference formation is an eventful process—one that unfolds over time in response to evolving experience.

The problem, of course, is to specify what kinds of events will be significant enough to alter existing beliefs. Without an indication of that, policy making might appear to be a random walk through history. All cases are singular, but this analysis of the decision to embark on EMU supplies some suggestions about the kinds of events likely to be important to the preference formation of governments. The impact of the economic downturn that began during the 1970s suggests that, while brief fluctuations in prosperity may leave little mark on a government's preferences, durable economic distress is likely to do so. After 1974, rates of growth in Europe remained at half the levels of preceding decades and, by 1980, that experience was inspiring radical reevaluation of existing policies. Major geopolitical realignments can act as similar solvents. In this case, the collapse of communism and the prospect of German reunification shifted the preferences in Germany and France in favor of monetary union. Not surprisingly, other studies suggest that the experience of war can have equally substantial effects (Barnett 1986).

More fine-grained analysis suggests there is also a texture to the interpretive encounter between experience and pre-existing beliefs, in which the sequencing of events matters. Once a new set of experiences have shifted the frame through which an issue is seen in the public arena, unless they reflect dramatic reversals, subsequent events tend to be interpreted in terms of that frame. The frame is refined rather than overthrown. This gives rise to something like a funnel of causation, in which a broad interpretation of major events and an associated set of preferences are developed in tentative terms and then consolidated as successive experiences are interpreted in the same terms (see Stone 1972). As these experiences build up, an interpretive frame becomes more widely accepted as the filter through which subsequent experience is to be interpreted, until shaken by a dramatic reversal of fortune that sets in motion a search for alternative interpretations.

We see this type of dynamic at work in the French case, where the disappointing experience of dirigiste policy in the 1980 to 1983 period under the first socialist government of the Fifth Republic inspired a radical reinterpretation of France's economic interests that shifted the government's preferences toward integration into competitive European markets. Partly as a result, when problems with the operation of EMS arose later on, the French response was not to consider withdrawing from it but to contemplate the advantages of monetary union. This was not a response to the narrowing of strategic alternatives, at least in the conventional sense of that term, but a more fundamental reconfiguration in the preferences of the French government with regard to European integration.[13]

Institutions are not irrelevant to this story. The impact of the European monetary system on the decisions of the member states to embrace monetary union highlights the influence of existing institutions over the formation of new ones. By the second half of the 1980s, the structures of the EMS were components of the status quo ante against which the value of monetary union was being evaluated. Existing institutions provide more than a setting for strategic interaction; they can define the opportunity costs against which proposals for change are weighed.

Similarly, if we were to look more closely at domestic debates about monetary union, we would see that political institutions structure the process through which collective actors, such as national governments, form their preferences. By distributing power among agencies with different interests and views of the world, political structures condition the weight attached to specific interests in governmental preference functions. It was important that a German chancellor interested in monetary union had enough power to outmaneuver a central bank more reluctant about entry, and Britain remained out of the EMS for some years because its prime minister had enough power to resist her chancellor's proposal to join. At several junctures, the structure of electoral politics also accelerated the movement of national governments toward monetary union.

However, the story I have told here is not primarily about how institutions structure action but about other factors that can induce changes in preferences. The move toward monetary union was one in which new institutions were established as the result of a process in which the fundamental preferences of governments shifted over time. That process can be read as an effort to maximize national well-being through strategic interaction, but to see it entirely in these terms would be to miss crucial dimensions of the causal dynamic whereby governments that were cool to the idea of monetary union in 1970 came to embrace it two decades later. Central to the dynamic was an eventful process in which actors reinterpreted their interests in light of national identities and in response to an unfolding set of experiences.

To adopt such a perspective, of course, is to complicate the tasks facing social scientists. At least one important tradition suggests that we should judge the adequacy of theories only by their predictive power, without inquiring into the formation of fundamental preferences (see Friedman 1968). But if preference formation has the characteristics I have adduced, it should be apparent that, by failing to examine it, we miss much of the action in the political world. As Weber (1949) pointed out decades ago, to impute preferences to actors without considering their perceptions of what they were doing is to populate the historical world with ahistorical actors, figments of our imagination, whose own political imagination escapes us.

It is time to remove fundamental preferences from the realm of assumption and make their formation the object of empirical political inquiry, but these formulations about that process are only a starting point for further investigation. By focusing on the malleability of fundamental preferences, the object of this chapter has been to inspire further reflection about the politics of preference formation, so that we can see, not only how institutions structure strategic preferences, but how shifts in preferences give rise to institutional change.

For comments on this chapter, I would like to thank the editors of this volume, Katerina Linos and Sidney Tarrow, and, for financial support, the MacArthur Foundation. Jonathan Laurence and Jane Lynch provided valuable research assistance.

Notes

1. To translate into an older language, preferences refer to an actor's perceptions of what is in his/her interest, and, I often use the terms interest and

preference interchangeably. Actors can be individuals or organizations, including governments, provided the latter have the capacity to act cohesively (Frey 1985).

2. The Marxist tendency to impute objective interests to groups that turned out to be amorphous collections of individuals with widely-variant self-understandings has been subjected to withering critique (see Somers 1996; McDonald 1996; Joyce 1980; Mitchell and Stearns 1974).

3. The term neo-classical here comprehends what is sometimes termed new classical economic theory.

4. For this reason, strategic preferences are often said to be "structurally-induced" preferences.

5. Although the brevity of this account means that I cannot explore it here, this type of organizational politics was a dimension of the process whereby the governments of Britain, France, and Germany formed their preferences over monetary union (see Dyson and Featherstone 1999; Balleix-Banerjee 1999).

6. It is beyond the scope of this analysis to specify the many types of uncertainties political actors face, although they include uncertainty about the nature of the outcomes of action as well as about the probabilities to attach to potential outcomes. As such, these uncertainties go well beyond known risks which can sometimes be treated analytically by specifying the relative risk-aversion of the actors.

7. For an analysis that distinguishes nicely between these two stages and examines both, see Moravcsik 1998, chap. 6. Of course, the actual agreement to create a monetary union also depended heavily on the second stage, when the member governments reached compromises about the institutional structure of the union, including its stability and growth pact.

8. Useful accounts of the relevant historical events can be found in Dyson (1994), Dyson and Featherstone (1999), Ungerer (1997), Szász (1999), Howarth (2001), and Kaltenthaler (1998). For a careful assessment of preference formation that parallels this one in some respects and differs in others, see Moravcsik (1998, chap. 6).

9. For a more detailed analysis of France with parallels to this one see Dyson (1999).

10. The dollar/deutschmark exchange rate went from 1.75 in June 1981 to 3.47 in February 1985.

11. Consider how Mitterrand justified his support for EMU in 1989: "Today, the strongest currency in Europe is West Germany's . . . should we live in a mark zone where only the Germans express themselves? . . . I would prefer an assembly, a meeting, a permanent conference of the different authorities where France could have its say on all aspects of economic policy" (quoted in Szász 1999, 108).

12. For a more complete discussion of the evolution of French thinking, see Moravcsik 1998, chap. 6.

13. Of course, closely associated with this was a process whereby these preferences were gradually "institutionalized," notably via the Single European Act. That shifted the strategies of many French firms, creating network externalities that made it more difficult for the government to reverse course (see Pierson 1996). That said, these institutional developments did not in themselves dictate entry into EMU. They are one part of a series of unfolding developments that consolidated the preferences of the French government for a set of pro-European policies.

References

Aeschimann, Eric, and Pascal Riché. 1996. *La Guerre de Sept Ans: Histoire Secrète du Franc Fort 1989–1996*. Paris: Calmann Lévy.

Anderson, Benedict. 1991. *Imagined Communities*. London: Verso.

Althusser, Louis. 1971. *Essays on Ideology*. London: Verso.

Attali, Jacques. 1995. *Verbatim: Tome 3. Chronique des Années 1981–1991*. Paris: Fayard.

Balladur, Edouard. 1988. *Europe's Monetary Construction*. Memorandum to ECOFIN Council. Paris: Ministry of Finance and Economics (January 8, 1988).

Balleix-Banerjee, Corinne. 1999. *La France et la Banque Centrale Européene*. Paris: Presses Universitaires de France.

Barnett, Corelli. 1986. *Audit of War*. London: Macmillan.

Bates, Robert. H. 1988. "Contra Contractarianism: Some Reflections on the New Institutionalism," *Politics and Society* 16(2): 387–401.

Bates, Robert, Rui de Figueiredo, and Barry R. Weingast. 1998. "Rationality and Interpretation: The Politics of Transition." *Politics and Society* 26(December): 603–42.

Bates, Robert H., Avner Greif, Margaret Levi, Jean-Laurent Rosenthal, Barry R. Weingast. 1998. *Analytical Narratives*. Princeton, N.J.: Princeton University Press.

Berman, Sheri. 1998. *The Social Democratic Moment*. Cambridge, Mass.: Harvard University Press.

Bleich, Erik. 1999. *Problem-Solving Politics: Ideas and Race Policies in Britain and France*. Ph.D. dissertation, Harvard University.

Blyth, Mark. 2002. *Great Transformations: Economic Ideas and Institutional Change in the Twentieth Century*. New York: Cambridge University Press.

Cohen, Eli. 1996. *La Tentation Hexoganale*. Paris: Fayard.

Cukierman, Alex. 1993. *Central Bank Independence*. Cambridge, Mass.: The MIT Press.

Duckenfield, Mark Edward. 2000. *Flight of the EMU: Business Groups and the Politics of Economic and Monetary Union in Germany and the United Kingdom*. Ph.D. dissertation, Department of Government, Harvard University.

Dyson, Kenneth. 1994. *Elusive Union: The Process of Economic and Monetary Union in Europe*. London: Longman.

———. 1999. "EMU, Political Discourse and the Fifth French Republic: Historical Institutionalism, Path Dependency and 'Craftsmen' of Discourse." *Modern and Contemporary France* 7(2): 179–96.

———. 2000. "Europeanization, Whitehall Culture and the Treasury as an Institutional Veto Player: A Constructivist Approach to Economic and Monetary Union." *Public Administration* 78(4): 897–914.

Dyson, Kenneth, and Kevin Featherstone. 1999. *The Road to Maastricht: Negotiating Economic and Monetary Union*. Oxford: Oxford University Press.

Eichengreen, Barry. 1997. *European Monetary Unification*. Cambridge, Mass.: The MIT Press.

Fratianni, Michele, and Jürgen von Hagen. 1992. *The European Monetary System and European Monetary Union*. Boulder, Colo.: Westview.

Frey, Frederick. 1985. "The Problem of Actor Designation in Political Analysis." *Comparative Politics* 17: 127–52.

Frieden, Jeffry A. 1991. "Invested Interests: The Politics of National Economic Policies in a World of Global Finance." *International Organization* 45(4): 426–51.

Frieden, Jeffry A., and Ronald Rogowski. 1996. "The Impact of the International Economy on National Policies: An Analytical Overview." In *Internationalization and Domestic Politics*, edited by Robert Keohane and Helen V. Milner. New York: Cambridge University Press.

Friedman, Milton. 1968. "The Methodology of Positive Economics." In *Readings in the Philosophy of the Social Sciences*, edited by May Brodbeck. New York: Macmillan.

Gamble, Andrew, and Gavin Kelly. 2002. "Britain and EMU." In *European States and the Euro*, edited by Kenneth Dyson. Oxford: Oxford University Press.

Garrett, Geoffrey. 1993. "The Politics of Maastricht." *Economics and Politics* 5(2): 105–25.

Garrett, Geoffrey, and Barry Weingast. 1993. "Ideas, Interests, and Institutions: Constructing the European Community's Internal Market." In *Ideas and Foreign Policy*, edited by Judith Goldstein and Robert Keohane. Ithaca, N.Y.: Cornell University Press.

Genscher, Hans-Dietrich. 1988. *Für die Schaffung eines Europäishen Währungsraumes und einer Europäishen Zentralbank*. Frankfurt: Bundesbank.

———. 1995. *Erinnerungen*. Berlin: Siedler.

George, Stephen. 1998. *An Awkward Partner: Britain in the European Community*. Oxford: Oxford University Press.

Goldstein, Judith, and Robert Keohane. 1993. "Ideas and Foreign Policy: An Analytical Framework." In *Ideas and Foreign Policy*, edited by Judith Goldstein and Robert Keohane. Ithaca, N.Y.: Cornell University Press.

Gowland, David, and Arthur Turner. 2000. *Reluctant Europeans: Britain and European Integration 1945–1998*. Harlow, Essex: Pearson.

Gramsci, Antonio. 1971. *Selections from the Prison Notebooks*. London: Lawrence and Wishart.

Grant, Charles. 1994. *Delors: Inside the House that Jacques Built*. London: Nicholas Brealey.

Grieco, Joseph. 1995. "The Maastricht Treaty: Economic and Monetary Union and the Neo-Realist Research Programme." *Review of International Studies* 21(1): 21–40.

Hall, Peter A. 1982. *The Political Dimensions of Economic Management*. Ph.D. dissertation, Department of Government, Harvard University.

———. 1986. *Governing the Economy*. Oxford: Polity Press.

———. 1987. "The Evolution of Economic Policy under Mitterrand." In *The Mitterrand Experiment*, edited by George Ross, Stanley Hoffman, and Sylvia Malzacher. New York: Oxford University Press.

———. 1989. *The Political Power of Economic Ideas: Keynesianism across Nations*. Princeton, N.J.: Princeton University Press.

———. 1993. "Policy Paradigms, Social Learning and the State: The Case of Economic Policy-Making in Britain." *Comparative Politics* 25(3, April): 275–96.

———. 1998. "Institutions, Interests and Ideas in the Comparative Political Economy of the Industrialized Nations." In *Comparative Politics: Rationality, Culture and Structure*, edited by Mark Lichbach and Alan Zuckerman. New York: Cambridge University Press.

———. 2001. "The Evolution of Economic Policy." In *Developments in French Politics 2*, edited by Alain Guyomarch, Howard Machin, Peter A. Hall, and Jack Hayward. Houndmills: Palgrave.

Hall, Peter A., and Robert J. Franzese, Jr. 1998. "Mixed Signals: Central Bank Independence, Coordinated Wage Bargaining and European Monetary Union." *International Organization* 52(5): 502–36.

Hall, Peter A., and Rosemary C. R. Taylor. 1996. "Political Science and the Three 'New Institutionalisms'." *Political Studies* 44(5): 936–57.

Howarth, David. J. 2001. *The French Road to Monetary Union*. Houndmills: Palgrave.

Jenson, Jane. 1989. "Paradigms and Political Discourse: Protective Legislation in France and the United States Before 1914." *Canadian Journal of Political Science* XXII(June): 235–58.

Joyce, Patrick. 1980. *Work, Society and Politics*. Rutgers, N.J.: Rutgers University Press.

Kaltenthaler, Karl. 1998. *Germany and the Politics of Europe's Money*. Durham, N.C.: Duke University Press.

Katzenstein, Peter, ed. 1996. *The Culture of National Security: Norms and Identity in World Politics*. New York: Columbia University Press.

Katznelson, Ira, and Aristide R. Zolberg, eds. 1985. *Working Class Formation: Nineteenth-Century Patterns in Western Europe and the United States*. Princeton, N.J.: Princeton University Press.

Kingdon, John W. 1995. *Agendas, Alternatives and Public Policies*, 2nd ed. Boston: Little, Brown.

Krotz, Ulrich. 2002. "Ties that Bind? The Parapublic Underpinnings of Franco-German Relations as Construction of International Value." *Working Paper* 02.4 of the Minda de Gunzburg Center for European Studies. Cambridge, Mass.: Harvard University.

Lakatos, Imre. 1970. "Falsification and the Methodology of Scientific Research Programmes." In *Criticism and the Growth of Knowledge*, edited by Imre Lakatos and Alan Musgrave. Cambridge: Cambridge University Press.

Lasswell, Harold. 1950. *Politics: Who Gets What, When How?* New York: P. Smith.

Lawson, Nigel. 1992. *The View from No. 11*. London: Bantam.

Markovits, Andrei, and Simon Reich. 1997. *The German Predicament: Memory and Power in the New Europe*. Ithaca, N.Y.: Cornell University Press.

McAdam, Douglas, Sidney Tarrow, and Charles Tilly. 2001. *Dynamics of Contention*. New York: Cambridge University Press.

McDonald, Terrence, ed. 1996. *The Historic Turn in the Social Sciences*. Ann Arbor: University of Michigan Press.

McNamara, Kathleen. 1998. *The Currency of Ideas*. Ithaca, N.Y.: Cornell University Press.

Milner, Helen. 1997. *Interests, Institutions and Information*. Princeton, N.J.: Princeton University Press.

Mitchell, Robert, and Peter Stearns. 1974. *Workers and Protest*. Boulder, Colo.: Flowers.

Moravcsik, Andrew. 1993. "Preferences and Power in the European Community," *Journal of Common Market Studies* 31(4): 473–524.

———. 1998. *The Choice for Europe*. Ithaca, N.Y.: Cornell University Press.

Mundell, Robert A. 1962. "The Appropriate Use of Monetary and Fiscal Policy Under Fixed Exchange Rates." *IMF Staff Papers* 9(March): 70–77.

North, Douglass C., and Barry R. Weingast. 1989. "Constitutions and Commitment: Evolution of the Institutions Governing Public Choice in Seventeenth Century England." *Journal of Economic History* 49(December): 803–32.

Oliver, Michael J. 1997. *Whatever Happened to Monetarism?* Brookfield, Vt.: Ashgate.

Pierson, Paul. 1996. The Path to European Integration: A Historical Institutionalist Analysis." *Comparative Political Studies* 29(2): 123–63.

Risse, Thomas. 2002. "Constructivism and International Institutions: Toward Conversations across Paradigms." In *Political Science: State of the Discipline*, edited by Ira Katznelson and Helen Milner. New York: W. W. Norton.

Rogowski, Ronald. 1989. *Commerce and Coalitions*. Princeton, N.J.: Princeton University Press.

Schön, Donald A., and Martin Rein. 1994. *Frame Reflection: Toward the Resolution of Intractable Policy Controversies*. New York: Basic Books.

Sen, Amartya K. 1978. "Rational Fools: A Critique of the Behavioral Foundations of Economic Theory." In *Scientific Models and Man*, edited by Henry Harris. Oxford: Oxford University Press.

Sewell, William H. 1996. "Three Temporalities: Toward an Eventful Sociology." In *The Historic Turn in the Human Sciences*, edited by Terrence J. McDonald. Ann Arbor: University of Michigan Press.

Shepsle, Kenneth A. 1989. "Studying Institutions: Some Lessons from the Rational Choice Approach." *Journal of Theoretical Politics* 1(2): 131–47.

Somers, Margaret. 1996. "Where is Sociology after the Historic Turn? Knowledge, Cultures, Narrativity, and Historical Epistemologies." In *The Historic Turn in the Social Sciences*, edited by Terrence McDonald. Ann Arbor: University of Michigan Press.

Stone, Lawrence. 1972. *Causes of the English Revolution*. New York: HarperCollins.

Stuart, Mark. 1998. *Douglas Hurd the Public Servant*. London: Mainstream.

Szász, André. 1999. *The Road to European Monetary Union*. Houndsmills, Basingstoke: Macmillan.

Thatcher, Margaret. 1993. *The Downing Street Years*. London: HarperCollins.

———. 1995. *The Road to Power*. London: HarperCollins.

Ungerer, Horst. 1997. *A Concise History of European Monetary Integration*. Westport, Conn.: Quorum.

Verdun, Amy. 2000. *European Responses to Globalization and Financial Market Integration*. Houndmills: Macmillan.

Walsh, James I. 2000. *European Monetary Integration and Domestic Politics: Britain, France and Italy*. Boulder, Colo.: Lynne Rienner.

Weber, Max. 1949. *The Methodology of the Social Sciences*, translated by E. Shils and H. Finch. Glencoe, Ill.: Free Press.

Wendt, Alexander. 1999. *Social Theory of International Politics*. New York: Cambridge University Press.

Young, Hugo. 1998. *This Blessed Plot: Britain and Europe from Churchill to Blair*. London: Papermac.

6

Persuasion, Preference Change, and Critical Junctures: The Microfoundations of a Macroscopic Concept

Barry R. Weingast

The relationship between historical institutionalism (HI) and rational choice institutionalism (RCI) remains unclear, clouded by a range of myths and mutual misunderstandings. My purpose in this chapter is threefold. First is its broad methodological purpose: to show that these methods are not antithetical but complementary. Indeed, I will demonstrate several points of contact between the two approaches and thus that they have much in common. Second is the narrow methodological purpose: to draw on concepts from HI to enrich RCI; notably, to apply the concept of a critical juncture, an important macroscopic principle used by historical institutionalists, in rational choice terms. Other HI concepts will also have a role in the application, including structure, contingency, the role of ideas, and the formation of actor's preferences over appropriate actions. Third is to draw on RCI to provide the microfoundations for critical junctures.

To help explain large-scale processes, historical institutionalists appeal to several concepts, including path dependence and critical junctures (Thelan 1999). Scholars have begun to provide the microfoundations for various conceptions of path dependence. W. Brian Arthur (1989), Paul David (1985), and Douglass North (1990), for example, use RCI techniques. Paul Pierson (2000) draws on a combination of HI and RCI methods. RCI scholars also employ a wide range of related concepts without using the path dependence label (see, for example, Greif's 2005 analysis of institutional elements and cultural beliefs).

No analysis parallels that for path dependence which studies the microfoundations of critical junctures. How do they work? What are the mechanisms by which critical junctures occur and how do they constrain behavior?

I develop here a political model of persuasion that predicts a set of circumstances that produce discontinuous political change.[1] The model assumes the existence of a pivotal decision-maker, whose support is necessary to preserve the status quo. If this pivot decides instead to support an alternative policy, then the status quo will change. The central importance of the pivot reflects the idea that some people are most committed to the prevailing idea and others are most committed to the new idea, but that neither is politically strong enough to prevail. Between these two groups is a third—moderates whose support is necessary for one of the sides to maintain political control. As these moderates or pivots go, so too does the politics. Contests of this type occur all the time in politics.

The purpose of the model is to study the conditions under which political entrepreneurs can persuade the pivotal political decision-maker to change her mind about the appropriate political actions—in particular, to take a political stand likely to provoke revolution or civil war.

Political scientists using a range of approaches emphasize the importance of preference change, persuasion, and the role of ideas in politics (Goldstein and Keohane 1993; Pierson 1994; Skocpol 1979). Yet no accepted model of this process exists.

I address these concerns by providing a model of persuasion and the role of ideas in politics. Under well-defined conditions, rational individuals change their mind in the face of evidence, and in so doing often change the political ends they pursue and the policies they prefer.

Some terminological clarification is useful at this point: Many non-rational choice political scientists use the label preference change to describe a situation in which an actor's preferred action, policy, or strategy change. Clearly, in these settings, preferences over political ends and policies change. In the common use of the term, preferences, this label is literally true—individuals' preferred choices change. But rational choice theorists do not call this preference change because it is not underlying and basic preferences that change here. Instead, what changes are the induced preferences over strategies about how to best achieve basic ends. An analogy with a canonical economic example makes this distinction clear. Based on their preferences and market prices, individuals make choices of what goods and services to purchase. As the prices change, so do their choices. Even though both prices and choices change, however, the underlying preferences do not. Returning to the political example, new information or changing circumstances have the power to alter the relative attractiveness of various choices and may therefore change an individual's preferred actions or strategies, though this information does not change underlying preferences.

In the model that follows, I assume that individuals have a mental model of the political world in which they live (Denzau and North 1994) and, further, that one particular model—the prevailing idea—dominates in the sense that most individuals share this model about their world. The prevailing idea typically has a range of implications for what policies and institutions are best for the society. In addition, there may be one or more new or challenging ideas that represent alternative mental models for interpreting the world and typically have very different policy consequences than the prevailing idea.

I assume that, at some initial period, a prevailing idea dominates the society. At the same time, various political entrepreneurs attempt to persuade others that one of several new ideas that imply a range of new political ends and policy changes should replace the prevailing idea.

Under what conditions are people persuaded to abandon the prevailing idea and begin to act in accord with a new one? The critically important part of the model is the political pivot, the individual or small group of individuals whose decision about whether to support the prevailing idea or a new challenging idea determines whether the new idea remains stable or not.

Most new ideas fail to attract much support among the general population. The reason is twofold: first, many people have a stake in the prevailing idea; and, second, even if the new idea promises additional benefits beyond the prevailing idea, typically little evidence supports the new idea and, also typically, there is something to be lost by pursuing the new idea when it turns out to be wrong.

For individuals to adopt a new idea, they must find it a persuasive way of organizing the world. In the rational choice perspective, this requires not only that the new idea have logical and emotional appeal, but that evidence supports the idea as a viable model of the world. As I suggest, a central aspect of political persuasion is that events beyond the direct control of the political entrepreneurs advocating the new idea help confirm the entrepreneur's views.

The model draws on a simple approach to learning under uncertainty. Associated with each new idea is a probability π that it is true. For most ideas, π is sufficiently low so that few people beyond a small cadre of advocates take it seriously. But on occasion, the right combination of new ideas and events persuade a much larger group of people to support the new idea.

The approach is designed to suggest the conditions under which the political pivot will switch allegiance from supporting the prevailing idea to the new idea. The model shows that, for a pair of prevailing and challenging ideas, there is a critical probability threshold, π^*, such that the political pivot will switch to embrace the new idea and its policy consequences if the probability that the idea is true rises above the critical threshold, i.e., when $\pi > \pi^*$. For π to rise above its initially low level, evidence must arise that makes the idea more likely to be true.

I derive an important comparative statics result drawn from the "rationality of fear" model (de Figueiredo and Weingast 1999, Weingast 2005): this result shows that, as the stakes of the controversy rise, the critical threshold, π^*, goes down. Indeed, when the stakes are asymmetric—that is, when the costs of failing to act under the new idea are quite large—π^* can be quite low, much closer to 0 than to 1.

The perspective shows that two dynamics can affect people's beliefs about a new idea. First, as noted, new evidence may arise that increases the likelihood that the idea is true. Second, people's perceptions of the stakes may change so that rising stakes lower the critical threshold probability π^*.

When the political controversy involves the sources of credible commitments to protecting critical economic and political rights, the stakes are typically quite high, since these involve people's livelihoods, way of life, and sometimes their lives.

The approach provides a rational choice interpretation of the historical institutionalist idea of critical junctures (Collier and Collier 1991; Katznelson 2003; Thelen 1999). When perceptions about the likelihood of the new idea's validity rise above π^*, the pivot switches sides to support the new idea, accepting its policy implications. The result is discontinuous political change.

I apply this approach to the American Revolution (Rakove, Rutten, and Weingast 2005, de Figueiredo, Rakove, and Weingast 2005). A central question for this event concerns how a relatively small group of radicals were able to persuade the much larger group of moderates, who wanted nothing more than to live in peace and maintain the status quo, to fight a war of revolution against Great Britain.

Reflecting the underlying international structure, one idea prevailed—for several generations, most colonists believed that the British were a benevolent, if remote presence and that they posed no problem to the American colonies. Before 1763, no noticeable minority criticizing the British or the structure of the empire existed.

These ideas began to change when the international structure changed after Britain's defeat of France in the Seven Years' War (1756 to 1763). Until this war, the French threat had aligned the interests of the two sides of the Atlantic: both metropole and colonies needed each other to survive. With the demise of the French threat, this structure abruptly changed. For the first time in a hundred years, the British sought a degree of control over policies within the colonies, control delegated to the colonists over the previous century.

Radical critics emerged almost immediately after the imposition of the stamp tax in 1763, arguing that this tax represented the end of the world as they knew it; namely, that this tax represented a change in the constitution governing the empire and colonies (Greene 1986, Reid 1995). According to this argument, this precedent would enable the British to alter any domestic policy by end-running the source of American liberty, the colonial legislatures. The result, these Americans argued, would be tyranny and slavery.

Although most Americans disliked the stamp tax, few regarded it as the end of the world, and the new ideas about the larger issues fell on deaf ears. Most saw little evidence to persuade them at the prevailing ideas about the British were wrong.

The status of the new ideas changed, however, with the ongoing controversies of the next few years. At several points, the British sought to punish the Americans. In 1767, when New York refused to quarter British troops, the British suspended the colonial assembly and imposed martial law. In 1773, in response to the Boston Tea Party, the British passed the punitive acts, known in America as the intolerable acts, closing Boston Harbor, annulling Massachusetts's charter, suspending colonial law, and once again imposing martial law.

The radicals had begun by predicting that the British would interfere with colonial assemblies. Although these predictions seemed outlandish in 1763, the British in fact did just this in 1767 and 1773. This provided striking evidence in favor of the new idea (evidence in the sense that it raised the probability that the new idea was correct). Whatever the British reasons for their actions, they were no longer remote but instead a threatening menace.

By 1775, with the British refusing to produce any form of compromise, the moderates reluctantly changed their minds and came to support the radicals in a revolution. The essence of the model is twofold. First, evidence occurred to make the new idea—initially seemingly wildly at variance with people's experiences—seem plausible. Second, as sufficient numbers of moderates came to be persuaded by the idea, they altered their preferences over possible actions: they changed from supporting a "wait and see" policy to revolution.

This approach draws on several conceptions from HI. Most important, it draws on the idea of a critical juncture—the notion that massive change occurred. In doing so, the model both integrates this concept into RCI and provides the microfoundations for it. The role of ideas is critical to understanding people's preferences, and, moreover, people's preferences over actions changed as a result of changing ideas.

Several other concepts central to HI are critical for this story. First, the role of structure is important: the demise of the French threat affected the preferences of both sides of the Atlantic within the British empire. Second, considerable uncertainty existed about the nature of the world— no one had an adequate mental model of their situation, and thus people acted on ideas over which they had considerable uncertainty. Third, contingency is important: the radicals' ideas would not have had much effect on Americans had the British acted differently.

Constitutions and Commitments

Every society has a constitution in the sense that "rules of the game" exist. At one end are societies with formal, written constitutions that spell out both a range of citizen rights and a set of procedural constraints on government that help enforce those rights. At the other end are societies without one, in which the whims of a dictator are central to whatever rules there are. Yet societies based wholly on whimsy are rare. Because they fare quite poorly over the long run, even authoritarians have incentives to make rules that protect at least a subset of citizens to increase the overall size of the pie, as emphasized most clearly in Olson's (2000) "stationary bandit" approach (see also North 1981, chap. 3). Moreover, constitutions can protect a wide range of citizen rights and assets, whether religious or ethnic freedom, economic assets, or regional autonomy.

Constitutions that support stable rules of the game must somehow provide a credible commitment to those rules—that is, the constitution must somehow make it in the interests of political officials to honor the ideal (Elster and Slagstad 1988; Gibbons and Rutten 1997; North and Weingast 1989; Ordeshook 1992; Weingast 2005). When such incentives exist, we say that the constitutional provision is self-enforcing in the sense that public officials have an incentive to adhere to it.

My concern here is not whether a society's constitution is written or based on practice and precedent; nor whether the entire constitution is adhered to in practice or only part; nor whether the aspect of the constitution protects religious rights, civil rights, political rights, or economic rights. It is instead that, in any society, events that threaten the constitution or its underlying credible commitments raise the rationality of fear (de Figueiredo and Weingast 1999). I discuss the mechanism underlying this phenomenon in the next section and apply it in the following. For now, my point is that the stakes tend to be quite large when a situation threatens to undo parts of a constitution that protect what people consider most dear.

Put another way, people that fear for their assets, their sources of livelihood, their way of life (including their religious and ethnic identities), or their lives often resort to supporting extraconstitutional action (Weingast 2005). Examples are widespread, including Serbs living in

Croatia in 1989 and 1990, landholders in Chile in 1973 under the Allende regime, southern slaveholders on the election of Lincoln in 1860, or landholders and older industrialists in 1936 under the socialist government in Spain.

The perspective on constitutions implies that, during times of constitutional change, people will attend not only to the ideals of their constitution, but to the provisions that make it self-enforcing. What makes many conflicts confusing after the fact is that the regime took no direct action against a group that supported extraconstitutional action. Indeed, in most of the examples noted, it is not action by the regime, but the threat of such action that triggered extraconstitutional reaction.

The Political Economy of Ideas

Citizens face three sources of uncertainty in evaluating political issues, particularly those that arise outside of their everyday experience (such as a foreign threat). First is an incomplete understanding or mental model of the world. Second is incomplete knowledge of the facts, for instance, what is actually going on. Third is disagreement about the first two. These three are especially problematic when societies face external threats.

Uncertainty is acute during a major new crisis. Crises imply both high stakes and that rational individuals typically do not have the luxury of basing their actions on ideas or theories of the world that they know to be true without doubt (Denzau and North 1994; Hinich and Munger 1994). Instead, they must typically act on ideas or theories of the world whose probability of being true is considerably lower than 1. Major new social dilemmas typically confront citizens with the basis for serious doubt and uncertainty about what is going on and why.

Consider a potentially major but uncertain change in circumstances facing a society. Before any hint of change, a dominant understanding of how the world works generally or at least often prevails. For British citizens in the colonies before 1763, this understanding included central aspects of the British constitution, ideas about the sanctity of religious freedom in America, system of private property and (relatively) free market economy, and the structure of the empire that included ties to Britain as a means of protection against the pervasive French threat.

Suppose that the world begins to change. In the beginning, most citizens are likely to characterize the changes as modest, without profound impact. These individuals thus continue to rely on the prevailing (status quo) idea. Other analysts, however, may characterize the changes more radically—perhaps arguing that the changes represent a profound threat to the society. I refer to this characterization as the new or challenging idea. A minimal condition for widespread acceptance is that the new idea be logically and factually plausible. But logic and plausibility do not imply that the new idea persuades anyone. Indeed, most new ideas are never taken seriously enough to become the basis of much action.

A major problem with new ideas is that they are far too prevalent. A principal analytic question for any argument about the role of a new idea is that it answer the question: what determines when a new idea is taken seriously by a widespread group of citizens? And what coordinates the separate actions of many citizens in rejecting the status quo idea in favor of some new idea?

To answer these questions, I draw on the recent work of Robert Bates, Rui de Figueiredo, and Barry R. Weingast (1998) and de Figueiredo and Weingast (1999) to develop a series of propositions about the role of ideas. When faced with two or more competing ideas about their world that might be true, members of the society must decide which idea should be the basis for their actions.

To be more concrete about individual decision-making under this form of uncertainty, I ask when a given citizen will make decisions or favor action based on the new idea. Let π be the probability that this citizen believes the new idea to be true. With only two possible ideas, the probability that the prevailing or status quo idea is true is thus $1 - \pi$.

This approach yields four significant insights about the influence of ideas on political decision-making.

First, there is a critical threshold probability, π^* with the following property. If a citizen believes that the probability that the new idea is below π^*, then she will continue to rely on the prevailing idea. However, if circumstances change so that she believes that the probability that the new idea is correct is at least as great as π^*, then she will rely on the new idea for choice and action.

Second, the approach yields an important comparative statics result, or prediction about how an individual's choice will change in response to changing circumstances. The uncertainty about each idea implies that there is a cost for acting on the idea when it turns out to be wrong. The calculus of rational action in the face of this uncertainty turns out to hinge on the balance of these two costs.

As an illustration of these two costs, consider the problem confronting slaveholders in 1861 in the United States. Radical southerners argued that the North was a threat to the slaveholding system and that secession was the only way to protect it. After the seven states of the lower South had seceded (South Carolina, Georgia, Florida, Alabama, Mississippi, Louisiana, and Texas), the four states of the upper South had to decide whether to secede or stay in the Union (Virginia, North Carolina, Tennessee, and Arkansas). Both secession and remaining in the Union had costs of being wrong. Betting on the idea that the North was not a threat to slavery—hence not seceding—ran the risk that the North was in fact a threat to slavery. Betting on the idea that the North was a threat—hence seceding—ran the risk of fighting an unnecessary Civil War, unnecessary in the sense that the North was in fact not a threat so that secession and Civil War were not needed to protect slavery.

A parallel problem confronted Serbs in Croatia in the late 1980s. Were the Croats a threat to their existence? Not acting on this threat when the Croatians were bent on violence could prove deadly; but acting on it when it would not, in fact, otherwise materialize could provoke a violent reaction that spirals into full-scale ethnic conflict.

Let S be the stakes, defined as a ratio: the expected losses associated with acting on the old idea when it turns out to be false; relative to the expected losses associated with the new idea when it turns out to be false. Defined in this manner, the stakes reflect the relative costs of being wrong about the new idea. Holding constant for beliefs about probabilities, as the magnitude of the threat central to the new idea rises, so too do the stakes.

Bates, De Figueiredo, and Weingast show that, as the stakes rise, the threshold probability, π^*, goes down (1998). That is, as the stakes rise, the threshold for acting on the new view goes down. The reason is that, as the stakes rise, the expected costs of failing to act on the new idea rise. A threat whose expected consequences rise implies that citizens are more likely to act on the new idea. This comparative result holds constant for the degree of evidence favor the two views, and hence a given citizen's belief, π, that the new view is true.

The approach has a further implication. As the stakes get very large—that is, as the costs of failing to act on the new idea when it turns out to be true rise relative to the costs of failing to act on the old idea when it turns out to be true—the threshold probability, π^*, becomes much closer to 0 than to 1. The stakes are large when citizens believe their families and livelihoods are at risk.

The rationality of fear model implies that, for very large stakes, citizens may rationally act on a new idea even though they believe that the probability that the idea is true is significantly less than the probability that the prevailing idea is true. The reason is that citizens are not detectives or historians. They must weight their probability assessments by the value of the outcomes associated with the probabilities. With a large asymmetry in the stakes, enough so that the costs of being wrong about the new idea far exceed those of being wrong about the prevailing idea, citizens will support actions based on the new idea even though they believe it is less plausible (that is, if $\pi^* < \pi < .5$).

This approach to the role of ideas has, for proponents of a new idea, several implications about the task. Proponents need not convince people that they are right ($\pi = 1$) or even that their idea is more plausible than the prevailing idea ($\pi > .5$). They instead need to convince people that the expected value of acting on their idea is higher than that associated with the prevailing idea. The inequalities cited imply that the task for a proponent of an idea is more plausible than π^*. When the stakes are huge and π^* is closer to 0 than to 1, it can easily be that other ideas are more plausible.

The comparative statics result just noted also implies a heresthetics principle (Riker 1982, 1986) for proponents of new ideas: they have an incentive to raise the stakes because this makes it more likely that their ideas will be accepted. Promoters of new ideas are therefore often prophets of doom—or, in Norman Schofield's (2000) terms, prophets of chaos. Put simply, it is rational for proponents of a new idea to attempt to scare pivotal decision-makers since this fear affects the rationality calculus. Further, for a leader's attempts to raise the rationality of fear, they must focus on something that plausibly has large stakes.

The third implication of the approach is that, for newly proposed ideas to become the basis for action, they must be confirmed or validated by events external to their proponents in the following sense: events and other forms of evidence must occur that raise citizen beliefs that the idea is true.

The initial beliefs held by most citizens, π, that a new idea is true are likely to be very low. Most new ideas are therefore never taken seriously in large part because their associated probability of being true always remains low.

For a new idea to become the basis for action, something must alter the initial beliefs citizens hold so that the probability, π, rises from the initially low level to a level above the critical threshold level, π^*. For π to rise above π^*, in turn, events beyond the direct control of the new idea's proponent must occur that increase other citizens' beliefs that the new idea is true. We define as evidence those events that increase the likelihood of the new idea for citizens. This requires application of a statistical approach to decision-making based on Bayes's rule. Events thus need not prove that the new idea is true. Instead, events must make citizens believe that the new idea is more likely to be true.

Consider the example of Serbs living in Croatia in the late 1980s before the breakup of Yugoslavia. After the death of Marshal Tito, longtime head of Yugoslavia, the provinces began to assert more independence. Croatian Serbs naturally worried about how the Croatian majority would treat them.[2] Based on more than a generation of peaceful coexistence, these Serbs were likely to have had ex ante a very small possibility that the Croatians might be bent on violent discrimination or even genocide. Yet, because of the risk—and the history of episodic violence and genocide earlier in the century—Croatian Serbs attended closely to the majority's actions.

The Croatians drive for political independence from Yugoslavia, from Serbia in particular, illustrates this principle. By Bayes's rule, this drive raised the likelihood that the Croatians were bent on violence. The reason is that nongenocidal Croatians might seek independence, but not necessarily. On the other hand, Croatians bent on genocide would certainly do so. Thus, observing that Croatians seek independence increases the likelihood that they are bent on violence.

Fourth, this approach predicts discontinuous change in both political behavior and ideas. As long as the probability, π, that the new idea is true remains below the threshold, π^*, citizens continue to act on the old idea. If, however, events push the probability of the new idea above π^*, then citizens will switch discontinuously from acting on the old idea to the new idea. When the actions dictated by the competing ideas differ markedly, so will behavior. The discontinuity occurs because individuals instantaneously switch from the old idea to the new one as the evidence for the new idea raises above the probability threshold, π^*. When π rises above π^*, ideas that have long been the basis for action are suddenly discarded in favor of new ones.

The model provides a way of formalizing the concept of critical junctures used by many historical institutionalists (for example, Collier and Collier 1991, Thelan 1999). A critical juncture occurs when a major dislocation occurs in society, such as when people abandon previous views and come to hold new ones sufficiently different that the direction of politics transforms radically.

The model I use here provides the microfoundations for a critical juncture. In the context of a new idea being juxtaposed with an old idea, a critical juncture occurs when a series of events alter peoples beliefs so that the probability of a new idea being true rises from below π^* to above it. Once this threshold has been reached for the pivotal individual, the pivot's behavior changes and the society comes to reject the status quo prevailing idea and act on the new idea. When the new idea differs radically from the old idea, the pivot's switch implies a major reorientation in politics and political action.[3]

Implications

This approach to the role of ideas accords well with the findings of scholars who have long emphasized that it is not history that matters, but interpreted history. Specific ideas about the world and about the past affect how individuals view the world and hence the decisions they make.

Yet not just any interpretation will do. Only those that help people make sense of their world are useful. Scholarly proponents of the role of ideas typically fail to explain why one particular idea gains credence over thousands of other plausible ideas, as Judy Goldstein and Robert Keohane (1993) observe. The approach outlined here—and developed in Bates, de Figueiredo, and Weingast (1998) and again in de Figueiredo and Weingast (1999)—goes beyond the traditional arguments about the role of ideas to provide a deeper understanding of the conditions that particular ideas must satisfy for individuals to adopt and act upon them, and these involve Bayes's rule.

I leave abstract the nature of the threat to citizens about which the new idea arises. A class of threats that potentially invoke the rationality of fear are those that concern the credible commitments inherent in a constitution that protect what people (or some subset) in a society hold most dear. Threats to these commitments typically have large consequences. The rationality of fear model described here suggests that new ideas articulating a threat to these commitments come to be the basis for action when events consistent with them and not the prevailing idea occur so that people's beliefs about the veracity of the idea increase.

Taken together, the results of this perspective imply that conflicts involving new ideas often have an explosive characteristic. The reason is that proponents of new ideas, to succeed, have an incentive to raise the stakes. Often this involves provoking the majority or those in power so that a strong, negative reaction is consistent with their new idea and thus raises the probability it is true. As the stakes raise, the probability threshold, π^*, goes down, making it more likely citizens will switch to supporting the new idea and its consequences.

Finally, when the new idea differs radically from the prevailing idea, and when the pivotal decision-maker's beliefs that it rises above the probability threshold, π^*, the ideological basis for society, the type of politics, and the policies pursued all radically and suddenly shift. This provides the basis for a critical juncture.

The Role of Ideas in the American Revolution

Historians of the American Revolution argue that this revolution was fought over ideals.[4] Quoting one of the masters of the era, Gordon Wood, gives a flavor of the approach. Unlike many other revolutions, the origin of the American Revolution "lay not in the usual passions and interests of men" or in the overthrowing of a feudal yoke. Instead, it lay in "the Americans' world-view, the peculiar bundle of notions and beliefs they put together during the imperial debate" (Wood 1966, 162):

If the origin of the American Revolution lay not in the usual passions and interests of men, wherein did it lay? . . . Never before in history had a people achieved a "revolution by reasoning" alone . . . . The Revolution was thus essentially intellectual and declaratory. (162)

The Revolution becomes comprehensible only when the mental framework, the Whig world-view into which the Americans fitted the events of the 1760's and 1770's, is known. "It is the development of this view to the point of overwhelming persuasiveness to the majority of American leaders and the meaning this view gave to the events of the time, and not simply an accumulation of grievances," writes Bailyn, "that explains the origins of the American Revolution." (169)

Others in this historical tradition include Bernard Bailyn (1967), Greene (1986), Edmund S. Morgan (1956/1977), Jack Rakove (1979), and John Reid (1995).

Given this perspective, an explanation of how most American colonists came to embrace the radical new ideas introduced in the mid-1760s is a curious omission in the literature (Rakove, Rutten, and Weingast 2005). Americans in 1763 appeared remarkably heterogeneous, full of disagreement, and not at all inclined to adopt critical aspects of the Whig world view that would later compel them to support revolution. They disagreed, for example, about the role of religion in social and political life, slavery, and the west; they disagreed about the use of government for social control and over economic regulation.

At the end of the Seven Years' War (1756 to 1763), the prevailing idea among the American colonists was that the status quo within the empire was fine. Their rights, property, and liberty were protected by the British system and the British posed no apparent threat. Indeed, the British had shown a remarkable degree of deference to Americans, allowing them largely to govern their own domestic affairs. Dissensions from the prevailing view began to emerge as the British sought to reorient their policies following their victory over France in the Seven Years' War.

As historians emphasize, the British and the Americans in fact differed in their views about fundamental aspects of the structure of the empire, the constitution, the sources of liberty, and the rights of Americans (Greene 1986; Reid 1994). Furthermore, a range of differences subdivided Americans, some were international merchants while others lived in self-sufficient communities; others were part of religious sects that sought a safe haven in America; still others were slaveholders. These differences became apparent only over the course of the revolutionary crisis.

For our purposes, it is useful to divide Americans in a different way. In the beginnings of the crisis, a small group of radicals emerged that grew in strength and coherence over the revolutionary crisis. At the opposite end of the political spectrum were the loyalists. Neither was sufficient by itself to control the politics of the controversy. In between sat a large group of moderates, initially loyal to Britain. These moderates were the pivots: a revolution could happen only if they joined the radicals. Of course, these groups were hardly well formed in the beginning of the crisis, whereas by the mid-1770s they were well defined.[5]

Turning to the ideas, the Americans looked back to the English constitutional ideas of the late seventeenth century (Bailyn 1967; Greene 1986; Rakove 1996; Reid 1995). In this view, precedent was an important constitutional ingredient: long-standing practice in governance attained constitutional status. With respect to the empire, most Americans believed that its structure was federal (although they did not use this term): The British had control over the system-wide public goods, such as trade and security. The Americans controlled colonial policies covering the full range of domestic issues: contract and property law, religious freedom, slavery, taxation, and domestic social and economic regulation.[6] Further, this federal division of authority had evolved over a one hundred year period, with the British approving an increasingly wide range of powers to the American colonial legislatures.

These two elements in the colonists' mental model—the constitutional view emphasizing precedent; and the federal structure of the empire developed over a one hundred year period—combined to yield an important implication: by virtue of having endured and evolved over several generations, the federal structure of the empire had attained constitutional status. In particular, colonial legislatures protected the most important elements of American liberty—their property, religious freedom, and various other rights.

The constitutional structure of a federal empire provided a form of "bright line" commitment mechanism protecting American rights and liberties. The division of authority was relatively easy to police in the sense that deviations from it were easy to observe and thus easy to trigger defensive reaction by the other side. Americans thus believed that this political division of authority, rooting American law and government in the American colonial assemblies, protected their rights and liberties. Economically, they made their investments accordingly.

Historians emphasize that the British had very different views of these issues than the Americans (Greene 1986, Reid 1995). By the 1760s, the British had begun to develop what became the mature nineteenth century view of the constitution. This view emphasized parliamentary sovereignty over precedent. Friedrich Hayek (1960, chap. 11) concluded that this view implied that parliament was unlimited and unlimitable. Further, the British argued that, because sovereignty could not be divided, either they had it or the Americans did; and of the two possibilities, only the first was plausible.

The British interpreted the delegation of authority and discretion to American colonial legislatures not as a constitutional right but as a privilege that could be withdrawn. The British, therefore, did not believe themselves bound by constitutional constraints. If they had delegated Americans the discretion to govern themselves, this delegation could be removed.

Despite these large differences in understandings about American rights, the French threat provided the glue that held the British empire together. Put simply, both sides of the Atlantic needed each other and were willing to bear costs to ensure the public good of security. Respecting one another's rights in the federal division of power was thus self-enforcing under this regime (de Figueiredo, Rakove, and Weingast 2005).

The end of the Seven Years' War represented a major structural shift in the world: the French defeat removed them as a major threat to the British and especially to their empire. A simple bargaining framework suggests that, whatever the arrangements between colonies and metropole prior to the demise of the French, it was unlikely to be sustained afterward. Robert Tucker and David Hendrickson (1987), for example, suggest that America would inevitably move toward greater independence.

For their part, the British began to reorganize how they governed the empire. This was impelled in part by the sheer size and complexity of the new empire in comparison with the old, now including French Canada and parts of India. The more complex empire altered the British view of the American colonies within the larger structure. Prior to the Seven Years' War, the American colonies constituted the bulk of the empire, so that policies harming the Americans harmed the empire. After the Seven Years' War, the much larger empire implied that the British might well pursue policies that benefited the empire overall, though they might hurt one portion of it. Moreover, the British had to be concerned that disputes in one portion would inevitably have implications elsewhere. In particular, appearing weak in dealing with the American colonies would have implications for their ability to maintain control of French Canada.

These changes in international structure combined with the huge debt from the war motivated the British to intervene in various aspects of the Americans' domestic affairs in a way they never had before. It began when the British imposed a small, seemingly trivial tax.

The American radicals—"prophets of chaos" in Norman Schofield's

(2000) terms—argued that the new British policies in the empire represented a new and dangerous precedent, threatening life as the Americans knew it. The British policy was not about a small trivial tax, in the radicals' view, but a precedent-setting action that if successful would grant the British the power to control all aspects of American life. To the radicals, the British had become malevolent.

This was a clever political argument by the radicals attempting to garner support from others to oppose the tax. Looking beyond those who paid the tax, the radicals used the constitutional precedent interpretation to speak to everyone. Radicals claimed that everything of value—whether property, commerce, religious freedom, or slaves—depended on securing liberty through the constitutional provisions supporting the sovereignty of colonial legislatures in domestic colonial affairs. The new British behavior therefore threatened the foundations of American liberty—their colonial legislatures. Put in modern terms, the radicals argued that the British were seeking to undo the constitutional mechanisms that provided credible commitments to property, liberty, and their way of life.

Initially, the argument fell on deaf ears: most colonists ignored the radicals. The idea that the British were malevolent and out to take away American liberty simply did not match the world as most colonists had experienced it. Yet, over the next thirteen years, British actions provided evidence that favored the radicals' world view, causing a pivotal group of American moderates to switch sides and support revolution.

The model of the role of ideas and critical junctures applies here. The prevailing idea held that the British were benign (if remote) and would largely ignore the Americans. The radicals argued a new idea, that the British had become malevolent and bent on destroying the institutional mechanisms protecting American liberty. Initially, the probability, π, that the new idea was true was very low, far below the threshold, π^*, that would cause the pivotal colonists to act on the new idea.

Yet British actions changed this situation. A series of events served to raise the probability, π, that the radicals' ideas were correct. First, in reaction to American protests, the British repealed the Stamp Act. Simultaneously, however, they passed the Declaratory Act (1766), which told the Americans that, although they (the British) were removing the stamp tax, they had the right to impose such taxes if they saw fit. Although the British removed the tax, they not only failed to acknowledge the American view of the constitutional precedents granting Americans the right to control domestic colonial policy, they denied both this view of the constitution and that Americans had such rights, arguing instead that the metropole reserved the right to intervene at its pleasure.

Second, a major problem arose with respect to the British demands that the Americans quarter British troops. The colonial assembly of New York refused to provide for the quartering of troops. The British reacted in 1767 by suspending the New York colonial assembly and imposing martial law. This response demonstrated that, whatever their motive, the British were willing to attack American legislatures, colonial law, and the liberty these defined and protected.

Third, to add to the confusion in the colonies, if the French threat had disappeared, why did the British choose this moment to begin to maintain a huge standing army in the colonies? If the French threat had failed to motivate the British to have such an army, what could the army's purpose be? To many colonists, this policy appeared as a British excuse and that the troops were designed to compel compliance with harsher regulations.

Fourth, in response to changes in the regulation of tea duties in 1773, traders in Boston dumped tea in the harbor (the so-called Boston Tea Party). The British reaction was even stronger than against New York. In a series of Coercive Acts (1774)—known to many Americans as the intolerable acts—the British closed the port of Boston, disbanded the Massachusetts colonial assembly, annulled the colonial charter, and imposed the Justice Act allowing for jury trials in Britain for the prosecution of certain Americans.

However one might rationalize these British actions, they made it abundantly clear that the status quo view of British as a benign and remote presence could no longer be sustained. In terms of the model, all of these four events pointed in the same direction: raising the probability, π, that the British had become malevolent. In the mid-1760s, the radicals' argument that the British were out to destroy the institutional mechanisms protecting American liberty, the colonial assemblies in particular, seemed too far removed from experience to be plausible. By 1774, the British had demonstrated their willingness to do exactly what the radicals had predicted.

The British provided further evidence supporting the radicals' ideas. As Rakove (1979) emphasizes, American moderates bitterly hated the British willingness to impose punishments on all or large groups of Americans, including people not attempting to protest the British. Further, if the British were benign, why did they fail to offer a credible compromise? The fact that they failed to offer a compromise provided further evidence (in the Bayesian sense) that the radicals' views were correct.

In short, the "confirming evidence" altered the pivotal members' support to favor the radicals, leading to the path of revolution. In historical institutionalist terms, this moment represents a critical juncture: Americans' ideas and ideology changed markedly over the revolutionary crisis.

As the moderates came to believe the British were no longer benign, they reluctantly came to support revolutionary action against Britain, implying destruction of the empire as they knew it.

Interpretation

This brief account of the revolutionary crisis fails to do justice to the complexities of the revolutionary crisis. Yet it demonstrates an important element, namely, how the ideas of the radicals were peripheral in 1763 but became mainstream in 1776 (the dominant idea, as historians say, if not the unanimously held).

The approach helps explain why the moderates switched political allegiance from the British to the radical cause. Historians emphasize the role of ideas in the American Revolution but do not explain either why enough people came to embrace these ideas or why people were willing to fight and die for them. Lack of attention to what makes a constitution self-enforcing has led historians to an incomplete understanding of the role of ideas in revolutionary America (Rakove, Rutten, and Weingast 2005). Moreover, we show that this issue leads us precisely to the link between the realm of ideas and the realm of action. The British threat to the sources of credible commitment were precisely the link between the abstract ideas to the credible commitments protecting American liberties that became the focus of American historians.

The model shows why so many Americans came to take these ideas seriously. Although many of the British actions could be the result of other motives, the logic of Bayesian learning served to increase the moderate's beliefs, π, that the British were malevolent. The various British actions outlined, such as attacking American legislatures, raised π sufficiently so that, for many moderate Americans, it rose above π^*. This impelled them to alter their mental model and to oppose the British. If the British were benevolent, they may well have had legitimate motives to act as they did. That is, under some circumstances, a benevolent British might have acted this way. But if, as the radicals claimed, the British were malevolent, they would have acted this way with certainty. Given this logic, a range of British actions during the crisis served to raise the probability that the radicals were correct.

Moreover, other aspects of the theory are clearly present. From the beginning, the radicals argued that the stakes were high, covering everything near and dear to Americans. Their arguments focused on the heart of credible commitment mechanisms in the British empire: the system of federalism that allowed Americans to protect their liberties, including such diverse rights as religious self-governance, property, and slavery. Further, as the theory also predicts, the revolution exhibits discontinuous political change, as the moderates switched sides sometime between 1774 and 1776 to side with the radicals and wage revolution.

Finally, let me suggest that this contest was not solely about the prevailing idea against that of the radicals. Tories, at the opposite end of the political spectrum from the radicals, argued that the British were reacting legitimately to the radicals' provocation. They also argued that, no matter how bad the British were, the alternative was worse. The British had traditionally helped police colonial disputes, and these disputes, the Tories argued, were likely to explode if British authority were removed.

For the first decade of the controversy, moderates found these and related ideas sufficiently plausible that they sided against the radicals. This changed, however, with the British actions in the mid-1770s, leading the moderates, reluctantly (Rakove 1979), to switch sides.

Conclusions

I have developed an approach to one type of critical juncture and discontinuous political change. A central element to this approach is that political entrepreneurs attempt to persuade political pivots to adopt new ideas and hence to support radical action. Yet these entrepreneurs cannot succeed by rhetoric alone, in part because too many entrepreneurs compete for public acceptance with new ideas. To be accepted, the world view underlying a new idea must be confirmed, in the Bayesian sense, so that pivotal political actors come to believe it might be true.

The approach has four elements. First, the new idea has a probability of being true of π, which initially is typically so low as to be negligible. For each idea, there is a critical probability π^*, such that if $\pi > \pi^*$, the pivotal will support the new idea and its consequences for political action. Most new ideas in politics never meet this simple condition and thus never play a major role in politics. Second, for the probability that a new idea is true to rise above π^*, events must occur (beyond the direct control of the political entrepreneurs) that provide evidence in favor of the view. Third, as the stakes of the controversy rise, the critical probability, π^*, falls. Hence political entrepreneurs have an incentive to raise the stakes. In Schofield's (2000) terms, they are often prophets of chaos. Finally, the model exhibits discontinuous political change. When π rises above π^*, the pivot switches sides, often supporting radical action.

I applied this perspective to the American Revolution. In this case, the radicals professed a markedly new idea with implications for radical—indeed, violent if necessary—political action. By the mid-1770s, this action was increasingly focused on revolution, particularly in view of the fact that the British failed to offer any credible compromises.

All four elements of the theory apply to this case. First, the idea was initially held by only a small number of radicals. Second, political entrepreneurs attempted to raise the stakes by focusing on the credible commitments that protected a diverse range of rights that Americans held dear. Third, the British actions provided evidence that raised the probability that the new idea was likely to be true, that the British were no longer the remote, benevolent metropole. And, finally, when enough evidence accumulated to support the new ideas, the pivot switched sides, creating discontinuous political change.

This perspective thus develops a rational choice model of how ideas affect people's perceptions of their world and hence their preferences over action. Moreover, in each case, major changes in identity occurred.

Returning to our original purpose, the approach provides several points of contact between HI and RCI. I use the concept of critical junctures from HI to enrich an RCI analysis. In so doing, the approach also enriches HI by providing the microfoundations for this concept. The model applied to the American Revolution shows how a new set of ideas emerging from a political controversy served the ends of those who advocated them. Per the notion of critical juncture, these ideas also held the basis for turning the world upside down in sense of a radical departure from the status quo ante. In thirteen short years, Americans went from considering themselves British, and wanting nothing more than continuing to live in the empire as it then existed, to fighting a revolution against Britain.

Moreover, my rational choice interpretation encompasses several critical aspects of the HI approach. The role of structure is critical, as I noted in regard to the importance of the demise of the French threat, implying that the British empire became instantly more complex and saddled with a huge debt. This structural change altered the interests and perceptions of both sides of the Atlantic. Similarly, contingency plays a central role. Nothing, for example, was ordained about the British actions in America, or their response to the Americans' reactions. Had the British actions differed—for example, had they offered a compromise in the mid-1770s, a revolution would have been unlikely. Another element of contingency concerns the content of the radicals' ideas. Had these focused on a different aspect of the controversy—for example, not cleverly tying their own interests to others through the concept of credible commitment—these ideas might not have mixed with the British reactions in the right way to compel a change in beliefs as outlined here. Indeed, nothing in the historians' treatment suggests that these ideas inevitably emerged from the controversy.

Of course, this discussion is not a book. My purpose has been to focus on the mechanism underlying a central aspect of this case, namely, the critical juncture resulting in discontinuous change of the American Revolution. I believe that this central mechanism would carry the same weight in a far more extensive treatment, one that looked at a wider range of ideas and political interests among the colonists; a wider range of structural elements, including population change, the changing nature of the British mercantile system, the British restrictions on westward expansion; and provided a far more extensive narrative of events.

A major source of difficulty between HI and RCI types has been the differential use of the term preferences, with HI scholars often studying what RCI scholars call induced preferences—that is, preferences over strategies and choices. Once this difference is appreciated, then it becomes clear that both HI and RCI scholars regularly study circumstances in which these induced preferences change. In particular, my approach to the role of ideas shows how both beliefs and induced preferences over actions were not fixed but changed as a result of the ongoing interaction between British and Americans. Indeed, a strength of RCI is that it includes a technology for studying the mechanisms of such changes.

Let me end by addressing the issue of transportability of this approach to other contexts.[7] Specifically, this approach can be extended to other critical junctures in American history, including the rise of the so-called slave power conspiracy in the 1850s, helping both to create a sectional coalition to dominate American politics and to prompt southern secession; early twentieth-century Democrats proposing a greater role for the national government, failing to persuade the political pivot until the Great Depression of the 1930s; and the role of the civil rights movement, emphasizing social injustice to African Americans in the South, helped to convince the American political pivot in the late 1950s and 1960s to support a greater role for the national government in managing social, environmental, and health issues. In each case a new idea challenged the prevailing idea, but initially without success (where success is defined in the political model as the ability to persuade the pivotal political player). In each case, events occurred that changed the pivot's beliefs—the Kansas-Nebraska Act and Dred Scott decision for the slave power conspiracy in the 1850s, the Great Depression with its huge, sustained unemployment for the New Deal, and the television broadcasts of the brutal southern repression during the civil rights movement. And in each case, the new idea became the political motivator of dramatic new policies and political action. In this sense, each case can be called a critical juncture. The model here provides the mechanism emphasizing the microfoundations of these critical junctures.

The author thanks Rui de Figueiredo, Jeffrey Hummel, Ira Katznelson, David Laitin, Margaret Levi, William Sewell, and Kenneth Shepsle for helpful conversations.

Notes

1. This approach draws on my previous work (including de Figueiredo and Weingast 1999 on Yugoslavia; de Figueiredo, Rakove, and Weingast 2005, Rakove, Rutten and Weingast 2005 on the American Revolution; and Weingast 2005 on the circumstances providing for self-enforcing constitutions).
2. Bates, de Figueiredo and Weingast (1998) and de Figueiredo and Weingast (1999) explore these issues in the context of this case.
3. The approach discussed new ideas in a binary context—that is, just two possible ideas. This framework can easily be extended to include a prevailing idea and multiple new ideas. I will not work through all the implications here, but instead will only sketch it. Associated with each of the new ideas, i, is the subjective probability that it is true, π_i; and with the prevailing idea, π_o; where $\Sigma_{i=o,n} \pi_i = 1$. As before, for one of the new ideas to prevail, it must cross the threshold, $\pi_i > \pi^*$. All the same results now go through.
4. In this section, I summarize aspects of my larger project on the American Revolution (Rakove, Rutten, and Weingast 2005, de Figueiredo, Rakove, and Weingast 2005).
5. Rakove (1979) provides the best analysis of the politics underlying this era.
6. According to Morgan (1956/1977) for example, "For the Americans, the great thing about this empire, apart from the sheer pride of belonging to it, was that it let you alone" (8) and "Apart from trade regulations the laws the Americans lived by were made, as always, by their own representatives" (12).
7. I have elsewhere studied the application of this approach in an international context, specifically, to the breakup of Yugoslavia and its fall into ethnic warfare (Bates, de Figueiredo, and Weingast 1998 and de Figueiredo and Weingast 1999).

References

Arthur, W. Brian. 1989. "Competing Technologies, Increasing Returns, and Lock-In by Historical Events." *Economic Journal* 99(394): 116–31.

Bailyn, Bernard. 1967. *The Ideological Origins of the American Revolution*. Cambridge, Mass.: Belknap Press.

Bates, Robert, Rui de Figueiredo, and Barry R. Weingast. 1998. "Rationality and Interpretation: The Politics of Transition." *Politics and Society* 26(December): 603–42.

Collier, Ruth Berins, and David Collier. 1991. *Shaping the Political Arena: Critical Junctures, the Labor Movement, and Regime Dynamics in Latin America*. Princeton, N.J.: Princeton University Press.

David, Paul. 1985. "Clio and the Economics of QWERTY." *American Economic Review* 75(2): 332–37.

Denzau, Arthur, and Douglass C. North. 1994. "Shared Mental Models." *Kyklos* 47(1): 3–31.

Elster, Jon, and Rude Slagstad. 1988. *Constitutionalism and Democracy*. New York: Cambridge University Press.

de Figueiredo, Rui, and Barry R. Weingast. 1999. "Rationality of Fear: Political Opportunism and Ethnic Conflict." In *Military Intervention in Civil Wars*, edited by Jack Snyder and Barbara Walter. New York: Columbia University Press.

de Figueiredo, Rui, Jack Rakove, and Barry R. Weingast. 2005. "Rationality, Inaccurate Mental Models, and Self-Confirming Equilibrium: A New Understanding of the American Revolution." Working Paper, Hoover Institution, Stanford University.

Gibbons, Robert, and Andrew Rutten. 1997. "Equilibrium Institutions." Working Paper, Ithaca, N.Y.: Cornell University Press.

Goldstein, Judy, and Robert Keohane, eds. 1993. *Ideas and Foreign Policy*. Ithaca, N.Y.: Cornell University Press.

Greene, Jack P. 1986. *Peripheries and Center: Constitutional Development in the Extended Polities of the British Empire and the United States, 1607–1788*. New York: Norton.

Greif, Avner. 2005. *Institutions and the Path to the Modern Economy: Lessons from Medieval Trade*. New York: Cambridge University Press.

Hayek, Friedrich. 1960. *Constitution of Liberty*. Chicago: University of Chicago Press.

Hinich, Melvin, and Michael Munger. 1994. *Analytical Politics*. New York: Cambridge University Press.

Horowitz, Donald. 1985. *Ethnic Groups in Conflict*. Berkeley: University of California Press.

Katznelson, Ira. 2003. "Periodization and Preferences: Reflections on Purposive Action in Comparative Historical Social Science." In *Comparative Historical Analysis*, edited by James Mahoney and Dietrich Rueschemeyer. New York: Cambridge University Press.

Morgan, Edmund S. 1956/1977. *The Birth of the Republic, 1763–89*. Rev. ed. Chicago: University of Chicago Press.

North, Douglass C. 1981. *Structure and Change in Economic History*. New York: W. W. Norton.

———. 1990. *Institutions, Institutional Change and Economic Performance*. New York: Cambridge University Press.

North, Douglass C., and Barry R. Weingast. 1989. "Constitutions and Commitment: The Institutions Governing Public Choice in Seventeenth Century England." *Journal of Economic History* XLIX(December): 803–32.

Olson, Mancur. 2000. *Power and Prosperity: Outgrowing Communist and Capitalist Dictatorships*. New York: Basic Books.

Ordeshook, Peter C. 1992. "Constitutional Stability." *Constitutional Political Economy* 3(2): 137–75.

Pierson, Paul. 1994. *Dismantling the Welfare State?: Reagan, Thatcher, and the Politics of Retrenchment*. New York: Cambridge University Press.

———. 2000. "Increasing Returns, Path Dependence, and the Study of Politics." *American Political Science Review* 94(2): 251–67.

Rabushka, Alvin, and Kenneth A. Shepsle. 1972. *Politics in Plural Societies: A Theory of Democratic Instability*. Columbus, Ohio: Charles E. Merrill.

Rakove, Jack. 1979. *The Beginnings of National Politics: An Interpretive History of the Continental Congress*. Baltimore, Md.: Johns Hopkins University Press.

———. 1996. *Original Meanings*. New York: Alfred A. Knopf.

Rakove, Jack, Andrew Rutten, and Barry R. Weingast. 2005. "Ideas, Interests, and Credible Commitments in the American Revolution." Working Paper. Stanford, Calif.: Hoover Institution.

Reid, John. 1995. *Constitutional History of the American Revolution*. Abridged ed. Madison: University of Wisconsin Press.

Riker, William H. 1982. *Liberalism against Populism*. San Francisco: W. H. Freeman.

———. 1986. *The Art of Political Manipulation*. New Haven, Conn.: Yale University Press.

Schofield, Norman. 2000. "Constitutional Political Economy: On the Possibility of Combining Rational Choice Theory and Comparative Politics." *Annual Review of Political Science* 3(June): 277–303.

Skocpol, Theda. 1979. *States and Social Revolution*. New York: Cambridge University Press.

Thelen, Kathleen. 1999. "Historical Institutionalism in Comparative Politics." *Annual Review of Political Science* 2: 369–404.

Tucker, Robert W., and David C. Hendrickson. 1987. *The Fall of the First British Empire: Origins of the War of American Independence*. Baltimore, Md.: Johns Hopkins University Press.

Weingast, Barry R. 1995. "The Economic Role of Political Institutions: Market Preserving Federalism and Economic Development." *Journal of Law Economics, and Organization* 11(1): 1–31.

———. 1998a. "Constructing Trust: The Politics and Economics of Ethnic and Regional Conflict." In *Where is the New Institutionalism Now?*, edited by Virginia Haufler, Karol Soltan, and Eric Uslaner. Ann Arbor: University of Michigan Press.

———. 1998b. "Political Stability and Civil War: Institutions, Commitment, and American Democracy." In *Analytic Narratives*, edited by Robert Bates, Avner Greif, Margaret Levi, Jean-Laurent Rosenthal, and Barry R. Weingast. Princeton, N.J.: Princeton University Press.

———. 2005. "Self-Enforcing Constitutions: With An Application to Democratic Stability in America's First Century." Working Paper, Hoover Institution, Stanford University.

Wood, Gordon S. 1966."Rhetoric and Reality in the American Revolution." *William and Mary Quarterly*, 3rd. ser. 23(1): 3–32.

7

Endogenous Preferences About Courts: A Theory of Judicial State Building in the Nineteenth Century

Charles M. Cameron

National courts in federalist systems face a fundamental and recurring political dilemma: what is their role in relation to state governments and state judiciaries? Putting it more bluntly: who will have power? In many respects, this is the fundamental issue in the law of federal courts.

From this perspective, the history of federal courts in the United States presents a pretty puzzle: how can we account for the vast expansion of federal judicial power at the expense of the states'?

That such an expansion occurred is beyond doubt. In the early republic, the jurisdiction of federal courts was severely restricted, limited to cases involving the law of ships and shipping (admiralty), suits between citizens of different states (diversity cases), and suits between foreigners and U.S. citizens (alienage cases). With few exceptions, all else belonged exclusively to state courts. Federal judges themselves numbered but a handful. Supreme Court justices spent much of their time "riding circuit," traveling the miserable roads of the day. And, the clumsy hierarchical structure of the federal courts imposed by the Judiciary Act of 1789 limited the justices' ability to impress their rulings uniformly across geographically scattered subordinate judges. Not surprisingly, the social status of federal judges was low.[1] The weakness of the federal judiciary persisted at least until the Civil War. But then, the jurisdiction of federal courts over hitherto state matters underwent a tremendous expansion.[2] In addition, in the late nineteenth and early twentieth centuries Congress reorganized the judicial hierarchy, creating a structure that allowed much tighter control of the bottom by the top. The numbers and prestige of federal judges increased as well. The growth of the national administrative state after 1932 necessarily propelled the federal judiciary into myriad new areas previously ceded to the states. Finally, the explosion of federal judicial jurisdiction in the 1960s and 1970s (for example, by incorporating the Bill of Rights into the Due Process Clause) completed an astounding revolution in the power of the federal judiciary.

That the expansion of federal judicial power was consequential is also beyond question. A few examples will suffice. First, in the second half of the nineteenth century, the Supreme Court strove, largely success-fully, to create a continental free trade zone (Bensel 2000). To construct continental markets, the Court crafted new doctrines, invented new rights for property holders and companies, and severely restricted the powers of sovereign state governments. Second, federal courts severely limited the ability of the central government to raise revenue, effectively delaying the rise of a national welfare state. The Supreme Court's assault on the federal income tax in the late nineteenth century, which kept that source of revenue out of bounds for the federal government for a genera-tion, provides the most dramatic instance. Third, federal courts repeat-edly expanded, and in some cases contracted, national citizenship rights. For instance, after the Civil War, lower federal courts moved to create national citizenship rights for the freed slaves, rights that the U.S. Su-preme Court subsequently restricted (Smith 1997; Keyssar 2000). Finally, the role of the Warren Court in creating new national citizenship rights is an oft-told story. In all these examples, puissant federal courts pro-foundly altered the political economy of the United States and the rights of its citizens.

If one examines scholarly attempts to explain the course of federal judicial state building in the United States, one finds two distinct tradi-tions.[3] Neither takes federalism seriously. The first is a Congress-centered perspective, in which Congress constructs the federal judiciary. In this account, the federal judiciary is passive bystander with respect to new jurisdiction, always acted upon and rarely much of an actor. States and state interests make no appearance. The second is a court-centered per-spective, in which the Supreme Court itself constructs the jurisdiction of the federal courts (including limitations binding the hands of federal judges). In this account, the high court is the prime mover and Congress largely a spectator. Again, states play no role. Both accounts are able to point to significant episodes that seem to support their particular ana-lytic approach. But how satisfactory can federalism-free theories of fed-eral courts be?

Here I present a new theory of federal courts, drawing heavily on recent theoretical advances in the study of federalism (Cremer and Pal-frey 2002; Besley and Coate 2003). The model brings together the states, Congress, and the Supreme Court as jointly important actors in judicial state building. In the model, two distinct paths determine the jurisdiction of the federal courts: a delegation path in which a majority coalition of state delegates in Congress is the prime mover, and a unilateral action path in which Congress eschews that role and the Supreme Court assumes it instead. The model identifies circumstances in which one path or the other will predominate. I use the analytic lens of the model to examine a variety of episodes in federal judicial state building in the nineteenth century. These narratives serve less as a test of the theory than as a plausibility check and, perhaps, as down payment on more systematic inquiry in the future. Among the episodes I consider are controversies over the Fugitive Slave Act, apparent preference reversals by antebellum abolitionists and slaveholders, the passage of the Removal Act of 1875, and multiple twists and turns in the history of state sovereign immunity.

Before plunging into the analytics and history of judicial federalism, however, it is incumbent on me to explain how I will illustrate the themes of this book.

Deep Preferences, Induced Preferences, and Judicial Politics

How does the history of judicial federalism illustrate preferences and situations? Some gentle formalism facilitates precision about this question. Consider an actor with a vision of a good society, which I will call a deep preference. By choosing different means of action, the actor can alter the state of affairs that prevail, moving it closer or farther from her vision of a good society. What determines the actor's preferences for the different means, her induced preferences about means?

More precisely, denote different states of affairs as points (y) on a line (Y). Let $\bar{y}$ denote the actor's ideal state of affairs (her deep preference). Let her evaluation of actual states of affairs be given by $u(y;\bar{y}) = -(y - \bar{y})^2$. (The key point here is that the actor prefers states of affairs that are closer to her vision of the good society than farther from it.) Let X be the set of means available to the actor, with x indicating a specific means. Finally, let means of action affect states of affairs through a simple technology: $y = f(x;\theta)$, where θ denotes factors that affect the relationship between means and ends, which I will call structure.

Within this simple formalism, it is easy to understand the logic of the actor's preferences about means. Suppose for concreteness that $y = x + \theta$, with x and θ being real numbers.[4] It is easy to confirm that the actor's most preferred action is then $x^* = \bar{y} - \theta$.

This result is deeper than it initially appears. It shows clearly that the actor's (induced) preferences about means of action depend directly on her deep preferences about the ideal society ($\bar{y}$), but also equally directly on the structure relating means and ends (θ). Changes in either deep preferences or structure will change preferences about means. In this sense, preferences about means are endogenous.

In the jurisdiction game, the model is game theoretic rather than decision theoretic, unlike the simple example just given. The strategic complexity of American political institutions necessitates a move to game theory. Not surprisingly, the situation facing the actors is much more complicated than in the example. Nonetheless, the basic logic goes through.

More concretely, the actors include voters from slave states and voters from free states, who send representatives to Congress. These actors (and thus their delegates to Congress) have very different conceptions of the good society: their deep preferences are distinct. The means of action for the delegates in Congress is, strengthen or weaken federal courts. The structure, as elaborated in the model, is quite complex. It includes the externalities imposed on slave-holding voters and abolitionist voters by the opposing ways of life pursued in different states. It also includes the number of delegates from free and slave states in Congress, the decision rules in Congress used to choose policies, and the deep preferences of the high court (which are structure from the perspective of the congressmen). The model also includes the Supreme Court as an active player. It too has deep preferences about slavery (for example). The high court's means of action is, assert or refuse federal jurisdiction over state policy. Structure for the Court includes, critically, its enforcement costs for imposing policy on the states. The model then provides a framework for tracing out how changes in deep preferences and changes in structure drive the politics of federal judicial state-building—including changes in induced preferences about the power of federal courts.

Let me be clear about what is not in the model. It takes changes in deep preferences and structure as data, then works through the consequences for induced preferences and judicial state-building. It does not explain why structures or deep preferences about fundamental values change. But, endogenizing such changes is possible. For example, one could embed the jurisdiction game in an economic model of trade and growth, so that as interregional trade grows, externalities across states increase. This endogenous change in structure would then trace out into predictable struggles over federal judicial power. Alternately, one could at least in theory connect the jurisdiction game to a model of social movements. The rise of abolitionism, for example, as a social and political movement would alter endogenous deep preferences, with predictable consequences for the politics of federal judicial power.

Also missing from the story is a more subtle but intriguing notion: the co-evolution of preferences and institutions.[5] By this I mean, the expansion of federal judicial power will itself create voters and judges with altered deep preferences, whose deep preferences in turn feed back into changes in judicial institutions. For example, suppose newly empowered federal judges force changes in state electoral laws. The resulting change in state electorates may lead to the selection of different delegates to Congress. Nomination politics driven by the new delegates will then change the population of federal judges, who in turn act to alter federal jurisdiction again. Thus, over time deep preferences and judicial institutions would evolve together, toward stable points in which institutions and preferences fit together in a social-political equilibrium.

Many readers of this volume might prefer to see models of endogenously changing structures and deep preferences and co-evolving preferences and institutions. Me too! But one must walk (or stumble) before one can run. In that spirit, I turn to a more circumscribed but nonetheless rich model of judicial federalism.

Theories of Federal Courts

I have used the artful phrase judicial power without defining what I mean. By judicial power I mean the ability of a court system to formulate legal rules, modify them, use them to resolve a multitude of disputes, and make the resulting judgments stick. Many factors go into judicial power, including budgets, staffing, organizational structure, and autonomy in making procedural rules. But here I focus on jurisdiction, the formal ability to hear cases. Legal historian William Wiecek explains why jurisdiction must be the centerpiece in any account of judicial state building:

> To a court, jurisdiction is power: power to decide certain types of cases, power to hear the pleas and defenses of different groups of litigants, power to settle policy questions which affect the lives, liberty, or purses of men, corporations and governments. An increase in a court's jurisdiction allows that court to take on new powers, open its doors to new parties, and command the obedience of men formerly strangers to it its writ. Thus it is that in crabbed and obscure jurisdictional statutes a hundred years old we may trace out greats shifts of power, shifts that left the nation supreme over the states in 1876 and that gave the federal courts greater control over the policies of Congress than they had before the Civil War. (1969, 333)

There are two distinct analytic traditions concerning the jurisdiction of federal courts. The first, which might be associated with Felix Frankfurter's and William Landis's acknowledged masterpiece of twentieth-century legal scholarship, *The Business of the Supreme Court: A Study in the Federal Judicial System* (1927), emphasizes congressional warrants of jurisdiction. The second, which one might associate (somewhat symbolically) with Henry Hart and Herbert Wechsler's monumental work *The Federal Courts and the Federal System*, first published in 1953, emphasizes unilateral judicial action (Bator et al. 1988). In a fascinating recent article on judicial state building in the late nineteenth century, Howard Gillman clarifies and extends the Congress-centered approach (2002). In a sophisticated and ingenious paper, legal scholar Larry Kramer and political scientist John Ferejohn add a novel twist to both accounts, by emphasizing the way federal courts unilaterally restrict their own jurisdiction (2002).

The Congress-Centered Account

To focus on the essence of a Congress-centered account, I render it in a stark game theoretic fashion. The starting point for all that follows is the following observation: the default position in American federalism is that state governments and state judiciaries set their own policies, absent explicit federal authority and intervention. This essential fact about American federalism was the backdrop for struggles over the development of public infrastructure in the antebellum years, the fate of slavery and the civil rights of African Americans, the creation and regulation of national markets, and the construction of a powerful welfare state. To capture the notion of state policies, let the possible policy in a state be a point on the positive line—that is, in the interval $[0,\infty]$.

Figure 7.1 offers what I take to be a plausible formulation of the jurisdiction game implicit in Frankfurter's and Landis's book and somewhat more explicit in Gillman's recent analysis. First, Congress may pass legislation that extends federal judicial jurisdiction over a policy arena. If Congress does so, the Supreme Court sets a minimum floor policy F, a federal standard to be obeyed by the states.[6] For example, F might connote a basic level of procedural rights for recipients of welfare programs, a minimal level of rights for freed slaves,[7] a minimum degree of protection from state harassment for federal officials,[8] a minimal level of protection for creditors in bankruptcy cases,[9] a minimal degree of accessibility of public buildings for the handicapped, and so on. Each state is then free to set its own policy, but if the state policy does not lie at or above F (that is, in the interval $[F,\infty]$), the Court (following litigation) may reset the state's policy to F, possibly assessing a penalty against the state. If Congress does not extend jurisdiction to the federal courts, the states remain free to set whatever policy they wish, that is, they can set policy to any point in $[0,\infty]$ and the federal courts cannot intervene.

Figure 7.1   The Congress-Centered Account (Version 1)

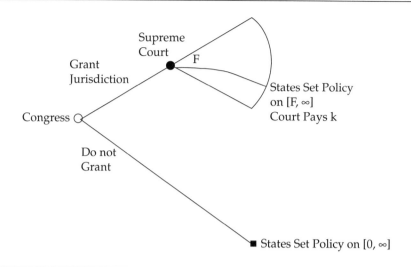

Source: Author's compilation.

In essence, the Congress-centered account is a delegation game: Congress creates authority and delegates it to the Supreme Court, which enforces it against the states (Bendor, Glazer, and Hammond 2001). To illustrate, consider Gillman's account (2002) of the Judiciary and Removal Act of 1875. This for the first time allowed the removal of cases with a significant federal question from state courts to federal courts. Critically, the act was passed by a lame duck Republican Congress facing the certainty of an incoming Democratic majority. In Gillman's view, which such prominent legal historians as Wiecek share, the economic nationalists of the Republican Party viewed the Republican-dominated federal judiciary as a reliable guarantor of property rights and laissez faire principles, especially in relation to state governments in the South, Midwest, and West. Hence, they conferred broad new jurisdiction on the federal judiciary, assuring acceptable enforcement of property rights in all the states, a level of enforcement the outgoing Republicans could not otherwise achieve. Of course, the incoming Democrats wished to repeal the act, and repeatedly tried to do so, but were continually hamstrung by divided party government. The Republicans of 1875 thus accomplished what the Federalists had tried but failed to do in 1801.[10]

In the Congress-centered account, Congressional lawmakers extend writs of authority to the federal courts when it serves the purposes of those who control the levers of power in Congress, and when the courts seem likely to be faithful agents. In this sense, the Congress-centered theory of federal judicial jurisdiction shares much with Congress-centered accounts of bureaucracy (McNollgast 1987, Epstein and O'Halloran 1999, Huber and Shipan 2002). Gillman goes a step further, identifying a majority political party as the key congressional actor. Thus, in his particular account, a dominant party shapes the jurisdiction of the federal judiciary so as to serve its partisan ends. But one need not be so heavily committed to a party-system view of American political history. Rather, the Congress-centered account is perfectly compatible with the view that representation in Congress is based on geography (Arnold 1979; Ferejohn 1974; Weingast, Shepsle, and Johnsen 1981). In this view, majority coalitions in Congress typically reflect shared economic and ideological interests across the states, rather than party per se. I will return to this point, because it affords an entrée for putting federalism back into the theory of federal courts.

Ferejohn and Kramer add an interesting twist to the Congress-centered account. They note that federal courts have been remarkably inventive in unilaterally restricting their jurisdiction. Hence, after Congress proffers jurisdiction to the federal courts, the Supreme Court may reject it (see figure 7.2).[11] But why should the high court limit its own power? In their account, the Supreme Court will do so to avoid bruising and potentially devastating confrontations with Congress. Of course, the Court could also do this simply by setting an innocuous federal standard—and if so, why limit jurisdiction? They provide an ingenious answer, which hinges on a collective action problem in the judicial hierarchy: lower court judges have an incentive to push warrants of authority into dangerous realms. In essence, lower court judges impose an externality on all federal judges should Congress respond to their provocations. But the Supreme Court faces the full impact of the many dangerous moves below, if Congress acts. Thus, the Court has an incentive to limit the rash actions of lower court judges by ruling dangerous policy arenas off-limits.

Obviously, this argument turns on the inability of the Supreme Court to police doctrine within the federal judiciary directly, a point that Ferejohn and Kramer (2002) do not establish.[12] In fact, it seems at odds with recent empirical scholarship, at least about the modern judicial hierarchy.[13] Moreover, there is a much simpler explanation, one that leaps irrepressibly from the pages of *The Business of the Supreme Court*: enforcement costs. As Frankfurter and Landis continually insist, every addition to the Court's jurisdiction brings a heavier workload. Every legal rule created under new jurisdiction burdens the courts with greater enforcement costs, especially when state governments resist assertions of federal authority.

Figure 7.2   Congress-Centered Account (Version 2)

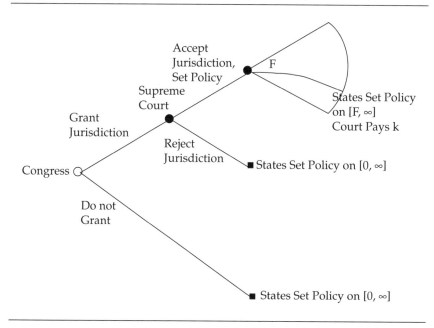

Source: Author's compilation.

Not surprisingly, the Supreme Court has created limitations on federal jurisdiction precisely to lighten a burdensome caseload. For example, Ferejohn and Kramer note,

> The advent of the regulatory state brought legislation creating countless new interests that had not been protected at common law, interests that invariably were shared by large numbers of people. At the same time, the Supreme Court recognized a myriad of new constitutional rights, also widely held, that likewise did not resemble traditional forms of liberty or property. These changes forced courts to address, in the words of one group of leading commentators, "who, if anyone, should be able to sue to ensure governmental compliance with statutory and constitutional provisions intended to protect broadly shared interests of large numbers of citizens." Taken for all they were worth, the new procedural and substantive regimes might have opened the doors of the courthouse to practically anyone unhappy with anything the government did. Instead, the Supreme Court circumscribed access to the judiciary by fabricating the doctrines of standing and ripeness. (2002, 1008–9)

Figure 7.3   The Court-Centered Account

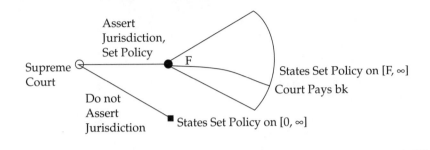

Source: Author's compilation.

Thus, in the context of the simple model of figure 2, imagine the Supreme Court faces a workload or enforcement cost k, associated with new warrants of jurisdiction and the declaration of new rights or national standards. To limit the adverse impact of enforcement costs, the Court might shrink its jurisdiction or (in the very stark version of the model I consider for clarity) eschew new jurisdiction all together.

The Court-Centered Account

The Court-centered account, in its baldest form, can be represented by the game in figure 7.3. Absent congressional action, the Supreme Court may simply assert jurisdiction and sets a federal standard F. It may also remain quiescent. In this case, F might be a minimal level of procedural rights for people in police custody, minimal rights for people incarcerated in state prisons, or a minimal absence of racial gerrymandering in electoral districts.

This rendering brings an obvious issue to the fore: what restrains the high court from assuming universal judicial authority and imposing all-encompassing federal standards on the states? Here, the standard accounts are silent. However, one answer involves raw power relations between the federal courts and the states' representatives in Congress. As Ferejohn and Kramer (2002) note, individual federal judges possess important protections, such as life tenure under good behavior; but the federal judiciary possesses relatively few. Thus, the judiciary is vulnerable if an assault on state sovereignty angers a majority in Congress.

In the area of jurisdiction, two examples of Congressional retaliation are often cited: the Reconstruction-era McCardle case involving military rule and habeas corpus, and the 1932 Norris-LaGuardia Act, which limits the ability of federal courts to use injunctions against labor unions.[14] The fact remains, though, that every other congressional effort to strip the Court of jurisdiction following a controversial ruling has failed. Of course, the paucity of jurisdiction-stripping legislation may simply reflect the skill of justices in avoiding controversy, not just the difficulty of enacting such legislation. And, as Ferejohn and Kramer (2002) note, by focusing on the most spectacular instances of court curbing, one misses more subtle expressions of congressional power, such as the limits on federal judicial discretion in sentencing.

Still, while conceding the very real possibility of congressional road rage, I explore an alternative explanation, one that is symmetric with the Congress-centered account sketched above: unilateral assertion of federal judicial authority over state policy inevitably levies an enforcement cost on the federal courts. Moreover, those costs are likely to be particularly onerous when the judiciary asserts jurisdiction unilaterally. When working in tandem with Congress, the federal courts generally share the enforcement burden with a federal regulatory agency, including the Justice Department. But when federal judges issue a judicial hunting license to themselves, they must bear the resulting workload and enforcement costs alone, or at least disproportionately. To capture these enhanced costs, replace k in the Congress-centered account with bk, where b is a parameter greater than one, capturing the workload and enforcement costs the federal judiciary must bear if it unilaterally asserts jurisdiction and sets a federal standard.

On this account, a principal brake on federal judicial activism is state resistance to federal encroachment, because greater resistance increases k and thus the enforcement burden bk borne by federal judges.[15] The prospect of massive resistance is apt to check the impulses of the Supreme Court, even on weighty matters, though, of course, not always. In much the same spirit, congressional restrictions on federal judicial capacity act as another brake on federal judicial activism. Examples include limiting the number of federal judges, and mandating procedures that make more difficult the efficient disposition of cases (for example, Congress required the Supreme Court to hear all appeals no matter how trivial, until well into the twentieth century). In the interests of simplicity and clarity, though, I will focus on judicial enforcement costs rather than congressionally imposed limits on judicial capacity.

A New Approach: The Jurisdiction Game

Figure 7.4 brings together both the Congress- and Court-centered accounts, in an obvious way. In the model, Congress may extend warrants of authority to the Supreme Court, which may accept or reject them. But

Figure 7.4 The Jurisdiction Game

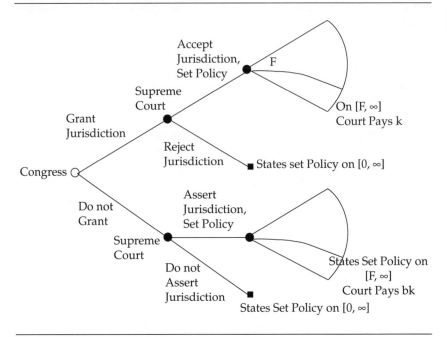

Source: Author's compilation.
Note: Prior to Congressional action, state voters elect congressmen.

if Congress does not act, the Court may assert authority unilaterally and announce a standard for the states. Following federal action, if any, the states set their policies and the federal courts pay an enforcement cost.

The jurisdiction game puts federalism back into the theory of federal courts in three ways. First, it departs from Gillman's assumption of a free-standing dominant party controlling Congress (2002). Instead, in the spirit of the new analytic literature on federalism (for example, Cremer and Palfrey 2002; Besley and Coate 2003), the model portrays each state as sending to Congress a delegate who faithfully pursues the interests of her constituents. In turn, the delegates (senators, as it were) decide whether to extend jurisdiction over an issue to the federal courts. Second, federal judicial policy directly affects the states, and hence the choices of the delegates (through anticipation). Finally, state resistance to federal judicial authority imposes costs on the federal courts. Thus, federal judicial action affects states; states interact directly with federal courts via resistance costs and indirectly through the actions of legislators in Congress, who anticipate judicial actions. The high court is both acted on by Congress, and acts itself to shape its jurisdiction.[16]

First, what do state voters, and thus their federal delegates in Congress, want? I assume the voters in each state have a preferred policy for their state. When the extant policy in the state deviates from this ideal policy, the state's voters suffer a loss. In addition, voters (and thus delegates) may care about policies in other states, because policies elsewhere impose burdens via externalities. The model emphasizes the burden imposed on voters in state 1 by policy in state 2, say, because state 1's residents believe state 2's policy is morally wrong, not just different from state 1's.

The logic of this situation drives delegates into three categories, given a minimum standard F that will be imposed by an empowered federal judiciary (see proposition 2 in the appendix). First are the nationalizers, who always favor extending jurisdiction to the federal courts. The critical fact about nationalizers is that their ideal policy is higher than that preferred by the Supreme Court. Thus, if the Court imposes its most preferred standard, the policy in the nationalizers' states will be unaffected because it is higher than the standard—but cross-state externalities from low policy states, who will be hit by the federal standard, will decline as the policies in those states ratchet upward.

Second are the states rightists. These delegates always oppose extending jurisdiction to the federal courts. States rightists have ideal points so low, relative to the Supreme Court, that a federal judicial standard not only hurts them directly; it does so indirectly by moving many other states away from their preferred position. Consequently, they oppose a national standard whether or not they care little about externalities—but sensitivity to externalities makes them oppose a federal judicial standard even more intensely.

Third are the moderates. These delegates have ideal points lower than the Supreme Court, but relatively close to it. They oppose a federal judicial standard, if they care only about policy in their state. But if they are sensitive to externalities from states with very low policies, they may nonetheless support federal jurisdiction, to bring the low-lying states in line with a policy they see as better, albeit imperfect.

What does Congress want? Because the state delegates constitute the Congress, their preferences, as aggregated through the rules, structures, and procedures of that organization, determine congressional policy action. In reality, committee jurisdictions, gate-keeping powers, minority filibusters, and presidential vetoes all play a role in aggregating the preferences of the delegates. But here, again in the interests of simplicity and clarity, I treat Congress as broadly majoritarian, so that the delegates determine congressional policy through pure majority rule. Thus, if the median member or delegate is, say, a states-rightist, Congress will favor a states rights policy. Obviously, the relative numbers of different types of delegates become critical for Congress's policy choice.[17]

What does the Supreme Court want? One assumes it has a most-preferred policy, and that it cares equally about policy in all the states. Given this straightforward assumption, the logic of the situation creates three varieties of federal courts (see proposition 1 in the appendix). The first is a retiring court, which will reject federal jurisdiction over a policy arena even if Congress offers it. (Of course, retiring courts never unilaterally assert jurisdiction). Retiring courts tend to prefer a low policy standard (so the benefits of a federal standard are low) or face massive resistance in the states if they accept jurisdiction. The second kind is a deferential court, which will accept jurisdiction if Congress proffers it but will not assert it unilaterally if Congress does not offer it. Such courts tend to favor higher standards and face substantial but bearable enforcement costs, but only if the Supreme Court works in tandem with federal regulators. The third kind is an activist court, which will assert jurisdiction even if Congress refuses to offer it. These courts stand to gain substantially from enforcing their preferred standard and face relatively low enforcement costs if they do.

Each of these judicial stances can be rationalized through a jurisprudential philosophy. Judicial reticence comports well with nullification, for example. More interestingly, deferential courts pursue the Progressive jurisprudence of a Frankfurter or Learned Hand, accepting a relatively activist role if, but only if, Congress requests it. Finally, activist courts can invoke the rights-oriented jurisprudence of a Warren, Fields, or Taney. From this perspective, jurisprudence is (arguably) endogenous to particular political configurations in the same way that administrative law doctrines appear to be (Shapiro 1988). But I will not pursue this point further here.

The three types of delegates (as median voter in Congress) intersect with the three kinds of high court to create outcomes (equilibria) in the jurisdiction game (detailed in proposition 4 in the appendix and in table 7.1). Activist courts always end up with jurisdiction; retiring courts never do; and deferential courts may or may not, depending on the lead of Congress.

The real payoff from the analysis comes in the comparative statics of the jurisdiction game. These involve both deep preferences and structure. As either change, they can impel the players from one equilibrium to another. Broadly speaking, the critical comparative statics will involve, first, changes in judicial preferences relative to state policies or in enforcement costs (state resistance) that move the Supreme Court across the spectrum from retiring, to deferential, to activist; and second, changes

Table 7.1   Equilibria in the Jurisdiction Game

	Activist Court	Deferential Court	Retiring Court
Nationalizer or pro-jurisdiction moderate Congress	Congress offers, Court accepts.	Congress offers, Court accepts	Congress does not offer, Court does not assert
States rightist or anti-jurisdiction moderate Congress	Congress does not offer, Court asserts	Congress does not offer, Court does not assert	Congress does not offer, Court does not assert

Source: Author's compilation.

in state preferences, changes in sensitivities to cross-state spillovers, or changes in the identity of the median voter in Congress, that move the median congress member from states rightist, to antijurisdiction moderate, to projurisdiction moderate, to nationalizer.

Playing the Jurisdiction Game: Congressional Delegation of Judicial Authority

As the discussion of the Removal Act of 1875 may have suggested, the delegation part of the story is often relatively straightforward. Here I will briefly illustrate it with brief vignettes from the antebellum period. In these cases, the jurisdiction game provides a framework for understanding how altered preferences or sensitivity to spillovers changed the politics of judicial state building.

In the years before the Civil War, the law of slavery was highly decentralized, allowing states considerable freedom in their own arrangements. In fact, this decentralized regime received special protection in the Constitution which, for example, prohibited Congress from banning the importation of slaves in the early years of the Republic. In the Deep South, of course, the law of slavery assumed ever more elaborate and savage forms. In the North, through statutes, constitutional provisions, and judicial precedents, nearly all states ended slavery. Many border states favored slavery, but with less fervor than in the Deep South.

State policy on rights for Negroes reveals that law in the North was antislavery, in the South proslavery, and in the border states (B) proslavery but less so than in the South (see figure 7.5). The Supreme Court was dominated by southerners, but the policy it would set (F) would proba-

Figure 7.5   Northern Abolitionists are Nationalizers in Terms of Rights
for Negroes, Southerners are States Rightists

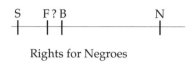

Source: Author's compilation.

bly be less pro-slavery than that prevailing in the southern states. In
these circumstances, most southerners in Congress were states rightists.
In the absence of much concern about slavery, moderates were generally
antifederal jurisdiction—their laws might not be touched by federal action and they were insensitive to the plight of slaves in the Deep South.
But notably abolitionists, who were acutely sensitive to the terrible situation of the slaves, were typically nationalizers. Federal courts represented
virtually the only way to alter laws in the South, and any intervention,
however tepid, would most likely be an improvement. Accordingly, abolitionist lawyers such as Salmon Chase exercised considerable ingenuity
trying to craft arguments in constitutional law that would support or
even require unilateral antislave action by the federal courts (Hyman
and Wiecek 1982). In fact, northern senators were typically staunch nationalizers (of course, economic concerns loomed large here). Not surprisingly, the Supreme Court remained unsympathetic to these arguments.

By about 1850, however, southerners began to see a problem with a
decentralized slave regime. Southerners traveling with their slaves
through northern states might find their "property" seized and declared
free. As interstate commerce and travel increased, the saliency of these
northern policies increased. Given the slavery-friendly leanings of the
Taney Court and the federal judiciary (Fehrenbacher 2001; Cover 1975),
many southerners began to reverse their adherence to states rights, instead advocating substantial expansion of federal judicial power over
state policy (Finkelman 1981).

Figure 7.6 illustrates how this remarkable preference reversal could
occur. The key is the policy dimension in question: protection of property rights in slaves. As shown, southern states had very high protection
for such property rights. Northern states had none. Northern disregard
for this kind of property right was of little concern to southerners so
long as North and South had little contact. But with the growth of cross-

Figure 7.6   Southerners are Nationalizers in Protecting Slave "Property"; Abolitionists become States Rightists

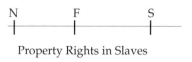

Source: Author's compilation.

state spillovers, federal jurisdiction began to appear attractive to southerners.

In September 1850, Millard Fillmore signed into law a new Fugitive Slave Act substantially expanding federal judicial power. Sensibilities in the North were rubbed raw as federal courts backed raids by slave catchers. Northern states enacted so-called liberty laws and state courts in the North resisted the slave-catchers. Southerners pushed for further expansions in federal authority—and northern senators (whose states in earlier years had been bastions of support for federal courts) began to echo the nullification doctrines espoused in South Carolina in the 1830s and encapsulated in the Virginia and Kentucky resolutions. Abolitionist Ohio Senator Benjamin Wade declared,

> I am no advocate for Nullification, but in the nature of things, according to the true interpretation of our institutions, a State, in the last resort, crowded to the wall by the General Government seeking by the strong arm of power to take away the rights of the State, is to judge of whether she shall stand on her reserved rights. (McDonald 2000, 175)

Later in the antebellum period Republicans tried to repeal Section 25 of the Judiciary Act, which gave the Supreme Court the power to apply judicial review to state legislation. This preference reversal by the abolitionists, and northern resistance to federal authority, is again easily understood in the context of figure 7.6.

In the years before the Civil War, southern courts adopted increasingly draconian slave policies. Some of the new rulings returned individuals freed during stays in northern states to slavery—which was, as might be expected, deeply offensive to northern sensibilities. Even worse, and almost incredibly, other rulings returned to slavery some individuals who had been voluntarily freed by their owners. By 1860, "the courts of the North and South had diverged to such an extent that a judicial secession had taken place" (Finkelman 1981, 183, and chap. 7 more generally). The political effect was to further inflame northern fears of a so-called Slave Power Conspiracy and engender even greater northern resistance to extensions of power to the slavery-friendly federal courts.

In the context of the jurisdiction game, the increasing extremity of the southern states suggested to northerners that the Supreme Court might move F (as shown in figure 6) to even higher levels. The northern response to this perceived threat was predictable.

Playing the Jurisdiction Game: Judicial Assertions of Authority

The unilateral action path has rarely been articulated as baldly as I have done, though implicitly it is a staple of textbook discussions of federal courts and constitutional law. Because of its novelty, I will illustrate this part of the jurisdiction game with a more extended look at the strange career of state sovereign immunity. I draw heavily on Orth's *The Judicial Power of the United States: The Eleventh Amendment in American History* (1987), which contains an exhaustive bibliographic essay on the subject, and his "The Interpretation of the Eleventh Amendment, 1798–1908" (1983).

In the early years of the republic, many states had reason to fear lawsuits by American Tories and British creditors whose property had been confiscated during the American Revolution. If these individuals could sue state governments and recover their property, the effect would be devastating for many who had loyally supported the revolution—and, no doubt, as their wrath sought a target, their representatives in state legislatures. It was with considerable interest, then, that state lawmakers followed the fate of the first important case heard by the fledgling Supreme Court, Chisholm v. Georgia (1793). In that case, Chisholm, a resident of South Carolina, sued the state of Georgia over a debt owed to an estate, of which he was the executor.

Chisholm invoked the original jurisdiction of the Supreme Court to hear "all cases . . . in which a state shall be party," so the case would be heard by the high court. Georgia, which denied that the Supreme Court had valid jurisdiction, declined to appear to defend itself. In lengthy opinions, the federalist dominated Supreme Court held that it properly had jurisdiction over the case. It also held that a state could indeed be sued in federal court by someone not a resident of the state. The intention behind the opinion was reasonably clear, and in some of the opinions (including that of Chief Justice John Jay) explicit: the Supreme Court would defend the rights of creditors, including foreigners, to facilitate the growth of "public credit" (in Hamilton's phrase). To do otherwise would lead to the exclusion of government from credit markets.

The case is easy to interpret in the framework of the jurisdiction game: the Supreme Court desired a very high degree of protection for creditors, declared that it had jurisdiction over the appropriate cases, and moved to impose a high standard on the states.

As predicted by the lone dissenter, Justice Iredell, the opinion unleashed a fire storm in the states and in Congress. Within three weeks, both houses of Congress had proposed the Eleventh Amendment. Within a year, twelve of the fifteen state governments—the necessary number— had ratified the amendment.[18] Even federalist strongholds like Massachusetts supported the amendment.

The Eleventh Amendment curtails the jurisdiction of federal courts in words that are anything but unclear: "The judicial power of the United States shall not be construed to extend to any suit in law or equity, commenced or prosecuted against one of the United States by citizens of another state, or by citizens or subjects of any foreign state." And from 1795 to 1823, the Supreme Court took the amendment on its face value. But in 1824, the Supreme Court under Chief Justice John Marshall found a new way to read the amendment.

Without a doubt Marshall, a staunch federalist, must have disliked the outcome of the Chisholm episode. In Osborn v. The Bank of the United States (1824) he devised a path around the plain meaning of the amendment. If someone sued an officer of the state, rather than the state itself, Marshall's court held, the Eleventh Amendment did not apply. In that case, federal courts could exercise jurisdiction and move policy in the correct direction.

An obvious question is, why did the Supreme Court again move to exert jurisdiction after the earlier rebuff? By 1824, the Revolutionary War debts were mostly a memory, no longer the third rail of American politics. In the years preceding Osborn, the Supreme Court had issued a series of rulings that, in essence, tested the waters without stirring up too much resistance.[19] By 1824, Marshall could interpret the Eleventh Amendment out of existence, assert federal jurisdiction over the relevant cases, and begin to impose tougher standards on the states. This remained the position of the Supreme Court for half a century, through the rest of the antebellum years, the Civil War, and Reconstruction. In fact, the Supreme Court affirmed and extended the Osborn doctrine as late as 1873 and 1876.[20]

The end of Reconstruction brought a new, and in many respects the most interesting, chapter in the history of state sovereign immunity. During Reconstruction, the governments in the southern states had issued debt at a furious rate. Southern bonds raised capital to fund public works, education programs, and social services for the freedmen—in other words, to create a new economy and a new society in the South.

Whether these plans could ever have worked remains a fascinating question. But, in the event, they failed in the face of terrorist resistance by whites in the South, corruption and incompetence by the new governments in the South, and waning northern enthusiasm for indefinite occupation of the South after the Panic of 1873. In short, the borrowed money was spent or stolen, the rebuilding failed, and one by one southern states were "redeemed" as the Democratic Party and former Confederates resumed power.

Needless to say, raising taxes and repaying debt issued by carpetbaggers for the benefit of ex-slaves had minimal appeal for the power brokers in the redeemed but impoverished South. (In fact, by late Reconstruction tax rates in many southern states were three to four times the pre-war levels). In state after state, reneging on the debts—repudiation—became a centerpiece of southern politics. The creditors holding the southern bonds were equally determined to get the money the states had solemnly pledged when they issued the debt contracts—and which the federal courts seemed obliged to enforce under the Osborn doctrine.

It is important to grasp what pro-creditor rulings by the federal courts implied: if southern legislators complied with the ruling, they would be obliged to pass laws raising taxes, actually gather the revenue from a hostile citizenry, and then positively disburse the funds to creditors. Shortly thereafter, the legislators would face the near-certain prospect of unemployment. On the other hand, if a state government refused to comply with a federal judicial order, what realistic prospect did a federal judge have of making the order stick? To do so would require raw federal force—marshals or troops, plus unending lawsuits and intense judicial supervision. After the election of 1876, raw force was exactly what the Hayes administration would never supply. Finally, if federal judges did not support the creditors, the bondholders would be left with worthless paper, because southern state courts would be extremely loathe to recognize their claims. (They could invoke sovereign immunity themselves.)

This situation is easily understood in terms of the jurisdiction game. First, the federal courts assert jurisdiction and enforce their preferred (pro-creditor) position against low policy states, at a time when state resistance is low (the Osborn case). Suddenly, however, state resistance to the federal standard skyrockets. Enforcement costs become huge. What are the courts to do?

The answer occurred in 1883 in Louisiana ex rel. Elliott v. Jumel, when the Supreme Court reluctantly concluded, contra Osborn, that the words of the Eleventh Amendment in fact mean what they seem to say. The Louisiana state government that had issued the debt in question had done practically everything possible to reassure creditors: amending the state constitution to require repayment, setting up an automatic tax to avoid annual appropriations, making diversion of those funds to any other purpose a felony, and depriving state judges of the power to enjoin the collection of the tax. But to no avail: the new state government refused to honor the debts. A creditor sued the state auditor, Jumel (as per Osborn), and petitioned the U.S. Supreme Court to issue a mandamus compelling the payment according to the original contract. The Court refused to issue the mandamus, declaring,

> The remedy sought, in order to be complete, would require the court to assume all the executive authority of the State, so far as it is related to the enforcement of this law, and to supervise the conduct of all persons charged with any official duty in respect to the levy, collection, and disbursement of the tax in question until the bonds, principal and interest, were paid in full. (107 U.S. 711, 727)

And this the Court refused to do.

A series of other rulings in the 1880s continued in this vein—with one telling exception. The Supreme Court ruled consistently against the state of Virginia and in favor of its creditors. The reason lay not in any special animus for the repudiators of the Old Dominion, or special affection for its creditors. Rather, the Reconstruction government of Virginia had hit upon a unique method for repaying bonds: Virginia bondholders could use the bonds in lieu of cash to pay state taxes. Given this state law, state bondholders themselves could enforce repayment in a radically decentralized way that required no ongoing federal judicial supervision. All the U.S. Supreme Court had to do to protect Virginia's creditors was to strike down new Virginia laws changing the repayment method! This it could do at little cost—and did do, over and over again.[21]

The final chapter in the story of state sovereign immunity may come as little surprise. Over time, passions over debt repudiation faded in the South, as bonds expired and creditors passed away. But the Supreme Court remained dominated by economic nationalists who strongly favored economic development and protection of corporations against populist or progressive state governments. Beginning about 1890 (in Hans v. Louisiana), the Supreme Court again found loopholes for escaping the reach of the Eleventh Amendment. After about 1894, the Court regularly enjoined state officers from taking actions adverse to interests of railroads. In essence, it reassumed the jurisdiction favored by John Marshall. To reach this end, several Supreme Court justices, such as Justice Bradley, adopted positions on state sovereign immunity at complete variance with those they had taken in the debt repudiation cases of the 1880s—a form of strategic behavior easily understood in terms of the jurisdiction game.

Conclusion

In federalist systems of government, expansions of national judicial authority inevitably come at the expense of states' legal and political autonomy. Consequently, the central political dynamic in federal judicial state-building is the struggle over national versus state power. Yet, existing theories of federal courts have been largely silent about this struggle. The object of this chapter has been to bring federalism back into the positive theory of federal courts.

The actual history of the jurisdiction, organization, and procedural operation of American federal courts is almost unbelievably convoluted. No single model can hope to explain everything about the law of federal courts, or even more than a small portion. Nonetheless, the virtue of the jurisdiction game—if it may be said to have any virtues—is to highlight the basic logic of the political choices facing judges, legislators, and voters as they wrestle with the allocation of judicial authority in a federalist system of government.

As I explained earlier, the approach taken in this chapter integrates institutions and preferences, but only to a degree. The model is arguably useful for exploring the *consequences* for federal judicial power of shifting moral passions (deep preferences), enforcement costs, and so on. At present, it says little about the origins of shifting passions and structure. Thus, in the cases I discussed, I emphasized the way structural changes— enforcement costs in the states or increased interstate commerce and travel—affected the politics of federal judicial power. I also emphasized the importance of shifting deep preferences, for example, over slavery. And, I acknowledged the importance of compelling ideas, for example, those that led nineteenth-century federal jurists to favor creditors over debtors whenever they could. But, given the focus of the model, I spent little time exploring (for example) the origins of abolitionism in nineteenth-century religious values; abolitionism's spread as a social movement; the intellectual roots of laissez-faire jurisprudence; or the diffusion of laissez-faire jurisprudence through the works of key treatise writers. This is not because these matters were unimportant for the history of judicial federalism in the United States—manifestly, they were important. A strength of the model is that it provides a framework for understanding how they could be.

The bare-bones jurisdiction game can be extended in many ways. For example, taking federal judicial enforcement costs out of the black box would surely be interesting. This would allow state citizens to play a more active role than simply as voters in congressional elections, and could illuminate the enforcement nexus between federal courts and federal administrative agencies (a hugely understudied subject, even in the area of electoral law). Extending the model to address federal judicial procedure and federal judicial organization, not just jurisdiction, could be quite interesting. As I mentioned, it might be very useful to better articulate the model of national lawmaking by incorporating more details about Congress and introducing a president with the veto power. From the perspective of preferences and situations, working harder to endogenize structure and deep preferences would be worthwhile. And, looming over the horizon is the fascinating prospect of co-evolving preferences and institutions.

Appendix: The Jurisdiction Game

The game form is that indicated in figure 7.4. The actors are voters in states, state delegates to Congress (for example, senators), and a Supreme Court. I seek sub-game perfect equilibria to the game. First, I recapitulate the assumptions in the text, impose some structure on preferences, and make some additional simplifying assumptions (some of which are quite strong).

The policy space in state i is $X_i = [0, \infty]$. The policy in place in state i is $x_i \in X_i$ and the most preferred policy for voters in state i is $t_i \in X_i$.[22] The utility function for the delegate from state i is:

$$-|t_i - x_i| - a_i \sum_{j \neq i} |t_i - x_j|$$

The coefficient $a_i \geq 0$ indicates the sensitivity of voters in i to cross-state spillovers or externalities from the policies in the other states. Note that this definition of externalities is essentially ideological or moral rather than economic: if all the states had the same policy, there could be still be cross-state externalities imposed on voters who believe the policy is wrong. (Think of slavery or abortion policy.) An alternative definition emphasizes what might be seen as economic externalities: $-|t_i - x_i| - a_i \sum_{j \neq i} |x_i - x_j|$. Here, externalities arise because other states have different policies, and this heterogeneity gives rise to transactions costs when voters from different states interact. (Think of railroad gauges or systems of weights and measures.) Both kinds of externalities are important, but here I focus on moral externalities.

The ideal policy for the Supreme Court is $t_j \in X$. Its utility function is $-\sum_i |t_j - x_i|$ if the Court has not assumed jurisdiction, $-\sum_i |t_j - x_i| - k$ if the Court has assumed jurisdiction after being offered it by Congress, and $-\sum_i |t_j - x_i| - bk$ if it has assumed it without being offered by Congress ($b > 1$). In other words, the Supreme Court cares about policy in all the states, equally.

The following lemma is obvious but useful:

Lemma 1   In the absence of federal jurisdiction, the voters in state i set policy to t_i. Given federal jurisdiction and standard F, voters in state i set policy to t_i if $F \le t_i$.

Proof. Follows from majority rule, and the non-binding nature of a minimum standard when voters prefer a higher one (Quod est demonstratum [QED]).

To avoid the complications and unnecessary distraction of modeling an enforcement game between the federal judiciary, the states, a federal regulatory agency, and litigants I employ the following costly compliance assumption: If the Supreme Court has set a standard F and $t_i < F$, policy in state i ultimately becomes F, but only after enforcement cost k is imposed on, or bk assumed by, the federal judiciary. This is relatively unobjectionable, but in the interest of simplicity I further assume k and bk are independent of F. This is clearly unrealistic and could not be maintained in most enforcement games. It is justified here only as a simplifying assumption that facilitates a focus on jurisdiction rather than judicial policy making per se.[23]

Given Lemma 1 and the costly compliance assumption, the following lemma follows immediately.

Lemma 2   If the Supreme Court accepts or asserts jurisdiction, it sets $F = t_j$.

Proof. F cannot lower the policy in high t states. It can only raise it in low t states, to F. Raising policy in a state above t_j imposes a loss on the Court. Hence, the best the Court can do is to set F to its ideal point, raising policy to t_j in all states whose policy would otherwise have been lower than t_j (QED).

I now consider the jurisdiction decision of the high court.

Proposition 1   If Congress has offered the Court jurisdiction, the Court will accept if and only if $k \le \sum_{t_i < t_j}(t_j - t_i)$. If Congress has not offered the Court jurisdiction, the Court will assert it if and only if $k \le \dfrac{1}{b}\sum_{t_i < t_j}(t_j - t_i)$.

Proof. If the Court has no jurisdiction, it receives $-\sum\limits_{t_i \leq t_j} (t_j - t_i) - \sum\limits_{t_i > t_j}(t_i - t_j)$ (using Lemma 1). If the Court accepts or asserts jurisdiction, the Supreme Court sets $F = t_j$ (Lemma 2), This yields utility $-\sum\limits_{t_i > t_j} (t_i - t_j) - k$ if jurisdiction has been offered and $-\sum\limits_{t_i > t_j} (t_i - t_j) - bk$ if not, a gain of $\sum\limits_{t_i \leq t_j} (t_j - t_i)$ at respective costs k and bk (QED).

For reticent courts, $\sum\limits_{t_i > t_j} (t_i - t_j) < k$, for deferential courts $k \leq \sum\limits_{t_i > t_j} (t_i - t_j) < bk$, and for activist courts $bk \leq \sum\limits_{t_i > t_j} (t_i - t_j)$ (QED).

I now consider the voting decisions of the state delegates in Congress. The following points about externalities are useful. Consider a distribution of state ideal points below t_j; call the lowest of these t_l and the highest t_h. If the Court assumes jurisdiction, it will move all these states' policy up to t_j. For any $t_i < \dfrac{t_l + t_j}{2}$, the resulting change in externalities must be adverse, since all other states below t_j will move to a point farther from i's ideal point than their initial position. And, for $t_i > \dfrac{t_h + t_j}{2}$, the resulting change in externalities must be favorable since all states below t_j will move closer. This argument establishes the existence of a type, between $\dfrac{t_l + t_j}{2}$ and $\dfrac{t_h + t_j}{2}$, for whom the resulting change in externalities is zero. For all higher types, the resulting change in externalities will be favorable, and for lower types adverse. (Note that this type might not be a member of the actual distribution of states.) Call this type $\hat{t}$.

Proposition 2 First, delegates whose ideal point is less than $\hat{t}$ always oppose federal jurisdiction. Second, delegates whose ideal point is greater than or equal to t_j always strictly favor federal jurisdiction, for any $a_i > 0$. Third, delegates whose ideal point is above $\hat{t}$ but below t_j favor or oppose jurisdiction, depending on the magnitude of a_i.

Proof. From the argument above, types below $\hat{t}$ suffer adverse externalities from federal jurisdiction. In addition, they suffer a direct policy loss from the change in policy in their state. Therefore, even if $a_i = 0$, these delegates oppose federal jurisdiction. Types at or above t_j escape the minimal standard; consequently, they suffer no direct policy loss. Since the ideal policy of these delegates lies above $\hat{t}$ (see above), they gain from the change in externalities. Hence, for any positive a_i, no matter how small, these delegates favor federal jurisdiction. Delegates whose ideal point lies above $\hat{t}$ but below t_j gain from the change in externalities but suffer a direct policy loss (that is, on balance states move closer to their ideal point than formerly, but the state's policy itself now diverges from its ideal). These states favor federal jurisdiction only if a_i is sufficiently large that the gain in externalities outweighs the direct policy loss (QED).

Part one of the proposition defines states rightists, part two defines nationalizers, and part three defines moderates. Let $\hat{a}$ be the critical level of sensitivity to externalities that pushes moderates to favor federal jurisdiction.

The following describes Congressional jurisdiction choice in which all state delegates behave sequentially rationally.

Proposition 3   If $k \leq \sum_{t_i < t_j} (t_j - t_i)$ and the median voter in Congress, one, has ideal policy greater than or equal to t_j and $a_i > 0$, or, two, has ideal policy greater than $\hat{t}$ and $a_i \geq \hat{a}$, Congress offers federal jurisdiction to the Supreme Court. Otherwise, it does not.

Proof. The proposition follows directly from Proposition 2 and standard voting theory. However, note the "vote no if indifferent assumption": Congress does not offer jurisdiction if it will be refused (in which case, the median voter who would otherwise favor jurisdiction will be indifferent about offering it), will not offer it if a majority of delegates oppose federal jurisdiction but the Court will unilaterally assert it (so a median voter who opposes jurisdiction loses nothing by offering it), does not offer if the ideal point of the median voter is greater than t_j but $a_i = 0$ (so the median voter neither gains nor loses from federal jurisdiction and is thus indifferent) (QED).

The following proposition, detailing equilibria, follows straightforwardly from combining Propositions 1 and 3.

Proposition 4   One, Congress offers jurisdiction and the Court accepts it when $k \leq \sum_{t_i < t_j} (t_j - t_i)$ and either conditions one or two in Proposition 3 hold. Second, Congress declines to offer jurisdiction and the Court unilaterally asserts it when $k \leq \dfrac{1}{b} \sum_{t_i < t_j} (t_j - t_i)$ and neither condition one nor two in Proposition 3 hold. Third, Congress declines to offer jurisdiction and the Court declines to assert it when $k > \sum_{t_i < t_j} (t_j - t_i)$, or when conditions one and two in Proposition 3 both fail and $k \leq \sum_{t_i < t_j} (t_i - t_j) < bk$ (QED).

I thank the participants in the Russell Sage Conference of April 12–13, 2002, especially John Ferejohn and the editors, for helpful comments on an early draft. I also thank Princeton's two marvelous Toms—Romer and Palfrey—for help with the analytics of federalism. Barry Friedman's insightful comments and voluminous but constructive criticisms sharpened the arguments in the paper, but not necessarily the way he wanted.

Notes

1. On the jurisdiction, structure, and capacity of the early federal courts, see Warren (1926), Frankfurter and Landis (1927), Surrency (1987), Holt (1989), and Goebel (1971).
2. On the Civil War and Reconstruction, see Hall (1975), Wiecek (1969), Kutler (1968), Hyman and Wiecek (1982), Frankfurter and Landis (1927), Fairman (1971), Avins (1966), and Friedman (2002).
3. I pass over functionalist accounts that invoke agent-free "historical inevitability" in one form or another. For examples, see Goebel (1971), Hall (1989), and Kagan et al. (1978).
4. They need not be. Readers who are interested in just how far one can push this formalism might consult Ashworth and Bueno de Mesquita (2005) and those references.
5. For a general discussion see Bowles (2004), and for a fascinating example involving the family as an institution see Fernandez, Fogli, and Olivetti (2002).
6. This formalism mirrors that in Cremer and Palfrey (2002).
7. For example, under the 1867 Habeas Corpus Act, which for the first time allowed federal courts to review the judgments of state courts, even those affirmed by state supreme courts, and apply habeas corpus. Many other Reconstruction statutes could be cited here, for example, the Civil Rights Acts of 1866 and 1871, and the 1871 Voting Rights Enforcement Act, among others.
8. For example, under the Habeas Corpus Acts of 1863 and 1866 and the Internal Revenue Act of 1866. These first two laws protected federal officials from suits for false imprisonment. They also voided all proceedings in state courts after a removal to a federal court, and made any person involved in such a void proceeding liable for damages and double costs. The latter act protected Treasury officials from hostile local courts. See Wiecek (1969, 338–39).
9. For example, under the Bankruptcy Act of 1867 and the Chandler Act of 1898.
10. In 1801, the outgoing Federalists not only passed the infamous Midnight Judges Act, but also reorganized the federal judiciary to make it more effective and gave it federal question jurisdiction, in the Judiciary Act of 1801. The first act of the incoming Republicans was repeal of the legislation (Ellis 1971).

11. A more nuanced rendering would allow the Supreme Court to restrict rather than reject jurisdiction. The reader should appreciate that this is my rendering of Ferejohn's and Kramer's argument; those scholars might view this game theoretic précis as a mischaracterization.

12. If the high court can police the lower courts effectively, then it need not restrict jurisdiction; it can just force policy to its most preferred alternative among those that will not provoke Congress. In the Ferejohn-Kramer account, the high court must limit federal jurisdiction to tie the hands of otherwise unreachable *lower* federal judges.

13. For an example, see Cameron, Segal, and Songer (2000), among others.

14. Epstein and Walker (1995) provide a game-theoretic analysis of McCardle.

15. A more finely articulated model would allow the states to set a resistance level k, and endogenously determine b through a federal-state enforcement game. But in the interest of maximum simplicity and clarity, I treat k and b as parametric.

16. In the appendix to this chapter, I impose enough structure on the jurisdiction game to allow an explicit solution.

17. One could elaborate a more finely articulated model with bicameralism, committees, filibusters, and vetoes. My reading of the history persuades me that doing so could cast additional light on federal judicial state-building. But I leave this to the future, as this paper's primary ambition is to put federalism (not, bicameralism, committees, filibusters, and vetoes) back into the theory of federal courts.

18. This response is exactly the kind discussed by Ferejohn and Kramer, and by Epstein and Walker (1995), which I have downplayed. The young Supreme Court had little experience with separation of powers games, which do sometimes have real bite.

19. These are detailed in Orth (1987, 34–40).

20. In Davis v. Gray (1873) and Board of Liquidation v. McComb (1876).

21. This is a very summary history of some extraordinarily intricate legal maneuvering. However, the details of the twists and turns, such as the special provisions in Supreme Court doctrine for creditors in the West and holders of county debt, confirm the picture of a court pursuing a pro-creditor policy when costs allowed, and compromising or retreating when state opposition was too formidable. See Orth (1987, chapters V-VII).

22. One may allow heterogeneous voters in each state, but this is just a distraction here.

23. If state compliance is simply assumed to be perfect (as in Cremer and Palfrey 2000), then it is hard to see why the judiciary would bear any costs k. But in that case, the federal judiciary would always assert jurisdiction, an uninteresting case. Hence, we require costly compliance, implying positive k.

References

Arnold, R. Douglas. 1979. *Congress and the Bureaucracy: A Theory of Influence.* New Haven, Conn.: Yale University Press.

Ashworth, Scott, and Ethan Bueno de Mesquita. 2005. "Monotone Comparative Statics in Models of Politics" Manuscript (January 18), Department of Politics, Princeton University.

Avins, Alfred. 1966. "The Civil Rights Act of 1875: Some Reflected Light on the Fourteenth Amendment and Public Accommodations." *Columbia Law Review* 66: 873–920.

Bator, Paul M., Daniel J. Meltzer, Paul J. Mishkin, and David L. Schapiro. 1988. *Hart and Wechsler's The Federal Courts and the Federal System,* 3rd ed. Westbury, N.Y.: The Foundation Press.

Bendor, Jonathan, Ami Glazer, and Tom Hammond. 2001. "Theories of Delegation," *Annual Review of Political Science* 4: 235–69.

Bensel, Richard. 2000. *The Political Economy of American Industrialization, 1877–1900.* New York: Cambridge University Press.

Besley, Tim, and Stephen Coate. 2003. "Centralized versus Decentralized Provisions of Local Public Goods: A Political Economy Approach." *Journal of Public Economics* 87(12): 2611–37.

Bowles, Samuel. 2004. *Microeconomics: Behavior, Institutions, and Evolution.* Princeton, N.J.: Russell Sage Foundation / Princeton University Press.

Cameron, Charles, Jeffrey Segal, and Donald Songer. 2000. "Strategic Auditing in a Political Hierarchy: An Informational Model of the Supreme Court's Certiorari Decisions." *American Political Science Review* 94(1): 101–16.

Cover, Robert M. 1975. *Justice Accused: Antislavery and the Judicial Process.* New Haven, Conn.: Yale University Press.

Cremer, Jacques, and Thomas R. Palfrey. 2002. "Federal Mandates by Popular Demand." *Journal of Political Economy* 108(5): 905–27.

Ellis, Richard E. 1971. *The Jeffersonian Crisis: Courts and Politics in the Young Republic.* New York: W. W. Norton.

Epstein, David, and Sharyn O'Halloran. 1999. *Delegating Powers: A Transactions Cost Politics Approach to Policy Making Under Separate Powers.* New York: Cambridge University Press.

Epstein, Lee, and Thomas G. Walker. 1995. "The Role of the Supreme Court in American Society: Playing the Reconstruction Game." In *Contemplating Courts,* edited by Lee Epstein. Washington, D.C.: CQ Press.

Fairman, Charles. 1971. *Reconstruction and Reunion, 1864–88, Part One.* Oliver Wendell Holmes Devise History, vol. 7. New York: Macmillan.

Fehrenbacher, Don E. 2001. *The Slaveholding Republic: An Account of the United States Government's Relations to Slavery,* edited by Ward M. McAfee. New York: Oxford University Press.

Ferejohn, John. 1974. *Pork Barrel Politics*. Stanford, Calif.: Stanford University Press.

Ferejohn, John, and Larry Kramer. 2002. "Independent Judges, Dependent Judiciary: Institutionalizing Judicial Restraint." *NYU Law Review* 77: 962–1039.

Fernandez, Raquel, Allessandra Fogli, and Claudia Olivetti. 2002. "Marrying Your Mom: Preference Transmission and Women's Labor and Education Choices." NBER Working Paper 9234. New York: National Bureau of Economic Research.

Finkelman, Paul. 1981. *An Imperfect Union: Slavery, Federalism, and Comity*. Chapel Hill: University of North Carolina Press.

Frankfurter, Felix, and James M. Landis. 1927. *The Business of the Supreme Court*. New York: Macmillan.

Friedman, Barry. 2002. "Reconstruction's Political Court." *Georgetown Law Journal* 91(1): 1–65.

Gillman, Howard. 2002. "How Political Parties Can Use the Courts to Advance Their Agendas: Federal Courts in the United States, 1875–1891." *American Political Science Review* 96(3): 511–24.

Goebel, Julius. 1971. *History of the Supreme Court of the United States: Antecedents and Beginnings to 1801*. Oliver Wendell Holmes Devise History, vol. 1. New York: Macmillan.

Hall, Kermit L. 1975. "The Civil War Era as a Crucible for Nationalizing the Lower Federal Courts." *Prologue* 7(3): 177–86.

———. 1989. *The Magic Mirror: The Law in American History*. New York: Oxford University Press.

Holt, Wythe. 1989. "'To Establish Justice': Politics, the Judiciary Act of 1789, and the Invention of the Federal Courts." *Duke Law Journal* 1989(6): 1421–1526.

Huber, John, and Charles Shipan. 2002. *Deliberate Discretion? Institutional Foundations of Bureaucratic Autonomy*. New York: Cambridge University Press.

Hyman, Harold, and William M. Wiecek. 1982. *Equal Justice Under Law: Constitutional Development 1835–1875*. New York: Harper and Row.

Kagan, Robert A., Bliss Cartwright, Lawrence M. Friedman, and Stanton Wheeler. 1978. "The Evolution of State Supreme Courts." *Michigan Law Review* 6: 961–1005.

Keyssar, Alexander. 2000. *The Right to Vote: The Contested History of Democracy in the United States*. New York: Basic Books.

Kutler, Stanley I. 1968. *Judicial Power and Reconstruction Politics*. Chicago: University of Chicago Press.

McDonald, Forrest. 2000. *States' Rights and the Union: Imperium in Imperio, 1776–1876*. Lawrence: University of Kansas Press.

McNollgast [Weingast, Barry R., Matthew McCubbins, and Roger Noll]. 1987. "Administrative Procedure as Instruments of Political Control." *Journal of Law, Economics, and Organization* 3: 243–77.

Orth, John V. 1983. "The Interpretation of the Eleventh Amendment, 1798–1908:

A Case Study of Judicial Power." *University of Illinois Law Review* 1983(2): 423–54.

———. 1987. *The Judicial Power of the United States: The Eleventh Amendment in American History.* New York: Oxford University Press.

Shapiro, Martin. 1988. *Who Guards the Guardians?* Athens: University of Georgia Press.

Smith, Rogers. 1997. *Civic Ideals: Conflicting Visions of Citizenship in U.S. History.* New Haven, Conn.: Yale University Press.

Surrency, Erwin C. 1987. *History of the Federal Courts.* Dobbs Ferry, N.Y.: Oceana Publications.

Warren, Charles. 1926. *The Supreme Court in United States History*, vol. 2, *1836–1918.* Boston: Little, Brown.

Weingast, Barry R., Kenneth A. Shepsle, and Christopher Johnsen. 1981. "The Political Economy of Benefits and Costs: A Neoclassical Approach to Distributive Politics." *Journal of Political Economy* 89: 642–64.

Wiecek, William M. 1969. "The Reconstruction of Federal Judicial Power, 1863–1875." *American Journal of Legal History* 13: 333–59.

PART III

Categories

8

Inducing Preferences Within Organizations: The Case of Unions

Margaret Levi

Why are some union members—to use Vladimir Lenin's (1902/1963) terminology—economistic but others commit time and resources to social justice causes that will benefit others as much, if not more, than themselves? Labor unions are important collective action organizations with which members form identifications and grounds for ethical reciprocity (Levi 1997) based on the establishment of a shared normative framework. Unions vary in terms of the preferences and beliefs they encourage or engender among members: business unions tend to induce economistic preferences and social movement unions class consciousness and ideological commitments to the welfare of workers more generally. This preliminary investigation of leadership and institutional differences across several labor organizations considers how governance, bargaining, and workplace institutions play a role in ordering and inducing membership preferences and the evolution of social commitments. The focus is particularly on institutions that facilitate member participation and those that make leaders accountable to members.

I compare the International Longshore and Warehouse Union[1] (ILWU) under Harry Bridges, to the International Brotherhood of Teamsters (IBT) under James R. Hoffa. The emphasis is on these leaders, but they are to be understood as emblematic of the dominant group and philosophy within their unions. I hope to develop an account that identifies key factors in explaining the majority preference of ILWU members for a member-led union and political activism. The ILWU and IBT of the 1930s through the early 1970s make for a particularly interesting comparison. Both emerged from the transport sector of the economy and had a long history of militant and effective strikes. Both redesigned themselves in the turbulent years of the 1930s. Both experienced ideological conflicts among those on the far left and those more committed to a conservative, business union model. Both had to deal with a multiplicity of employers rather than a single corporation. In both the members fit the portrait of "the traditional mainstay of trade unionism" (Richards 2001, 19): they were almost all white, male, and blue-collar, industrial labor. Moreover, over time both unions have come to incorporate workers who hold very different jobs and have different demographics.

Howard Kimeldorf (1988) undertook a somewhat similar analysis, comparing the radical and participatory ILWU and the corrupt, conservative, and repressive International Longshoremen's Association (ILA). He concludes that variations in the working class cultures of the West and East coasts (also see Johnson 2000; Nelson 1988), industrial structure, and organization of the employers explain the differences between the two unions. Structural and historical variables certainly can have a critical effect on the variation in union styles. I shall address them throughout and particularly in conclusion, when I consider alternative accounts to my own. My purpose here, however, is to demonstrate the importance of union governance and work-related institutions in establishing, cementing, and even reproducing a particular union style.

My argument represents an application of David Kreps's (1990) theory of corporate culture, that is, a set of principles that constitute the identity of the organization and establish the rules to guide the behavior of hierarchical superiors when they face unforeseen contingencies. For these principles to constitute the basis of an effective corporate culture, they must be communicated to all involved in the organization and their implementation observable post hoc. The organizational leaders establish their trustworthiness and reliability through reputational mechanisms built on these principles (also see Miller 1992). They sustain their reputation and that of the organization by upholding these principles even in circumstances when it might not be in their short-term interest and even when they are not "first best" or efficient (Kreps 1990, 127–28).

The Kreps model requires modification when applied to unions rather than to firms and even universities, Kreps's other example. Firms have employees and universities student-clients, who have joined an ongoing enterprise that they or their predecessors in those roles did not create and do not manage. Union members can also, of course, join an ongoing labor organization, and there is a hierarchical distinction between leaders and rank-and-file. Nonetheless, it is union members who create and recreate the union over time. The leaders are selected by the members rather than selecting their hierarchical subordinates, as is the case of students and employees. This means that the union culture depends in part on the continued support of the majority of rank-and-file and the transformation or exclusion of those who do not. To achieve support, leaders may recruit only those with like-minded principles. More often, and certainly in the instances of the IBT under Hoffa and the ILWU under Bridges, creating the corporate culture requires winning active approval of these principles from the members. The linkage between the leadership, the union's institutions, and its popular base varies, however, just as it does in the governance of democratic political parties and states (Levi 1997).

When the concept of corporate culture is transplanted from firms to unions, the principles that define the corporate culture become signaling devices about the kind of leaders the unions have, the kinds of behaviors expected of union members, and the stances the unions will take with employers and competitors. They are sustained not only by the benefits that flow from a reputation for upholding these principles but also by institutionalized and credible commitments. Kreps (1990, 128) notes that involvement in such a culture may change the preferences of the leaders and the members. I find some evidence suggesting that they do. The reasoning behind Kreps's claim is that continued employment in the firm requires a certain preference ordering, as revealed in behavior, which then may be internalized, if it was not already.

The preference set chosen is often in tension with alternative preference orderings not only among competing factions within the group but, often, within individuals. There is a well-known literature on this kind of problem. Both Schelling (1978) and Elster (1979), for example, have addressed the issue of conflicts between immediate satisfaction and long-term benefit. The resolution of the tension may require a commitment, which "drives a wedge between personal choice and personal welfare" (Sen 1977, 329).

There can also be a conflict between personal preferences and those that serve the common welfare. Sanchez-Cuenca (2005) offers a possible means to model this process. For him the problem is the tension between choices over particular objects and preferences over what the preference ordering itself should be. He labels this second preference over choices and argues that it involves conceptions of self, identity, and principle rather than the satisfaction of an immediate desire. Individuals have reasons or principles for their preference over choices, and sometimes we consider these principles normatively good or socially productive and sometimes not, as when zealots—even those raised in a religious tradition that values life—engage in murderous terrorism.

The conflict exists because there are several criteria of choice. The agent will have to integrate these several pressures into a final, consistent preference order, and she will choose according to it. Rational choice provides an impoverished view of the agent by focusing exclusively in this last state of the decision process, when the agent has arrived at a final preference order that overcomes the previous conflict. But there is nothing in rational choice theory that forces us to analyze only this last stage. The whole process can be examined. (Sanchez-Cuenca 2005) [Emphasis in original].

Preferences over choices can occur for any number of reasons. One explanation, explored here, is that a leadership, selected for its competence and then proving it in ways that significantly improve the lives of the members, has not only provided evidence of its type but also demonstrated the value of certain kinds of strategies that allowed the union to achieve its ends. Given the combination of its proven value and uncertainty associated with alternative leaders and alternative strategies, the proven leadership is retained. Moreover, the members then empower the leadership to establish a constitution, a set of institutional arrangements, and thus the beginnings of a corporate culture for the labor organization. This culture then reinforces or possibly creates a particular preference ordering among the large majority of the members. Members and leaders commit to follow the principles of the corporate culture because they prefer to have the preferences embodied in the culture or because the institutions precommit them to at least act as if they have those preferences if they are to survive and thrive within the union.

An effect is that some members go beyond rationalizing the preference ordering embodied in the institutionalization of the leader's preferences to actually holding those preferences themselves—if they did not before.

Organizational Culture in Unions

Corporate—or what I label organizational—cultures in unions are initiated and reinforced at critical moments in the history of the union when a leadership cohort emerges and proves its effectiveness by solving the critical strategic problems of recruiting members, managing and winning strikes, achieving recognition and the right to bargain collectively, and securing a first contract.[2] This is what constitutes leadership competence, which is then reinforced by continuing success in improving the economic and work conditions of the union membership. This leadership cadre is then empowered to write or revise the constitution of the union and to establish or reinforce institutions that will maintain the union's organizational culture. However, the organizational culture survives its founding leaders and membership cohort only to the extent that it builds institutions that reinforce and reproduce the culture.

A revised Kreps model (1990; also see Miller 1992) for unions yields four key elements for the survival of a organizational culture:

communication of a consistent set of principles by leaders to members

institutions that embody and enforce those principles

observable implementation of those principles by leaders, even when they appear to be against the short-term interests or preferences of the leaders

observable support for and enforcement of the principles by members themselves

Here we consider two distinct kinds of union organizational cultures, embodied in the ILWU on the one hand and the Teamsters on the other. The initial problem is to clarify what the defining principles are. There are a series of obvious distinctions between the two. The IBT formed alliances with racketeers, as did the ILA; the ILWU did not. The IBT practices a form of business or job unionism with an emphasis on wages, hours, working conditions, and benefits. The ILWU practices a form of social unionism, valuing jobs and benefits but reveling in its commitment to political and social activism. Teamster political action is national, involving lobbying on behalf of workers in the United States and perhaps Canada. The ILWU is international in both its concerns and its actions. It supports not only other nations' port workers, with whom its own job actions are intimately linked due to the nature of shipping (Levi and Olson 2000; Turnbull 2000), but also the struggles of workers worldwide. The IBT restricts membership participation in the elections of international officers and approval of contracts; the ILWU encourages full rank-and-file participation. But which of these factors, if any, are causal? That is, which define the organizational culture and thus help produce the other distinctive features of the unions, including the preference orderings of the members?

Both unions, indeed nearly all successful unions, uphold the principle of improving the economic welfare of their members, but differ in how they implement it. The Teamster leadership pledged to use whatever means were available, including organized crime, sweetheart deals with employers, corruption of governmental authorities, and strong-arm tactics against dissenting members as well as rival unionists. IBT leaders, and quite notably Hoffa, also insisted on top down and centralized government. Finally, they upheld and practiced a form of business unionism, narrowing their concerns to the material and job-based interests of their members.

The ILWU leadership likewise pledged to raise the standard of living of its members, but its principles permitted only the means consistent with social responsibility to membership and its sense of class warfare. Thus there were to be no sweetheart deals with organized crime or employers. Three other principles have also been central to the ILWU identity: a strong emphasis on member-led policy making, a commitment to economic and racial egalitarianism within the union, and a form of internationalism that requires not only support of workers worldwide but also the use of union power to influence American policy in international conflicts.

Having a preference for improving one's welfare, which both kinds of unions emphasize, is not problematic theoretically. Lenin (1902/1963) long ago argued that economism captured the natural preferences of workers; only leadership and education would induce them to seek a wider class conflict. Nor has he been alone in that assessment. Indeed, many analysts of unions and of human behavior more generally would agree with Mancur Olson (1965) that, at least for analytic purposes, it is sensible to assume that most individuals will act on the basis of their calculation of material benefits (in which Olson includes social pressure), not their ideological goals. From this perspective, the existence of business unions is the expectation, but unexplained is the variation among business unions in terms of their forms of governance, their tolerance of racketeering, their militance, their racism, and the like. Lenin emphasized the importance of persuasive leadership and educative techniques for building a class rather than narrow workplace consciousness. My account suggests institutions are also required to sustain the kinds of commitments to egalitarianism, social justice, and participatory democracy that the ILWU organizational culture demands.

There are important examples of social unions, as in South Africa and Brazil (Seidman 1994), that have proved essential for bringing about fundamental change in their countries. Even in the advanced industrial democracies, there are exemplars of social unionism. In some cases, illustrated by the Wobblies, the Industrial Workers of the World, their demise is due to government repression and continued employer resistance; they were simply too radical and militant to tolerate. Many of the unions in Britain began with a socialist platform—although few currently retain such commitments. In the United States, social unions tend to be fewer proportionally among the population of unions than are the business unions, but their impact can still be significant for effective bargaining and democratic governance (Stepan-Norris and Zeitlin 1991, 1995, 1996, 2002). Understanding the conditions under which they can survive provides a window into understanding the conditions supportive of contentious politics, participatory democracy, and other situations in which ethical concerns assume a high place in the preference ordering of the citizens of organizations and states.

Selecting the Union's Leader

The organizational culture of a union emerges from the interactions of the union's leadership and its rank-and-file membership. The culture is generally the one the leader prefers and then institutionalizes, but it is the members who select the leaders. On what grounds do they make that selection?

Rank-and-file members have to make assessments prospectively about leadership trustworthiness.[3] There are two hypothesized aspects of this evaluation: beliefs about leadership competence and beliefs about leadership stances on other dimensions members may value—for example, honesty, social commitments, and race. Let us assume that competence is a valence issue and that the others are position issues.[4] At first glance this translates into choosing a leader based on a relatively simple preference order:

1. Competent and shared position

2. Competent and opposite position

3. Incompetent and shared position

4. Incompetent and opposite position

All else being the same, union members prefer a union leader who is competent and shares their positions. Payoffs to hiring (or electing) and firing (or voting out of office) follow from this. However, the decisions that interest us are taking place at critical moments in the history of the union. During these periods, competence outweighs all other considerations. Members select the leadership who prove their trustworthiness by solving the central strategic problems confronting the union. To repeat, these are organizing the members, running a successful strike, winning collective bargaining rights, and bargaining a contract that significantly improves the members' welfare.

This can be modeled as separating and pooling equilibria.[5] For illustrative purposes, let us specify the leader's position as honest versus corrupt. The rank and file uses behavioral evidence to separate the competent from the incompetent and the corrupt from the uncorrupt. At time T^0 the principal, defined here as the median union member, has to choose an agent, defined here as a union leader. The members prefer a competent leader who will deliver good collective bargaining contracts and successfully organize strikes (if need be) to an incompetent agent. At the point of selection, the members make an assessment but lack certainty as to the leader's type. There is some probability α that the leader is incompetent.

At time T^1 the leader has to deliver a benefit to the members. It is then the leader must decide whether to engage in corrupt practices and make money or not. There are two kinds of rents of corruption assumed in this model. The first, earned by an incompetent leader, are personal, benefiting only him. The second increases the pie to the members; the leader benefits by proving his worth to the union and, perhaps, by an additional kickback. This often means involving a third party, such as the Mafia, which derives a rent from the employer, who is compelled to provide more to the union members.

Although the members can observe whether the leader was competent in the past, they are not sure whether he (or she) is or will be competent in the future. However, they may be able to observe whether the leader is involved in corruption and whether it serves their interests as well as his. Thus, at T^3, the principal decides whether to entrust the agent or to fire him and select a new agent.

The implication of this discussion is that, particularly at critical moments, members will do all they can to ensure that they have competent leadership. However, it does not preclude the possibility that the positions the leader takes may affect assessments of competence. For example, linkage with organized crime may enhance the leader's capacity to achieve employer compliance. Alternatively, a commitment to egalitarianism may increase the solidarity and militance of the union.

The Cases

The history of American trucker and longshore labor organizations is a history of competing factions, which vary in both competence and views about the role of unions and the connections of leaders with political parties, economic interests, and the like. Issues of racketeering and corruption have influenced elections in both unions (Kimeldorf 1988; Stier 2002). Important reformist elements and radical groups have challenged the leadership of the IBT, and conservative groups have exercised political muscle within the ILWU, which is itself a break-away organization from the parent ILA.

Positions may have been salient[6] in some elections, but the reputation for competence appears to have dominated the initial selection of James

R. Hoffa as president of the IBT, from 1957 to 1971, and of Harry Bridges as president of the ILWU, from 1937 to 1977. Hoffa and Bridges were extremely competent in managing strikes and in bargaining good contracts for their members. Both used strikes to disrupt the normal chain of the delivery of goods. Trucks, particularly those engaged in long haul, can disrupt national trade, and the inhibition of ships being loaded, unloaded, or refitted seriously impairs international as well as national trade. Both had proven track records in effective organizing, strike management, and collective bargaining.

As a young warehouseman in the early 1930s, Hoffa had been innovative in his use of strikes and effective as an organizer. He learned from Farrell Dobbs, business agent of the Trotskyite Minneapolis local, and a leader of the 1934 Minneapolis "teamster rebellion" (Dobbs 1972) major new techniques in organizing long haul truckers and warehousemen (Moldea 1978, 28–30; Russell 2001, 33–47; Sloane 1991, 18–22). Hoffa used these techniques to great advantage, first in Detroit and then nationally. In 1964, as president of the IBT, he negotiated the first national contract with the trucking companies.

Hoffa allied himself with organized crime, which helped him get good contracts for the men. Hoffa did not, however, ensure that all the rents of corruption went to his members; he did get a kickback. Nonetheless, his men believed—and most probably it is true—that they did better with than without Hoffa's pact between organized labor and organized crime. Hoffa's strategy was a successful application of a strategy developed by others. Instead of spending his time organizing potential members, he devoted most of his effort to organizing the industries themselves (Russell 2001; Sloane 1991). He did this by refusing to deliver or pick up from businesses that refused to sign union contracts, and he also used threats and protection rackets backed up by the Teamster's own thugs as well as the mafia's.

Bridges was instrumental in running one of the major events in U.S. labor history, the 1934 strike along the entire West Coast waterfront, which won recognition for the coastwide union and, as a result of a federal arbitration decision, a hiring hall jointly run by the union and the employers. He held important offices in his local and on the bargaining team that won the 1934 strike before breaking from the International Longshoremen's Association in 1937, helping to found the ILWU, and becoming its first and long-serving president. In 1960, Bridges negotiated the Modernization and Mechanization Agreement, which eased the introduction of containerization in the ports while ensuring extraordinary compensation for the rank-and-file workers who would ultimately be displaced. Bridges was untouched by even the smallest whiff of corruption. His competence was based on the enduring solidarity of the longshore workers and their strategy of retaining control over the workplace and the waterfront jobs.

Hoffa and Bridges had each established their competence and their commitment to the union cause. Moreover, they continued to demonstrate considerable capacity to deliver good collective bargaining agreements in terms of wages, working conditions, and hours. Their members flourished materially during both regimes. Both were chosen for and continued to demonstrate their competence; constituents could estimate with a high probability that each would prove competent in the future. The members of the IBT even knew with some certainty that Hoffa was corrupt, given highly publicized charges and evidence. The members of Bridges's union knew with some certainty that he was not. What made them acceptable was less whether they were honest or corrupt but whether they were competent. Their competence, that is the capacity to deliver the goods, was the basis of member perception of their trustworthiness and reliability.

The unions, however, were quite different. Both inherited and confirmed distinct rules of governance and styles of leadership. The members of both the IBT and the ILWU kept these highly competent leaders in office, but the mechanisms of selection were quite different. So were the positions the leaders held on a range of social and political questions. These unions came to embody two very different organizational cultures. Creating and even sustaining the organizational culture depended on the demonstrated competence of the leadership faction that advocated the principles of the culture. Competence is a necessary but not sufficient condition to maintain an organizational culture; maintenance also depends on the establishment of institutions that members continue to support.

Selecting and Sustaining the Union's Organizational Culture

There may well be cases of union leaders who are simply clean and competent—or not. However, the more interesting cases are those, such as Hoffa and Bridges, where the voters must determine what they value in addition to confidence about the delivery of a good contract. What price are the members willing to pay and for what kinds of return? By the standard economic account, all that matters are the material costs and benefits. However, ethical concerns might also enter the calculus, at least if the material losses are not too high (Levi 1997; Stoker 1992). Moreover, individuals may form preferences over choices that they then institutionalize through an organizational culture, composed of principles, rules of governance and other devices. This, I claim, is what both the IBT and the ILWU did.

Hoffa ran a business union. In principle, his concerns were limited to issues directly related to the hours, wages, working conditions, benefits, and job security of his members. Although the IBT did get involved in lobbying—its headquarters is a huge "labor temple" near Congress—its focus was on what aided those who paid their dues to the union; this often required advocacy of protectionist and military interventionist policies. Bridges, in contrast, advocated social unionism. He cared about the working class and the poor as a whole and not only his own particular members. Although he worked hard on job-related matters, he also involved his members in political and social issues far removed from their daily lives. His commitments to internationalism and racial justice were legendary and deep.

Of course, these descriptions are far too pat. Hoffa became very involved in the anticommunist campaigns, within the labor movement and worldwide. Bridges may have facilitated the political activism of his members, but the ILWU is not a socialist union in any meaningful sense (Wellman 1995, 10). Nor does either union possess an uncontested organizational culture. Both possess serious dissident factions and always have.

In general, however, the IBT members acquired a leadership that asked them only to act in their material interest, but they had to be willing to accept top-down governance and corrupt officials. For many, the material return was evidently worth the material cost, and any puzzle disappears according to the standard account of the economistic actor. For others, the costs of defection were too great, given the strong-arm tactics of the union, and—by the same reasoning—the puzzle again disappears. Nonetheless, as in any population, there was wide variation among the IBT members concerning the acceptability of corruption as well as on political and social issues.

The members of the ILWU got good contracts, but they were also subject to a steady stream of exhortations to act altruistically on behalf of others. At the extreme, they were being pushed to transform their preferences to value the welfare of others as highly—or almost as highly—as their own. Why would they agree to that? Many unions are initially militant and participatory, and members may exhibit a high degree of identification with the union, "which is likely to take precedence over the many other conflicting interests and activities that compete for a worker's free time" (Seidman 1953, 221–22). The puzzle here is why and how the ILWU sustained that kind of identification, especially among those who were neither confirmed communists nor syndicalists. Because this for many is the more perplexing puzzle, the following narratives provide more detail on the ILWU than the IBT.[7]

Hoffa and the IBT

The fundamental principles of the organizational culture Hoffa helped establish for the Teamsters had three facets: improving the economic well-being and working conditions of the members, protecting and building the union, and doing this with a hierarchical structure. These justified his relationship with the Mafia and made him dismiss rank-and-file democratic participation within the union or political activism by the union as obstructionist or irrelevant.

Hoffa did not create the organizational culture of the Teamsters, but he was the key player in institutionalizing it against the threats of a competing vision that Farrell Dobbs of Minneapolis represented. The secession of the Minneapolis local from the IBT and its alignment with the CIO made it an alternative organization to which other dissident Teamsters could turn. Hoffa, as henchman of then IBT President Daniel J. Tobin, masterminded and ran the campaign to ensure that Dobbs and the other Minneapolis radicals did not pose a continuing challenge to the Teamster culture (Russell 2001, 79–82; Sloane 1991, 28–31). The literal battle in the streets of Minneapolis was joined by the federal government, to whom Tobin had appealed. Key members of the Minneapolis leadership, including Dobbs, were indicted under the Smith Act, convicted, and jailed.

With the victory over the left secured, Tobin and his successors, Dave Beck and Jimmy Hoffa, reasserted their preferred organizational culture, and the majority of the members came to support it. Its principles included strong top-down leadership, business unionism, and doing anything necessary to improve the welfare of the workers and protect the union from raiders. Moreover, these principles were clearly communicated to members through both the speeches and the actions of the leadership. For example, unlike Bridges, Hoffa discouraged the union from engaging in actions, economic or political, not specifically related to conditions of employment (although he did, as did so many other union leaders of the time, try to rid the ranks of communists). He made clear his respect for the effectiveness of a Dobbs and of a Bridges but also expressed incomprehension about their political ideologies and their eagerness to involve their members in issues not directly related to the members' own wages, working conditions, and hours.

The rules for making decisions about officers and about contracts supported this culture. The IBT followed a fairly general practice within the labor movement. Elections for major office and approval of contracts were by roll call votes of the representatives to the convention and not the rank and file. Bargaining was done by a relatively small committee tightly controlled by the leadership. The leadership was granted wide discretion to act as it saw fit.

Hoffa observably implemented these principles. He was a strong and tough leader, effectively expanding the union and improving the lot of the Teamsters and the other workers brought into the union. He got things done, and he exuded confidence. He also was very accessible to his members. His door was open, and his telephone number available. He gave favors and aid often and easily. He agreed to lead the campaign to discredit and destroy his friend and mentor Farrell Dobbs even when it was against his personal preference—albeit arguably in his long-term interest. His role confirmed Hoffa's reputation as someone committed to upholding the union's organizational culture. That Jimmy Hoffa worked closely with organized crime when necessary also signaled his commitment—and the Teamster commitment more generally—to do whatever it took to improve the lot of the working man. He engaged in actions that incurred great personal costs if it served the interests of his members; his celebrated conflict with Robert Kennedy is illustrative.

Of course, while Hoffa was ensuring that his membership benefited from the relationship with organized crime, he did as well. He was convicted in 1964 of jury tampering and of fraud in handling of union benefits; in 1967 he began serving a thirteen-year prison sentence, which President Richard Nixon commuted in 1971 under the proviso that he not be active in the union until 1980.

Why would members prefer a leader who acted in such ways? They demonstrably did. In 1961, despite mounting government revelations about him, Hoffa insisted that the union abide strictly by the Landrum-Griffin election requirements and handily won a very clean election—and was voted a tremendous raise (Russell 2001, 215). Despite his conviction for raiding their pension funds, the membership allowed Hoffa to retain his union presidency until 1971, when the provisions of the commutation required him to give it up. A. H. Raskin, who covered labor organizations for the *New York Times* and a regular Hoffa critic, conducted an unscientific survey of the membership in 1971 and found that Hoffa, who was in prison at the time, was regarded as a hero and martyr (Russell 2001, 223–24). One quote seems to sum up the preference ordering: "For what he did for the driver, I'd take a chance on him again. If he robbed a little, what the hell" (Russell 2001, 224). His legal trials and convictions, especially those that Kennedy provoked, were interpreted by many as a consequence of Hoffa's successes in bargaining and in challenging the power of employers and government (Russell 2001; Sloane 1991; Stier 2002, 146–47).

In return for what he delivered, Hoffa required from his members their militance as needed and their loyalty. There is little question that Hoffa, as well as other Teamster leaders, enforced the organizational culture with strong-arm tactics. Nonetheless, the reelections of Hoffa, the homage still associated with the Hoffa name (and skillfully employed by his son in his successful election campaign), and the persistence of the kind of philosophy of unionism that Hoffa embodied are indicators of the extent to which members supported and continue to support the union organizational culture Hoffa helped develop and sustain. Jimmy Hoffa and his coterie would do all that was necessary to provide good contracts and to keep the Teamsters a strong, independent union, wealthy in numbers and money. In return, members reelected them and seem to have accepted their way of doing things.

Bridges and the ILWU

ILWU International President Harry Bridges, Secretary-Treasurer Louis Goldblatt, and others in the leadership cadre institutionalized a very different kind of organizational culture. Their principles were equally clear and consistent. The ILWU was to be rank-and-file driven, egalitarian, and internationalist. This meant that membership voice on contract terms and policy issues were determinative, even when union leadership disagreed. It also required the commitment to ensuring that union members had relatively equal pay, hours, and voice. It demanded racial justice. The culture also implied recognition of a labor movement and worker interests beyond the shores of the United States, not only among other dock workers but in the whole range of occupations, and promoted the use of union power to influence American foreign policy.

Bridges and others in the leadership communicated the principles of this organizational culture through speeches, discussions in union conventions and meetings, and columns in the *Dispatcher*, the union paper. They built on existing union institutions and created additional ones to enforce these principles. The governance structure, the hiring hall and the rules regulating dispatch, the coastwide bargaining process, and the constitutional provisions for racial equity were the basis of the union's organizational culture.

Governance

Even before the ILWU came into existence in 1937 with the split of most of the West Coast locals from the ILA, the Pacific Coast District was distinctive in its radicalism and democracy (Kimeldorf 1988; Nelson 1988). The ILWU's constitution only slightly modified the District's.[8]

Bridges and his membership continued the tradition of highly autonomous locals with relatively few officers. Some locals restrict officers to two consecutive terms. There is no term limit for international officers, but an age rule was eventually introduced, in part as a response to Bridges's continual reelection. By 1938 recall of the international officers was reformed so that only 15 percent of the membership was sufficient to initiate a recall, at least as long as they were spread through several locals. All officers, national and local, are elected by the entire membership, and within a very short time period the process was refined to ensure secret and secure ballots. In addition, there were regular, generally biennial conventions. Representatives of locals attended, and there was often fierce debate about important questions of governance, union policy, and more general politics.

Another important institution of ILWU governance is the coastwide[9] caucus, which further ensures member-driven decisions and relatively equal influence across the locals. Regular meetings of the caucus and the importance of its concerns helps reproduce union solidarity, at least within the longshore division it serves. The caucus is instrumental in unifying workers who perform diverse tasks, work in different ports, and possess distinctive backgrounds. It is also the body that formulates bargaining demands through a complex process beginning with locals and eventually ending up coastwise. The bargaining is then done by a team, which is selected from among a larger set of representatives of all the relevant locals and is required to report back regularly to the caucus.

The president and other international officers are accountable to the caucus, which therefore exercises significant constraint on leadership discretionary action. The ILWU further ensures that its officers' interests are aligned with those of members by limiting international officer pay, which constitutionally cannot exceed a small increment above the highest paid member of the union (and still cannot). The ease of recall provides further reinforcement of the union's principles and accountability.

The Hiring Hall and the Rules of Dispatch

Perhaps the most important ILWU institution is the hiring hall. It evolved with the ILWU's efforts to regularize work on the waterfront. Labor had been totally casual, meaning that all work was temporary and, often, very short term (Turnbull 2000). Compounding the ills of casualization, when work was found it most frequently required workers to work consecutive eight-hour shifts, until the ship was loaded or unloaded. In fact, the representatives of the bosses would hire people on a daily basis in something called a shape-up, in which all who were interested would gather around the hiring agent, who would then pick favorites or accept bribes in return for a job. The agent would regularly refuse employment to union sympathizers. On the job, the slightest offense could result in firing or blackballing from future jobs.

Through strikes and negotiation, Bridges facilitated the creation of a hiring hall, which the unions ran for the employers and which the employers funded; it effectively controlled the production process at the point of production. Perhaps its most important function was reproducing relative equality of pay and work by regulating the access to the number of hours worked through a complicated but equitable dispatch system.[10] Given the high unemployment caused by the Great Depression, the Bridges leadership group also urged the elimination of the so-called steady man, someone who held a permanent position, and for a rotation that ensured that all union members would get work and earn relatively equal amounts. The goal here was to match the practice of political democracy with the outcome of economic democracy. The ILWU membership voted in favor of this plan and has largely maintained it since—despite continuing pressure for change.

The hiring halls also have important socializing functions. These are heated rooms where the workers gather and where work is assigned by criteria established by the union. Not only does the hiring hall put job assignment in the hands of the workers, it also creates a location where the rank-and-file meet regularly. It sets up a locus for discussions of union business and for political education. There are always newspapers, books, and information available and flowing. The hiring hall is critical to introducing new workers to the ways of the ILWU.

Observable Leadership Implementation of the Principles

Bridges signaled strong moral commitments to a progressive agenda that included economic and racial equality, for those outside as well as inside his union. He was a self-proclaimed socialist. There is no question about his extraordinary honesty and competence, but he did not find it sufficient to attend only to the hours, wages, and working conditions of his membership. He attempted to ensure his members got the best possible contract for the time, but also urged them to become citizens in a wider labor and social movement, to expend efforts on behalf of others not integral to their union or its important allies. His internationalism, remarkable among American union leaders, became—over time—a defining feature of the union.

Bridges often sacrificed his short-term interests to demonstrate his commitments to the principles of the ILWU organizational culture. He was jailed—albeit for shorter terms and distinct offenses from Hoffa's.

His criminal trials mostly arose from his affiliation with the Communist Party, alleged and unproved in Bridges's case. Bridges, Australian by birth, was the subject of repeated efforts by the U.S. government to deport him and imprison him for offenses related to alleged membership in the Communist Party of the United States. Three of the cases went all the way to the U.S. Supreme Court before being dismissed for lack of credible evidence.

At the governance level, he was assiduous in his efforts to halt discriminatory behavior in the locals towards workers of color, even when this created problems for him with important locals in San Pedro and Portland (Kimeldorf 1988, 144–48; see also Nelson 2001). Moreover, the ILWU, under Bridges's leadership, aggressively organized workers of color, most notably in the Hawaii plantations and warehouses.

Bridges also upheld the principle of a member led union even when it was against his personal preference. A research team at the University of Washington is documenting instances of this at the convention.[11] The most telling is his management of the 124-day strike in 1971. He had argued against the strike but lost. He led it, as was his job, and his predictions proved true about having a worse contract after the strike than what had been offered before. He had upheld the principles of the organizational culture of the ILWU even when he felt the result was inefficient, costly, and mistaken.

Membership Support

Harry Bridges served as president of the ILWU for forty years, from 1937 to 1977. This in itself is evidence of membership support, particularly given the high level of electoral turnout and the existence of factions within the organization. Recent presidents have served single or double terms at most.

Other evidence of member support and enforcement of these principles is revealed in member actions, sometimes at their own initiative and sometimes in response to the initiatives of the titled officers. They fought hard to retain the hiring hall, coast wide bargaining, and work rotation in the face of strong employer attack; both longshore defense of these institutions and employer attack continue to this day. Their electoral turnout and participation at meetings was high. It is lower now but fluctuates with the competitiveness of the election and other factors that intensify member interest.[12]

They not only demonstrated commitment to and enforcement of the principles that protected their prerogatives at the workplace and in the union, they also engaged in actions in support of social justice and internationalist causes. The ILWU closed down the ports to prevent scrap iron being shipped to Japan in the days before Pearl Harbor out of suspicion that Japan would soon be the enemy, suffering loss of salary and threat of jail time for doing so. They have refused to ship grapes in support of the farm workers' boycott and refused to unload South African vessels to protest apartheid. They closed West Coast ports on November 30, 1999 in protest of the WTO meetings now memorialized as the Battles in Seattle, and they closed ports as part of the campaign to free Mumia. They regularly act to support longshore workers around the world as well as in the United States; the Charleston Five is one example. They have stood nearly alone among the large U.S. unions in their support of changing China's trade status (Levi and Olson 2000).

Discussion

Why were the preference orderings of the members of these two unions so different? The argument presented here emphasizes the importance of the distinct organizational cultures of the unions. Their elected leadership communicated and observed different principles and enforced and reproduced them with different institutions and rules.

For most unions at the level of development of those under investigation here, a great deal of personal trust of leaders exists initially as an effect of the multilayered and thick network of relationships essential to building the union and engaging in the strikes and other job actions required to win initial recognition and contracts. Certainly that is true for Hoffa and Bridges.

One factor not fully explored yet here but clearly of empirical consequence is the external attacks on the union leaders.[13] Bridges's prosecution by the federal government may have enhanced membership's positive perceptions of his trustworthiness; his willingness to stand up for his principles certainly signaled his moral and ideological commitments. As in Hoffa's case, the effect appears to have been to solidify the organizational culture in opposition to those who were attacking their union presidents. Both unions also had conflicts with the AFL, the CIO, and then the AFL-CIO.

Despite similarities in some aspects of the relationship between the leaders and their members, over time the institutional differences between more and less participatory unions begin to have consequences, possibly even for preference formation and maintenance. The ILWU and the IBT are emblematic of the distinction between unions that are fairly participatory in their deliberations and their negotiations and those whose governance arrangements are more top down but whose officers are still subject to periodic elections. The ILWU has a whole series of procedures that ensure that demands are formulated with considerable membership input and discussion. The IBT certainly holds large conventions and elicits membership input in other ways, but the procedures are designed to give the leadership a great deal of day-to-day autonomy from membership. In both unions, the titled officers must run for office, but Teamster elections have several times been invalidated by federal authorities.

The existence of participatory institutions helps explain how Bridges's principles were internalized by so many of the ILWU members who did not hold them before and were supported even by those who questioned them. The explanation of the Bridges phenomenon lies at least partially in the willingness of the leadership to delimit its power and ensure transparency of actions to gain credibility and win the confidence of their members.[14] The combination of successful bargaining, self-created controls on behavior, and increased accountability provides these leaders with moral suasion over their members. They are in fact altruists of the sort Chong (1991) describes as crucial to generating civil rights protests. They had already demonstrated their competence. That alone, as the Hoffa case also reveals, was probably enough for continued reelection. But they wanted more. They wanted socially conscious members.

On the one hand, the institutional arrangements of participatory democracy create considerable monitoring and fairly tight reins on the leaders' actions. They inhibit private information and delimit leadership discretion—at least as long as membership participates. Under these conditions, the leader is trustworthy but only because there is little option to be anything but. On the other hand, a leader who has protected, even nourished, the participatory apparatus signals his commitments to a set of principles. He has shown respect for the process and for the members' opinions, and has revealed his character through the process of communication (Mackie 1998).

A less participatory union relies more on after-the-fact controls in the form of elections. On the one hand, a leader may have a large degree of discretion, partially as a result of a relative monopoly over private information and the capacity to manipulate information and outcomes. Elections provide most of the constraints on leadership behavior. On the other hand, less participatory unions tend to be more hierarchical, which may undermine the establishment of personal trustworthiness.

In the case of the Teamsters, Hoffa clearly had considerable discretion and leeway in action. His contract delivery also earned him a reputation as a trustworthy representative. He did, however, evoke an oppositional group, eager to oust him out of power and establish a more democratic regime. Bridges also faced opposition at times, but the disagreements were over substantive issues, such as the Modernization and Mechanization Agreement, or over political issues, not over process.

In participatory unions, leadership leeway may actually be restricted, even when members have considerable confidence in their leaders. And so it was in the ILWU. The requirements that membership be involved in establishing contract demands, negotiating, and approving the final contract limited Bridges's discretionary behavior. However, by submitting to such constraints, indeed in establishing such constraints on themselves, they gained two major benefits. First, trusted leaders may be granted greater constituent tolerance even if they head the union during failed strikes, the negotiation of poor contracts, and so forth. When a strike or contract was not all that the members—the principal—hoped, the principal has to share the blame with its agent.

Second, having earned the reputation of reliability may matter for a range of decisions leaders must make, and it may increase the influence of leaders in union deliberations. Trusted leaders may have greater authority and persuasive powers within the union meetings and among the bargaining team. Certainly, Bridges did. Their trustworthiness derived in part from rank-and-file personal knowledge of and ongoing relationships with them; they stayed close to and were involved with the membership both as officials and as men. In addition, the continuing communication that arises with participatory democracy may be, as Gerry Mackie claims, "the best way to subdue deception" (1998, 92), increase transparency, and thus engender trustworthiness.

Moreover, the respect Bridges demonstrated, personally and institutionally, for the membership seems to have enhanced their assessment of his trustworthiness. One of the consequences of the perceived trustworthiness of the Bridges group and the relations of trust and solidarity they helped create among the membership was their effectiveness in persuading members to act outside of their narrow self-interest. Certainly, this is an extraordinarily solid union. Recall the slogan of the ILWU: "An Injury to One is an Injury to All."

Bridges helped his members sustain and order a set of preferences distinct from the majority of the IBT. In the ILWU being a good union member involved a willingness to give money, time, and effort on behalf of causes far distant from the bread and butter concerns of the job. The hiring hall facilitated this culture by providing a location for self-education and joint deliberation, and the other participatory institutions of the union furthered the evolution of progressive unionism. This was, of course, Bridges's aim; he was committed to fundamental social and economic change to ensure political and economic equality of all. He achieved his goals by tying his own hands, by limiting his discretionary power, increasing his trustworthiness and reliability, signaling his principles, and thus enhancing his persuasive and political power.

Alternative Explanations

A number of other factors may also be critical in accounting for the variation in these unions. Among the most important and most often cited are

1. distinct demographic characteristics of the workers that make them more susceptible to one kind of organizational culture than another

2. pre-existing ideologies among the workers

3. industrial structure

4. the organization of the employers

5. the role of the state, locally and nationally

Some of these factors are the ones Kimeldorf (1988) emphasizes in his comparison of the ILWU with the mob-ridden International Longshoremen's Association (ILA) on the East Coast. A brief consideration of some additional cases of waterfront unions makes it possible to better assess the role of the first two factors. Consideration of the others will have to await another paper and further research.

Kimeldorf (1988) argues that one reason the ILWU was so different than the one from which it broke away, had to do with the demographics of the two groups. The ILWU drew primarily from among Protestant Scandinavians. The ILA drew primarily from Irish and Italian Catholics. Yet, there are reasons to doubt this explanation. The Tacoma longshoremen stayed in the ILA for more than a decade and a half after the other West Coast locals broke away. Yet, their ethnic and racial characteristics were no different than that of Portland or Seattle, and they, too, had a history of radical unionism. What distinguished Tacoma was its longer tradition of the hiring hall and its somewhat older workforce (Bamberger 2005). Even more interesting is the comparison of the Australian waterfront workers with those in East Coast ports of the ILA. They were virtually the same in religious and national background—yet the organizational cultures of several of the most important of these unions closely resembled the ILWU.

The ideological influences are not so easy to dismiss. Both Kimeldorf (1988) and Nelson (1988) distinguish the ILWU by its historical roots in the Wobblies, a tradition the East Coast waterfront workers did not share. Although the Wobblies were not a major influence in Australia, other syndicalist labor organizations were. Moreover, in both countries and on both coasts, the Communist Party was a presence. While it failed to take hold in the ILA, it left its mark on the ILWU and many other American unions; its influence is highly correlated with more democratic and participatory unions (Stepan-Norris and Zeitlin 1991, 1995, 1996, 2002).

Communism is a critical factor in the biographies of two of the most legendary Australian waterfront union leaders, Paddy Troy and "Big Jim" Healy.[15] Both were avowed communists. Between 1947 and 1972, Paddy Troy served various terms as secretary of the Coastal Dock Rivers and Harbour Works' Union (CDRHWU), later, the Ship Painters and Dockers' Union of Western Australia (SPDU), and, still later, the Maritime Services Union.[16] "Big Jim" Healy presided over the Waterside Workers Federation of Australia (WWF)[17] from 1937 until his death in 1963. Each experienced serious faction fights and red baiting within their union and went to jail for their beliefs.[18] Both ran extremely militant and democratic unions, and both had hiring halls.

What made these unions so similar to the ILWU and so different from the ILA was the instantiation, at the critical moment of the institutionalization of the union, of democratic principles and rules by which the leaders and the members were held to account. By developing democratic procedures and encouraging participation and by building a reputation based on that, Troy and Healy clearly differentiated themselves from Joe Ryan and others in the ILA. Moreover, they made similar credible commitments as their counterparts in the ILWU. Their pay was tied to that of their members, and they remained clearly working class. Elections were free and open. Troy was often defeated. Healy continued to win but was often challenged. Convention debate in the WWF was as lively as that of the ILWU.

This brief comparison suggests that a full explanation of union difference requires a more complex account. While ethnic and religious differences do not appear to be causal, locally grounded ideologies and working class cultures are. In addition, a variety of structural and political factors, not yet investigated, may also be crucial to understanding the origin and choice of the original organizational culture and to the success or failure of factions that challenge it. Even so, it seems clear that the institutionalization of the organizational culture is essential to its survival and maintenance.

Conclusion

This simplified narrative accentuates initial leadership and the institutions they create. These unions are far more complex than these descriptions indicate. Both extended their membership base beyond the core set of workers that gave them their original start. By expanding the short haul trucking division, which includes the UPS employees, and organizing various service and governmental workers, the Teamster leadership created a base for a renewed challenge to its organizational culture. By bringing in the warehouse workers, the cannery workers, the inland boatmen, and the Hawaii plantation, hotel, and restaurant workers, the ILWU leadership both created new supports and new challenges to its organizational culture. The process of incorporating new kinds of workers and of resolving various faction struggles within both unions deserve further elaboration in order to better understand the nature of organizational culture and its adaptations. There is also an interesting story to be told about the conflictual relationships between the Teamsters and the ILWU in their battle for the warehousemen in 1937 and in their later positive interactions as they explored the possibility of building a larger transport union. If that effort had succeeded, there would certainly have been major consequences for the organizational cultures of both unions.

What remains notable nonetheless is the survival of both the ILWU and Teamster organizational culture, well beyond the presidencies of Bridges and Hoffa. Despite stresses and strains and even some severe cracks, there is remarkable persistence. There are also changes. The Teamsters appear to be clearing up the related charges of racketeering and rigged elections. The ILWU is experiencing some dwindling in participation at meetings.

The participatory unions may create norms that the leader internalizes as well as obeys. In the case of democratic unions defined only by their electoral processes, there is a greater chance for a leader who once had a normative commitment to the common good of the membership to become more narrowly self-interested, for the iron law of oligarchy to take effect (Michels 1962; Voss and Sherman 2000). But the logic of the argument above also suggests that the most dangerous situation for members may be one in which they rely on participatory mechanisms, lack effective after the fact controls, and then fail to ensure participation.

Both Hoffa and Bridges created organizational cultures that their members came to support and that ordered the members' preferences over choices. Members preferred or came to prefer, whatever their initial preferences, the preference ordering the leaders represented. It also seems to be the case that both leadership groups succeeded in institutionalizing that culture. But it is equally apparent that stress lines in these cultures appear when the initial leaders and those like them are no longer active. The strength of Teamsters for a Democratic Union reveals different preferences among some of the IBT membership than those of the Hoffa faction. The decreasing radicalism and activism of the ILWU reveals new or changed preferences among that membership as well.

Preferences and preference orderings are not immutable. They are, however, sticky. Nonetheless, they are subject to manipulation and transformation in ways we are only just beginning to explore. The implications are that neither economism nor social activism are givens; they are often the product of the institutions, credible commitments, and principles embodied in a organizational culture that itself requires nurturance to be sustained.

The initial research for this paper was funded by the Russell Sage Foundation project on Trust and Trustworthiness. I have benefited from comments on earlier drafts by participants in the RSF Conference on "Preferences in Time," organized by Ira Katznelson and Barry Weingast, and those attending colloquia at the University of Michigan, *Wissenschaftszentrum Berlin für Sozialforschung* (WZB), Northwestern University, University of Nebraska, Princeton University, the Juan March Institute, the Max Planck Institute for the Study of Societies, the University of California, Berkeley, and Harvard University. I am also grateful for the careful, critical readings by David Soskice, Andrew Richards, Ignacio Sanchez-Cuenca, Peter Evans, Maria Victoria Murillo, Stuart MacIntyre, Patrick N. Troy, Michael Honey, and, George Lovell. I especially want to acknowledge the contributions of David Olson, John Ahlquist, and other members of the Harry Bridges Center for Labor Studies Working Group on *Union Democracy Reexamined*: community advisors Ron Magden, Eugene Vrana, and Joseph Wenzl; graduate students Barry Eidlin, Gillian Murphy, and Todd Tavares; and undergraduates Nowell Bamberger, Randy Eng, Adam Goodwin, Devin Kelly, Natalie Qwist, and Elisabeth Zamora.

Notes

1. Originally, the name of the union was International Longshoremen's and Warehousemen's Union. The name was made gender-neutral by a vote of the convention in the late 1990s.
2. This claim has some elements in common with the argument about critical junctures put forward by Collier and Collier (1991).
3. Karen Cook, Russell Hardin, and I have developed arguments about the role of and contexts for trust and trustworthiness in a jointly authored book (2005). My argument here is informed by this joint work although the statements made here are mine alone.
4. Eric Schickler suggested this framing of the problem.
5. The initial idea of a separating equilibrium came from David Soskice. Ignacio Sanchez-Cuenca, John Ahlquist, and I are now developing the implications of Soskice's suggestions and attempting to develop a formal model.

6. Interestingly, this was the case in the very first IBT election in 1903 (Stier 2002, 52–53).
7. The larger project will be equally attentive to the IBT.
8. I thank Gene Vrana for pointing this out to me.
9. Coastwise is the ILWU term of art, but I am using the more familiar term here.
10. Wellman (1995, 71–72) offers an excellent description of the dispatch system used by Local 10 in San Francisco.
11. For more information on this project, see *Union Democracy Reexamined* website, http://depts.washington.edu/ilwu/ (accessed April 15, 2005).
12. See the powerpoint presentation, "Rank And File Democracy: Tradition And Trends" on the *Union Democracy Reexamined* website, http://depts.washington.edu/ilwu/ (accessed April 15, 2005).
13. Wellman (1995) considers this a very important factor for understanding ILWU working class culture, though he claims its effect was by means of the isolation it caused.
14. This follows a line of reasoning developed by Ferejohn (1999) and then by Alt (2002).
15. My evidence on Troy comes principally from Stuart MacIntyre's (1984) excellent monograph and from discussions with Troy's son, Patrick N. Troy. My evidence on Healy and the WWF comes from a variety of secondary sources (Beasley 1996; Bull 1998; Lockwood 1990; Markey and Svensen 1996; Sheridan 1994) as well as extensive research in the archives of the Maritime Union of Australia, available in the Noel Butlin Archives, Australian National University.
16. The union was deregistered on a number of occasions, and each time other unions moved in to claim some of its workers. Although it became increasingly small, it also became more narrowly a waterfront union and increasingly militant. Conversation with Professor Patrick N. Troy, July 21, 2002.
17. The WWF became part of the Maritime Union of Australia (MUA) in 1993.
18. This occurred in 1941 before he belonged to Coastal Dockers' Union. According to his son, the jailing of Troy was due to allegations that he sold a Communist Party (CP) paper, which was legal at the time but later proscribed. Moreover, Troy had not actually sold the paper. Nor was he a CP member at the time because the party was illegal; he belonged before and after.

References

Alt, James E. 2002. "Comparative Political Economy: Credibility, Transparency, Accountability and Institutions." In *The State of the Discipline: Power, Choice, and the State*, edited by Ira Katznelson and Helen Milner. New York: W. W. Norton.

Bamberger, Nowell. 2005. "Waterfront Unionism in Seattle and Tacoma, 1887–1958: A Comparative Study in Radicalism." Undergraduate paper in the Department of Political Science, University of Washington, Seattle.

Beasley, Margo. 1996. *Wharfies: A History of the Waterside Workers' Federation of Australia*. Rushcutters Bay, NSW: Halstead Press.

Bull, Tas. 1998. *Life on the Waterfront*. Sydney: HarperCollins.

Chong, Dennis. 1991. *Collective Action and the Civil Rights Movement*. Chicago: University of Chicago Press.

Collier, Ruth Berins, and David Collier. 1991. *Shaping the Political Arena*. Princeton, N.J.: Princeton University Press.

Cook, Karen S., Russell Hardin, and Margaret Levi. 2005. *Cooperation Without Trust?* New York: Russell Sage Foundation.

Dobbs, Farrell. 1972. *Teamster Rebellion*. New York: Monad Press.

Elster, Jon. 1979. *Ulysses and the Sirens*. London: Cambridge University Press.

Ferejohn, John. 1999. "Accountability and Authority: Toward a Theory of Political Accountability." In *Democracy, Accountability and Representation*, edited by Adam Przeworski, Susan Stokes, and Bernard Manin. New York: Cambridge University Press.

Harry Bridges Center for Labor Studies. "Working Group on Union Democracy Reexamined." Available at: http://depts.washington.edu/ilwu/ (accessed April 15, 2005).

Johnson, Victoria. 2000. "The Cultural Foundation of Resources, the Resource Foundation of Political Cultures: An Explanation for the Outcomes of Two General Strikes." *Politics & Society* 28(3): 331–65.

Kimeldorf, Howard. 1988. *Reds or Rackets? The Making of Radical and Conservative Unions on the Waterfront*. Berkeley: University of California Press.

Kreps, David M. 1990. "Corporate Culture and Economic Theory." In *Perspectives in Positive Political Economy*, edited by James Alt and Kenneth Shepsle. New York: Cambridge University Press.

Lenin, Vladimir I. 1902/1963. *What is to be done?* Translated by S.V. Utechin and P. Utechin. Oxford: Clarendon Press.

Levi, Margaret. 1997. *Consent, Dissent and Patriotism*. New York: Cambridge University Press.

Levi, Margaret, and David Olson. 2000. "The Battles in Seattle." *Politics & Society* 28(3): 217–37.

Lockwood, Rupert. 1990. *Ship to Shore: A History of Melbourne's Waterfront and Its Union Struggles*. Sydney: Hale & Iremonger Pty.

MacIntyre, Stuart. 1984. *Militant: The Life and Times of Paddy Troy*. Sydney: George Allen & Unwin Australia Pty.

Mackie, Gerry. 1998. "All Men Are Liars: Is Democracy Meaningless?" In *Deliberative Democracy*, edited by Jon Elster. New York: Cambridge University Press.

Markey, Ray, and Stuart Svensen. 1996. "Healy, James." In *Australian Dictionary of Biography*, edited by John Ritchie. Melbourne: Melbourne University Press.

Michels, Robert. 1962. *Political Parties*. New York: The Free Press.

Miller, Gary. 1992. *Managerial Dilemmas*. New York: Cambridge University Press.

Moldea, Dan E. 1978. *The Hoffa Wars: Teamsters, Rebels, Politicians, and the Mob*. New York: Paddington Press.

Nelson, Bruce. 1988. *Workers on the Waterfront: Seamen, Longshoremen, and Unionism in the 1930s*. Urbana: University of Illinois Press.

———. 2001. *Divided We Stand: American Workers and the Struggle for Black Equality*. Princeton, N.J.: Princeton University Press.

Olson, Mancur. 1965. *The Logic of Collective Action*. Cambridge, Mass.: Harvard University Press.

Richards, Andrew. 2001. "The Crisis of Union Representation." In *Can Class Still Unite? The Differentiated Work Force, Class Solidarity, and Trade Unions*, edited by Guy Van Gyes, Hans de Witte, and Patrick Pasture. Burlington: Ashgate.

Russell, Thadeus. 2001. *Out of the Jungle: Jimmy Hoffa and the Remaking of the American Working Class*. New York: Alfred A. Knopf.

Sanchez-Cuenca, Ignacio. 2005. "Preferences Over Choices." Unpublished paper, prepared at the Juan March Institute, Madrid.

Schelling, Thomas C. 1978. *Micromotives and Macrobehavior*. New York: W. W. Norton.

Seidman, Gay W. 1994. *Manufacturing Militance: Workers' Movements in Brazil and South Africa, 1970–1985*. Berkeley: University of California Press.

Seidman, Joel. 1953. "Democracy in Labor Unions." *Journal of Political Economy* 61(3, June): 221–32.

Sen, Amartya K. 1977. "Rational Fools: A Critique of the Behavioral Foundations of Economic Theory." *Philosophy and Public Affairs* 6(4): 317–44.

Sheridan, Tom. 1994. "Australian Wharfies 1943–1967: Casual Attitudes, Militant Leadership and Workplace Change." *Journal of Industrial Relations* 36(2): 258–84.

Sloane, Arthur A. 1991. *Hoffa*. Cambridge, Mass.: The MIT Press.

Stepan-Norris, Judith, and Maurice Zeitlin. 1991. "'Red' Unions and 'Bourgeois' Contracts?" *American Journal of Sociology* 96(5): 1151–1200.

———. 1995. "Union Democracy, Radical Leadership, and the Hegemony of Capital." *American Sociological Review* 60(6): 829–50.

———. 1996. "Insurgency, Radicalism, and Democracy in America's Industrial Unions." *Social Forces* 75(1): 1–32.

———. 2002. *Left Out: Reds and America's Industrial Unions*. New York: Cambridge University Press.

Stier, Anderson & Malone, LLC (Stier). 2002. "The Teamsters: Perception and Reality. An Investigative Study of Organized Crime Influence in the Union." Prepared for the International Brotherhood of Teamsters. New York: Stier, Anderson & Malone, LLC.

Stoker, Laura. 1992. "Interests and Ethics in Politics." *American Political Science Review* 86(2): 369–80.

Turnbull, Peter. 2000. "Contesting Globalization on the Waterfront." *Politics & Society* 28(3): 367–91.

Voss, Kim, and Rachel Sherman. 2000. "Breaking the Iron Law of Oligarchy: Union Revitalization in the American Labor Movement." *American Journal of Sociology* 106(2): 303–49.

Wellman, David. 1995. *The Union Makes Us Strong: Radical Unionism on the San Francisco Waterfront.* New York: Cambridge University Press.

9

Preference Formation in Transitional Justice

Jon Elster

Transitional justice refers to the judicial process of coming to terms with the past in the transition from one political regime to another. It includes, notably, trials, administrative and professional purges, restitution of property, and compensation for suffering. Examples of transitions to, or returns to, democracy that have addressed these issues include:

- the demise of the Athenian oligarchs in 411 and again in 403 B.C.
- the restoration of democracy after 1945 in countries occupied by the Germans during World War II
- the return to or introduction of democracy after 1945 in the main Axis countries (Germany, Japan, Italy) and their more or less voluntary allies
- the fall of military dictatorships in southern Europe in the mid-1970s
- the return to or introduction of democracy after 1989 in numerous countries in Eastern Europe
- the recent fall of the dictatorships in many Latin American countries, notably Argentina, Chile and Bolivia
- the transition to democracy in South Africa

There is also one important case of transitional justice in the restoration of monarchy, namely, the French Restoration after the fall of Napoleon. Actually, this complex process had two phases. The first occurred between Napoleon's demise in 1814 and his return from Elba in 1815, and was characterized by surprising leniency. The second, much more savage, took place after the end of the Hundred Days. Even then, however, the much-maligned Louis XVIII successfully resisted many émigré claims that would have divided France and undermined social stability.

When thinking about initiating a process of transitional justice the new democratic leaders must choose among a number of options. First, there is the choice whether to have a process at all or rather to draw a thick line between the past and the present.[1] Given that a decision is made to go ahead with a process, there is a choice among many different modalities. One can define wrongdoing broadly or narrowly. One can aim at severe or lenient punishment of wrongdoers thus defined. One can define suffering and victimization broadly or narrowly. One can opt for generous or mostly symbolic compensation of victims thus defined. In addition to these substantive choices, there are numerous procedural decisions to be made, such as whether to enact retroactive legislation or extend the statute of limitations.

These choices are shaped by preferences. They are also shaped by many other things: beliefs, constraints, bargaining power. Here I focus on the role of preferences, although I shall also consider their interaction with other determinants of choice. Rather than treating preferences as given, I shall look into processes of preference formation. This approach seems especially called for in these extraordinarily turbulent situations. Although they certainly contain elements of "politics as usual" that do not require much by way of preference explanation, much of the motivational dynamics emerges from the transition itself.

Preferences and Motivations

I distinguish between preferences and motivations. The former I define as a preference ordering over policy options, policy being used in a broad sense that includes issues for individual as well as collective decisions. The latter are the more fundamental psychic forces that underlie the preferences. As I explain elsewhere (Elster 1999), I follow the seventeenth-century French moralists in distinguishing among three motivations: emotion, reason, and interest.[2]

The motivations may also be classified from a different perspective, as outcome oriented and non–outcome oriented. Interest-based action is always outcome oriented. Emotion-based action sometimes is, and sometimes not. Reason-based action sometimes is as well, and sometimes not. The first of these three statements does not require much explanation. Interest is the pursuit of advantage—money, power, esteem. Assuming rationality, action is chosen to promote the agent's interest as efficiently as possible. Emotion-based action often springs directly from the action tendency that accompanies the emotion (Frijda 1986). When I strike to hit someone who has hit me (or when I stumble over a stone and kick it in return), there is nothing I want to bring about by my action. When I turn away from someone in contempt or run away in fear, my action does not have a well-defined end for which it is the best means, or even a means. Other emotions can induce instrumentally rational behavior. The Holocaust was an act of hatred carried out with ruthless efficiency. Impartial, reason-based action, finally, can be consequentialist as well as nonconsequentialist (or deontological).

The link between motivation and preference may be immediate or belief mediated. An outcome-oriented motivation needs to be supplemented with causal beliefs to yield a policy preference. More simply: to achieve an end you need to form a belief about means to that end. This is true of the pursuit of the common interest as well as of private interest. Many non–outcome oriented motivations yield direct policy preferences. If I believe I have a duty to tell the truth, my preference for truth-telling over lying is an immediate consequence. Yet the implementation of duties and rights is often limited by costs (Holmes and Sunstein 1998) and other facts of life, such as the impossibility of undoing the past.

We have motivations over motivations, or meta-motivations.[3] If we go on a diet, some of us would prefer saying to others and to ourselves that it is for health reasons rather than admitting that it is for the sake of vanity. More generally, most societies rank motivations in a normative hierarchy. In our society, it's better to marry for love than for money. Among the ancient Greeks, acting for the sake of the polis was best, acting for revenge second-best, acting out of interest third-best. and acting out of envy worst. In many Western societies, the desire for impartial retribution is ranked above the desire for revenge, but in feuding societies this ranking is reversed. In our time, most Americans probably believe it is better to act for charitable than for selfish motives, but Tocqueville (1840/1969, 526) claimed that the Americans he met had the opposite ranking.

I suggest something along the following lines. Human beings have first-order motivations that induce specific policy preferences and meta-motivations that induce a desire to be swayed by specific first-order motivations. Most of all, we would like to have our cake and eat it too: to be able to justify our preferred policy by our preferred motivation. And often we can do this. If my vanity induces me to go on a diet, I can tell myself a story that my decision is really induced by my desire to be healthy. Or consider the motivation to donate to charity. If others give much, I may adopt a utilitarian theory of charity that would justify small donations on my part. If others give little, I may adopt a reciprocity theory of charity, which would also justify small donations. In either case I can satisfy my material interest and my self-image as not being moved only by material interest.

Let me now focus more directly on policy preferences, and distinguish three cases: individual policy choices not observed by others, individual choices observed by others, and collective policy choices. In the first case, the agent simply acts on his substantive policy preferences. Shopping for food is a paradigm example. In the second case, complications arise because the agent also has to consider how others might reward or punish him for the choice he makes. If he abstains from taking revenge when social norms make it mandatory, he could suffer severe social ostracism. If he chooses to make public rather than private donations to charity, it may reveal that he is more concerned with the esteem of his peers than with the welfare of the beneficiaries. To take an example closer to the topic of the paper, if a person engages in spontaneous transitional justice, such as tarring and feathering collaborators[4] or cutting the hair of women who engaged in "horizontal collaboration" with the enemy (Virgili 2000), the motivation may be to assure his peers about his patriotic motivations rather than to punish those who lack them.

The third case offers further complications. In group policy choices, individual preferences have to be aggregated to yield the collective decision. Here aggregation is used in a broad sense that includes not only voting, but also arguing to(ward) consensus and bargaining. In most actual cases, all three mechanisms are involved. Because arguing rarely yields consensus, one may have to take a vote. Because decision making often involves more than a single issue, voting opens for bargaining in the form of logrolling. By including arguing among the mechanisms of aggregation I want to highlight the fact that motivations, beliefs and preferences can be changed during the decision-making process.

Emotion-Based Preferences in Transitional Justice

The downfall, defeat, or implosion of an authoritarian or totalitarian regime cannot fail to provoke strong emotions. I first discuss some evidence or indicators that emotion—quite generally speaking—does have a causal role in shaping transitional justice, before proceeding to a more fine-grained discussion of the causal impact of particular emotions.

Two features of emotions are especially relevant in the present context. First, emotions induce urgency, which I define as a preference for earlier action over later action, independent of the timing and size of the rewards. Second, emotions have tendency to decay in intensity over time. As we shall see, the anticipation of the second tendency may induce the first. Before making that connection, however, let me discuss the two phenomena separately.

In transitions to democracy, there is often an urgent demand for justice. Objectively, other matters such as economic reconstruction might suffer more from delay. Subjectively, punishment of the former oppressors and collaborators becomes the more urgent task. The number of extralegal executions after World War II in France and Italy, around 10,000 in each country, is one indicator.[5] The French practice of establishing summary martial courts to prevent people from taking justice into their own hands is another (Novick 1968, 146). The widespread practice in all German-occupied countries of cutting the hair of women who had had relations with Germans is even more telling,[6] because they presented no possible risk that could justify immediate action on prudential grounds. In the first period after Liberation, there was in several countries increasing popular frustration with the slowness of legal prosecutions against collaborators.

The Japanese war trials are another example of the impact of urgency. The trial of General Tomoyuki Yamashita ignored due process and *mens rea* requirements, in favor of strict liability (Cohen 1999). In his dissenting Supreme Court opinion, Justice Frank Murphy observed that

> No military necessity or other emergency demanded the suspension of the safeguards of due process. Yet [Yamashita] was rushed to trial under an improper charge, given insufficient time to prepare an adequate defense, deprived of the benefits of some of the most elementary rules of evidence and summarily sentenced to be hanged. In all this needless and unseemly haste there was no serious attempt to charge or prove that he committed a recognized violation of the laws of war. (cited in Taylor 1981, 163)

Needless haste is indeed the essence of urgency, as I have defined it. Even where there is nothing to be lost and something to be gained by waiting, the psychic momentum of the emotion may prove too strong.

The sense of urgency, like the emotion itself, decays with time. The short half-life of emotion shows up in two ways. First, the desire for retribution is blunted if the most serious acts of wrongdoing occurred long before the transition.[7] In the first French Restoration, even the regicides who had voted for the execution of Louis XVI were exempt from prosecution. In the second Restoration, those among the regicides who had joined Napoleon during the Hundred Days were exiled. In some of the German-occupied countries, the worst crimes were committed shortly before Liberation. In Italy, Denmark, and France, new and more oppressive occupational regimes were created after 1942 and 1943. In 1944 and

1945, the Germans often engaged in scorched-earth tactics as they retreated. In any case, no occupation lasted more than five years. By contrast, when the East European communist regimes fell in 1989 and 1990
they had been in existence for fifty years and the worst atrocities were
in a relatively remote past. There was not, therefore, the same urgent
demand for retribution. The Spanish transition of 1976 to 1978 also fits
this pattern.

Second, the retributive emotions decay if there is a long delay between
the transition and the trials. In trials in German-occupied countries after
World War II, sentencing was almost invariably more severe in the initial
stages than after two or three years.[8] Other explanations are also possible, however. Aristotle observed that "men become calm when they have
spent their anger on someone else. This happened in the case of Ergophi-
lus: though the people were more irritated against him than against Callisthenes, they acquitted him because they had condemned Callisthenes
to death the day before" (*Rhetoric* 1380b 11–13; see also Seneca, *On Anger,*
I xviii).[9] A third explanation relies on the common observation that war
situations tend to induce a general devaluation of human life, which
makes the death penalty seem less extreme than under normal circumstances.[10] After a while, other priorities and evaluations will predominate. Although I believe the first account is the most plausible, each of
the others may also have some explanatory power. Note, however, that
none of them is compatible with reason or interest as the main sources
of preference formation in transitional justice.

Could there be a causal link between the urgency of transitional justice and the tendency for emotions to decay with time? If the actors
anticipate that they will feel less strongly in a few years' time, would
they not have an incentive to impose severe punishments while their
emotions are still at peak level? In Belgium, on the basis of the experience from World War I, "it was believed that after a while, the popular
willingness to impose severe sentences on the collaborators would give
place to indifference" (Huyse and Dhondt 1993, 115). Hence some Bel-
gians wanted the trials to proceed as quickly as possible, before passion
was replaced by reason or interest. In France, many felt that the purges
had to be carried out immediately because "it was necessary to act before
the voices of timidity reasserted themselves" (Novick 1968, 39). In a related argument, President Alfonsín decided in 1983 that "the trials should
be limited to a finite period during which public enthusiasm for such a
program remained high" (Nino 1996, 67). These cases rest on what is
called hot-to-cold empathy, and hence go counter to the claim that
agents in an excited state are unable to imagine that their emotion will
cool off (Loewenstein 1996). Although significant from a theoretical point
of view, they are not typical. Urgency may sometimes be due to the

anticipation of decay, but mostly it is simply an indissociable part of the action tendency of emotion.

I now proceed to classify the emotions that arise in transitional justice in a more fine-grained way. Among the agents involved are, first, the perpetrators or wrongdoers: agents, collaborators, and leaders of the pre-democratic regime that committed acts of wrongdoing. Second are the victims: those who suffered as a result of these acts. Third are the (internal) resisters: those who fought or dissented from the regime, publicly or clandestinely, with words or with weapons. Fourth are the neutrals: nonvictims who neither cooperated with the regime, nor helped the victims, nor joined the resisters. Fifth are the beneficiaries of wrongdoing: those who, while not themselves wrongdoers, were made better off as a result of wrongdoing.[11] A given individual may fall in more than one category. Under the Nazi regime or Nazi occupation, some victims did not resist, but others did; some resisters were not victims, but others were. In South Africa, some liberal resisters to apartheid were also its beneficiaries.[12] A fortiori, neutrals can also benefit.[13] In South Africa, even firms that had no direct part in repressive practices benefited from the abundant availability of cheap black labor (TRC 1999, vol. 4, 19).[14] Wrongdoers may or may not be beneficiaries; the East German border guards who killed escapees to the West certainly did not derive any benefit from the regime and their place in it.

Ideally, one ought to consider the emotions felt by individuals in each of these categories toward individuals in each of the others. I mainly limit myself, however, to emotions that target wrongdoers, with some but not much attention to how they are modulated by the status of the subject who is experiencing them. The main emotions are: anger, two varieties of indignation, hatred, and contempt. Although in actual situations these emotions may fuse with one another in analytically intractable ways, I will treat them, somewhat artificially, as distinct and separate. The emotions have different cognitive antecedents and induce different action tendencies. Each action tendency also corresponds, at least roughly, to a specific set of legal and institutional reactions.

Consider first the cognitive antecedents. A feels anger toward B when he believes that B has harmed him without a good reason. The anger may be weaker or stronger depending on whether A believes that B's behavior was negligent, reckless, or deliberate. In the last case, that of deliberate infliction of harm, the strength of the emotion may also depend on whether A believes that B wanted to harm him or that he simply didn't care whether he was harmed as a means to, or a side effect of, B's pursuit of other ends. What I shall call Cartesian indignation is the emotion A experiences when he sees B harming C without a good reason (Descartes 1985, Art.195). Compared to anger, indignation is an impersonal emotion and typically a weaker one.[15] What I call Aristotelian indignation is the emotion triggered in A by the belief that B enjoys an undeserved fortune (*Rhetoric* 1386 b). Although this concept overlaps with the Cartesian one, neither is included in the other.

Whereas anger and Cartesian indignation are triggered by A's belief that B has done a bad action, hatred and contempt are triggered by the belief that B has a bad character. The antecedent of hatred is the belief that A's character is evil; that of contempt, that it is inferior or base. Followers of Hitler thought Jews evil but Slavs inferior (Goldhagen 1996, 469). The distinction between action and character may seem problematic, at least if one believes that a claim that someone has a bad character can be supported only by pointing to his bad actions.[16] Yet in some cases, such as sadistic torture, we tend to think that a single action provides sufficient evidence of an evil character.[17] The same problem arises for contempt and the correlative feeling of shame. The paradox of shame is that it "involves taking a single unworthy action or characteristic to be the whole of a person's identity" (Lindsay-Hartz, de Rivera, and Mascolo 1995, 297). As for the distinction between hatred and contempt, perhaps it can be exemplified by the different emotions we feel toward someone who positively wants the destruction of other human beings and toward someone who simply doesn't care whether they are destroyed or not.

To summarize, we react to the chronically bad with hatred, to the chronically weak with contempt, to the occasionally and intelligibly weak with anger or Cartesian indignation, and to the undeservedly fortunate by Aristotelian indignation. We feel hatred for torturers and denunciators. We feel contempt for the opportunists who would enter the Nazi Party or the Communist Party to get jobs they could not otherwise obtain. We feel anger towards the South African lawyers who failed to speak out against apartheid (the vast majority) or toward the Norwegian sheriffs who joined the National Socialist Party (again a vast majority) because they would lose their jobs if they didn't. We feel Aristotelian indignation towards the beneficiaries of wrongdoing, such as economic collaborators in German-occupied countries, the white liberal elite in South Africa under apartheid, or Swiss banks that profited from the bank accounts of Jews who did not survive the Holocaust. After the French restorations, many felt the same way toward those who had purchased émigré properties after they had been confiscated by the revolutionary authorities.

These emotions have different action tendencies. Aristotle says that "much may happen to make the angry man pity those who offend him, but the hater under no circumstances wishes to pity a man whom he once hated; for the one would have the offenders suffer for what they have done; the other would have them cease to exist" (*Rhetoric* 1382a,

2–16). This observation, while accurate, is incomplete. If A is angry at B, he wants B to suffer through his, A's, agency. If B is injured in a car accident, this will not slake A's desire for vengeance. In hatred by contrast, agency is not essential. What matters for the anti-Semite is that Jews cease to exist, whether it be through his or someone else's agency. Also, hatred may result in the desire to expel the object of the emotion rather than to destroy it. Thus ethnic cleansing may take the form of mass deportations rather than genocide.

Cartesian indignation is similar both to hatred and to anger. The indignant person wants the target of the emotion to suffer, but because the agent is not himself the victim of the target, the agency is immaterial. The person who is subject to Aristotelian indignation wants the undeserved fortune to be confiscated: again, agency is immaterial. Although the agent can hardly fail to perceive that the target will suffer as a result, this effect will be the goal of action only if the target is himself a wrongdoer rather than merely the beneficiary of wrongdoing.

Contempt—the action tendency of which is ostracism—is more similar to anger. The contemptuous man refuses to have any personal dealings with the target of his contempt. Unlike what occurs with hatred, the fate of the target is not his concern. Expressions of contempt can also take another form, however. Often they occur spontaneously, as when we turn away from someone who shows immoderate fear in the face of danger. The effect, though not the intention, of such behavior is to induce shame in the target.

In transitional justice, these five emotions map into distinct legal and administrative reactions. Anger induces a demand for long prison sentences, and Cartesian indignation a demand for somewhat shorter sentencing.[18] Aristotelian indignation triggers demand for restitution of undeserved gains and for punitive action if the target himself had a hand in the unjust transactions. Hatred induces a demand for the death penalty, and contempt a demand for the imposition of civil indignity, that is, loss of civil rights.[19] If we accept the Kantian view that retribution is a form of recognition of the offender as a moral agent, nonprosecution may also be an expression of contempt.[20] The demand for the dismissal of tainted individuals from public service may reflect anger or contempt, depending, as I said, on whether they are condemned for their actions or for their character. Empirically, the correspondence between emotional and legal reactions may be hard to establish. As I said, these emotions tend to fuse with another. Also, as I argue later, emotions are not the only source of preferences in transitional justice. Furthermore, even when they are the predominant source, they may enter into conflict with the meta-motivations of the agent.

After the transition, those who remained neutral may be targeted for their passivity and be at the receiving end of contemptuous reactions. More important, the guilt they feel for having done nothing may strengthen their demand for retribution, as if their post-transition aggression toward the wrongdoers could magically undo their pre-transition passivity. The tendency for the neutrals, those in the gray zone between collaboration and resistance, to be especially vindictive seems a general phenomenon.[21] Carlos Nino cites disgusted reactions to the hypocrisy "when those who were silent in the past suddenly become vociferous advocates of retroactive justice" (1996, 39). In Belgium, the draconian measures imposed by Antoine Delfosse, minister of justice in the exile government, "may have their origin in a need to stifle doubts created by his behavior during the first months of the occupation" (Huyse and Dhondt 1993, 69). In Italy after 1944, suspect judges might lean over backward to prove their patriotism (Domenico 1991, 179). In France, a defense lawyer explained the severity of the first sentences by "the fact that many jurors were latecomers to the resistance and were eager to demonstrate a zealousness which they had not shown earlier. Later, when the deported came back from Germany, one had much more thoughtful jurors who . . . did not feel the need to prove themselves" (Lottman 1986, 272). The "résistants de septembre,"[22] who suddenly emerged from their passivity after the liberation of the territory in August 1944, were often more zealous in the harassment of women who had had relations with the Germans (Virgili 2000, 111–15, 208–9). Commenting on the difference in outlook that separated de Gaulle from the Resistance, A. J. Liebling wrote:

> Every Frenchman feels in some degree guilty for the debacle of 1940—if only because he let himself be bamboozled into a sense of security before it happened. But the traitors personify the guilt of all, which makes the honest men all the more bitter against them. In punishing the traitors, the French were punishing part of themselves. Only he who feels himself without guilt is reluctant to cast the first stone; he lacks the requisite imagination. General de Gaulle, the most self-righteous of Frenchman, was one of the least vindictive against the erring brothers. (cited in Novick 1968, 157 n.3; see also Lacouture 1985, vol. II, 140)

In such cases, guilt is transmuted into aggression toward the wrongdoers. In other cases, guilt may turn into aggression toward the victims. Commenting on the psychology of the purchasers of confiscated émigré property after the original owners came back in 1814 and 1815, de la Gorce writes: "There are some forms of remorse which become twisted and turn into hatred. The history of the Restoration can be summarized in the famous saying: 'Whoever has offended cannot forgive'" (1926, 162–63).[23] Prideful individuals may find it harm to admit and therefore to undo the damage they have done.

Reason-Based Preferences in Transitional Justice

I understand reason as any impartial, dispassionate and disinterested motivation that aims at promoting the common good or protecting individual rights. First I deal with the tension between forward-looking and backward-looking approaches to the treatment of perpetrators, and then consider how the same tension can arise in dealing with the claims of victims.

Nonconsequentialist, backward-looking, or retributivist (I use these terms as synonyms) conceptions of punishment emphasize that the severity of punishment must match that of the crime. In the case of transitional justice, the consequences of wrongdoing are often so momentous that severe punishment follows automatically once the requisite subjective conditions (mens rea) have been established. Those who reach the same conclusion on consequentialist grounds typically rest their argument on a deterrent effect. Severe punishment of dictators and their collaborators is supposed to act as a precedent that will deter future would-be dictators from taking power, in part presumably because others will be deterred from assisting them. This was, for instance, Justice Robert Jackson's position during the Nuremberg trials: they were needed "to make war less attractive to those who have the governments and the destinies of peoples in their power" (cited in Taylor 1992, 55). Henri Donnedieu de Vabres, a French member of that International Military Tribunal, stressed the function of the Nuremberg judgment as an incomparable precedent. Otto Kirchheimer, who cites this phrase, goes on to comment that "the incomparable precedent would backfire, however, if it induced the leaders of a future war to fight to the bitter end rather than surrender and face the possible future of war criminals" (1961, 325 n. 29).

The precedent argument does, in fact, have a number of flaws. Suppose (implausibly) that severe punishments in the present will indeed install the appropriate belief in potential coup-makers that they will be harshly punished if they take power illegally and are then deposed. It is extremely unlikely that the deterrence effect of this belief will reduce the chance of an illegal seizure of power to zero. In a given case, a rational would-be dictator might find that the expected benefits from taking power exceed the costs, even when the latter are inflated by the prospect of severe punishment. Some aspiring dictators may be fanatics rather than opportunists, and care little about their personal fate. Given that some illegal seizures of power are likely to occur, Kirchheimer's observation applies forcefully. In this perspective, the net effect of severe penalties in the present on human rights violations in the future is essentially indeterminate (Elster 1999, chap. 1). On the one hand, some rational would-be dictators will be deterred from taking power. On the other hand, those who actually do take power will hang on to it longer and apply more violent means to retain it, reasoning that they might as well be hanged for a sheep as for a lamb.[24]

Let me now contrast the deontological argument for severe punishment with consequentialist arguments for leniency. A purely pragmatic argument for leniency is related to the fact that transitional justice often takes place in societies that have been ravaged by war (as after 1945) or by a massively inefficient economic system (as after 1989). In Western Europe, there was a need for large-scale economic reconstruction; in Eastern Europe, for transition to a market economy. In both cases, it was widely believed that the unfettered pursuit of retributive justice might interfere with these tasks. In Western Europe, this belief justified a low rate of prosecutions for economic collaborations with the Germans,[25] as well as a generally modest level of purges in the administration. In France, the provisional government offered the sibylline statement that in purging the administration "it is good to show intransigence but only to the extent that it does not interfere with the functioning of the services" (cited in Rousso 2001, 532).[26]

In Germany itself, denazification was initially envisaged at a large scale. To take an extreme example: to address the particularly delicate problem of the severely tainted judiciary it was at one point envisaged "closing all German courts for ten years and replacing them with a 'colonial' system, so that a new generation of judges could be educated in the meantime" (Müller 1991, 201). In the actual course of events, only two judges of the Third Reich were convicted (Rothleutner 1994, 488). This extremely low number was due not to concerns for efficiency, but to Nazi judges refusing to condemn their own. Yet here, as in other sectors, a primary reason that the denazification program had to be scaled down was that it would otherwise have interfered with the economic necessities of running the country.

In the former GDR the impact of these pragmatic considerations on the rate of decommunization is clear if one compares purges in different Länder. "Among the state governments, a rift soon appeared between Saxony and the four other new Länder on the definition of criteria [for dismissal from public service of those who had worked for the state security]. The Saxons argued for the application of the strict criteria in use in Berlin, where intransigence was facilitated by the on-site availability of alternative (western officials). Officials from the four other Länder argued for more flexibility" (Sa'adah 1998, 218; for the special case of dismissal vs. retention of judges, see Quint 1997, 187). In Poland, it has been argued that decommunization was frustrated by the fact that the new leaders "had no choice but to rely on the experience and cooperation of many former nomenklatura members" (Walicki 1997, 195). Tucker argues, however, that the nomenklatura did not in fact have much useful expertise (2000).

A more principled argument for leniency rests on the need for national healing and reconciliation. In this respect, the South African Truth and Reconciliation Commission has a somewhat ambiguous status. Being part of a negotiated agreement between the apartheid leadership and the African National Congress, the commission cannot really be characterized as a pulled punch on the congress's part. The reconciliation agreement between the oligarchs and democrats in Athens in 403 B.C. is also somewhat ambiguous, since the treaty was set up under Spartan supervision. Yet, by and large, the victorious democrats seem to have been genuinely motivated by a desire to reduce the level of antagonism in the polis. A general amnesty covered all but the most prominent in the oligarchy. Even these could avoid prosecution by submitting to euthyna, the routine scrutiny to which officials were exposed upon leaving office. To assure them a fair scrutiny the treaty specified that it would be carried out only by taxable citizens, as Aristotle writes in *The Politics and Constitution of Athens*, thus ensuring that the oligarchs would be well represented, rather than by a random selection from all citizens, as was the normal practice (39). There is a stark contrast with transitional justice in France and Denmark after 1945, where perpetrators faced juries in which victims were overrepresented[27] (Lottman 1986, 225; Tamm 1984, 133–35).

In Eastern Europe after 1989, there have been many voices for drawing a thick line between the past and the present, to avoid endless civil strife. The first post-communist prime minister of Poland, Tadeusz Mazowiecki, wanted to follow the Spanish model, but could not impose it (Walicki 1997, 188). The former Hungarian president Arpad Gontz several times referred vindictive legislation to the constitutional court, which routinely struck it down (Halmai and Scheppele 1997; see also Schwartz 2000, chap. 4). Objecting to the Czech purges (lustration), President Havel said in a 1993 interview: "It is enough that people were afraid of the secret police for 40 years. They should not be afraid that someone will reveal something about them in 15 years' time" (Michnik and Havel 1993). These ideas rest on the contested causal premise that we cannot move forwards unless we forget the past. Others have argued that we cannot move forward unless we first address the past.[28] Comparing processes of transitional justice after 1945, the French model is closer to the first and the Norwegian closer to the second.

Let me now turn to the tension between forward-looking and backward-looking arguments in dealing with victims and their suffering. The backward-looking argument, once again, is simple: society has a duty to undo the harm done to the victim. If possible, the undoing should restore the state that existed before the wrongdoing. Illegally expropriated property, in particular, should be given back to its original owners. If restoration is physically impossible, as in loss of liberty, damage to health or blocked career advancement, undoing requires full compensation. If full compensation is financially impossible, the allocation of partial compensation to victims has to be in accordance with principles of distributive justice.

The only case in which anything like a pure backward-looking policy has been applied is that of property restitution. Among the post-communist processes of transitional justice, Czechoslovakia and the Czech Republic have been the most adamant in respecting the rights of the original owners to get their property back in kind. As Vojtěch Cepl explains (1991), several reasons are involved: a philosophically based respect for the rights of the original owners (a backward-looking argument), a desire to send a signal to foreign investors that property rights will be protected (a forward-looking argument), and a desire to reduce the chances that the property would end up in the hands of the former nomenklatura (a form of punishment). In the former GDR, the Kohl government's adherence to the "strong property principles of conservative ideology" that also led to an emphasis on restitution in kind (Quint 1997, 153). Among the exceptions the most significant was laid down in the unification treaty, viz. that property expropriated during the period of Soviet occupation (1945 to 1949) would not be returned to the original owners.

Compensation for other forms of suffering or harm has ranged from symbolic to substantial, but has never been anything like full. The grounds for compensation in the West German federal restitution law of 1956, included harm to life, harm to body and health, harm to freedom, harm to possessions, harm to property, harm through payment of special taxes, fines, and costs, harm to career advancement, and harm to economic advancement. Compensation for these harms varied. For each month of deprivation of freedom, victims received the normal lump sum payment for false imprisonment, 150 DM (about $75). To compensate for harm to career, persecutees received civil servant pensions corresponding to one of the four civil service classes, depending on their position before the start of persecution (Pross 1998, 50–51; see also Elster 2004, chap. 6, for conundrums raised by compensation for counterfactual harm). Following the second German transition of 1989 and 1990, former political prisoners in the GDR could receive 300 DM for each month of imprisonment, and an additional 250 DM per month of imprisonment for those who resided in the GDR until November 9, 1989, the day the Berlin Wall was opened. Those who can show that they suffered interruption or denial of career for political reasons get assistance for reeducation and a small monthly payment (Quint 1997, 222–25).

Clearly, these reparations go only a small way toward undoing the harm. The reason is obvious: full compensation, whatever that might mean, would be too expensive. Even in the affluent Germany after 1990, "many asserted that any attempt to provide real compensation for [the effects of discrimination] would be quixotic and beyond the resources of the treasury of the Federal Republic" (Quint 1997, 224). The history of compensation schemes after 1945 and after 1989 revolves around this tension between the rights-based claims of the victims and the financial means and needs of the state. Legislative assemblies, faithfully assisted by lower courts, agencies and experts, have consistently sought to limit the grounds for compensation and the amounts of compensation.

Forward-looking arguments may be invoked to limit restitution as well as compensation. The Hungarian constitutional court used an explicitly forward-looking argument when it declared, in the first compensation case (decision reproduced in Sólyom and Brunner 2000, 114) that favoring original landowners was justified if and only if "it can be proved that with the preferential treatment of former owners the distribution of state property will yield a more favourable overall social result than equal treatment would." The German "unification treaty provided that a former owner can be denied a return of expropriated property if the property is needed for urgent investment uses that would yield general economic benefits in Eastern Germany" (Quint 1997, 129).

The rebuttal in 1995 by the Czech constitutional court of a petition to secure the restitution of formerly German-owned property seized after 1945 presents an especially interesting case. To grant the claim would open a floodgate of similar demands from the survivors and heirs of the almost three million Germans expelled from Czechoslovakia after World War II. To return properties in kind would have meant social turmoil. To offer more than symbolic compensation might bankrupt the country. These compelling reasons were not, however, the ones cited by the court. Instead, it made what Istvan Pogany calls a "deeply emotive judgment" about historical justice:

In the 1930s, a fateful decade for the Czechoslovak Republic, each of its citizens could have realized, or rather should have realized, that right here, under the veil of propaganda and lies on the part of Nazi Germany, one of the crucial historical clashes between propaganda and totalitarianism was taking place, a clash in which everyone bore responsibility together for the position they adopted and the social and political role they undertook, that is, the role of a defender of democracy or an agents of its destruction. . . . This applies as well to the German citizens in pre-war Czechoslovakia, and to them in particular, for the conflagration which Nazism unleashed was in large part the work of their nation and its leaders. All the more so should they have manifested their fidelity to the Czechoslovak Republic whose citizens they were (cited in Pogany 1997, 153).

This vindictive statement is based on an imputation of collective guilt. A few years earlier, the court had upheld similarly vindictive legislation by parliament, namely, the lustration law of 1991. The law blocked access to certain public offices for individuals who had been members of or served in communist organizations, with no need to show individual wrongdoing.[29] In these anti-Nazi and anticommunist decisions the preferences of the court appear to be based on emotion, not on reason.

Interest-Based Preferences in Transitional Justice

The two obvious places to look for interest-based preferences in transitional justice are among perpetrators and victims of property expropriation. The former want to avoid or minimize punishment, the latter to get their property back. Neither preference need be based exclusively on interest. In perpetrators, interest may be reinforced by fear. The preferences of former owners may be based in justice as well as in interests. I ignore the first, a relatively minor complication. The second is very important, and I will therefore discuss it shortly.

If the interest of the perpetrators in avoiding punishment is to have causal efficacy, they must be part of the decision-making process that shapes transitional justice. This may come about in one of two ways. If the transition to democracy is negotiated between the leaders of the old regime and the new democratic forces, the former invariably try to ensure immunity from prosecution after the transition. This pattern characterizes the southern European transitions of the mid-1970s as well as those of South Africa and many Latin American countries. Even if the transition occurs because the pre-democratic regime is defeated or implodes, the old leaders may be able to shape the form of transitional justice if they are allowed to participate in the democratic process. This pattern characterizes many post-communist transitions.

A military dictatorship or a regime based on coercive repression may enact self-immunity legislation to protect itself against future prosecution. In two of the following four cases they failed; in two they succeeded. In the trials of the Greek military after 1974, the Court of Appeal accepted the retroactive interpretation of the ambiguously worded amnesty law, which the military had wrongly believed would give them impunity (Alivizatos and Diamandouros 1997, 43–44).[30] In Argentina, General-President Reynoldo Bignone signed a self-amnesty law five weeks before the first free elections in 1983. After the elections, it was nullified by Congress in a unanimous vote (Nino 1996, 90–102).[31] In Chile, the military junta enacted an amnesty law in 1978. It was protected by the 1980 constitution, which sought to immunize itself against change by giving a prominent role to the military. After the democratic forces won the 1990 election it was upheld by the Chilean constitutional court and served as a deterrent for prosecution of wrongdoers until human-rights groups discovered a loophole in the law that allows the courts to treat some disappearance cases as kidnappings, a crime that has no statute of limitations. In Uruguay, the electorate voted in a 1989 referendum to uphold an amnesty law that the new democratic regime had enacted shortly after coming to power in 1986. It is widely believed that the law was passed as part of a negotiated deal for the transition (Linz and Stepan 1996, 154).

In South Africa, negotiations between the apartheid regime and the African National Congress concluded in 1993 with agreement on an interim constitution. In a last-minute addition to that document a postamble stated that "amnesty shall be granted in respect of acts, omissions and offences associated with political objectives and committed in the course of the conflicts of the past." Later, the conditions for amnesty were spelled out in the mandate of the Truth and Reconciliation Commission. Although in retrospect one can cite good reasons for the choice of amnesty, including the unfeasibility of large-scale trials and the need for national healing (Boraine 2000, chap. 8), there is little doubt that the 1993 decision was imposed by the interest of the former elite. After the transition, respect for the decision is, paradoxically, enforced by the interest of the black majority. It is widely and, I think, correctly believed that more radical prosecution of the white elite than allowed for in the Truth and Reconciliation mandate would trigger beliefs about a Zimbabwe scenario for Western investors and capital holders, to the detriment of economic development.

Perpetrator interests had minimal causal efficacy in post-1945 transitions. Economic collaborators could to some extent hold the country to ransom, by dragging out proceedings until the overriding concern for national reconstruction caused their cases to be dropped. More serious wrongdoers, however, had no leverage. In the post-1989 transitions, agents and collaborators of the communist regime have been able to shape transitional justice through the participation of ex-communist parties in democratic politics. In Czechoslovakia, Vaclav Havel deliberately opted for proportional elections, against his personal preferences for majority voting, in order to ensure a place for the ex-communists in the first freely elected parliament. Although this decision may have been fatal for the constitution-making process and for the unity of the federation, it does not seem to have affected transitional justice. In other countries, though, the presence of communists in parliaments and in the government have had a demonstrable impact on the scope of transitional justice. When ex-communist parties are in power but expect to lose the next elections, they enact mild lustration laws by appealing to a pivotal median party, thus preventing harsher legislation favored by hard line anticommunists (Nalepa 2005).

Although many transitions take place in an atmosphere of national unity, it usually does not take long before party interests, over and above those involving members of the pre-democratic regime, come to the forefront. After the transition, political parties may engage in a "more retributive than thou" competition for electoral gain or, on the contrary, seek to minimize the extent of transitional justice. Also, parties may seek to disqualify the voters of other parties on grounds of collaboration with the former regime. Some examples follow.

In German-occupied countries after World War II, party politics played an important role in shaping transitional justice. In several countries, the intransigent attitude of the Communist Party after Liberation forced other parties to take a similar stance, so as not to be outdone electorally in anti-Fascism (for France, see Novick (1968), 179; for Denmark, Tamm 1984, 259; for Belgium, Huyse and Dhondt 1993, 153). In Belgium, members of the opposition suffered loss of civil liberties just before strategic elections, intended to deprive them either of their right to vote or their right to stand for office (Huyse and Dhondt 1993, 31, 151–52). The political landscape was complicated by the division between the Flemish and Wallon communities, and the role of Flemish nationalism. Whereas the socialists wanted to use severe retroactive measures to eliminate Flemish nationalists from the voter register, the Catholic party promoted clemency to prevent the formation of a Flemish nationalist party that might drain votes from the Catholics (181–82). In Italy, the Communist leader Palmiro Togliatti came back from Moscow with the intention of collaborating with the middle classes. "An intensive purge could hardly be in the best interests of this policy" (Woller 1998, 539).

In Germany and Austria after 1945, the presence of a large electorate with a Nazi past was a key factor in politics. In Germany, once the Allies had handed transitional justice over to the Germans, electoral politics set severe limits to what could be done. Even the Social Democrats had to take account of the fact that the bulk of their supporters had a murky past (Giordano 2000, 95; Frei 1999, 56). Commenting on the high number of early releases of war criminals in Austria, Winfried Garscha writes:

> One of the reasons for this remarkable clemency was the fact that the 500,000 former members of the Nazi party represented an attractive voters' reservoir. In 1945 they had temporarily lost their right to vote. Before the elections of 1949, when they were allowed to vote again, a disgraceful run on the Nazi votes began. The two big parties, the conservatives and the socialists, were keen on proving that they acted on behalf of the "soldiers generation." (1997)

In Eastern Europe, the electoral usages of transitional justice (competition among noncommunist parties has been most striking in Poland). Andrzej Walicki refers to a group of

> ambitious and power-hungry politicians, who saw themselves as representing Solidarity's right and could draw upon at least two reasons for deep personal frustration: the first was their marginalization at the Round Table talks, and the second, the failure of Mazowiecki's government to offer them a satisfactory share of power. The leading figure in this group, Jaroslaw Kaczynski . . . was not interested in historical justice. Above all, he wanted to oust Mazowiecki from power, and this, he thought, could best be done by accusing his followers of the proverbial "softness of communism." Kaczynski also hoped to use radical decommunization as a means of placating Poland's industrial workers: a broad change of personnel in industrial management though the elimination of the old nomenklatura, he thought, would give them "moral compensation" for the inevitable moral losses resulting from accelerated marketization. (1997, 191, 193)

Transmutation

I have tacitly assumed that emotion, reason, and passion are distinct and stable motivations. It is time to muddy the waters, and to consider how one motivation may undergo a transmutation into another (Elster 1999, 2). In transitional justice, interest and revenge are usually perceived as inferior motivations (see earlier Preferences and Motivations). There is, therefore, a normative pressure on those who are animated by these motivations to present them, to themselves and to others, in the guise of justice. More subtly, there is a pressure to resolve tensions between the desire for substantive justice and the desire for procedural justice, so as to be able to accomplish both.

Earlier I defined interest-based preferences as the pursuit of advantage. That definition, while useful in many cases, is too narrow in others. Often, interest and reason blend into ideology. This is particularly striking in the context of property restitution. After the transition in 1989, the strongest demands for restitution of landed property came from the party of the Independent Smallholders, who

> sought restitution in a very specific and limited sense—reversion to the property relations on agricultural land found in 1947. The date is crucial; it fell after the post-war land reforms which resulted in the redistribution of land from the large estates to peasants and agricultural labourers, but before the Communist-dictated process of enforced collectivisation. The 1947 fate also fell comfortably after the confiscation of Jewish-owned property (including agricultural land) and after the expulsion of much of the Volksdeutsche from Hungary. Thus, for the Smallholders, restitution was seen as a means of reconstituting a particular social order in Hungary, one characterised by a pronounced emphasis on the agrarian sector and by a comparatively egalitarian and homogeneous (i.e. Hungarian) peasant-oriented culture. (Pogany 1997, 156)

The Smallholders no doubt believed themselves to be motivated by the general interests of Hungarian society rather than by the class interests of small landowners. This is the pattern of many ideological beliefs. As Marx noted, "one must not form the narrow-minded notion that the petty bourgeoisie, on principle, wishes to enforce an egoistic class interest. Rather, it believes that the special conditions of its emancipation are the general conditions within which alone modern society can be saved and the class struggle be avoided" (1852/1977, 130).

Commenting on the German debates over property restitution after 1989, Peter Quint makes a similar observation. Referring to 1992 governmental guidelines that privileged former owners of the land confiscated during the Soviet occupation period, he writes:

> This important political battle to some extent resembles an old-fashioned class struggle: in many cases it pitted the large land owners or their descendants against persons who had actually worked the land. . . . Moreover, the 1992 guidelines reflected political and ideological concerns, as

they favored largely conservative private investors over the suspect successors of the former [agricultural collectives]; they also incorporated the
deeply ingrained preference in Western Germany for individual rather
than cooperative ownership in agriculture. (1997, 140)

In other cases it is professional rather than (merely) economic interest
that is dressed up in the garbs of principle. This is especially striking
when judges are asked to screen or condemn themselves on the basis of
their implication in the pre-democratic regime. In South Africa (Dyzenhaus 1998, 138–50) as well as in Poland (Schwartz 2000, 63), judges have
resisted outside interference by appealing to the need for an independent
judiciary, in spite of the complete lack of independence that most of the
same judges showed under apartheid or communism. In the case of Hitler's judges, the retroactive adoption of legal positivism served the same
purpose: "Although it was clear to every jurist during the Nazi era . . .
that National Socialist legal doctrines were the exact opposite of legal
positivism, the claim that judges and prosecutors were merely following
the law and that, after all, this was how they had been trained by their
democratic professors during the Weimar Republic became a blanket excuse for the whole profession" (Müller 1991, 220).

In transitional justice, transmutation can make it difficult to distinguish among three attitudes toward wrongdoers: the emotionally based
desire for revenge, the desire for substantive justice, and the desire for
transitional justice (Sa'adah 1998, 145 ff). As noted earlier, the fact that
the demand for justice tends to decay with time suggests that it has a
strong emotional underpinning. In addition, there is an internal tension
within the desire for justice itself. In democracies that emerge from law-
less regimes, whether authoritarian or totalitarian, the new leaders often
want to show their adherence to the rule of law and the Rechtsstaat. The
post-1945 trials in Western Europe were shaped by this consideration. In
Norway, the use of summary trials was dismissed as an expression of an
unacceptable Nazi mentality (Andenæs 1980, 62). In Belgium, internment
practices were severely criticized for resembling how things were done
"on the other side of the Rhine" (Huyse and Dhondt 1993, 100). In
France, retroactive legislation was condemned as a Vichy practice (Lottman 1986, 50),[32] and anonymous denunciations—another Vichy custom—were not accepted (186).

The desire for legality often goes together with a strong desire for a
large fraction of the collaborators to be convicted. As Peter Novick remarks about France, "side by side with this passionate longing [for retri-
bution] was the attachment of résistants to those principles of justice and
equity which distinguished them from the rulers of Nazi Germany and

Vichy France" (1968, 141). Istvan Deák (2000) notes that in post-1945 Hungary, the Minister of Justice insisted "both on the need to observe strict legal procedures and on the need to exercise revolutionary political justice." In many cases, however, there is a conflict between the desire for procedural justice and the desire for substantive justice, between the desire to demarcate oneself from the earlier regime and the desire to punish the regime as severely as it deserves. Former East German dissident Bärbel Bohley's now-famous statement made this clear: "We expected justice, but we got the Rechtsstaat instead" (cited in McAdams 1997, 240).

New democracies can resolve the dilemma in one of three ways. First, one can insist on respect for basic legal principles such as a ban on retroactive legislation or an extension of the statute of limitations. This has, for instance, consistently been the approach of the Hungarian Constitutional Court after 1989 (Halmai and Scheppele 1997; Schwartz 2000, chap. 4). Second, one can frankly and openly accept the need to violate these principles in an unprecedented situation. After 1945, Denmark and Holland adopted explicit retroactive legislation, a procedure that was probably facilitated by the fact that neither country has a ban on retroactivity in the constitution. Third, and this is the most common procedure, one can use subterfuge to try and have it both ways. In 1948, a Belgian commentator wrote that "the Dutch system [of specifically permitting retroactivity] is more sincere than ours. The Belgian legislator pretended to adhere to the principle of non-retroactivity in criminal law. In reality [the Penal Code] . . . was made increasingly severe by so-called interpretative laws" (Mason 1952, 130; see also House and Dhondt 1993, 28–29, 64–65, for retroactivity of much Belgian legislation). The same year, a Dutch law professor "criticized the French who—in order to avoid retroactive penalties—called the often severe sanctions of the new 'national indignity' crime 'losses of rights' instead of penalties. 'This seems to me a mere playing with words; a confiscation of one's entire property, or even a loss of certain rights, is as much a . . . [penalty] as say a fine or the deprivation of liberty" (Mason 1952, 130; for retroactivity of French legislation see also Novick 1968, 146 and Lottman 1986, 51–52).

The trials of the border guards in the former GDR arguably rested on legal subterfuge. To comply with the clause in the unification treaty that prosecution could only target acts that were crimes under East German as well as West German law, the Federal Supreme Court of Germany reconstructed an ideal law of the GDR from supralegal principles of natural law. Peter Quint comments on this decision:

> For all their earnestness and complexity, opinions of this sort seem to be
> lacking in candor. The court creates an ideal law of the GDR, through the

use of techniques and principles resembling those current in the Federal Republic, solely for the purpose of saying that this hypothetical construct was "really" the law of the GDR and therefore its application today is not retroactive. . . . It would seem much more direct and honest to say: The law of the GDR as it actually existed was unacceptable and therefore we are applying a new law to these cases. Perhaps under prevailing interpretations of the Unification Treaty . . . that acknowledgment could mean the end of these cases, but these issues nonetheless deserve a more general consideration. (1997, 203)

Conclusion

I have focused on the formation of preferences that generate a demand for or a resistance to measures of transitional justice. Typically, these preferences can be linked to the location of the agents in the autocratic political system that preceded the transition. Wrongdoers, beneficiaries from wrongdoing, victims, resisters, and neutrals tend to have systematically different preferences with regard to what should be done. To understand how these preferences generate political decisions to carry out or to refrain from transitional justice, we must locate the same agents within the post-transitional institutions. What power do these institutions confer on them to enact policies that reflect their preferences? I cannot do full justice to this question, but the following comments may serve as a brief summary.

At one extreme, the former wrongdoers may be well placed to block or limit transitional justice. This is notably the case when they retain control over the repressive apparatus, as in many Latin American transitions. In South Africa, the economic power of the white elite has forced the political majority to pull their punches. In these cases, the incoming democrats have had to content themselves with the establishment of truth commissions and, in some cases, financial compensation to victims. Most wrongdoers have gone free.

At another extreme, the former wrongdoers are largely excluded from political life after the transition. This was notably the case after 1945, in Germany and in the countries allied with or occupied by Germany. In West Germany, allied pressure led to the ban on the neo-Nazi party. Indirectly, though, the Nazi elite was able to exercise political influence through two of the smaller political parties. In Austria and Belgium, Nazi members or sympathizers were disenfranchised. In other German-occupied countries, many collaborators lost the right to vote.

Between the extremes we find the post-1989 transitions in Eastern Europe. Although the communist parties did not retain any leverage from the former regime, they were allowed to reestablish themselves, and in several countries actually went on to form the government. In many places, transitional justice is still at the heart of political conflict. In Hungary and Poland, ex-communist parties in power have even proposed mild purges (lustration) of former communists to preempt harsher measures by the predicted non-communist winners of the next elections (Nalepa 2005).

Future episodes of transitional justice are likely to be heavily shaped by international institutions, as shown by the complex processes in Sierra Leone, Cambodia, and East Timor. Endogenous transitional justice will also become less important as national courts assume international jurisdiction. The forms of transitional justice I have discussed—in which a society has to come to terms with itself—may be a thing of the past. National institutions and the preferences of domestic actors will continue to matter, but they will no longer be decisive.

Notes

1. The Spanish transition of 1978 is the best-known instance in which there was a conscious decision not to have any form of transitional justice (Aguilar 2001).
2. For a reference to these three motivations at work in transitional justice, see a mid-1783 letter from the New York Chancellor Robert Livingston to Alexander Hamilton: "I seriously lament with you, the violent spirit of persecution which prevails here and dread its consequences upon the wealth, commerce & future tranquillity of the state. I am the more hurt at it because it appears to me almost unmixed with *purer patriotic motives*. In some few it is a blind spirit of *revenge & resentment*, but in more it is the most *sordid interest*" (cited in McDonald 1982, 75; italicized phrases correspond to reason, emotion and interest, respectively).
3. This idea is unrelated to the concept of meta-preferences introduced by Sen (1977). An example of his approach would be a person with two different preference orderings, one for eating over dieting and one for dieting over eating, and a meta-preference favoring the latter. In my example in the text, the meta-motivation amounts to a preference for preferring dieting over eating on grounds of health over having the same preference ordering on grounds of vanity.
4. This was a standard treatment of loyalists during and to some extent after the American War of Independence (van Tyne 1902/2001, 61, 241, 295). It also occurred occasionally in the Liberation of France in 1944.
5. Rousso cites a slightly smaller figure for France (2001, 501), and Woller a slightly larger one for Italy (1996, 279).
6. In France, the only country for which the phenomenon has been systemati-

cally studied, the number may be around 20,000 (Virgili 2000, 74–78;. for a survey of the practice in the other countries, see 271–78).

7. This is one of the factors cited as affecting the strength of the demand for retribution (Nino 1996, 126–27). Indicating factors that increase it by [+] and those that decrease it by [-], the others are: (1) the heinousness of the crimes [+]; (2) absolute and relative quantity of the abuses [+]; (3) social identification with victims of the abuses [+]; (4) social identification with perpetrators of abuses [-] and (5) diffusion of responsibility [-]. To these I would add (6) pre-democratic regime imposed by a foreign power [+]; (7) diffusion of knowledge about the abuses [+]; (8) absolute and relative prosperity of perpetrators after the transition [+] and (9) time span between transition and trials [-]. I treat the last factor separately in the text.

8. For Norway, see Johs Andenæs (1980, 229); for Denmark, see Tamm (1984, chap.7); for Holland, see Mason (1952, 187 n.36); for Italy, see Domenico (1991, 178); for Belgium, see Huyse and Dhondt (1993, 231). Huyse and Dhondt consider and reject the objection that the trend could be an artifact of the most serious crimes having been tried first. The only exception is France, for which Novick (1968, 164 n.12) finds no evidence for the hypothesis of progressive leniency of sentencing, but is not able to rule it out.

9. Commenting on the 1945 execution of a member of the extreme-right government of Ferenc Szálasi, László Karsai writes: "There must have been two main reasons behind the execution of Pálffy: his trial was among the first to be held and his relationship with Szálasi was ideologically closer than that of Szakváry or Hellebronth. One might add that had he not descended from a great historic family and had he been tried in the second half of 1946, after the people's judges' thirst for blood had been quenched, he may well have received only a life sentence" (2000, 243; see also Huyse and Dhondt 1993, 119; and Frijda 1994).

10. For a general discussion of this tendency, see Slovic (2000, chap.24.) For examples from transitional justice, see Huyse and Dhondt (1993, 49) and Andenæs (1980, 182). A World War II story provides a telling illustration. In August 1945, five thousand German prisoners of war participated in minesweeping operations in Norway. One hundred and eighty-four of them were killed during the operations. Although this practice was almost certainly a violation of the Geneva convention, nobody paid much attention to it at the time.

11. To my knowledge, the first to emphasize the distinction between perpetrators and beneficiaries was Mamdani (1996/2001).

12. Thus David Dyzenhaus, a vocal opponent of apartheid before its abolition, writes that "the direct benefit of the ordinary violence of apartheid to all whites was a 'cushy' lifestyle, some (including myself) living in luxury virtually unmatched in the rest of the world" (1998, 12).

13. This is the claim of Lysias in the speech *Against Philon*, given when Philon

had to be approved by the Council before he could take the seat on it to which he had been chosen by lot. Lysias first says that nobody has the right to stay neutral in a civic strife such as the struggle between the oligarchs and the democrats in 403 B.C., and adds that Philon "had no intention of aiding the city, in such a position of her affairs; his purpose was to make a profit out of your disasters."

14. However, there are two competing narratives: one that saw "apartheid as part of a system of racial-capitalism [and] held that apartheid was beneficial for (white) business," and one that claimed "that apartheid raised the costs of doing business, eroded South Africa's skill base and undermined long-term productivity and growth" (TRC 1999, vol. 4, 19).

15. Fehr and Fischbacher (2003) show that in experiments where individuals are allowed to punish those who behave unjustly, at some cost to the punishers, "third-party punishments" by external observers are typically weaker than "second-party punishments" by the victims of the injustice. Yet even third-party punishments are surprisingly strong.

16. Anti-Semitism, when it rests on the premise that the evil of Jews is intrinsic, "in their blood," does not need evidence of bad action; it also follows that Jews cannot be redeemed by good actions.

17. There is a clear difference between noninstrumental torture (sadism) and torture to gather information. Reading the account of a self-confessed torturer of the latter variety in Aussaresses (2001), it is not obvious to me that he was an evil man. What he did was wrong, and he should have been punished, but less severely than sadistic torturers. My intuitions on this point are not strong, and certainly less firm than those of the Italian Corte di Cazzatione, which reversed a number of convictions for gruesome crimes on the grounds that there were others that were still worse (Woller 1996 388–89). Thus "A most unfortunate and grotesque distinction was drawn between 'ordinary' tortures and tortures that were particularly 'atrocious'. Using this formula the courts were able to pardon the following crimes: the multiple rape of a woman partisan; a partisan tied to a roof who was punched and kicked like a punch-bag; electric torture on the genitals applied though a field telephone. On this last case, the Corte di Cazzatione ... ruled that the tortures 'took place only for intimidatory purposes and not through bestial insensibility'" (Ginsborg (1990, 92). The contrast could not be greater with the claim of the French Communists that "résistants who under torture gave information to the Germans were 'objectively' traitors and had to be punished as such" (Novick 1968, 179).

18. "Even liberal states are more likely to seek justice for war crimes committed against their own citizens, not against innocent foreigners" (Bass 2000, 8). After 1945, the target of American reactions to Nazi crimes is summarized as "the war first, the Holocaust second," with particular "concern over war crimes committed against American soldiers" (173, 177). The attitude of the

cabinet member (Henry Morgenthau) who was most outraged at Nazi atrocities of the Jews was explained by another member (Henry Stimson) as "Semitism gone wild for vengeance" (152, 167). Morgenthau was Jewish. Whereas other members of Roosevelt's administration felt anger for what the Germans had done to Americans and at most indignation at what they had done to the Jews, Morgenthau felt anger at the Holocaust because he identified himself with the victims.

19. The sentence of national indignity adopted in many countries after World War II varied a great deal. In France, the disqualifications included loss of the right to vote and to hold elective office; a ban on public employment, exclusion from leading functions in semi-public corporations, banks as well as newspapers and radio; and exclusion from the legal and teaching professions (Novick 1968, 148–49). In Belgium, they included loss of political rights, but also of the right to exercise the professions of doctor and lawyer, priest, journalist or teacher, as well as exclusion from leading functions in any organization whatsoever (Huyse and Dhondt 1993, 30–33). In Holland, courts could deprive collaborators of the right to vote and to be elected; to serve in the armed forces; to hold government positions; and the right to exercise certain occupations. As a separate measure, loss of citizenship and hence of property was imposed on forty thousand Dutch men and, as an automatic consequence, on their wives (Mason 1952, 64–68). In Norway, the legislation was Draconian, including the loss of the right to own real estate, but practice was generally lenient (Justis-og Politidepartmentet 1962, 426–29). In Denmark, comparable measures were proposed but not adopted (Tamm 1984, 590–92). Further variations arise in the duration of disqualifications, ranging from five years to life, and in whether they could be applied separately or only en bloc.

20. Claus Offe (personal communication) made this observation in the context of the low level of prosecution of leaders and agents of the former GDR.

21. Although I cannot cite written sources for the post-1989 East European transitions, many conversations with knowledgeable individuals in the region suggest that the tendency operated there as well. In the Algerian transition to independence, the most vindictive in the killing of harkis (Algerians who had collaborated with the French) were those who had joined the National Liberation Front at a very late date, even after Independence (Hamoumou 1993, 250; Méliani 1993, 57). In an analogy to the "septembrists" who joined the French resistance after Liberation in August 1944, these were referred to as "marchians" because they joined the Front after the Evian agreements in March 1962.

22. Referring to France, Belgium, and the Netherlands, Lagrou writes that "the definition of what and who had been elements of the resistance, accommodation or collaboration became one of the most vehemently debates political issues of the post-war years" (2000, 25). In France, the National Assembly

adopted in March 1950 legislation saying that to obtain the coveted carte du combattant one had to prove active involvement in the resistance beginning at least ninety days before the Normandy landings; to benefit from the similar Belgian act any activity before the landings was sufficient (45, 51).

23. In his exhaustive treatment of the subject, Gain asserts that "it would be more correct to say that the purchaser, looked down upon and despised by the former owner, envied and ridiculed by his neighbor, retreated into a defiant isolation vis-à-vis the regime and, until 1830, gladly posed as a victim" (1928, vol. I, 348). These motivational nuances are hard to assess.

24. Thus "the early actions of the Alfonsín regime in prosecuting the former military rulers stimulated some Uruguayan military to back away from their commitment to relinquish power" (Huntington 1991, 103). The same argument is stated in an editorial in *The Economist* of August 31, 1996: "It is probably true that neither the generals who run Myanmar, nor President Suharto in Indonesia, nor the Communist Party in China, will be encouraged to move towards democracy by the fate of Messrs Chun and Roh. After all, Mr Roh ceded power as gracefully as any military man can. Now he has fallen victim to the process of democratisation that he helped to foster. The moral drawn by Asia's nervous dictators may well be that, when democrats are at the door, lock them up rather than usher them in."

25. For several reasons, small firms were disproportionately targeted. Trying large firms took more time, partly because the cases were more complicated and partly because large firms could afford good lawyers who would drag out their cases through appeals. This time factor was doubly decisive in explaining why large firms were then rarely prosecuted: the demand for retribution decayed with time, and the imperatives of reconstruction made it very costly to have big firms in legal limbo.

26. On the basis of new evidence, Rousso states that the traditionally cited number of 11,000 administrative sanctions (for a population of forty million) may have to be doubled. For Belgium (population ten million) Huyse and Dhondt cite a total of 10,000 sanctions (1993, 39). In the former East Germany (population sixteen million), there were forty-two thousand dismissals from public service on grounds of collaboration with the state security service (McAdams 2001, 73).

27. In Belgium, too, members of the resistance claimed a central place in judging the collaborators, but with less success (Huyse and Dhondt 1993, 72, 90–93).

28. This tension between what she calls the "institutional strategy" and the "cultural strategy" is the central theme of Sa'adah (1997; see also Boraine 2000, 15).

29. The text of the law, together with a memorandum critical of the law (written by Herman Schwartz, Lloyd Cutler and Diane Orentlicher) are found

in Kritz (1995, vol. 3). The court's decision to uphold the law, with some modifications, is also reproduced there.

30. The importance of the issue is brought out by the following comment: "to the extent that the phrasing of the amnesty decree appeared to include principals of the authoritarian regime and thus provided them with an additional incentive to remain quiescent, it afforded the incoming civilian leadership precious breathing space during which to proceed with the implementation of its democratization strategy" (Alivizatos and Diamandouros 1997, 59 n.42).

31. Yet in his efforts to implement transitional justice President Alfonsín remained heavily constrained by the continued presence of the military.

32. François Mauriac saw in the willingness of Albert Camus to adopt retroactive laws "the corrosive effect of four years of fascist rule" (Sa'adah 1998, 54).

References

Aguilar, Paloma. 2001. "Justice, Politics and Memory in the Spanish Transition." In *The Politics of Memory*, edited by Alexandra B. de Brito, Carmen Gonzaléz-Enríquez, and Paloma Aguilar. Oxford: Oxford University Press.

Alivizatos, Nicos C., and P. Nikiforos Diamandouros. 1997. "Politics and the Judiciary in the Greek Transition to Democracy." In *Transitional Justice and the Rule of Law in New Democracies*, edited by James McAdams. Notre Dame, Ind.: University of Notre Dame Press.

Andenæs, Johs. 1980. *Det Vanskelige Oppgjøret*. Oslo: Tanum-Norli.

Aussaresses, Paul. 2001. *Services spéciaux: Algérie 1955–57*. Paris: Perrin.

Bass, Gary Jonathan. 2000. *Stay the Hand of Vengeance*. Cambridge, Mass.: Harvard University Press.

Boraine, Alex. 2000. *A Country Unmasked*. Oxford: Oxford University Press.

Cepl, Vojtěch. 1991. A Note on the Restitution of Property in Post-Communist Czechoslovakia. *Journal of Communist Studies* 7: 368–75.

Cohen, David. 1999. "Beyond Nuremberg: Individual responsibility for war crimes." In *Human Rights in Political Transitions*, edited by Carla Hesse and Robert Post. New York: Zenith Books.

Deák, Istevan. 2000. "Political Justice in Austria and Hungary after World War II." Unpublished manuscript, Columbia University.

Descartes, René. 1985. "Passions of the soul." In *The Philosophical Writings of Descartes*, vol. I. Cambridge: Cambridge University Press.

Domenico, Roy P. 1991. *Italian Fascists on Trial*. Chapel Hill: University of North Carolina Press.

Dyzenhaus, David. 1998. *Judging the Judges, Judging Ourselves: Truth, Reconciliation and the Apartheid Legal Order*. Oxford: Hart Publishing.

Elster, Jon. 1999. *Alchemies of the Mind*. Cambridge: Cambridge University Press.

―――. 2004. *Closing the Books*, Cambridge University Press.

Fehr, Ernst, and Fischbacher, Urs. 2003. "Third Party Norm Enforcement." Working Paper No. 106. Institute for Empirical Research in Economics, University of Zürich.

Frei, Norbert. 1999. *Vergangenheitspolitik*. Munich: Deutsche Taschenbuch Verlag.

Frijda, Nico. 1986. *The Emotions*. Cambridge: Cambridge University Press.

―――. 1994. "The Lex Talionis: On vengeance." In *Emotions: Essays on Emotion Theory*, edited by S. N. Goozen, N. E. van de Poll, and J. A. Sergeant. Hillsdale, N.J.: Lawrence Erlbaum.

Gain, André. 1928. *La restauration et les biens des émigrés*. Nancy: Société d'Impressions Typographiques.

Garscha, Winfried R. 1997. "The second Austrian Republic and the sequels of the Nazi dictatorship." Lecture at the Harriman Institute, Columbia University, New York (October 16). Available at http://www.doew.at/secondaustrian.htm.

Ginsborg, Paul. 1990. *A History of Modern Italy*. Harmondsworth: Penguin.

Giordano, Ralph. 2000. *Die Zweite Schuld*. Köln: Kiepenhauer und Witsch.

Goldhagen, Daniel. 1996. *Hitler's Willing Executioners*. New York: Alfred A. Knopf.

de la Gorce, Pierre. 1926. *Louis XVIII*. Paris: Plon.

Halmai, Gabor, and Scheppele, Kim Lane. 1997. "Living Well Is the Best Revenge: The Hungarian Approach to Judging the Past." In *Transitional Justice and the Rule of Law in New Democracies*, edited by James McAdams. Notre Dame, Ind.: University of Notre Dame Press.

Hamoumou, Mohand. 1993. *Et ils sont devenus harkis*. Paris: Fayard.

Holmes, Stephen, and Cass Sunstein. 1998. *The Cost of Rights*. New York: W. W. Norton.

Huntington, Samuel P. 1991. *The Third Wave: Democratization in the Late Twentieth Century*. Norman: University of Oklahoma Press.

Huyse, Luc, and Steven Dhondt. 1993. *La répression des collaborations*. Bruxelles: CRISP.

Justis-og Politidepartmentet. 1962. *Om Landssvikoppgjøret*. Gjøvik: Mariendals Boktrykkeri.

Karsai, László. 2000. "The People's Courts and Revolutionary Justice in Hungary, 1945–46." In *The Politics of Retribution in Europe*, edited by I. Deák, J. Gross, and T. Judt. Princeton, N.J.: Princeton University Press.

Kirchheimer, Otto. 1961. *Political Justice*. Princeton, N.J.: Princeton University Press.

Kritz, Neil J., ed. 1995. *Transitional Justice*, vols. I–III. Washington, D.C.: U.S. Institute of Peace Press.

Lacouture, Jean. 1995. *De Gaulle*. Vols. I–III. Paris: Seuil.

Lagrou, Pietre. 2000. *The Legacy of Nazi Occupation*. Cambridge: Cambridge University Press.

Lindsay-Hartz, J., J. de Rivera, and M. F. Mascolo. 1995. "Differentiating Guilt and Shame and Their Effects on Motivation." In *Self-Conscious Emotions*, edited by J. P. Tangney and K. W. Fischer. New York: The Guilford Press.

Linz, Juan, and Alfred Stepan. 1996. *Problems of Democratic Transition and Consolidation*. Baltimore, Md.: The Johns Hopkins University Press.

Loewenstein, George. 1996. "Out of Control: Visceral Influences on Behavior." *Organizational Behavior and Human Decision Processes* 65: 272–92.

Lottman, Herbert. 1986. *L'épuration*. Paris: Fayard.

Mamdani, Mahmood. 1996/2001. "Reconciliation Without Justice." *Southern African Review of Books* No. 46. Reprinted in *Religion and Media*, edited by Hent de Vries and Samuel Weber. Stanford, Calif.: Stanford University Press.

Marx, Karl. 1852/1977. *The Eighteenth Brumaire of Louis Napoleon*. In *Marx and Engels Collected Works*, vol. 11. London: Lawrence and Wishart.

Mason, Henry L. 1952. *The Purge of Dutch Quislings*. The Hague: Martinus Nijhoff.

McAdams, A. James, ed. 1997. *Transitional Justice and the Rule of Law in New Democracies*. Notre Dame, Ind.: University of Notre Dame Press.

———. 2001. *Judging the Past in Unified Germany*. Cambridge: Cambridge University Press.

McDonald, Forrest. 1982. *Alexander Hamilton*. New York: W.W. Norton.

Méliani, Abd-El-Aziz. 1993. *Le drame des harkis*. Paris: Perrin.

Michnik, Adam, and Vaclav Havel. 1993. "Confronting the Past: Justice or Revenge?" *Journal of Democracy* 4: 20–27.

Müller, Ingo. 1991. *Hitler's Justice*. Cambridge, Mass.: Harvard University Press.

Nalepa, Monika. 2005. "The Power of Secret Information: Transitional Justice After Communism." Ph.D. diss., Department of Political Science, Columbia University.

Nino, Carlos. 1996. *Radical Evil on Trial*. New Haven, Conn.: Yale University Press.

Novick, Peter. 1968. *The Resistance Versus Vichy*. London: Chatto and Windus.

Pogany, Istvan. 1997. *Righting Wrongs in Eastern Europe*. Manchester: Manchester University Press.

Pross, Christian. 1998. *Paying for the Past*. Baltimore, Md.: The Johns Hopkins University Press.

Quint, Peter. 1997. *The Imperfect Union*. Princeton, N.J.: Princeton University Press.

Rothleutner, Hubert. 1994. "Deutsche Vergangenheiten verglichen." In *Die Normalität des Verbrechen*, Festschrift für Wolfgang Scheffler zum 65. Geburrtstag, herausgegeben von Helge Grabitz, Klaus Bäustlein, Johannes Tuchel, Berlin: Edition Hentrich.

Rousso, Henry. 2001. *Vichy. L'événement, la mémoire, l'histoire*. Paris: Gallimard.

Sa'adah, Anne. 1998. *Germany's Second Chance*. Cambridge, Mass.: Harvard University Press.

Schwartz, Herman. 2000. *Constitutional Justice in Central and Eastern Europe*. Chicago: University of Chicago Press.

Sen, Amartya K. 1977. "Rational Fools: A Critique of the Behavioral Foundations of Economic Theory." *Philosophy and Public Affairs* 6(4): 317–44.

Slovic, Pail. 2000. *The Perception of Risk*. Sterling, Va.: Earthscan Publications.

Sólyom, Laszlo, and G. Brunner. 2000. *Constitutional Judiciary in a New Democracy*. Ann Arbor: University of Michigan Press.

Tamm, Ditlev. 1984. *Retsopgøret efter Besættelsen*. Copenhagen: Jurist-og Økonomforbundets Forlag.

Taylor, Lawrence. 1981. *A Trial of Generals*. South Bend, Ind.: Icarus Press.

Taylor, Telford. 1992. *The Anatomy of the Nuremberg Trials*. New York: Alfred A. Knopf.

Tocqueville, Alexis de. 1840/1969. *Democracy in America*. New York: Anchor Books.

TRC. 1999. *Truth and Reconciliation of South Africa Report*. London: Macmillan.

Tucker, Aviezer. 2000. "Paranoids May Be Persecuted: Post-Totalitarian Transitional Justice." *European Journal of Sociology* 41(1): 56–100.

Van Tyne, Claude. 1902/2001. *The Loyalists in the American Revolution*. Safety Harbor, Fla.: Simon Publications.

Virgili, Fabrice. 2000. La France "virile." *Les femmes tondues à la libération*. Paris: Payot.

Walicki, Andrzej. 1997. "Transitional justice and the political struggles of post-Communist Poland." In *Transitional Justice and the Rule of Law in New Democracies*, edited by James McAdams. Notre Dame, Ind.: University of Notre Dame Press.

Woller, Hans. 1996. *Die Abrechnung mit dem Faschismus in Italien 1943 bis 1948*. Munich: Oldenbourg Verlag.

———. 1998. "The Political Purge in Italy." In *Modern Europe after Fascism*, edited by S. Ugelvik Larsen. New York: Columbia University Press.

10

What the Politics of Enfranchisement Can Tell Us About How Rational Choice Theorists Study Institutions

James Johnson

The emergence of democracy arguably is the single most important political phenomenon of the twentieth century.[1] And the right to vote, interpreted rather expansively, is as close to a defining component of contemporary democratic institutions as we might find.[2] There is now a virtual international consensus that only mental deficiency (however arbitrarily defined) and age afford grounds for restricting the franchise. Indeed, there is no agreement across democracies about whether even prison inmates, nonresidents, or noncitizens can rightly be excluded from the vote (Blais, Massicotte, and Yoshinaka 2001). This is a remarkable if usually flawed, often precarious, and hardly preordained accomplishment.[3] I use an historical sketch of the politics of enfranchisement in the United States and elsewhere to focus discussion of the tasks rational choice theorists face in analyzing institutional emergence and change.[4] This sketch focuses attention on supply-side issues and suggests that even in instances when the eventual outcome is normatively attractive, such as the emergence of universal suffrage, we need not abandon the standard view of political actors as primarily strategic and self-interested.

Institutions are sets of rules (for example, roles, procedures, offices) that emerge from and subsequently structure social and political interaction. They can be informal and decentralized (for example, various norms and conventions), formal and centralized (for example, legally mandated and monitored arrangements) or, more plausibly, a mixture of the two (think of how everything from families to the Congress or the Supreme Court operate in the United States). In either case, however, institutional rules specify not simply such things as what can be done, by and to whom, and when, but also what happens when the rules are breached and who is to do what to whom in such circumstances.[5] It is of course a crucial part of any institution to identify such third parties. Informal social norms may require all or most members of a community to react to noncooperation. More formal, centralized institutions, by contrast, typically will assign this task to particular officials. This is unimportant for present purposes. In this sense institutions differ from bare behavioral regularities.[6] Institutional rules often demand that individuals act in ways that run counter to their immediate or even longer term interests or preferences. It thus is crucial to see that institutions ultimately must be self-enforcing—that is, that they must rest on the mutual expectations of relevant participants. In other words, we must be able to account not only for institutional equilibria, those persistent patterns of interaction that institutions induce, but must also establish that such outcomes are generated by arrangements that themselves are equilibrium institutions (Shepsle 1989, 138; Weingast 1996). This complicates matters because there typically will be several, perhaps many, feasible ways of institutionalizing social and political interaction. Consequently, any given institution and the larger arrangements of which it is a component represent large-scale coordination equilibria in some underlying, usually ongoing, strategic interaction (Calvert 1995a, b).

In many ways this characterization begs the entire point of exploring the differences and potential complementarities between so-called historical and rational choice versions of institutionalism. For on some accounts the most salient theoretical difference between the two approaches emerges precisely around the question of whether institutions are best conceptualized in equilibrium terms in the first place (Thelan 1999). But even having focused attention on this difference, it remains difficult to keep clear on what is at stake theoretically. In part this is because once they distance themselves from the more extreme criticisms of equilibrium accounts, historical institutionalists themselves confront just those issues of the reproduction, stability, and persistence of institutional arrangements that are especially auspicious topics for equilibrium-based rational choice approaches (Thelan 1999, 391–401).[7] In part, though, and more to the point in this discussion, it is difficult because rational choice theorists are remarkably unclear about the role that equilibrium plays in their work. So rather than criticize historical institutionalists my aim here is to clarify the tasks rational choice theorists confront when they study institutions. This endeavor is analytically prior to any confrontation between or synthesis of "rational choice" and "historical" institutionalism—for the simple reason that there is no consensus about what rational choice institutionalism actually means.

A passage from Schelling provides a useful point of departure:

An equilibrium is a situation in which some motion or activity of adjustment or response has died away, leaving something stationary, at rest, "in
balance," or in which several things that have been interacting, adjusting
to each other and to each other's adjustment, are at last adjusted, in balance, at rest. . . . An equilibrium can be exact or approximate. It can be
always approached but never quite achieved, the potential equilibrium itself continually changing. And equilibrium can be partial or more complete, short run or long run. . . . The point to make here is that there is
nothing particularly attractive about an equilibrium. An equilibrium is
simply a result. It is what is there after something has settled down, if
something ever does settle down. The idea of equilibrium is an acknowledgment that there are adjustment processes; and unless one is particularly
interested in *how* dust settles, one can simplify analysis by concentrating
on what happens after the dust has settled. (Schelling 1978, 25–26)

Schelling himself calls the study of what happens once the dust has
settled equilibrium analysis. Among rational choice theorists this involves identifying both the set of possible equilibrium outcomes to some
strategic process and the conditions needed to sustain those equilibria.
This typically is done in game theoretic terms and relies on the concept
of Nash equilibrium or its progeny. But notice that Schelling also clearly
differentiates this analytical task from both the explanatory task of exploring how an equilibrium actually emerges and the normative task of
assessing any such outcome. On the explanatory front we must worry
about how any given equilibrium is achieved, about the mechanisms
that lead relevant actors to arrive at just this particular outcome and not
another. This task is especially pressing given the existence of multiple
equilibria in nearly any repeated game.[8] Stated simply a rational choice,
explanation requires that we identify "a social mechanism" understood
as "an interpretation, in terms of individual behavior, of a model that
abstractly reproduces the phenomenon that needs explaining" (Schelling
1998, 33).[9] On the normative front, given the exigencies involved in the
strategic processes that generate some equilibrium, the mere fact that it
emerges as the solution to a game in no way implies that it is justified.
Indeed, those exigencies—which minimally can include power differentials among actors and unforeseen contingencies—often pose an especially heavy burden of justification and one quite easy to misplace. If we
hope to avoid doing so we need to attend to the consequences that a
given equilibrium sustains and the conditions under which it generates
those consequences
    A considerable part of the disagreement that emerges between ratio-
nal choice and historical institutionalists stems from the propensity of

rational choice theorists themselves to be unclear about just what they are doing when they study equilibrium behavior, and particularly from their tendency to conflate the distinct tasks—analytical, explanatory, and normative—they confront. To get a feel for these distinctions and for how easy it is to blur them, the next section addresses a familiar version of equilibrium analysis—microeconomic analysis of market institutions. While economists typically are preoccupied with how competitive markets generate equilibrium outcomes, their analysis directs attention to the question of how market institutions themselves are sustained in equilibrium. Discussion of how analysis, explanation, and normative assessment co-mingle in standard microeconomics helps to underscore the multiple tasks that confront equilibrium-based theories generally and the efforts of rational choice theorists to account for institutional emergence and change in particular. The third section offers some empirical ballast—a very brief historical sketch of how universal suffrage emerged as an equilibrium institution. I use that sketch in the subsequent two sections to focus discussion of how rational choice theorists explain and justify equilibrium institutions. Section four explores the ways that the most prominent forms of rational choice institutionalism tacitly build normative justification into their purportedly "positive" accounts. Section five turns to the "moral" or "ethical" explanation that rational choice theorists (among others) sometimes advance for the emergence of normatively attractive institutions, such as universal suffrage. One substantive conclusion to be drawn from both sections is that, in the case of enfranchisement at least, there is little reason to worry too much about other-regarding preferences or how they might change over time. In conclusion, I offer some ideas about more plausible ways to account for the ways principles work in politics.

Analyzing Markets: A Textbook Account

This section reviews how microeconomists conduct equilibrium analysis of markets. It focuses on a particular textbook account.[10] Although this may seem an odd way to proceed, it will perhaps seem less so if we recall two things. First, rational choice theorists in political science regularly invoke microeconomic analysis of markets as inspiration for their enterprise.[11] And, more important, markets are institutions in just the sense we have identified—as mechanisms for coordinating ongoing social interactions (Kreps 1990a, 5–6, 187–98; Lindblom 2001).

It is important to distinguish among three concepts—exchange, competition, and markets—that economists and political theorists too often conflate. Exchange is pervasive in social life. It occurs whenever two or more individuals transfer goods or services among themselves. Exchange, however, does not automatically imply market interactions. These emerge from the need to predictably coordinate exchange in multilateral, increasingly impersonal settings (Lindblom 2001, 37). Only after exchange starts to occur under certain specifiable conditions do we observe either the institutionalized interactions characteristic of markets or the normatively attractive outcomes that economists attribute to them. These conditions operate to establish and sustain varying degrees of competition among parties to exchange relations. One virtue of standard microeconomic analysis is that it clearly identifies these conditions.

In standard textbook versions, microeconomists can in general show that an equilibrium generated by competitive market always yields a Pareto efficient allocation. They also can show that any such allocation constitutes an equilibrium. These results, roughly speaking, are the fundamental theorems of welfare economics (Kreps 1990a, 199–202, 286–89). They establish the existence and attractiveness of market equilibrium. This is a remarkable convergence. As Kreps remarks: "You should now be hearing choirs of angels and choruses of trumpets. The 'invisible hand' of the price mechanism produces equilibria that cannot be improved upon" (1990a, 200). Colorful imagery aside, the substantive points are both uncontroversial and important: the most basic results of microeconomics are not explanatory, and they straddle normative and analytical enterprises. This is not problematic, provided that we remain confident that the analytical account is plausible. But when we attend to the "can" in the first two sentences of this paragraph, such confidence appears largely to be a matter of faith. What does it mean to say economists can do these things? Here it is helpful to ask two subsidiary questions. What, more precisely, are economists doing? And what conditions do their arguments presuppose? In addressing these questions we can illustrate how the three tasks of institutional analysis are related and why it is important not to confuse them.

Consider the first question. What economists offer is an analysis of the existence and characteristics of equilibrium outcomes. Two features of this analysis are important. First it focuses on the normative features of equilibrium outcomes that competitive markets generate. The conclusion that those outcomes cannot be improved upon justifies whatever patterns they sustain. Second, this analysis in no way explains how markets generate such nice equilibria. In other words, this demonstration "doesn't provide . . . any sense of how markets operate. There is no model here of who sets prices, or what gets exchanged for what, when, and where" (Kreps 1990a, 195–98). This is because what economists offer "is a reduced form solution" (195) that "describes what we imagine will be the outcome of some underlying and unmodeled process" (187). Standard microeconomic accounts offer little understanding of precisely how "market/exchange mechanisms" operate (195).[12] Kreps thus admits that the claim that economic agents will find their way to equilibrium in a decentralized process is a "rather heroic assertion." He suggests, conversely, that it "seems natural to think that we could increase (or decrease) our faith in the concept of Walrasian equilibrium if we had some sense of how markets really do operate" (187). Progress on this task can be made "only if we are more specific about the institutional mechanisms involved" in market interactions (190).

It is not that economists have not generated some good work on that score. Quite the contrary. But the "exploration of more realistic models of markets is in relative infancy" (Kreps 1990a, 190, 195, 197).[13] Moreover, that work encounters difficulties both in explaining how the price mechanism generates equilibrium outcomes and in demonstrating how equilibria attained in particular settings retain the attractive normative properties of competitive equilibria that economists can establish in the general case.[14] To appreciate the difficulties here we need to turn to the second question.

Economists can establish the existence of normatively attractive equilibria only under reasonably restrictive conditions. Some of these are purely technical and can be set aside.[15] Others revolve around the adequacy of efficiency as a normative criterion.[16] They can be set aside as well because market institutions can, for purposes of argument, be justified in terms of their efficiency-enhancing effects.[17] The conditions that remain are meant to ensure that no producer's or consumer's choice exerts significant influence on the choices of other agents. In other words, standard microeconomic models capture exchanges under conditions that are sufficiently competitive that we reasonably can interpret them as transpiring between agents who are free and equal.[18]

The conditions necessary to ensure this are not easy to relax (Myles 1995, 48–49). They fall into two categories. The first concerns the role of information and time in market exchange (Kreps 1990a, 193–95). These can be relaxed if we incorporate futures markets and increasingly clairvoyant agents (Kreps 1990a, 216f; Myles 1995, 48–49).[19] Awareness of the constraints that information and time impose on economic exchange prompt economists to focus on the transaction costs involved in processes of search and monitoring. This in turn provided the impetus for a large literature on economic institutions.[20] This literature largely is concerned with the ways that information and time constraints produce inefficiencies. What is less often noted is that whereas transaction costs affect all parties in an economic exchange, their burdens typically are distributed unequally. For example, information imperfections typically confer advantage on one party in ways that clearly subvert equal status and thus threaten the normative attractiveness of any outcomes. I will later suggest that the rational choice literature on institutions often approaches its explanatory task by seeking to show that institutions function to mitigate transaction costs. To the extent that it does so this literature tacitly but systematically intermingles its normative and explanatory tasks.

The second category of conditions is meant to establish the sort of competitive environment needed to ensure that individuals choose independently and so to preclude such things as externalities, monopolies, and public goods. These conditions, in other words, are meant to ensure that agents who populate these models are parametric in the sense that they all are more or less equally situated price takers (Kreps 1990a, 202, 264–65; Myles 1995, 20). Absent such conditions, not only will market competition potentially generate an inequitable distribution along the efficiency frontier (the normative problem we set aside earlier), but we cannot generally rely upon it to generate efficient outcomes at all (Kreps 1990a, 202–4, 288–92). To return to an earlier image, the "choirs of angels and choruses of trumpets" we hear will sound increasingly dissonant.

The aim of this discussion is not to challenge the basic analytical results of microeconomics. It is instead simply to underscore the highly conditional nature of those results and to suggest how awareness of those conditions prompt us to ask how they are embodied in existing institutional arrangements and whether, and if so how, those institutions shape economic exchange into competitive markets. In short, the analytical results prompt us to ask properly explanatory questions. Likewise, calling attention to the conditional nature of microeconomic analysis is not meant to challenge the economist's preferred normative criterion— efficiency—with some other criterion—for example, equity—but rather to illustrate how attention to those conditions prompt us to ask properly normative questions about whether and when the economists' normative claims are warranted on their own terms.

Textbook microeconomic analysis, then, prompts us—for both explanatory and normative reasons—to inquire into the "institutional framework" of market interaction (Kreps 1990a, 190). This, as it turns out, is a complex undertaking. On the one hand, standard accounts readily acknowledge that the proper operation of markets presupposes an exogenous institutional framework, including well-defined property rights and enforceable contracts (Kreps 1990a, 263; Myles 1995, 20, 48–49). On the other hand, it is less commonly acknowledged that, because they offer only reduced form analyses, microeconomic accounts do not properly address the task of explaining how an informal institutional framework of roles, norms, and prerogatives defines the scope and operation of markets. It is a truism that markets cannot themselves produce institutional arrangements of the first sort. There is also little reason to suspect that they can generate institutions of the second sort. But we cannot understand how markets in fact operate without specifying how informal institutions and decentralized exchange interpenetrate to establish the sort of internal "trading environment" that allows us to treat markets as institutions (Swedberg 1994).

Economists, then, offer a highly technical analysis of market competition that they use to sustain a set of normative judgments. They do not, however, do much by way of explaining how markets work. They thus exemplify how important it is for those who proffer equilibrium-based theories to keep their analytic, explanatory, and normative tasks distinct. Are we offering analytical results or an explanation? Are our conclusions—whether analytical, explanatory, or normative—based on highly restrictive assumptions? Are we relying on the same theoretical edifice to undertake explanatory and normative tasks? And, if so, are we being explicit about how we are doing so? Casual empiricism suggests that economists are nowhere near as careful about these matters as they should be. But rational choice theorists who analyze institutional emergence and change in equilibrium terms also are especially prone to elide the distinction between equilibrium analysis, explanation, and normative assessment. The tendency to conflate explanation and justification has led to two sorts of error. First, contributors to the rational choice literatures on institutions more or less systematically smuggle normative justifications into their purportedly explanatory or positive accounts by tacitly assuming a set of favorable but highly restrictive initial conditions. They thereby greatly underestimate the burdens of justification. Second, when they actually pursue normative tasks, rational choice theorists of various persuasions often sketch ethical or moral explanations of large-scale institutional change. They thereby neglect the valuable explanatory leverage that rational choice accounts in fact afford.

The Politics of Enfranchisement

It will help to develop a historical sketch of how Western polities converged on one particular political institution—nearly universal adult male suffrage. To do so, we conveniently can turn to Alexander Keyssar's recent history of franchise in the United States (2000). This is a complex account and I attend primarily to a particular question during the initial period (from 1790 to 1850) of this history. Keyssar asks not only "why was the franchise broadened—and broadened so dramatically?" but also, and much more pointedly, "why did voting members of the community sometimes elect to share their political power with others?" (33, 37). His response to both questions is the same—one or another part of the socially and politically privileged (those already enfranchised) "saw themselves as having a direct interest in enlarging the electorate" (37). Sometimes social elites saw enfranchisement as a quid pro quo for the military service of the lower classes but, importantly, they saw this "not simply as a question of fairness . . . but also as a matter of security." They hoped, as it were, to buy continued protection. Sometimes elite perceptions reflected material advantage—when, for example, residents of sparsely populated territories hoped to use easy enfranchisement to attract additional settlers "and in so doing raise land values, stimulate economic growth, and generate tax revenues." Sometimes—and perhaps most commonly after about 1820—political elites supported an enlarged electorate simply because they perceived it as to their partisan advantage in electoral terms (37–42).

This focus on narrow material interests, whether economic or political, is not the only relevant portion of Keyssar's analysis. He also makes clear that, although by about 1855 most jurisdictions had first removed various property and then even taxpaying restrictions on the suffrage, this was not because the already enfranchised were deeply committed to anything like universal white male suffrage. Indeed, the wide franchise that existed in the United States by the mid-nineteenth century was, on Keyssar's account, almost entirely "an unintended consequence of changes in the suffrage laws" (2000, 68). The expansive franchise resulted from the fact that suffrage reforms typically were enacted with the expectation that they would extend voting rights only to "respectable" members of the population, to settlers who, even if property-less, intended to purchase and work the land. Although conservatives resisted suffrage reforms out of fear that large groups of propertyless, immigrant workers would threaten property rights, neither they nor those promoting suffrage reform accurately foresaw the rise in immigration, industrialization, and urbanization that would in fact generate a massive and largely foreign-born working class.[21] The crucial point is that neither conservatives nor reformers would have supported granting voting rights to the latter group and, as a result, no "deliberate and conscious decision" was ever made to enfranchise them (2000, 69).

As Keyssar makes clear, the historical dynamic actually was quite different.

> The relatively early broadening of the franchise in the United States was not simply, or even primarily, the consequence of a distinctively American commitment to democracy, or of a belief in the insignificance of class, or of a belief in extending political rights to the subaltern classes. Rather the extension of voting rights occurred—or at least was made possible—because the rights and power of those subaltern classes, despised and

feared in the United States much as they were in Europe, were not an issue when suffrage reforms were adopted. The American equivalent of the peasantry was not going to be enfranchised in any case, and the social landscape included few industrial workers. What was exceptional about the United States was an unusual configuration of historical circumstances that allowed suffrage laws to be liberalized before men who labored from dawn to dusk in the factories and the fields became numerically significant actors. (70)

Elites, then, supported an expanded franchise, when they did, largely for self-serving reasons. Only the opacity of the future—the fact that combined mass immigration, industrialization, and urbanization truly was an unforeseen contingency—ensured that their support generated outcomes that they found alarming.[22] They were left to fight a rearguard action in hopes of restricting the franchise. And, over the seventy years from 1850 through 1920 that is just what they did, with great vigor and significant success. The result was a concerted, "sustained, nationwide contraction of suffrage rights" in which, through a variety of mechanisms, "millions of people—most of them working class and poor—were deprived of the right to vote in municipal, state, and national elections" (Keyssar 2000, 169–70).[23]

There is no need here to pursue the history of suffrage in the United States any further. But it is important to note that from a comparative perspective the broad pattern Keyssar traces was hardly unique. Collier, for instance, discerns three historical "paths toward democracy" where mass enfranchisement is one crucial criterion for defining democracy (Collier 1999).[24] Each shares important features of Keyssar's account. Along the first of these paths politically excluded middle-class constituencies sought enfranchisement "to gain their own political inclusion and to oppose the hegemony and dominance of the politically privileged traditional elite and/or corporate groups" (34). Along the second path political elites supported an expanded franchise because they "calculated that a suffrage extension would play into their hands in the electoral arena and that it would help them with their political agenda" (55). As in the United States, along neither of these paths did "the popular classes in general and the working class in particular" (76) play a substantial role in securing expanded suffrage. And, again as in the American case, along neither path did reformers anticipate that "power would effectively pass to the majority" (34).

The third, more recent of Collier's paths toward democracy consists of what she labels "joint projects" in which the working classes played a significant role in securing broadened suffrage in strategic contexts

where other social strata and political organizations were pursuing independent objectives. But here Collier is quite clear about two things. First,
in this pattern political reforms—including enfranchisement—were in
critical ways "driven by the positive strategies of other groups and political parties as they sought either to protect their own electoral position
or to pursue some other goal such as national autonomy" (Collier 1999,
172). Second, while in these cases large portions of the working class
already were enfranchised, further enfranchisement to a significant degree once again represented a move in "a political game of partisan competition" in which socialist and labor parties sought to enhance their
electoral prospects (108–9). Consequently, Collier warns against taking
an overly simplistic view of enfranchisement on the basis of even this
pattern of joint projects. It is a historical mistake, she insists, to portray
the emergence of mass suffrage as the culmination of a narrative that
stars "the lower classes playing an inclusion game in which they wrest
the concession of their own participation." For franchise extensions were
not only typically a by-product of interactions animated by partisan or
other political interests. Mass enfranchisement often also was an unintended by-product in the sense that "it was not necessarily the lower
classes who were the main actors even with regard to their own inclusion." In these cases the lower classes obtained the franchise because
"the middle classes fought for a broad suffrage that essentially by default
included the working class" (190–91).

As in the United States then, the politics of enfranchisement in Europe
and Latin America has a seemingly peculiar structure. A uniform, normatively attractive outcome—an expansive franchise that more or less
approximated universal suffrage—emerged historically as a stable if contested feature of democratic polities. As the supply-side accounts that
Keyssar and Collier advance make clear, it hardly emerged as the result
of some campaign for fairness, equality or justice. Instead it emerged as a
largely unintended by-product of ongoing, relatively unstructured strategic interactions among individuals and groups who not only were motivated by a narrow interest in establishing or consolidating political or economic advantage at the expense of rivals but whose relatively myopic
political judgments were, in crucial cases, further confounded by eventual-
ities that they not only did not but arguably could not have anticipated.

Analyzing, Explaining, and Assessing
Institutional Change

What lessons might rational choice institutionalists derive from the politics of enfranchisement? A basic problem is that there is no consensus
about the basic mechanisms that animate rational choice accounts of any-

thing. Some theorists, for instance, defend the standard view that intentional individual actions caused by reasons (beliefs and desires) represent the basic mechanism in rational choice theories (Elster 1986). Others reject this internalist view and instead endorse an externalist one on which various sorts of environmental constraint or pressure actually animate rational choice accounts (Satz and Ferejohn 1994).[25] Not surprisingly, this philosophical disagreement is echoed among rational choice accounts of institutional emergence and change. All of these accounts portray institutions as equilibrium outcomes generated by interactions among strategically rational agents. But, as was the case with standard microeconomic analysis, this does little to explain how institutions actually emerge.

Calvert's (1995a, b) abstract game theoretic argument reveals the analytical structure of rational choice institutionalism.[26] He depicts institutions as sets of rules sustained as equilibria (and so as self-enforcing) of some underlying repeated game (1995a, 228–33; 1995b).[27] He represents the basic underlying game as an indefinitely repeated, N-person prisoner's dilemma in which players are randomly matched for pairwise interactions. He then models a set of increasingly complex versions of this game in each of which he identifies threshold values for the discount parameters of players, the size of N and, eventually, the costs of communication that sustain a variety of cooperative equilibrium outcomes, both noninstitutional and institutional. These outcomes all involve some more or less elaborate variation on conditional cooperation in which players opt to cooperate today in light of the credible threats others can make to retaliate against noncooperators in future interactions. They range from what we might call specific reciprocity, in which mutual cooperation emerges and persists in what we might call institutionally unbound contexts, through the sorts of generalized reciprocity characteristic of informal social norms, and on through increasingly formalized institutions that incorporate first multilateral communication, then centralized communication, and finally centralized communication coupled with protections against higher order malfeasance.

This is in many ways a remarkable demonstration. But notice that, as Calvert himself acknowledges, his analysis does not explain the emergence of any social or political institutions. He instead generates an existence result that, by identifying the conditions under which they can emerge, establishes the possibility of equilibrium institutions. The difficulty, of course, is that—as with nearly any repeated game in which players discount the future—the games Calvert examines generate multiple equilibria. The resulting and unavoidable coordination problem sets the basic explanatory task for institutional analysis. Which, if any, of the available equilibrium institutions will in fact emerge from social and political interaction? And how—in terms of which mechanism or mechanisms—might we best explain the way institutions emerge and change? These are critical questions if we aspire to fulfill the explanatory ambitions of institutional analysis (Calvert 1995a, 228). They are questions that Calvert explicitly leaves unanswered.[28]

At least three broad types of explanation exist among rational choice accounts of institutional emergence and change (Knight 1995). Moreover, although each account builds on the analytical scaffolding that Calvert constructs, each invokes quite different explanatory mechanisms, and each more or less tightly and more or less explicitly integrates explanatory and normative considerations. What follows is the barest sketch of these positions.

The first explanation invokes decentralized coordination on social or political conventions and has informed accounts of the genesis of language (Lewis 1969), the emergence of social norms (Ullman-Margalit 1977) and constitutional politics (Hardin 1999; Ordeshook 1992, 1993). On this account, relevant actors converge more or less arbitrarily on one among several feasible ways to coordinate their ongoing interactions. The resulting equilibrium is collectively beneficial in that it is Pareto-superior to generalized lack of coordination. As a result, rational agents will adapt to this arrangement over time.

The second explanation relies on a market based account of exchange and competitive selection to account for how rational agents voluntarily contract with one another in order to establish a set of rules (for example, some regime of property rights) that will govern their ongoing interactions (North 1990a, 1990b; Eggertsson 1990). The resulting institutional arrangement is collectively beneficial in that it works to minimize the transaction costs involved in measuring, monitoring, and enforcing agreements. And, all things equal, rational actors will change institutions in collectively beneficial ways under pressure of competitive selection—if exogenous factors alter circumstances in such a way that some alternative institutional arrangement will generate greater collective benefit, rational agents will coordinate again on that alternative.

The third explanation depicts institutions as the by-product of bargaining interactions among asymmetrically endowed social and political agents (Knight 1992). Here the underlying mechanism is the pursuit not of collective benefit but of distributional advantage. Institutions typically (but not always) emerge as the unintended by-product of strategic contests through which rational actors seek to constrain the choices available to others. More precisely, strategic actors seek to establish rules that structure future interactions in ways that increase the probability that they will generate from among the feasible equilibrium those outcomes most favorable to themselves. The credibility of these strategies derives from asymmetrical bargaining power.[29]

Knight (1995) provides a concise comparison of these competing explanations. He establishes that the conditions under which the bargaining approach holds (for example, differential bargaining power grounded in systematic resource asymmetries) are significantly less restrictive than those demanded by either the coordination or the contract/selection approaches (for example, decentralized emergence, voluntary compliance, symmetrically endowed actors). The point is that Knight is persuasive if only because, while he does not insist that social and political actors never will act for the collective benefit, he rightly indicates that insofar as we view them as strategically rational we must recognize that the conditions under which they are likely to act in such public regarding ways remain relatively restrictive. As a result, we have ample reason to accord analytical priority to the bargaining account of institutional emergence and change that he advances.[30] The problem, of course, is that, as an explanatory theory, the bargaining account exacerbates the normative task that rational choice institutional confront.

It is easy enough to see why this is so. Consider the coordination and contract and selection explanations. They do not generate this perplexity. Any institutional arrangement that emerged under the relatively attractive conditions these explanations presuppose would be presumptively justifiable. Indeed, a common feature of studies that advance such explanations is that, because they posit actors motivated by the collective benefits institutions afford and because they attribute convergence over time to anonymous or benignly arbitrary environmental forces, proponents of these accounts build normative inferences (for example, about the efficiency or functional efficacy of some institutional arrangement) directly into their preferred explanation of institutional emergence.[31] By highlighting the stringency of initial conditions required to make either sort of explanation plausible, Knight warns against making any such direct inferences. Yet, while the bargaining approach he advances as an alternative is analytically more plausible than its competitors, it generates an especially heavy burden of justification. Indeed, insofar as institutions emerge under conditions presupposed by the bargaining account (for example, asymmetrically situated actors pursuing distributional advantage), it is difficult to see how we might ever envision the emergence of normatively justifiable institutions. In particular it is unlikely that our account of the genesis of institutions will afford clues as to their normative qualities.

What bearing does this treatment of rival rational choice accounts have on the discussion in earlier sections? Recall Kreps's confession: we likely would have substantially greater faith in the analytical and normative results of standard microeconomics if we had a plausible explanation of how markets really do operate. This, however, would require abandoning reduced form analysis and explaining both how market institutions induce equilibrium outcomes and how markets themselves emerge as equilibrium institutions. And this, in turn, requires that we explain the genesis in particular cases of the exogenous framework of social, political, and legal institutions needed to sustain competitive markets and of the internal institutional features that constitute the trading structure of actual markets. Because institutions of both sorts, like public goods generally, are characterized by strategic interdependencies, it is unlikely that they might be provided by markets. There thus is scant reason to suppose that those who produce and sustain them will be motivated by efficiency or some other aggregate benefit.[32] Indeed, to the extent that we consider the bargaining account of institutional emergence and change more robust than its competitors, we ought to anticipate that both the exogenous institutions that sustain markets and the internal institutional structure of markets themselves will reflect the distributional advantage of the relatively powerful. We thus have little reason for optimism about the prospects that these institutions will both emerge in a decentralized fashion and embody the "nice" normative characteristics that textbook microeconomics attribute to market equilibrium. The upshot, while perhaps somewhat ironic, seems hard to resist. To the extent that we make progress in explaining how markets do emerge and operate our faith in the standard microeconomic analytical and normative results likely will diminish rather than increase.

When we turn to the politics of enfranchisement a similarly ironic conclusion emerges. The bargaining approach nicely captures the essential features of how that politics occurred across the United States, Europe, and Latin America—primarily as the unintended by-product of ongoing, unstructured conflict among political and economic actors in pursuit of narrow advantage, whose short time frames were, in the United States at least, exacerbated by unforeseen contingencies. The irony (one not lost on elites who realized too late the democratic excesses into which their strategic pursuits had led them and who then vigorously sought to marginalize the newly enfranchised) is that this process generated an outcome that, however unintentionally, benefited the relatively powerless. The bargaining account typically would not lead us to expect this sort of distributive pattern. And even in cases such as this, in which the ultimate outcome is normatively attractive, the bargaining account raises a significant burden of justification. It would, in particular, warn us against presuming that universal suffrage was the product of a concerted campaign for fairness, equality or justice.

Invoking Moral Motivations

Political theorists, rational choice theorists prominent among them, regularly attribute the expansion of the franchise over the course of the nineteenth and twentieth centuries to moral or other motivations. These claims come in various forms and with different degrees of strength. In each case, however, the theorist uses franchise extension to illustrate how, more broadly, we might justify institutional transformations.

We are told, for example, that "extensions of the franchise themselves must surely require a hefty dose of precisely such direct moral appeals to people's moral principles" (Goodin 1992, 87). Likewise, we are told that "the main political reforms of the last century" including especially extension of suffrage were necessarily animated by a conception of justice. The reasons for this are relatively simple. If a proposed reform "is perceived as fundamentally just" those who advocate it and those whom they are able to convince "will be willing and motivated to put up with the cost of transition and of experimenting with different modes of implementing it." And, conversely, adversaries of the reform will be disarmed because "if a reform is widely perceived as fundamentally just, it is difficult to oppose it in more than a half-hearted way" (Elster 1989, 203). Finally, we are told that suffrage extension is the sort of large-scale institutional change that is susceptible to ethical explanation in the precise sense that such an account would invoke the injustice of political exclusion to explain why restrictive voting regimes are unstable and so, why they are replaced by increasingly broad suffrage (Cohen 1997, 92–96).[33]

Claims such as these raise two obvious questions. First, how are we to understand "moral motivations"? And, second, how do the conditions under which some institutional change occurs bear on the tasks of explanation and normative justification? We can consider these questions in turn.

How are we to understand what counts as moral motivation here? One easily can think of a range of possible answers to this question. We might start with a baseline contrast that sees franchise extension as part of a self-interested strategy on the part of a more or less unified elite. On this view enfranchisement constitutes an anticipatory reaction on the part of elites hoping to legitimize their power and prerogatives in the face of potential popular challenges and, in the extreme, revolution (Freeman and Snidal 1982; Acemoglu and Robinson 2000a, b).[34] At the other end of the spectrum we might see suffrage reform as driven by moral motivations of the sort that Weber captures in his notion of value-rational action. Here relevant actors—whether agitators among the disenfranchised, the audiences to whom they appeal, or reform-minded elites—advocate enfranchisement on a principled basis regardless of both the costs to themselves and the prospects of success (Weber 1922/ 1968, I: 25). Intermediate positions would include actors motivated by sympathy (essentially an externality in their utility function) or, alternatively, by a genuine, if more or less constrained, commitment to fairness or some other ethical norm that might induce counter-preferential choice (Sen 1982, 92, 93–4).

Elster approximates Weber's position. and in that respect his view is more demanding than Cohen's or Goodin's. He insists that enfranchisement was not "supported mainly by instrumental considerations" but instead was motivated by something like "the noninstrumental right to equal concern and respect" that animates contemporary liberal theories of justice (Elster 1989, 203). His claim is dictated in large part by his larger theoretical purposes. Elster hopes to disarm antirationalist skeptics—whether conservatives like Oakeshott, or so-called classical liberals like Hayek—who question the very possibility of systematic institutional reform. He concedes that reform proposals often imply what he calls "hyper-rationalism," but claims that they nevertheless can be justified in non-instrumental terms. Hence his claim that franchise extensions, in fact, were motivated by noninstrumental, moral considerations.

By contrast, Cohen's account appears in some way less demanding. In particular, it does not obviously presuppose that actors in Weberian fashion abandon instrumental considerations. Institutional change emerges, at least in part, because unjust institutional arrangements are unstable and so do not afford viable means of coordinating ongoing social and political interactions. Restricted suffrage, for example, therefore conflicts with the interests of excluded groups and, insofar as these groups (such as workers, women, or racial minorities in the United States) are disadvantaged relative to the enfranchised, it is unjust.[35] This injustice severely restricts the viability of any state that seeks to maintain a restricted franchise, because recognition of injustice will motivate political opposition and/or because it generates political conflicts that disadvantage the state in economic or military interactions with other states.[36] When exclusionary suffrage arrangements are portrayed as unjust, that depiction itself, on Cohen's account, has independent explanatory force insofar as it induces relevant actors (for example, the politically excluded and their actual and potential political allies) to oppose them as unjust and/or because it thereby places states with restricted franchise at comparative disadvantage.

This is a provocative thesis. According to Cohen it is the injustice itself of the institution "and not simply the consequences of the fact that some people come to think of it as wrong" that provides the crucial explanatory factor (1997, 95). Fortunately for my purposes, it is unnecessary to assess the basic claim Cohen defends, namely that—contrary to prevailing varieties of political realism—it is just possible that right does indeed make might.

The brand of ethical explanation he advances depends crucially on the motivational force of recognized injustice. Here he is committed to nothing so strong as the position Elster holds. It is entirely possible that the disenfranchised, and especially their allies, act in instrumental terms on the basis of something like what Sen calls commitment. Under relevant circumstances political actors might just behave in other regarding ways to end or reform so-called unjust arrangements.

Goodin, by contrast to both Elster and Cohen, is a utilitarian. He hopes to defend his overall view indirectly. His conception of moral motivation resembles Sen's notion of commitment. He advances the very strong claim that reforms aimed at "extending the franchise" are "wholly explicable in the minimally moralized terms of simple reciprocity." Yet while he insists that reciprocity in such settings is at best a "first cousin" to deontological motivations of the sort that Elster invokes, neither does he reduce it to simple non-myopic self-interest of the sort that sustains conditional cooperation in repeated games (for example, Taylor 1987).[37] For him, simple reciprocity is a moral motivation just insofar as it moves relevant agents take an action because it is principled or fair (Goodin 1992, 87, 85, 26–35).

As with Elster's and Cohen's, Goodin's position reflects his larger theoretical commitments. He is concerned with identifying the conditions under which institutions and practices will generate good outcomes. And, to that end, he states,

> I do suppose that if we are going to secure morally desirable outcomes, then the best way to do so—over the long haul, anyway—is by encouraging people to act on morally worthy motives.
>
> The pragmatic point I see as central is just this. We want to get people to do the right thing *regularly* and *systematically* and the surest way to do that has to be to get them to do the right thing for the right motives. (1992, 9)

Hence, on Goodin's account it is some appreciation for simple reciprocity or some sense of fairness rather than abstract moralizing and philosophical argument that motivated suffrage reforms. And this is important to his account because he wants to claim that universal suffrage is justified (in the sense that it generates good outcomes) because this provides new voters with a reason to act fairly and responsibly once enfranchised.[38] The reciprocal threat to use of the franchise in a retaliatory fashion can provide a barrier, on his view, to the most blatant forms of oppression and exploitation and so protect liberty and rights.

Elster, Cohen, and Goodin each are preoccupied with justifying progressive political change in the face of one or another form of skepticism. They thus seek to establish that the road to justice (as embodied in expansive franchise) has been paved with good intentions. The problem is not that they are concerned with this normative task, which is, after all, one that theorists of institutions cannot avoid. And it surely is best to approach this task directly rather than tacitly building normative justifications into our explanatory accounts, as both the convention and contract/selection accounts of institutional emergence and change tend to do.

The problem with each of their accounts is that they seem to barely connect with what we know of the history of enfranchisement. Moral motivations—what commonly are taken to be "other-regarding" preferences—play an insignificant role in the history of why elites willingly extended suffrage rights to the disenfranchised enfranchisement—at least as Keyssar and Collier depict that history.[39] Moreover, Elster, Cohen, and Goodin largely dispense with the analytical leverage that the bargaining account of institutional emergence and change affords. The problem, then, is not that universal suffrage—like other equilibrium institutions—requires no justification. Rather it is that accounts that invoke moral motivations to both explain and justify progressive reforms, simultaneously risk advancing historically implausible, analytically impoverished explanations and leading us to misconstrue the burden of normative justification.

Concluding Speculations

It seems most useful to conclude by raising two speculative issues. The first is explanatory and highlights the importance of figuring out how social and political actors "do things with principles" (Nozick 1993). The second is normative. It suggests how we might harness the analytical advantages of bargaining explanations of institutional emergence and change to the task of justification. Each reflects the need to recognize and keep distinct the analytical, explanatory, and normative tasks that political theorists confront.

Speculation One

Nothing I have said thus far implies that when we observe political interactions we see no moral or ethical language, no invocation of principle. It raises only the issue of whether and how such discourse enters into political dynamics. Here is how I suspect moral claims—to fairness, reciprocity, justice, and so forth—work in politics. Actors invoke principles. These, as Nozick points out, "support subjunctive inferences" in the sense that they present a new case as similar to a current or past case, and therefore in need of similar treatment, (Nozick 1993, 5; Kreps 1990c). Principles typically are supported by a scaffolding of interests. The concern for interests provides claims of principle with their force.[40] But contrary to what Nozick (1993, 10) and Kreps (1990c) claim, I suspect that in politics the role of principle is less to bind ourselves than to constrain others. This suspicion follows simply from the bargaining approach to institutional analysis. When a political actor invokes a principle, he or she is trying to get others to acknowledge that if they treated some past or ongoing case (this population or that issue) like this, then they ought also to treat this new case (a new population or issue) in the same or similar manner.[41] The problem is that in asymmetrical bargaining such claims often have scant impact when addressed by the disadvantaged to the advantaged. The disadvantaged and their allies surely make such principled claims. Such claims are critical to any sort of successful political mobilization. And the advantaged may well act in ways that (intentionally or otherwise) further the sorts of reform the disadvantaged advocate. But none of this means that the advantaged act for "moral" or "ethical" reasons. Indeed, the history of franchise expansion suggests the contrary. Universal suffrage emerged across the United States, Europe, and Latin America despite the intentions of enfranchised elites. Yet, in a dynamic sense, none of this might preclude the disadvantaged and their allies from invoking principles to make similarity arguments in some future interaction. Notice, too, that none of this involves establishing or changing preferences in any direct sense. Principles of fairness or justice operate on this view—much as symbols do—in a broadly cognitive manner. They induce relevant actors to attend to or imagine possibilities.[42]

Speculation Two

The bargaining approach to institutional analysis seems more robust than its competitors in analytical terms. But because it presupposes that most institutions emerge as the by-product of interactions characterized by marked, systematic power differentials, it generates a daunting burden of justification. If all or most institutions emerge this way, how might we envision justified or even justifiable institutional arrangements? The first thing to notice is that, unlike competing approaches, the bargaining approach highlights the need for justification rather than, as it were, building it more or less tacitly into the explanatory enterprise. But it also suggests three features that will hold of any plausible strategy of justification. First, it will be consequentialist. It will not rely on some interpretation or reinterpretation of institutional genesis. It instead will point out the good, bad, or indifferent consequences of coordinating on-going interactions in one or another way. Second, it will constrain that consequentialism by examining the initial conditions from which outcomes emerge. As a result, and, third, it will be political in the sense that it will lack external foundations: it will require a process of argument and counter argument that, constrained by suitably defended but nonetheless contestable criteria, will address not only institutional arrangements, but the very principles by which we seek to justify them (Knight and Johnson 2002).

Notes

1. For instance, Amartya Sen reports that when queried about "the most important thing that had happened in the twentieth century" he pondered numerous candidates but "did not, ultimately, have any difficulty in choosing one as the preeminent development of the period: the rise of democracy" (Sen 1999, 3). And in celebration of "the dramatic expansion of democratic governance over the course of the century" Freedom House (1999) issued a fin-de-siecle report proclaiming the twentieth as Democracy's Century.

2. Hence the Freedom House report referred to in the previous note defines electoral democracies in terms of "the standard of *universal suffrage* for competitive multiparty elections" (Freedom House 1999, 2, stress added). Compare Lipset and Lakin (2004, 19) who offer the following, avowedly minimalist conception of democracy: "An institutional arrangement *in which all adult individuals have the power to vote*, through free and fair competitive elections, for their chief executive and national legislature" (stress added).

3. I hope it goes without saying that the formal right to vote often is subverted either explicitly or tacitly by other factors. For frank admission of this see Lipset and Lakin (2004, 81–82).

4. That the politics of enfranchisement is a special case of my broader concern with institutional change should be clear. "If democracy is . . . understood as a particular set of institutions, democratization, in turn, is understood as the introduction, adoption, or installation of those institutions, or the events that lead to the introduction or adoption of the institutions that constitute a democratic regime" (Collier 1999, 24). As an integral component of democratization enfranchisement, on this general view, is the process however contingent and unintentional of institutionalizing rights to participate among increasingly large segments of the population.

5. This typically will require a response by actors not party to the particular interaction.

6. This is true even of simple rules of reciprocity. Here see Taylor (1987).
7. For an example of an extreme view, see Orren and Skowronek (1996). For a more or less orthodox rational choice reaction, see Fiorina (1996).
8. Practicing political scientists typically treat the question of how individual actors coordinate on some equilibrium as a more or less straightforward technical matter and choose to ignore the "muddy philosophical issues" (Kreps 1990b, 35–36) it raises. Although these issues do bear mentioning I will not pursue them here. See Binmore (1990), Gibbons (1997), Myerson (1999), and Rubinstein (1991).
9. On the importance of properly specifying the mechanisms that animate rational choice explanations see Little (1993) and Johnson (2002b).
10. For present purposes I rely almost exclusively on a single recent textbook account (Kreps (1990a). This textbook is especially valuable for my purposes because it not only is written by an esteemed economist but is unabashedly "chatty" (Kreps 1990a, xvi). It consequently is considerably more explicit on matters that concern me here than are comparable texts. Compare Mas-Colell, Whinston, and Green (1995).
11. Hence we are told that rational choice approaches promise "a theory of politics no less sophisticated and comprehensive than the theory of markets found in economics" (Ordeshook 1986, x). See also Riker (1990, 177–81).
12. In other words, "why the economy should actually reach the equilibrium is not entirely clear" (Myles 1995, 25–26). While this is true for standard microeconomics it is less clearly the case for recent work by sociologists (Swedberg 1994) or economic historians (Greif 1997) even though in any particular case it is an open question whether the equilibria we actually observe retain the normative properties of the standard micro-economic analysis.
13. Greif (2003) provides a snapshot of relevant work.
14. It is important, in other words, not to presume that a move from general to partial equilibrium analysis satisfies the demand for realistic models. Partial analyses simply recapitulate both the explanatory shortcomings and normative character of more general approaches. What if we want to try to explain how the price mechanism generates an equilibrium in particular cases? First, moving to partial equilibrium analysis is not terribly helpful insofar as it too neglects underlying institutional mechanisms (Kreps 1990a, 263–64, 286). In essence it simply amounts to shifting the markets surrounding those under scrutiny into the "larger social and political environment which general equilibrium takes as given" (263–64). Second, we cannot assume that the particular case will have the attractive normative properties that the general equilibrium argument establishes. That however is pretty much what partial equilibrium analysis does. Since it focuses on some particular realm of exchange it takes all others as given. It thus allows the analyst to assume that the interactions under consideration in fact meet the restrictive

conditions presupposed by nice equilibrium outcomes and to not ask one way or the other about all the other interactions that a general equilibrium argument would encompass (279–84). But from the vantage point of general equilibrium analysis (to say nothing of a more fully political analysis) this process of extraction clearly is artificial and thus is a theoretical move for which the analyst must offer a plausible defense. Otherwise there is no reason to expect that whatever equilibrium emerges in particular cases is normatively attractive in even efficiency terms.

15. For instance, the general equilibrium results presume a set of technical assumptions about consumer preferences—they are "convex, continuous, nondecreasing, and locally insatiable" (Kreps 1990a, 199–200, 287).

16. The second welfare theorem is sensitive to the initial distribution of endowments. Depending on how endowments are distributed (or redistributed) at the outset, market exchange can generate efficient but highly inequitable outcomes. This observation often generates normative arguments about the degree and feasibility of establishing such initial equity (Kreps 1990a, 200). This is not the place to discuss the relative importance of equity and efficiency as normative criteria. But particular cases—such as analysis of markets in women's sexual or reproductive labor (Satz 1992, 1995)—suggest how extensive redistribution would have to be in order to establish initial conditions of equity. Once we concede that what Satz (1992, 110) calls "the background conditions of gender inequality that characterize our society" include pervasive social, cultural and political dependencies as well as economic inequalities, the political task of establishing the requisite initial equity rightly appears immense.

17. For one alternative normative defense of markets, see Sen (1993).

18. Here I have in mind something like what economists take as the "the natural meaning of 'competition,' that each participant in the market is so small that he will have no effect on the behavior of others" (Stiglitz 2002, 467). Put otherwise, to the extent they exist, the conditions of competitive exchange operate to mitigate asymmetries of power.

19. The extent of the strain is the subject of disagreement among economists. Some, like Stiglitz (2002), claim that even small amounts of imperfect information derail standard microeconomic arguments. As he says, even if we acknowledge the fact that information is costly "economies with information imperfections would not be Pareto efficient" and there will always be feasible political "interventions in the market that could make all parties better off" (Stiglitz 2002, 477–78).

20. See Williamson (1985), North (1990), Eggertsson (1990), and so forth. Kreps (1990a) clearly traces the connections between standard microeconomic analysis and the transaction cost economics that underlies much of the recent rational choice literature on institutions.

21. The "prospect of a society dominated by manufacturing and cities teeming

with hundreds of thousands of poor, rootless workers did not seem credible to most Americans in 1820 or even 1840" (Keyssar 2000, 49).

22. An "unforeseen contingency" consists of an eventuality that ex ante relevant actors have not considered. While the meaning of unforeseen contingency is subject to some dispute, it commonly is accepted that it is not meant simply to capture events or circumstances that an actor considers but to which she assigns a low or zero probability (Dekel, Lipman, and Rustichini 1998, 524; Nelson and Winter, 1982, 66). So it is not simply that relevant actors failed to anticipate some event or state of affairs but that in some sense they could not have anticipated it. It is not just that things happen that we didn't imagine. Rather it is that things occur that were not imaginable.

23. For the details of this historical process see Keyssar (2000, 77–172). I would add two caveats here. First, this relatively narrow focus in no way implies that the politics of voting rights in the United States or elsewhere has been unproblematic in subsequent periods. Second, the fact that active resistance to an expansive franchise diminished after about 1920 does not mean that elites were reconciled to popular participation. It instead reflected a set of factors—demographic, political and legal—that rendered a broad franchise less threatening (230–37).

24. The first two paths largely were nineteenth-century phenomena and traversed both Europe and Latin America, examples of the third path cluster in Europe in the first third of the twentieth century (Collier 1999, table 2.1). For summaries of her analysis, see Collier (1999, 33–36, 54–55, 75–81, 108–9, 171–73, 185–91).

25. Critics respond that the "externalist" position verges on incoherence (Hausman 1995). For a plausible argument—more or less intermediate between the internalist and externalist positions—that while structural or environmental factors can have causal efficacy they must ultimately work by influencing the beliefs, preferences, information, or capacities of individuals see Little (1993).

26. Calvert's papers are especially useful insofar as his explicit aim is to articulate the theoretical structure that informs several influential historical accounts that claim political institutions emerge and change to facilitate the creation and stabilization of markets (North and Weingast 1989; Milgrom, North, and Weingast 1990; and Greif, Milgrom, and Weingast 1994).

27. Calvert actually is somewhat ambiguous on this point. He pointedly suggests that *"Institution* is just a name we give to certain parts of certain kinds of equilibria." In that sense he tacitly seeks to dispense with any reference to the rule-like features of institutions. Yet he also characterizes such equilibrium institutions as "no more than a regular behavior pattern sustained by mutual expectations about the actions that others will take when anyone violates the rule—whether the violation be defection, lying, nonpayment of

fees, extortion, or malfeasance in office. The institution is just an equilibrium" (Calvert 1995b, 74, 73). And here his definition of institution clearly is parasitic on the recognition that they are composed of rules which on any conception must amount to more than a mere behavioral regularity. This last observation is in keeping with Calvert's own claim that there is "no better" way to conceive of institutions than as rules (Calvert 1995a, 217).

28. Calvert (1995a, 70, 80–82) professes to be agnostic among variety of accounts that might explain the emergence of equilibrium institutions. Here I only hope to highlight the analogy between Calvert's analytical exercise and standard microeconomic analysis. The crucial point is that neither analytical exercise is explanatory.

29. For a systematic discussion of this notion of power see Dowding (1996).

30. The claim here is not that the convention or contract-competitive selection approaches are false, but that they are likely to produce plausible explanations of institutional genesis in a relatively narrow range of cases. Although political scientists rarely explicitly assess the empirical performance of competing explanatory mechanisms his position appears empirically persuasive. The few studies that compare rival rational choice accounts of institutional emergence conclude that the bargaining account is more robust empirically than its competitors (for example, Allio et al. 1997; Binder and Smith 1998). That said, brute induction is unlikely to settle this matter in any definitive way. For some indication of the persistent theoretical difficulties see Knight and North (1997).

31. This is perhaps clearest when theorists characterize a range of social and political institutions—families, the rule of law generally or enforceable contracts and property rights in particular, various constitutional provisions such as federal arrangements or separation of powers, and even democracy—as "market preserving" (Weingast 1995) or "market supporting" (McMillan 2002, 11). For this characterization sustains efforts to explain and, tacitly, to justify institutions primarily in terms of how they contribute functionally to the operation of markets. The tacit premise in this line of reasoning is that the markets in question operate under conditions that at least approximate those highlighted in the standard microeconomic account and that the relevant institutions help, intentionally or otherwise, to minimize transaction costs that otherwise would jeopardize those conditions.

32. As Kreps (1990c), for instance, does in his discussion of the way actors establish the "principles" that constitute what he calls corporate culture.

33. In fairness to Cohen it is important to note that I am extrapolating from what he makes as a passing remark. He is primarily concerned to offer an ethical explanation for the demise of slavery. For a contrary view see Kaufman and Pape (1999). This is not the place to pursue the competing accounts of the demise of slavery. It also should be clear that Cohen is signifi-

cantly less concerned with rational choice accounts than is either Elster or Goodin. That said his account trades explicitly on the notion that unjust institutions are unstable precisely in the sense that, because they operate contrary to the interests of some significant portion of the relevant population they provide members of that group reason to subvert—actively or passively—the offending institutional arrangements.

34. Notice that this baseline account differs in several respects from the historical sketch presented in section three. In many ways it buys into just the sort of game of inclusion scenario against which Collier warns.

35. Cohen's argument is actually more complex than this. He claims that an institutional arrangement (that is, restricted franchise) is unjust insofar as, first, it operates contrary to the interests of some group (that is, the disenfranchised), and, second, that group is powerless relative to other groups (that is, the enfranchised) as evidenced by the fact that their disadvantaged position could not be sustained by free, uncoerced agreement.

36. Cohen acknowledges that this competitiveness argument relies on environmental pressures that may or may not actually obtain. In this respect his account demonstrates a degree of self-awareness lacking in many rational choice accounts.

37. Taylor (1996) has subsequently offered a brief for the importance of moral motivations.

38. As Keyssar makes clear, historically this has come down to anxiety about whether, once enfranchised, the poor will expropriate the rich either directly or by electing a government that enacts confiscatory tax policies. This prospect, of course, preoccupied nineteenth century observers of various political persuasions who hardly envisioned moral motivations as a sufficient brake on material interest (Macaulay 1935, 189–90; Marx 1973, 264; Constant 1988, 215). But there also are many other possible accounts for "Why the Poor Do Not Expropriate the Rich" (Roemer 1998; Putterman 1997; Wallerstein 1997; Shapiro 2002). None of these accounts presume widespread moral motivations either.

39. If moral motivations *were* at work we would have a difficult time, explaining in the American case, the reversal of inclusionary trends in the aftermath of the Civil War. This is a problem for each of the accounts I've sketched in this section. Elster (1989, 203), as already noted suggests that moral considerations disarm opponents of reform, making it difficult to sustain more than half-hearted resistance. Goodin (1992, 95–97) and Cohen (1997, 130) likewise claim that in cases where moral or ethical explanations have purchase we ought not see reversal of progressive trends.

40. This is true of much of our normative lexicon—--but in the current context it will suffice to point out that it is true of both rights and representation. On rights see Waldron (1993, 11). On representation see Pitkin (1967, 209).

41. This suggestion is just the alternative against which Goodin is arguing.

42. This suggests that principles often are deployed as strategic resources. In such instances one party to the interaction is trying to get relevant others to see the current situation or group as like this and not like that. In the politics of enfranchisement in the United States this often meant endeavoring to portray some disenfranchised population as being like the already enfranchised and not like slaves (Shklar 1991, 25–63). And in this sense it is unnecessary to theoretically distance the politics of recognition from strategic and instrumental concerns. See Johnson (2000; 2001; 2002a; 2002b).

References

Acemoglu, Daron, and James Robinson. 2000a."Why Did the West Extend the Franchise?" *Quarterly Journal of Economics* 114(4): 1167–99.

———. 2000b. "Democratization or Repression." *European Economic Review* 44(4–6): 683–93.

Allio, Lorene, Mariusz Dobek, Nikolai Mikhailov, and David Weimer. 1997. "Post-Communist Privatization as a Test of Theories of Institutional Change." In *The Political Economy of Property Rights*, edited by David Weimer. Cambridge: Cambridge University Press.

Binder, Sarah, and Steven Smith. 1998. "Political Goals and Procedural Choice in the Senate." *Journal of Politics* 60(2): 398–416.

Binmore, Ken. 1990. *Essays of the Foundations of Game Theory*. Malden, Mass.: Blackwell Publishing.

Blais, André, Louis Massicotte, and Antoine Yoshinaka. 2001. "Deciding Who has the Right to Vote." *Electoral Studies* 20(1): 41–62.

Calvert, Randall. 1995a. "Rational Actors, Equilibrium and Social Institutions." In *Explaining Social Institutions*, edited by Jack Knight and Itai Sened. Ann Arbor: University of Michigan.

———. 1995b. "The Rational Choice Theory of Social Institutions." In *Modern Political Economy*, edited by Jeffrey Banks and Eric Hanushek. Cambridge: Cambridge University Press.

Cohen, Joshua. 1997. "The Arch of the Moral Universe." *Philosophy & Public Affairs* 26(1): 91–134.

Collier, Ruth Berins. 1999. *Paths Toward Democracy*. Cambridge: Cambridge University Press.

Constant, Benjamin. 1988. "Principles of Politics Applicable to all Representative Governments." In *Political Writings*, edited by Biancamaria Fontana. Cambridge: Cambridge University Press.

Dekel, Eddie, Barton L. Lipman, and Aldo Rustichini. 1998. "Recent Developments in Modeling Unforeseen Contingencies." *European Economic Review* 42(3–5): 523–42.

Dowding, Keith. 1996. *Power*. Minneapolis: University of Minnesota Press.

Eggertsson, Thráinn. 1990. *Economic Behavior and Institutions*. Cambridge: Cambridge University Press.

Elster, Jon. 1986. "The Nature and Scope of Rational Choice Explanation." In *Actions and Events*, edited by Ernest LePore and Brian McLaughlin. Oxford: Blackwell Publishing.

———. 1989. *Solomonic Judgments: Studies in the Limitations of Rationality*. New York: Cambridge University Press.

Fiorina, Morris. 1996. "Looking for Disagreement in All the Wrong Places." In *Nomos XXXVII: Political Order*, edited by Ian Shapiro and Russell Hardin. New York: New York University Press.

Freedom House. 1999. *Democracy's Century: A Survey of Global Political Change in the 20th Century*. New York: Freedom House.

Freeman, John, and Duncan Snidal. 1982. "Diffusion, Development and Democratization: Enfranchisement in Western Europe." *Canadian Journal of Political Science* 15(2): 299–329.

Gibbons, Robert. 1997. "An Introduction to Applicable Game Theory." *Journal of Economic Perspectives* 11(1): 127–49.

Goodin, Robert. 1992. *Motivating Political Morality*. Oxford: Blackwell Publishing.

Greif, Avner. 1997. "Microtheory and Recent Developments in the Study of Economic Institutions Through Economic History." In *Advances in Economics and Econometrics*, vol. 2, edited by David Kreps and Kenneth Walks. Cambridge: Cambridge University Press.

———. 2003. "Review of Fligstein, *The Architecture of Markets*." *Contemporary Sociology* 32(2): 148–52.

Greif, Avner, Paul Milgrom, and Barry Weingast. 1994. "Coordination, Commitment, and Enforcement." *Journal of Political Economy* 102(4): 745–76.

Hardin, Russell. 1999. *Liberalism, Constitutionalism, and Democracy*. New York: Oxford University Press.

Hausman, Daniel. 1995. "Rational Choice and Social Theory: A Comment." *Journal of Philosophy* 92(2): 96–102.

Johnson, James. 2000. "Why Respect Culture?" *American Journal of Political Science* 44(3): 405–18.

———. 2001. "Inventing Constitutional Traditions: The Poverty of Fatalism." In *Constitutional Culture and Democratic Rule*, edited by John Ferejohn, Jack Rakove, and Jonathan Riley. Cambridge: Cambridge University Press.

———. 2002a. "Liberalism and the Politics of Cultural Authenticity." *Politics, Philosophy, and Economics* 1(2): 213–36.

———. 2002b. "How Conceptual Problems Migrate: Rational Choice, Interpretation, and the Hazards of Pluralism." *Annual Review of Political Science* 5: 223–48.

Kaufman, Chaim, and Robert Pape. 1999. "Explaining Costly International Moral Action: Britain's Sixty Year Campaign Against the Atlantic Slave Trade." *International Organization* 53(4): 631–68.

Keyssar, Alexander. 2000. *The Right To Vote: The Contested History of Democracy in the United States.* New York: Basic Books.

Knight, Jack. 1992. *Institutions and Social Conflict.* Cambridge: Cambridge University Press.

———. 1995. "Models, Interpretations, and Theories." In *Explaining Social Institutions,* edited by Jack Knight and Itai Sened. Ann Arbor: University of Michigan.

Knight, Jack, and James Johnson. 2002. "On the Priority of Democracy: Institutional Analysis and the Burden of Justification." Unpublished paper. New York: Russell Sage Foundation.

Knight, Jack, and Douglass North. 1997. "Explaining the Complexity of Institutional Change." In *The Political Economy of Property Rights,* edited by David Weimer. Cambridge: Cambridge University Press.

Kreps, David. 1990a. *A Course in Microeconomic Theory.* Princeton, N.J.: Princeton University Press.

———. 1990b. *Game Theory and Economic Modelling.* Oxford: Oxford University Press.

———. 1990c. "Corporate Culture and Economic Theory." In *Perspectives on Positive Political Economy,* edited by James Alt and Kenneth Shepsle. New York: Cambridge University Press.

Lewis, David. 1969. *Convention.* Cambridge, Mass.: Harvard University Press.

Lindblom, Charles. 2001. *The Market System.* New Haven, Conn.: Yale University Press.

Lipset, Seymour Martin, and Jason Lakin. 2004. *The Democratic Century.* Norman: University of Oklahoma Press.

Little, Daniel. 1993. "On the Scope and Limits of Generalizations in the Social Sciences." *Synthese* 97(2): 183–207.

Macaulay, Thomas Babington. 1935. *Speeches,* edited by G. M. Young. Oxford: Oxford University Press.

Manin, Bernard. 1997. *The Principles of Representative Government.* Cambridge: Cambridge University Press.

Marx, Karl. 1973. *Surveys from Exile: Political Writings,* vol. 1, edited by David Fernbach. London: Allen Lane.

Mas-Colell, Andreu, Michael Whinston, and Jerry Green. 1995. *Microeconomic Theory.* New York: Oxford University Press.

McMillan, John. 2002. *Reinventing the Bazaar: A Natural History of Markets.* New York: W. W. Norton.

Milgrom, Paul, Douglass North, and Barry Weingast. 1990. "The Role of Institutions in the Revival of Trade." *Politics and Economics* 2(1): 1–23.

Myerson, Roger. 1999. "Nash Equilibrium and the History of Economic Theory." *Journal of Economic Literature* XXXVII(3): 1067–82.

Myles, Gareth. 1995. *Public Economics.* Cambridge: Cambridge University Press.

Nelson, Richard, and Sidney Winter. 1982. *An Evolutionary Theory of Economic Change.* Cambridge, Mass.: Harvard University Press.

North, Douglass C. 1990a. "A Transaction Cost Theory of Politics." *Journal of Theoretical Politics* 2(4): 355–68.

———. 1990b. *Institutions, Institutional Change, and Economic Performance.* Cambridge: Cambridge University Press.

North, Douglass C., and Barry Weingast. 1989. "Constitutions and Commitment: The Institutions Governing Public Choice in Seventeenth Century England." *Journal of Economic History* XLIX(4): 803–32.

Nozick, Robert. 1993. *The Nature of Rationality.* Princeton, N.J.: Princeton University Press.

Ordeshook, Peter C. 1986. *Game Theory and Political Theory.* Cambridge: Cambridge University Press.

———. 1992. "Constitutional Stability." *Constitutional Political Economy* 3(2): 137–75.

———. 1993. "Some Rules of Constitutional Design." *Social Philosophy and Policy* 10(2): 198–232.

Orren, Karen, and Stephen Skowronek. 1996. "Institutions and Intercurrence." In *Nomos XXXVII: Political Order*, edited by Ian Shapiro and Russell Hardin. New York: New York University Press.

Pitkin, Hannah. 1967. *The Concept of Representation.* Berkeley: University of California Press.

Putterman, Louis. 1997. "Why Have the Rabble Not Redistributed the Wealth? On the Stability of Democracy and Unequal Property." In *Property Relations, Incentives and Welfare*, edited by John Roemer. New York: St. Martin's Press.

Riker, William. 1990. "Political Science and Rational Choice." In *Perspectives on Positive Political Economy*, edited by James E. Alt and Kenneth A. Shepsle. New York: Cambridge University Press.

Roemer, John. 1998. "Why the Poor Do Not Expropriate the Rich: An Old Argument in New Garb." *Journal of Public Economics* 70(3): 399–424.

Rubinstein, Ariel. 1991. "Comments on the Interpretation of Game Theory." *Econometrica* 59(4): 909–24.

Satz, Debra. 1992. "Markets in Women's Reproductive Labor." *Philosophy & Public Affairs* 21(2): 107–31.

———. 1995. "Markets in Women's Sexual Labor." *Ethics* 106(1): 63–85.

Satz, Debra, and John Ferejohn. 1994. "Rational Choice and Social Theory." *Journal of Philosophy* 91(2): 71–87.

Schelling, Thomas. 1978. *Micromotives and Macrobehavior.* New York: W. W. Norton.

———. 1998. "Social Mechanisms and Social Dynamics." In *Social Mechanisms*, edited by P. Hedström and R. Swedberg. Cambridge: Cambridge University Press.

Sen, Amartya K. 1982. *Choice, Welfare and Measurement.* Cambridge, Mass.: The MIT Press.

———. 1993. "Markets and Freedoms." *Oxford Economic Papers* 45(4): 519–41.

———. 1999. "Democracy as a Universal Value." *Journal of Democracy* 10(3): 3–17.

Shapiro, Ian. 2002. "Why The Poor Don't Soak the Rich." *Dædalus* (winter): 118–28.

Shepsle, Kenneth A. 1989. "Studying Institutions: Some Lessons from the Rational Choice Approach." *Journal of Theoretical Politics* 1(2): 131–48.

Shklar, Judith. 1991. *American Citizenship*. Cambridge, Mass.: Harvard University Press.

Stiglitz, Joseph. 2002. "Information and the Change of Paradigm in Economics." *American Economic Review* 92(3): 460–501.

Swedberg, Richard. 1994. "Markets as Social Structures." In *The Handbook of Economic Sociology*, edited by N. Smelser and Richard Swedberg. New York: Russell Sage Foundation and Princeton University Press.

Taylor, Michael. 1987. *The Possibility of Cooperation*. Cambridge: Cambridge University Press.

———. 1996. "Good Government." *Journal of Political Philosophy* 4(1): 1–28.

Thelan, Kathleen. 1999. "Historical Institutionalism in Comparative Politics." *Annual Review of Political Science* 2: 369–404.

Ullman-Margalit, Edna. 1977. *The Emergence of Norms*. New York: Oxford University Press.

Waldron, Jeremy. 1993. *Liberal Rights*. Cambridge: Cambridge University Press.

Wallerstein, Michael. 1997. "Comment." In *Property Relations, Incentives and Welfare*, edited by John Roemer. New York: St. Martin's Press.

Weber, Max. 1922/1968. *Economy and Society*, 2 vols. Berkeley: University of California Press.

Weingast, Barry. 1995. "The Economic Role of Institutions: Market Preserving Federalism and Economic Development." *Journal of Law, Economics and Organization* 11(1): 1–31.

———. 1996. "Political Institutions: Rational Choice Perspectives." In *A New Handbook of Political Science*, edited by Robert Goodin and Hans-Dieter Klingemann. New York: Oxford University Press.

Williamson, Oliver. 1985. *The Economic Institutions of Capitalism*. New York: Free Press.

PART IV

Synthesis

11

Combining Institutionalisms: Liberal Choices and Political Trajectories in Central America

James Mahoney

Scholars working in the field of historical institutionalism (HI) have explored how the formation of institutions during critical juncture periods may set countries on long-run paths of development that are not easily reversed (Collier and Collier 1991; Pierson 2000; Thelen 1999). One virtue of these path-dependent arguments is their sensitivity to the causal impact of temporally distant institutions and to the processes through which these institutions affect more contemporary outcomes. A common criticism, however, is that they fail to adequately theorize actor choices. Indeed, HI often treats critical juncture periods as moments of contingency when choices are highly efficacious but essentially unpredictable.[1]

Rational choice institutionalism (RCI) offers a basis for modeling actor choices during critical junctures as instrumental decisions made purposively in light of existing institutional arrangements. This approach can help historical researchers explain choices through a formal specification of the options, potential pay-offs, and preferences of actors. Those strands of RCI that embrace a thin theory of rationality and assume that actor goals must be specified in part through inductive research are especially compatible with HI (Bates et al. 1998), and can be combined with it to specify key dynamics during critical junctures in many path-dependent arguments.

Here I explore the contributions of combining institutionalisms by building on my work on liberalism and political development in Central America (Mahoney 2001). In *The Legacies of Liberalism,* I argue that the choices of liberal elites about how to modernize the state and agrarian sector in the nineteenth century set the countries of Central America on distinct paths of national development, culminating in remarkably different national political regimes. One criticism of the work, however, is its treatment of actor choices during the critical juncture period of liberal reform (for example, Prasad 2002). I now use the tools of RCI to enrich the analysis of the choices of liberal political elites. In particular, I suggest that liberal choices during this time can be heuristically modeled in light of liberals' subjective understandings of the outcomes, outcome utilities, and outcome probabilities associated with alternative choice options. Values for these components can be estimated through a historical analysis that explores the role of ideology, class position, and political goals in shaping liberal preferences.

Using this approach, I find that liberal choices concerning alternative policy options were strongly influenced by political aspirations to maintain state power. When liberal elites faced great political insecurity, they were likely to pursue a radical set of policies that extensively transformed existing state and class structures. By contrast, when liberal elites were more secure, they were motivated to follow a moderate set of reforms that only partially transformed pre-existing state and class structures. I also explore how this argument leads to a more general hypothesis that could be extended to other contexts in Latin America.

Liberalism and Its Legacies in Central America

In nineteenth-century Central America, the liberal reform period was initiated when political elites implemented policies designed to modernize the state and spur economic development through coffee and banana exportation. The elites who led this reform effort were called liberals because they opposed colonial and conservative institutions such as monarchial rule, trade monopolies, the Church, and the common land system. In turn, they advocated constitutional government (though not real democracy), free trade, a secularization of society, and private property. In these respects, Central American liberals were similar to liberals in Western Europe, though there were important differences as well.[2]

The liberal reform period corresponds with the world-historical environment when these countries began to export their primary products, thus opening the door to new possibilities in economic advancement. In particular, the market for coffee exploded in the nineteenth century, and technological improvements made it possible to profitably ship the highly perishable banana crop to distant markets. Because national political regimes in Central America at the time were organized as personal dictatorships and the chief executives wielded exceptional power, specific liberal leaders were positioned to steer their countries during this period. Legislatures functioned largely as rubber-stamp bodies designed to support the decisions of acting presidents; elections were either not held or were fraudulent affairs aimed at political legitimatization. Politics was the domain of individuals, and personal choices could be extremely consequential.

During the reform period, key liberal presidents[3] faced basic choices about how to modernize society, especially how to transform agriculture. I distinguish between the two agricultural modernization options that were alternatives to liberals: a radical policy option and a reform policy option. I argue that the choice to adopt either was a critical juncture that sent countries on long-run paths of development, ultimately culminating in the formation of dramatically different types of national political regimes (see figure 11.1).

To simplify, a radical policy option meant rapidly privatizing communal lands, promoting large agro-export estates, and using state coercion to secure labor. A radical policy option thus aimed to destroy existing communal landholding structures and replace them with export-oriented estates that relied on a dependent labor force. By contrast, a reform policy option involved selectively and gradually privatizing communal lands, promoting smaller farms dedicated to export crops, and less actively encouraging coercive labor. A reform policy option was therefore more moderately paced and entailed a transition to commercialized agriculture that was less disruptive to previous agrarian structures.

Different policy options were consequential because they produced new state and class institutions, which in turn had long-run effects on development. In Guatemala and El Salvador, where radical policy options were successfully implemented, highly militarized state apparatuses and highly polarized agrarian economies came into being. These institutions set the two countries on paths of development that culminated in democratizing movements that failed and were succeeded by brutally repressive military-authoritarian regimes. By contrast, in Costa Rica, where a reform policy option was successfully implemented, a modernized but nonpolarized agrarian economy and a state apparatus without a significant military were created. These institutions were essential to Costa Rica's eventual progressive democratic regime. Finally, in Honduras and Nicaragua, policy options were not successful. Liberals in those countries attempted to pursue specific policy options (a reform option in Honduras; and a radical option in Nicaragua), but episodes of foreign intervention led to the failure of liberal reform and no major structural transformations in the agrarian sector and the state. As a result, democratizing movements did not emerge in Honduras and Nicaragua and the countries were characterized by backward-looking traditional dictatorships for much of the twentieth century.

Figure 11.1   Summary of Legacies of Policy Options

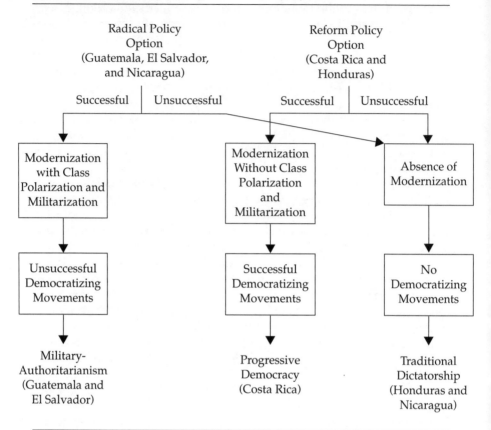

Source: Author's compilation.

Even from such a brief sketch, it is clear that actor choices play a prominent role in this HI argument. I will now explore the ways in which RCI might enrich an analysis of these choices, focusing on the liberal decision to adopt either a radical policy option or a reform policy option. Although these liberal choices were not the only variable shaping long-run development in Central America, they were a critical one—so much so that I argue different choices would have led the countries toward quite different outcomes. To the degree RCI can help us better understand these choices, then, it can contribute significantly to understanding long-run political trajectories in Central America.

Table 11.1   Components of Choice and Preference in Rational Decision Theory

Option	Outcome	Utility	Probability	Expected Utility
	$O^{1,1}$	$U^{1,1}$	$P^{1,1}$	$U^{1,1} \times P^{1,1}$
C^1	$O^{1,2}$	$U^{1,2}$	$P^{1,2}$	$U^{1,2} \times P^{1,2}$
	$O^{1,3}$	$U^{1,3}$	$P^{1,3}$	$U^{1,3} \times P^{1,3}$
	$O^{2,1}$	$U^{2,1}$	$P^{2,1}$	$U^{2,1} \times P^{2,1}$
C^2	$O^{2,2}$	$U^{2,2}$	$P^{2,2}$	$U^{2,2} \times P^{2,2}$
	$O^{2,3}$	$U^{2,3}$	$P^{2,3}$	$U^{2,3} \times P^{2,3}$

Source: Adapted from Little (1991, 41).

A Heuristic Model

Rational decision theory is helpful for formulating a simple model of liberal choices. As table 11.1 illustrates, this theory emphasizes the following elements as the components shaping an actor choice: the behavioral options available to the actor; the specific outcomes that might be generated if a particular option is carried out; the utility associated with each of these specific outcomes; and the probability that a given outcome will take place if a particular option is selected. One can arrive at the expected utility of each outcome by multiplying utility and probability. For utility maximizing actors, the best option corresponds to the one with the greatest sum of expected utilities. For risk adverse actors, the preferred option corresponds to the one with the best-worst outcome.

From the HI perspective, there is nothing wrong with abstractly formulating a model of actor decision making like this one. Historical institutionalists will insist, however, that each key component—options, outcomes, utilities, and probabilities—be specified through a historically grounded analysis that makes inferences about actors' subjective experiences. In this sense, HI assumes that the values of the different components of the model do not reflect objective reality, but instead the

Table 11.2   Preference Structure for Actors Adopting a Radical
             Policy Option

Option	Outcome	Utility (1= Least)	Probability (1 = Lowest)	Expected Utility (1 = Least)
Radical policy	Overthrow of liberal rule	Very negative (1)	Very unlikely (2)	Slightly negative (2)
	Unstable liberal rule	Positive (3)	Likely (4)	Positive (4)
	Stable liberal rule	Very positive (4)	Unlikely (3)	Positive (4)
Reform policy	Overthrow of liberal rule	Very negative (1)	Unlikely (3)	Negative (1)
	Unstable liberal rule	Marginally positive (2)	Likely (4)	Marginally positive (3)
	Stable liberal rule	Positive (3)	Nearly impossible (1)	Marginally positive (3)

Source: Author's compilation.

subjective understandings of the actor in question. In fact, an actor's assessment of the probabilities may be quite removed from reality, but that
inaccurate assessment will nevertheless serve as the basis for rational
decision making.[4]

In decision theory, the concept of preference refers narrowly to the
utilities associated with different possible outcomes. However, HI also
treats the actor's understanding of the possible choice options, different
outcomes, and the probabilities associated with these outcomes as components of an actor's preference. Under this broader definition, the expression preferences and situations might refer to the idea that historical
circumstances shape a wide range of components of actor choice, not
only utility functions.

Here I offer simple models for understanding liberal choices in Central America. Table 11.2 attempts to specify the components of prefer-

Table 11.3   Preference Structure for Actors Adopting a Reform
Policy Option

Option	Outcome	Utility (1= Least)	Probability (1 = Lowest)	Expected Utility (1 = Least)
Radical policy	Overthrow of liberal rule	Very negative (1)	Likely (4)	Very negative (1)
	Unstable liberal rule	Positive (3)	Unlikely (3)	Marginally positive (3)
	Stable liberal rule	Very positive (4)	Nearly impossible (1)	Marginally positive (3)
Reform policy	Overthrow of liberal rule	Very negative (1)	Very unlikely (2)	Slightly negative (2)
	Unstable liberal rule	Marginally positive (2)	Likely (4)	Marginally positive (3)
	Stable liberal rule	Positive (3)	Unlikely (3)	Marginally positive (3)

Source: Author's compilation.

ence that characterize liberal actors who pursue a radical policy option. By contrast, table 11.3 tries to characterize the components of choice among actors who pursue a reform policy option. The codes in the models are derived from the historical discussion that follows; they are inductively formulated estimates grounded in the historiography. In using induction and historical analysis this way to guide a rational choice account, I essentially follow the programmatic agenda of the Analytic Narratives project (Bates et al. 1998), which I believe substantially overlaps with long-standing HI emphases.

In both tables, key liberal rulers are faced with two options: a radical policy option and a reform policy option. In turn, each option is associated with three possible outcomes: first, instability that leads to the overthrow of the liberal order; second, unstable but sustained liberal rule; and, third, stable and sustained liberal rule. The utilities associated with each outcome are identical in each table. For a radical policy option, which ceteris paribus all liberals prefer, the utilities are specified as very negative for instability and overthrow, as positive for instability but continued liberal rule and reform, and as very positive for stability with liberal rule and reform. For a reform policy option, which is less preferred, the utilities for the same outcomes are specified as very negative, marginally positive, and positive. The figures also offer a simple ordinal ranking of the outcomes according to their desirability to liberals.

Tables 11.2 and 11.3 are different with respect to the probabilities that liberals associate with each outcome. Those actors whose preferences are summarized in table 11.2 view the consequences of a radical policy option as follows: outcome A is very unlikely, outcome B is likely, and outcome C is unlikely. By contrast, those actors whose preferences are summarized in table 11.3 view the consequences of a radical policy option differently: outcome A is likely, outcome B is unlikely, and outcome C is nearly impossible. Similarly, the actors with the preferences of table 11.2 view the consequences of a reform policy option as follows: outcome A is unlikely, outcome B is likely, and outcome C is nearly impossible. By contrast, those with the preferences in table 11.3 see the consequences of a reform policy option differently: outcome A is very unlikely, outcome B is likely, and outcome C is unlikely. These differences in perceived probabilities in turn explain why actors adopt different policy options.

A radical policy option is the rational choice in table 11.2, whereas a reform policy option is the slightly better choice in table 11.3. This is true if the decision maker chooses the option with the greatest expected utility or if the actor chooses the option in a risk-averse fashion that avoids a catastrophic outcome. For example, in table 11.2, a radical policy option has a positive expected utility (that is, the average of slightly negative + positive + positive), whereas a reform policy option has a neutral to negative utility (that is, the average of negative + marginally positive + marginally positive). Likewise, the probability of a catastrophic outcome (that is, liberal overthrow) occurring is lower if a radical policy option is adopted. In this sense, in table 11.2, a radical policy option is the best choice under most decision-making rules. By contrast, a reform policy option will be preferred given the preferences in table 11.3.

I build an empirical argument that illustrates how the decision structure of table 11.2 approximates liberal choices in Guatemala, El Salvador, and Nicaragua, which all followed a radical policy option. By contrast, the decision structure of table 11.3 applies more to liberals in Honduras and Nicaragua, which followed a reform policy option. I show how thinking in terms of the components of rational decision theory (that is, options, outcomes, probabilities) can be helpful in examining alternative hypotheses that seek to explain liberal behavior. Using these components to frame the discussion makes it possible to state more precisely how alternative factors likely affected liberal decisions. In addition, as we shall see, the use of these models points toward at least one testable hypothesis that could be applied to liberal reform throughout nineteenth-century Latin America: the extent of liberal policy transformation is positively related to the extent of political threat facing liberals.

Three Approaches to Preference Formation

In the historiography on Central America, three distinct understandings of liberal goals and motivations can be found: as ideological actors, as class actors, and as political actors. These understandings are worth considering here, for they parallel more general approaches to explaining the sources of actor preferences in the social sciences.[5] In addition, a discussion of these alternatives helps provide empirical grounding to the estimates presented in the models.

Ideological Beliefs

One approach to preference formation is to understand actors as ideological carriers motivated by a set of principled beliefs. Scholars who explore the ramifications of basic cultural systems, such as the Enlightenment or Marxism-Leninism, often use this kind of analysis. The approach also is found in the work of those who suggest particular actors are inspired to action by deeply held normative convictions, perhaps personally formulated in a unique way. In the HI literature, such ideological beliefs are studied through historical analysis that looks at the idioms and expressed commitments of concrete actors. Historical institutionalists believe that such an approach is more likely to bear fruit than an analysis that abstractly attributes an overarching ideological frame to an actor (see Skocpol 1985; Swidler 1986).

Historians of Central America have suggested that the liberal ideology found in the nineteenth century can be used as a guide to explaining liberal behavior. They point out that the conflict between liberals and conservatives mirrored an ideological split within the region's elite. For example, according to the distinguished historian Ralph Lee Woodward, Jr., liberals and conservatives "were factions of a landholding and bureaucratic elite, but they reflected fundamentally different perceptions on how best to develop their country" (1984). On the one hand, the conservatives favored policies that would preserve the aristocratic landholding elites in their traditional, dominant roles, but also, in noblesse oblige fashion, assured the peasants of a degree of protection, especially against exploitation by the Liberal modernizers. . . . [Conservatives] emphasized traditional Hispanic values and institutions, especially the Roman Catholic Church . . . . While they welcomed some expansion of agricultural exports, which allowed them a few luxury imports, they were sensitive to the danger of upsetting native labor and land tenure patterns. (292)

On the other hand, the liberals

wished to modernize Central America through emulation of the economic and political success of Western Europe and the United States from the late eighteenth century forward. These "modernizers" rejected traditional Hispanic values and institutions, especially the Church, and espoused classical economic liberalism, opposing monopolies while encouraging private foreign trade, immigration, and investment. They emphasized exports, and treated the rural masses and their land as the principal resources to be exploited in this effort. (292–93)

Although Woodward supports this broad characterization of liberal and conservative ideology with considerable evidence, revisionist historians have emphasized that the ideologies were hardly sacredly held beliefs (see Gudmundson and Lindo-Fuentes 1995). For example, individuals could and did switch sides in the struggle between liberalism and conservatism as circumstances warranted. And few liberals were so committed to their beliefs that they were unwilling to violate ideological principles when given powerful inducements to do so.

The simple fact is that many ideologies can be and are cast aside in the face of other, more important competing interests. When treating historical ideologies as the source of actor preferences, then, one must always probe the degree to which these principled beliefs will be maintained when the actor is confronted with competing interests. When ideological principles and other core interests (for example, class interests or personal political interests) clash, actors frequently will forgo the former to pursue the latter. Of course, when ideological principles and core interests are consistent,[6] it is easy for actors to behave consistently with their ideology. Although one may wish to hold up such behavior as illustrating the power of ideology, it often makes more sense to view the behavior as following the other core interests.[7] Like most other historical institutionalists, I favor a cautious approach to understanding the power of ideology, one that avoids the temptation of overestimating its role at the expense of other (not ideologically defined) interests.

In Central America, ideology surely had a role to play during the liberal reform period, though not likely one that can fully explain the different policy choices of liberals. Ideological beliefs almost certainly shaped the range of possible options that liberal actors contemplated seriously. For example, liberals did not contemplate any options that involved maintaining the political and economic status quo, as their conservative predecessors had. Rather, they considered only change, whether radical or reform.[8] In fact, although many of their core interests were similar, conservatives and liberals differed significantly in their ideology. This difference helps explain why liberals contemplated choices that conservatives never even considered appropriate.

However, ideology is far less effective at explaining why liberals decided to pursue a radical or a reform policy option. From the existing sources, it is difficult to glean any specific difference in the principled beliefs of liberals across countries that might explain variations in policy choice. Instead, all key liberals appear to have had similar and relatively constant principled beliefs about what was appropriate for modernizing society. In particular, they favored a rapid and thoroughgoing transformation of society in which the colonial and conservative order was more or less completely replaced. In this sense, other things being equal, they favored a radical policy option on principled grounds. Given that they did not all end up choosing a radical policy option, however, it is clear that other things were not equal.

In short, I argue that ideology helped define the set of options that liberal actors considered seriously, but ideology had little causal role beyond this contribution. In general, I think this argument is consistent with what many institutionalists already believe about ideology and preference formation—ideological commitments may define the parameters of contemplated possibilities, but only rarely are the final movers of actor choices.

Class Position

A second approach locates the source of actors' preferences with the class positions of those actors. Analysts who adopt this approach are not of one mind, however. For some, class position affects preferences through a socialization process in which individuals learn the tastes and habits that characterize their socioeconomic grouping. Here the assumption is that, because of sociocultural differences, members of different classes may value different things (for example, Bourdieu 1984).[9] For others, class position shapes preferences because it affects the material opportunities available to actors. With this orientation, actors are assumed to value similar things, such as economic power and material resources, but their different class positions are seen as social institutions that provide different economic opportunities and incentives (for example, Elster 1985; Przeworski 1985; Wright 1997). Because of these different opportunities and incentives, actors of different classes will have different (induced) preferences.

Scholars of Central American politics often apply a Marxist version of class analysis consistent with the second view. Class position is defined by an actor's relationship to the productive process, and class is understood to shape behavior by leading actors to be concerned with material well-being and providing them with economic incentives to maximize this interest. Using such a framework, analysts have argued that the division between liberals and conservatives can be studied as a class division (Dunkerley 1988; Paige 1997). Liberals are understood to represent that class faction most involved in the production of new agro-export products, especially coffee. By contrast, conservatives are viewed as representing traditional landowners outside the emerging agro-export economy. From these class positions, differences in preferences can be derived: conservatives should favor the socioeconomic status quo, including trade monopolies, existing land tenure relationships, and a strong role for the Church. By contrast, liberals should favor free trade, land privatization, and the removal of corporate entities, such as the Church, that stand in the way of capitalist entrepreneurship. Furthermore, within the liberal faction, those especially well situated to take advantage of agrarian commercialization should favor an especially radical set of transformations. Thus, one would expect that key liberal leaders who followed a radical option would be especially well positioned to profit from the production, processing, and export of major primary products. This should be less true of those who pursued a reform option.

Although intuitively plausible as an explanation of liberal choices, this account is not supported by the bulk of empirical evidence. The argument assumes that liberals were members of an agro-export elite, and, within that category, those liberal presidents who enacted a radical policy option were well situated to reap benefits from agrarian commercialization. However, only two key liberal presidents, Barrios in Guatemala and Guardia in Costa Rica, can actually be considered full members of the agro-export elite (Williams 1994, 212–19), and they followed contrasting policy options, that is, a radical policy in Guatemala and a reform policy in Costa Rica. Of the remaining liberal presidents, none was deeply involved in the agro-export landholding, with the possible exception of Zelaya in Nicaragua, whose father was an important coffee planter. When all is tallied, a class-based explanation is problematic for those liberal presidents not seriously involved in export agriculture (El Salvador and Honduras), or for those who stood to personally benefit from a radical policy but ended up following a reform policy (Costa Rica).

In fact, if one looks beyond particular liberal presidents, consistent evidence does not support the idea that liberals and conservatives occupied distinct positions within the productive process. Rather, sometimes both came from the same agrarian elite (Gudmundson and Lindo-Fuentes 1995; Mahoney 2001). In Nicaragua, for example, much of the conservative leadership was deeply involved in coffee production, the economic base from which liberalism should have developed. In Honduras, liberals emerged in an economic context that did not feature any major agro-export economy. Finally, in Guatemala, El Salvador, and Costa Rica, the liberal movement was born before export agriculture was consolidated, suggesting that liberalism did not depend on a new class structure.

To summarize, historical institutionalists will often entertain the idea that actor preferences reflect underlying economic interests and are ultimately rooted in class position. They will insist, however, that empirical evidence support these ideas before they reach firm conclusions. In the case of Central America, historical evidence appears to contradict the notion that liberal preferences and liberal policy choices were products of underlying class structure.

Political Power

In a final perspective, analysts link actor preferences to the needs of gaining, maintaining, and augmenting personal political power. Actors are assumed to have a basic interest in political power, and this interest is typically understood to derive from the demands of the institutional environment of the actors. Thus, in the RCI literature, scholars often assume that elected politicians have an interest in maintaining political office because their continued status as elected politicians demands it (for example, Geddes 1994). Likewise, comparative-historical analysts who work on early modern Europe sometimes suggest that states have an interest in self-preservation because those that do not may be "selected against" in the course of warfare (Tilly 1990; cf. Waltz 1979). In both examples, a selection mechanism helps ensure that actors with a specific preference are present in a particular institutional environment.

Although this approach is not commonly offered in the literature on Central America, we have good reason to believe that it may make sense for the liberal reform period. In turbulent nineteenth-century Central America, leaders rose or fell according to how successful they were at using resources to preempt or defeat armed challenges to their rule.

Leaders who chose to ignore the imperatives of maintaining power were selected against in this environment—that is, the failure to exhibit a concern with self-preservation and power expansion would almost always lead to the removal of a liberal leader. Thus, had liberals been uninterested in maximizing power, they never would have gained control of government in the first place, much less have gone on to lead administrations with enough longevity to enact far-reaching reforms.

The need to pursue power was closely linked to the fact that there were no civil institutions to maintain political order during the liberal reform period. Leadership transfer from one dictator to another occurred largely as a result of coercive pressures in which an acting president stepped down in the face of potentially life threatening challenges. Those who sought to oust liberal presidents were usually rival elites who mobilized an armed movement from the peasant population living near their local base of power. A key goal of all liberal presidents was to defeat these rival elites.

Liberals would not likely adopt a given policy option if they believed an alternative policy would better serve their interests in maintaining power. How well a particular policy option might do so depended in part on the existing political environment, including the level of threat facing liberal presidents. These levels were rooted in the strength of conservative opponents and the cohesion of the liberals. In Guatemala, El Salvador, and Nicaragua, liberals were more divided and conservatives were stronger than elsewhere in Central America (Mahoney 2001). As a result, a key goal of liberals was to build up the state to defeat the existing serious political threats. A radical policy option was appropriate because it involved establishing tight control of the countryside and marginalizing enemies by reorganizing property relations in the countryside. A reform policy option did not entail building up the military and extending the state, and thus may well have left these presidents vulnerable to overthrow. In the context of a high level of threat, then, a radical policy was more consistent with liberal power goals.

In Honduras and Costa Rica, the challenge to liberals from conservatives and other political elites was less extensive. Here a radical policy option may have been more destabilizing than a reform option. In particular, in the absence of a severe threat, a radical policy risked creating large-scale social upheaval and opposition from among those groups who opposed major transformations. In this context, the more modest reform policy was the safer and wiser choice, even though it was less desirable for ideological reasons. More specifically, given a low threat, a reform policy allowed liberals to safely implement certain reforms with only a low probability of triggering enough opposition to risk their overthrow.

Evidence from the Central American cases suggests that liberal decision makers did contemplate choices in light of these kinds of considerations. For example, we know that Barrios in Guatemala implemented land and labor reforms with a close eye on their effects vis-à-vis securing state control of hostile areas. He often would not implement reforms in areas where he felt doing so would generate more opposition than it prevented (McCreery 1994, 238; Williams 1994, 63). Likewise, while Honduran liberal reformer Marco Aurelio Soto may initially have been ideologically disposed toward a radical policy option, he likely did not pursue it because doing so would have created intense resistance from the rugged settlers in the isolated villages of rural Honduras.[10] Even the moderately inclined reformer Dr. Rafael Zaldívar of El Salvador ended up following a radical policy option when political challenges seemed to make this the more secure course (Mahoney 2001, 115–16, 124–30).

To conclude, liberals were concerned with political survival and maximizing power, and contemplated policy options in light of these concerns. When liberals encountered serious political threat, a radical policy better enabled them to preserve power. By contrast, when threat was minimal, a reform policy was more consistent with maintaining power.

Revisiting the Heuristic Models of Liberal Choices

Let us now revisit the heuristic models, asking how the discussion of preference formation can help to elaborate them. Reviewing the empirical basis for each major element of the models—options, outcomes, utilities, and probabilities—is the easiest course. We can then reflect more generally on the strengths and weaknesses of the models.

Empirical Grounding of the Models

The analysis of preference formation suggests that ideological beliefs played a role in the formulation of the policy options that liberal actors considered seriously (see table 11.4). Liberal ideology defined the menu of possible behaviors that were considered reasonable options (that is, radical and reform policy options) and filtered out as unreasonable other options such as maintaining the status quo. Indeed, had liberals chosen to maintain the status quo, they would not have qualified for membership in the category liberal as defined in nineteenth-century Central America. In this sense, liberal ideology was constitutive of liberals in Central America, and it ensured that liberals would decide between options that entailed some kind of transformation, whether radical or reformist.

Both a radical and a reform option were evaluated in light of the

Table 11.4   Sources of Preferences for Liberals

Option	Outcomes	Utilities	Probabilities
Liberal ideology shapes the choice between radical and reform options.	Outcomes associated with each option are evaluated according to their political consequences for liberal leaders.	Both ideology and political considerations affect the utility values of each outcome.	The probabilities of outcomes reflect actors' understandings of the level of threat posed by opposition forces.

Source: Author's compilation.

possible outcomes associated with them. Liberals did not know in advance exactly what would happen if a particular option was selected. They had to make decisions based on their subjective assessments of what might happen.[11] We have good reason to believe that they were concerned with outcomes related to their political and power goals, especially given that nearly all previous efforts at enacting liberal reforms had produced instability and eventually the defeat of liberal presidents. Political and power considerations thus were a key second filter that defined the three outcomes specified here: overthrow of the liberal order, liberal rule with instability, and liberal rule with stability.

The utilities associated with the different outcomes were closely tied to the liberal concern with maximizing political power, though ideology was relevant here too. The worst possible outcome was overthrow of the liberal order. This would mean not only the failure to successfully implement liberal changes (very negative from an ideological perspective), but also—and more important—the defeat of the particular liberal president (very negative from a personal power perspective). In the models, therefore, the utility associated with overthrow is set at very negative. The best outcome for liberals was stable liberal rule, which accorded with both their ideological preference to see liberals in power and their preference to personally rule without serious challenges. In the models, this outcome is represented with positive designators, though it was especially valued when it accompanied a radical policy (favored by liberals on ideological grounds). Finally, the outcome of unstable liberal rule is viewed as desirable, and thus receives a score of positive for a radical policy and a marginally positive for a reform policy (only marginally positive because the combination of instability and limited liberal transformation was not a particularly desirable outcome). Again, these designators and the ordinal rankings that accompany them are inferences, but they nevertheless are grounded in historical evidence.

The probabilities associated with each outcome are understood to reflect liberals' subjective assessments of the likelihood of each outcome occurring. My assumption is that liberals had reasonable knowledge of the level of threat facing their administrations, and that they implicitly calculated the probability for each outcome in light of this threat. Thus, the probabilities in table 11.2 are rough estimates for the likelihood of each outcome when political threat was high, whereas the probabilities in table 11.3 are rough estimates of the likelihood of each outcome when political threat was low. Overall, the argument is that differing levels of threat drove the differing probabilities in the two models, making it rational to select a radical policy when threat was high and rational to select a reform policy when it was low.

This hypothesis could be developed into a more general proposition for all of Latin America—that is, the extent of state and agrarian transformation during the liberal reform co-varies with the extent of political threat facing key liberal rulers. The liberal reform period had its own pace and rhythm in South America and Mexico, and it is debatable whether the period represented a critical juncture for them as it did for Central America. Even so, one would expect to find some support for this hypothesis if the argument about the sources of liberal choices presented here is indeed correct.

Contributions to HI and RCI

Although I have suggested that there is an empirical basis for accepting the heuristic models offered here as approximations of reality, it is essential to recognize that the models do not fully capture the complexity of reality. In fact, each of the elements in the models is a simplification of the cognitive process through which liberals arrived at policy choices. For example, as far as I know, liberals did not directly discuss radical and reform policy options, and we cannot be certain that they explicitly deliberated about whether to follow a more radical or a more moderate set of reforms.[12] Likewise, liberals might not have explicitly considered the three outcomes associated with each option identified here. Rather, they may have gauged outcomes in terms of a continuum ranging from overthrow by enemies to complete stability with many gradations in the middle. Models are necessarily simplifications of reality, and the risk of missing key aspects of reality is understood.

Nevertheless, the models do offer a more precise account of actor choice than is often found in the HI literature on critical junctures and path dependence. For example, a historical institutionalist might be tempted to assert that the level of threat facing liberals led them to select either a radical or a reform policy. This assertion has an element of truth, but it is incomplete. It fails to identify the mechanism though which level of threat translates into a particular actor choice. As we have seen, rational decision theory enables one to conceptualize this mechanism in terms of subjective actor beliefs about the possible options available for selection, the outcomes associated with those options, and the utility and probability of those outcomes. Making this rational choice mechanism explicit makes it possible to state more precisely why level of threat affects actor choice.

At the same time, I have tried here to ground actor choices more thoroughly in history than is perhaps true of many analyses in the RCI tradition. Rational choice theorists will often assume that actors' subjective understandings of possible outcomes and their probabilities correspond with objective reality (that is, there is risk in making choices, but no uncertainty about the risk probabilities involved). With this approach, it is not necessary to theorize how an actor defines outcomes and probabilities, because these aspects of actor choice can be measured independently of the actor's subjective consciousness. Likewise, rational choice theorists may simply assume without much justification the utility values that an actor holds vis-à-vis possible outcomes. Such an approach makes it possible to build models without knowing too much about the actor whose behavior is being modeled. But it is precisely this lack of historical grounding that seems inadequate in the HI tradition.

Combining rational choice and historical institutionalism offers possibilities for a positive-sum synergy between the two traditions. Scholars affiliated with RCI stand to benefit from the concern of HI with empirically justifying assumptions about actor goals and assessments. Moreover, HI can contribute to RCI by identifying those specific periods when actor choices are especially consequential and thus need to be carefully modeled. For their part, scholars in the field of HI can benefit from the concern of RCI with rigorously modeling the mechanisms through which actors make choices during key historical periods. The biggest impediment to furthering this synergy is the strict separation of scholars into the RCI and HI camps. Fortunately, this division will be hard to maintain in the future if scholars who combine institutionalisms achieve important gains in substantive understanding.

Notes

1. These periods are "essentially" unpredictable because many path-dependent analysts assume that critical junctures are not inherently random;

rather they are unpredictable in relationship to prevailing theory. For a discussion see Mahoney (2000).

2. One critical difference concerned the size of the middle classes that supported liberal movements: they were tiny in Central America, but they made up the core of liberalism as a movement in Europe. This difference was linked to the varying levels of economic development in the two regions.

3. One or two liberal presidents in each country enacted policy legislation that defined the overall direction of change for the entire period. These key presidents were: Justo Rufino Barrios (1873 to 1885) in Guatemala, Rafael Zaldívar (1876 to 1883) in El Salvador, Braulio Carrillo (1838 to 1842) and Tomás Guardia (1870 to 1882) in Costa Rica, Marco Aurelio Soto (1876 to 1883) in Honduras, and José Santos Zelaya (1893 to 1909) in Nicaragua.

4. There are various reasons why an actor's assessment may not correspond to reality (see, for example, Elster 1989). Imperfect information is of course one, but assessment biases stemming from ideological convictions, charged emotions, habituated action, and other kinds of predispositions (for example, biological urges) can lead actors to ignore valid information and thereby make inaccurate assessments of possible outcomes and their probabilities. In my view, none of this necessarily means that actors behave irrationally or that the core assumptions of rational choice theory are violated. As far as I am concerned, the hard core of rational choice theory is nothing more (or less) than the idea that individuals are purposive and instrumental. Beyond this, rational choice theory (like other potentially useful general theories) has no empirical content independent of bridging assumptions. For a discussion, see Mahoney (2004).

5. At this point, the social sciences have no general theory of preference formation. In the view of HI, scholars should strive to identify plausible variables (for example, class position) that offer partial accounts of the sources of actor preferences and their evolution over time. However, a full-blown theory of individual preferences likely would have to explore the interaction between human genes and human environments. In this sense, evolutionary psychology may provide the most promising avenue for the construction of a truly general theory of preferences.

6. The nature of nonideological core interests is debated, though the class and power interests discussed are often considered examples.

7. In practice, it may be impossible to fully disentangle the relative contribution of principled ideology versus core interests. However, in the view of HI, a close inspection of real actors and their beliefs may provide the best vantage point for attempting to do so.

8. In this sense, liberals were not fully instrumental actors. That is, they excluded from consideration certain possible options without regard for their consequences.

9. The concern of scholars such as Weber (1922/1968) and Giddens (1973) with the social closure of classes is consistent with this emphasis on socialization as a basis of preference formation.

10. One can glean this interpretation by comparing the work of Valenzuela and Argueta (1978) with the description of highland villages in Guevara-Escudero (1983).

11. In this sense, risk was present in liberals' decisions. That is, even if they selected an option to maximize utility (or to avoid the worst possible outcome), there was still a chance that they would be overthrown.

12. However, some evidence does suggest that they did explicitly consider this issue. For example, Marco Aurelio Soto in Honduras was aware of both the reformist model of Costa Rica and the radical model of Guatemala. Soto appears to have consciously decided to pursue a reformist model like that of Costa Rica.

References

Bates, Robert H., Avner Greif, Margaret Levi, Jean-Laurent Rosenthal, and Barry R. Weingast. 1998. *Analytic Narratives*. Princeton, N.J.: Princeton University Press.

Bourdieu, Pierre. 1984. *Distinction: A Social Critique of the Judgment of Taste*. Cambridge, Mass.: Harvard University Press.

Collier, Ruth Berins, and David Collier. 1991. *Shaping the Political Arena: Critical Junctures, the Labor Movement, and Regime Dynamics in Latin America*. Princeton, N.J.: Princeton University Press.

Dunkerley, James. 1988. *Power in the Isthmus: A Political History of Modern Central America*. London: Verso.

Elster, Jon. 1985. *Making Sense of Marx*. Cambridge: Cambridge University Press.

———. 1989. *Solomonic Judgments: Studies in the Limitations of Rationality*. New York: Cambridge University Press.

Geddes, Barbara. 1994. *Politician's Dilemma: Building State Capacity in Latin America*. Berkeley: University of California Press.

Giddens, Anthony. 1973. *The Class Structure of Advanced Societies*. London: Harper and Row.

Gudmundson, Lowell, and Héctor Lindo-Fuentes. 1995. *Central America, 1821–1871: Liberalism Before Liberal Reform*. Tuscaloosa: University of Alabama Press.

Guevara-Escudero, José Francisco. 1983. "Nineteenth-Century Honduras: A Regional Approach to the Economic History of Honduras." Ph.D. dissertation, New York University.

Little, Daniel. 1991. *Varieties of Social Explanation: An Introduction to the Philosophy of Social Science*. Boulder, Colo.: Westview Press.

Mahoney, James. 2000. "Path Dependence in Historical Sociology." *Theory and Society* 29(4): 507–48.

————. 2001. *The Legacies of Liberalism: Path Dependence and Political Regimes in Central America*. Baltimore, Md.: Johns Hopkins University Press.

————. 2004. "Revisiting General Theory in Historical Sociology." *Social Forces* 83(3): 459–90.

McCreery, David J. 1994. *Rural Guatemala, 1760–1940*. Stanford, Calif.: Stanford University Press.

Paige, Jeffery M. 1997. *Coffee and Power: Revolution and the Rise of Democracy in Central America*. Cambridge, Mass.: Harvard University Press.

Pierson, Paul. 2000. "Increasing Returns, Path Dependence, and the Study of Politics." *American Political Science Review* 94(2): 251–67.

Prasad, Monica. 2002. Book Review of *The Legacies of Liberalism*. *American Journal of Sociology* 107(6): 1639–40.

Przeworski, Adam. 1985. *Capitalism and Social Democracy*. Cambridge: Cambridge University Press.

Skocpol, Theda. 1985. "Cultural Idioms and Political Ideologies in the Revolutionary Reconstruction of State Power: A Rejoinder to Sewell." *The Journal of Modern History* 57(1): 86–96.

Swidler, Ann. 1986. "Culture in Action: Symbols and Strategies." *American Sociological Review* 51(2): 273–86.

Thelen, Kathleen. 1999. "Historical Institutionalism and Comparative Politics." *Annual Review of Political Science* 2: 369–404.

Tilly, Charles. 1990. *Coercion, Capital, and European States, AD 990–1990*. Cambridge, Mass.: Basil Blackwell.

Valenzuela, José Reina, and Mario Argueta. 1978. *Marco Aurelio Soto: Reforma liberal de 1876*. Tegucigalpa: Banco Central de Honduras.

Waltz, Kenneth. 1979. *Theory of International Politics*. Boston: Addison-Wesley.

Weber, Max. 1922/1968. *Economy and Society*. 2 vols. Berkeley: University of California Press.

Williams, Robert G. 1994. *States and Social Evolution: Coffee and the Rise of National Governments in Central America*. Chapel Hill: University of North Carolina Press.

Woodward, Ralph Lee, Jr. 1984. "The Rise and Decline of Liberalism in Central America." *Journal of Interamerican Studies and World Affairs* 26(3): 291–312.

Wright, Erik Olin. 1997. *Class Counts*. Cambridge: Cambridge University Press.

Index